High on God

JAMES K. WELLMAN, JR.

KATIE E. CORCORAN

KATE J. STOCKLY

High on God

How Megachurches Won the

Heart of America

OXFORD

UNIVERSITY PRESS

OXFORD
UNIVERSITY PRESS

Oxford University Press is a department of the University of Oxford. It furthers
the University's objective of excellence in research, scholarship, and education
by publishing worldwide. Oxford is a registered trade mark of Oxford University
Press in the UK and certain other countries.

Published in the United States of America by Oxford University Press
198 Madison Avenue, New York, NY 10016, United States of America.

Library of Congress Cataloging-in-Publication Data
Names: Wellman, James K., author. | Corcoran, Katie E., author. | Stockly, Kate J., author.
Title: High on God : how megachurches won the heart of America / James K. Wellman, Jr.,
University of Washington, Katie E. Corcoran, West Virginia University,
Kate J. Stockly, Boston University.
Description: New York : Oxford University Press, 2020. |
Includes bibliographical references and index.
Identifiers: LCCN 2019009821 | ISBN 9780199827718 (hardcover) |
ISBN 9780190065102 (epub)
Subjects: LCSH: Big churches—United States. | United States—Church history.
Classification: LCC BV637.9 .W45 2020 | DDC 277.3/083—dc23
LC record available at https://lccn.loc.gov/2019009821

9 8 7 6 5 4 3 2 1

Printed by LSC Communications, United States of America

This book is dedicated to Brooke Wellman, who creates peace and joy, as well as the blessing of our new daughter, Simone James Wellman, born the day after I finished that last sentence of this book. JKW
To my son Aden, you are my sunshine. KEC
For my dad, who in both his life and death taught me grace, courage, and gratitude. And for my mom, my hero. KJS

CONTENTS

Preface: Am I High on God?   ix

Acknowledgments   xix

PART I   **Desire Is the Heart of Religion**

1   Megachurch: The Drug That Works   5

2   The Problem of Cooperation and *Homo Duplex*   15

3   Interaction Rituals and Embodied Choice Theory   23

4   Defining Religion: Sacred Moral Communities   33

5   Megachurch: An American Original (Almost)   37

6   Congregations in a Time of Change   63

PART II   **Pistons of Desire and Power: Cracking the Megachurch Code**

7   The Micro-sociology of Interaction Rituals within Megachurches   79

8   Desire for Acceptance and Belonging   89

9   Desire for Wow, or Hacking the Happy   99

10   Desire for a Reliable Leader   115

11   Desire for Deliverance   137

12   Desire for Purpose in Service   153

13   Desire to Re-member   171

PART III   **The Dark Side of Megachurches: How Some Deceive and Destroy**

14   Dissecting Megachurch Scandals   189

15   Conclusion: Havens of Health or Habitats for the Prosperity Gospel?   215

Postscript from the Pews   229
Appendix A: Data, Methodology, and Descriptive
   Statistics   231
Appendix B: How Is God "Like a Drug"?
   Exploring the Evolution of Social Affects and
   Oxytocin   251
Appendix C: Megachurch Scandals   293
Bibliography   301
Index   321

PREFACE: AM I HIGH ON GOD?

T HIS BOOK HAS been a long time coming. It was delayed for personal reasons, in which I (James K. Wellman, Jr.) took time to care for myself and my family. But in coming back to this project, a surge of energy seized me and we began to think of this book as not just about American megachurches, but about the nature and character of human beings as they experience and embody their religion. This exploration has been my life journey, a search that has been full of bumps and bruises, but also moments of exhilaration. So, for us, this is a book about megachurches but it is also, more profoundly, a book about the contours of human religiosity.

Along the way, we rediscovered Émile Durkheim as the father of the sociology of religion—humans must make and dwell in worlds, and these worlds, for better or worse, are sacred. Durkheim's notion of *homo duplex*[1] became a definitive way for us to understand human beings as they construct, negotiate, and sometimes destroy religious worlds. World building, of whatever kind, is a sacred act, but nonetheless one that is full of ambivalence, promise, and trouble. American megachurches are one way that humans have tried to navigate this tension. From our research, megachurches have been enormously successful in resolving this multivalent challenge. How do they

---

[1] Émile Durkheim, *The Elementary Forms of Religious Life* (New York: Free Press: 1995 [1912]); Émile Durkheim, "The Problem of Religion and the Duality of Human Nature," translated by R. A. Jones and W. P. Vogt, in *Knowledge and Society: Studies in the Sociology of Culture Past and Present* vol. 5, 1–44 (Elsevier Science Unlimited, 1984 [1913]).

do it, and what is it about their structure and rituals that makes so many feel as if they are high on God?

In this Preface, I describe an experience that I had while conducting this research, which helped me connect, existentially, with the question, "What does it mean to be high on God?" For many scholars of religion, especially sociologists, religious ecstasy seems like an epiphenomenon: an illusion that is talked about as something "they" do, but not always believed or taken with great seriousness. We will take this experience very seriously in this book. As authors, we take religious experience to be something quite real, as a phenomenon that is as valid as any experience in human life. In fact, religious emotions and ecstasy have, in many ways, throughout history and across the world (including in twenty-first-century America), played a formative role in shaping human lives and cultures. In this way, humans, it seems to us, are *homo religiosus*.[2] People build and place their trust in unseen worlds to which they pray, in which they find meaning, and about which they doubt and ask questions. American megachurches are simply a rather delicious exemplar of how human beings are *homo religiosus*—doing what we explain in this book, getting high on God.

So, here is an example of how the experience of the God-high might manifest—even in a scholar (myself), even as I fully intended to remain a neutral observer.

I have been studying, going to, and preaching at churches for most of my life. I've visited nearly every conceivable form of church. And so to visit a megachurch is nothing out of the ordinary. Indeed, my first book was a study of a liberal Protestant megachurch—a rare breed I might add.[3] So when I visited one of the twelve megachurches that we explore in this book, I knew what to expect. It was a typical Sunday and I was there to witness and experience all five of the services offered that Sunday. I estimate that I witnessed around 12,000 people come through the doors that day; most were on the youthful side, but they were of every ethnicity and racial background. The ethnic diversity stunned me—every imaginable ethnic blend mixed together as if all the tensions in our country never existed. It struck me to watch a young white woman and an African American teenager dance to the worship music, utterly caught up in the moment, as they stood only one row away from each other. I thought about how remarkable this combination was, both

[2] Mircea Eliade, *The Sacred and the Profane: The Nature of Religion* (New York: Harcourt, Brace & World, 1959).

[3] James K. Wellman, Jr., *The Gold Coast Church and the Ghetto: Christ and Culture in Mainline Protestantism* (Champaign: University of Illinois Press, 1999).

historically and culturally, especially given that Martin Luther King, Jr. once said that 11 a.m. on Sunday is the most segregated hour in America. From the perspective of my own liberal Protestant tradition, which incorporates the teachings of the social gospel, *this* is the kingdom of God.[4] A holy habitation where harmony mediates all classes, races, and social divisions.

As is common for megachurches, this church had renovated an old warehouse and remodeled it, nicely I might add, into a modern theater with stage and lighting gear that compete with the most sophisticated venues I have experienced. They executed the show—and it *was* a show—with great mastery and professionalism. HD screens loomed across the front. From any angle in the theater, no matter where one was sitting, attendees could see every pirouette of the singers and every strum of the (electric) guitar. The close-ups of the lead singer invited listeners to feel her pathos. But what struck me about her was that she seemed depressed and even desperate. My intuition was supported by the fact that at midday she began to lose her voice, and by the fourth service she was encouraging the congregation to sing along with her and for her. I thought, "Wow, why don't they give her a break?"

The other soloist was a young Hispanic man, whose voice stunned me. He stood in front of us like a Southern Hispanic god. I kept thinking about his ethnic history, and wondering by what Catholic tributary he was nurtured into this quite remarkable future. All my dreaming was taking place as a prelude to what was coming—the senior pastor. His beauty struck me as he strutted onto the stage, all decked out in stone-washed jeans and a casual but stylish dress shirt; his broad smile and energy immediately captured and enchanted the audience. He clapped his hands, saying, "How are you? How are you? How are you?" And I thought, "I am good." And, truth be told, when I saw his picture online before attending the service, I had thought, "This guy is not very impressive." Well, in person, his eloquence and intelligence struck me with some force. I was smitten.

His sermon engaged me not only because of his charisma and his winning personality, but also because it made sense. He covered familiar ground, arguing that proof of God's existence is found in the beautiful design of nature (a classic theological argument): if we see order around us, there must be a designer. And intuitively, on a certain level, this makes sense. Though, as Kant has shown, no necessary inference can be drawn about a first cause, but I didn't expect the pastor to be reading German philosophy.[5]

[4] See Walter Rauschenbusch, *A Theology for the Social Gospel* (New York: The MacMillan Company, 1917).
[5] See Immanuel Kant, *Critique of Pure Reason* (Cambridge: Cambridge University Press, 1998 [1781/1787]).

At the end of the "talk," he began the altar call. He proclaimed that our "sinful blood is damning," and that only "the innocent blood of the savior Jesus Christ can cover us." This is hardly original or unusual; the blood atonement theory is nearly universal throughout megachurches. When individuals responded to the altar call by coming forward to the stage, the pastor would prance across the platform, saying, "God bless you, God bless you, God bless you." The "audience," who were instructed to pray, had their eyes closed; I did not. It appeared to me that his machine-gun rapid-fire "God bless you"s acted as a kind of reverse-action pepper spray that lifted people and propelled them to come down front and be saved at the altar.

By the third service of the day, I had settled into my role as a "participant observer." I looked at every detail of each service, scribbled notes throughout, and did my best to blend in with the young multi-ethnic sweep that rose and danced all around me. The bass drum literally beat on my chest cavity—I thought, maybe I am too old for this kind of thing. After all, the only demographic not represented at the services were post–sixty-year-olds. It seemed clear that this was a young person's game.

During the third altar call, as my head leaned into my note taking, I realized that, unbeknownst to my researcher mind, my body had invited itself to get up and go forward for the altar call. I literally felt a power in my limbs rising and going down to join the train of those moving toward the stage to seize the pastor's hand—to catch one of the pastor's "God bless you"s. The act came utterly involuntarily—the force of it stunned me. My mind began a negotiation: on the one hand, "Why not? Who would be hurt if I went to the altar?" and on the other hand, "This is unethical! You are doing research! It would be professionally embarrassing."

The whole experience lasted a minute or two. I decided not to go, at which point I forcibly pulled the energy that had prompted me to walk down the aisle back up into my head, and the feeling finally stopped. As I relaxed back into my seat, I thought, "Well, that was a close call."

I am familiar with altar calls, and I can see how they function as deeply emotional forms of engagement, for good and ill. But the power of suggestion from the pastor surprised me and caught me off guard. His charisma and the pull of that service became a somatic marker empirically verified in my body.[6] I thought later, "This is what it's like to be high on God."

Religious ecstasy is not the product of some detached rational assent to a philosophical idea—it is a full-body experience. The affective energies and

[6] Antonio Damasio, *Descartes' Error: Emotion, Reason, and the Human Brain* (New York: Penguin Books, 1994).

emotional valences that characterize religious ecstasy are the primary focus of our study of megachurches. These experiences can engender powerful benefits as well as important dangers, both of which we will explore. In both cases, the body is where the somatic marker imprints. The conscious mind merely negotiates and, in the long run, rationalizes the physiological experience.

In this book, our focus is on the dynamics of desire. Desire is in the body, and so affect and emotion rule this territory. In the past, because of my own training in the power of the mind and rationality, I have been suspicious of emotion and the body. However, over this last decade, research has shown that many of our thoughts, decisions, and beliefs are reactions to what our body either wants or rejects. We sometimes critique certain rational explanations as ex post facto—after the fact—but our growing suspicion suggests that conscious thought is in fact *exclusively* ex post facto. We experience a problem or a situation and our bodies spring into action: our heart races, our hands sweat, a surge of adrenaline floods our bloodstream. We interpret these physiological events as evidence, and they propel us to respond quickly. Only later—perhaps milliseconds, minutes, or a month later—do we rationalize our behavior, choices, and explanations.

My attention to *desire* came by way of René Girard's early work, *Deceit, Desire and the Novel*.[7] Girard intuited the triangular nature of desire in his study of classic novelists. He argued that a person sees what the other desires and they mimic it, molding a genuine desire within them. A triangle is formed between the person, the other, and what becomes, through the person's mimicry of the other, their mutual object of desire, thus setting up a rivalry between the two desirers—we compete with those whom we mimic. During the altar call, my desire to touch the pastor's hand mimicked those who had already responded, and our shared desire to participate in the aura of religious ecstasy that exuded from the stage mimicked the pastor's performance. I, too, wanted to touch the pastor's hand, to be washed in Jesus's blood. I saw what others desired and that desire sprung up in my own body. Thus, what we desire is always mediated—either externally or internally, either by models out there or models that we have internalized.

So, for instance, this is the essence of advertising: one may or may not want a new Mac laptop, but when one sees another wanting this particular laptop design, one's desires are stimulated and the passions rise. The lust for a computer is banal of course, but the causal matrix can be compared to the imitation of the Christ: one experiences that another wants the Christ, and one

---

[7] René Girard, *Deceit, Desire, and the Novel: Self and Other in Literary Structure*, translated by Yvonne Freccero (Baltimore: Johns Hopkins University Press, 1966 [1961]).

begins to want what that person wants. And that person develops an intent to have it through imitation, at times even unto death. We might be saying to ourselves, even now, "Well, that is not me, I want things because I want them, not because of others." And, of course, Girard would say, yes, the culture has constructed that myth of individuality, so even our rationalization of desire is a mimicked response. We easily fool ourselves into thinking that our desires come first. And marketing knows this truth: all purchases are personalized, and only those of unique tastes, like our own, would want these things. So, this circle of desire binds us and deceives us, and for Girard, this mimetic tornado leads to crisis and competition, which all cultures must manage and channel. No one avoids this mimetic circle of desire, and since it starts in the body, the mind uses ex post facto reasoning to save our pride.

All of this, by the way, is perfectly captured in a scene from *Monty Python's Life of Brian*:

BRIAN: Look, you've got it all wrong! You don't need to follow me, you don't need to follow anybody! You've got to think for yourselves! You're all individuals!

THE CROWD (IN UNISON): Yes! We're all individuals!

BRIAN: You're all different!

THE CROWD (IN UNISON): Yes, we are all different!

MAN IN CROWD: I'm not.[8]

For instance, why do I want to study and write on megachurches? Most liberals despise these institutions and many of our readers will likely also feel this way (mimicking, as it happens, this liberal judgment). The most typical remark that we receive is that these places are dens of consumerism and false-messianic profit takers, which represent a brand of Christianity that is below us. Even worse, they may even view the "superstitious" theology and "unconstrained" worship styles as a form of primitivism. My sense is that for many, these judgments are based on hearsay, and on the news stories of particular megachurches that have gone astray or become utterly craven in their appeals. Many such churches exist.[9] Perhaps even jealousy of megachurch success rumbles amidst these reactions, as well as ignorance of what actually occurs in these churches. These reactions and uninformed hostilities are partly what we aim to overcome. To be sure, we will engage very serious critiques of megachurch culture in the final part of the book, but first, our

---

[8] *Monty Python's Life of Brian*, directed by Terry Jones (London: HandMade Films, 1979).
[9] See Kate Bowler, *Blessed: A History of the American Prosperity Gospel* (New York: Oxford University Press, 2013).

task will be to "normalize" megachurches as a part of what humans do when they do religion. And perhaps, even more than this, what humans do because that is what we are pulled to do in our condition of being, using Durkheim's felicitous phrase, *homo duplex*.

As humans, we swim in desires that are borrowed and framed in us, often without much foreknowledge. And this quintessentially human desire to participate in and merge with the desire of the other is an evolved mechanism that enables us to build the social coalitions imperative for our species' survival. We must construct and merge with groups, ideas, and constructs bigger than ourselves, which Durkheim calls the *sacred*. We explore this tendency more fully in Part I. The underlying thesis of this book is that humans, in order to survive, desire to join something bigger than themselves. The self is never enough; we must move out and participate in Durkheim's sacred. But this desire for communion is in constant tension with our desire to be distinct, an independent self, so harmony in togetherness is rarely easy, no matter how much we want it. It is the complicated work of culture. We will argue that religion is one of the primary ways humans exercise and enact this desire.

But what about my own desires when it comes to these churches? Well, I notice that I feel some forms of envy when I'm at some of these churches. "Wow, look at their success. Their leaders seem so powerful and persuasive. Why can't I be that way?" This passes, of course, but then I sometimes think, "Hey, these folks look truly happy with their religion. Why can't I be like that?" And, I sometimes feel, "Wow, look at how much actual good they are doing." And I ask, "Why are liberal religionists so pretentious and self-righteous? They talk about social action and social justice, but in reality, they do little of it, particularly when compared to these megachurches."[10]

To make my point, the weekend I was at the megachurch where I experienced this bodily desire to touch the hand of the pastor, the church reported that the day before, they had sent out 600 volunteers to completely refurbish an entire city park, something city officials said would take them five years to complete. On top of this, the pastor announced that the church had given out free vouchers to their thrift and food warehouse to all 2,000 police officers and firefighters in the city, encouraging them to give the vouchers to those in need. This was real, direct social service to many of the neediest people in this midsize city. I began to desire to be a part of what this church had done; my body wanted to touch the pastor's hand, to be somehow be close to him

[10] See James K. Wellman, Jr., *Evangelicals vs. Liberals: The Clash of Christian Cultures in the Pacific Northwest* (New York: Oxford University Press, 2008).

as an embodied symbol of charisma and goodness. I wanted to be close to, as Randall Collins names, a special individual like this pastor, the "energy star," the source of that power, which felt like a power of love, a power to forgive, a power to persuade so many to serve their communities and those in need.

And true to this process, in reading the nearly 300 transcriptions of megachurch focus groups and interviews, the people in these churches were doing what I was doing, catching the desire of the energy stars in theirs churches, wanting what those charismatic figures wanted. Particularly in churches that were at the height of their growth, peaking as it were in popularity and power, congregants' references to these charismatic figures constructed them as sacred objects. Yes, the Bible was talked about and songs were sung, but the sacralization of leadership was something we noticed consistently. The construction of pastors as sacred objects of ultimate desire formed and informed our research about megachurches. With their charismatic leadership and example of holy desire at the helm, megachurches are motivated to acts of service that benefit themselves, each other, and their communities.

Out of this fierce fire of charisma and catalyzed sacred communities, we emerged with a slightly edited version of my own definition of religion, adding the Durkheimian notion of a moral community:

Religion is the socially enacted desire for the ultimate that binds a group into a moral community.

Our sense is that humans first and foremost want or need energy that constructs stable social groups. Often, religion offers that opportunity, though other social forms can do this as well. Empirically humans want and desire forms of what Collins calls "emotional energy." They also want it to last—and religion tends to make the claim of unlimited permanence. This powerful claim draws many—like a magnetic pull, summoned to an ultimate source that appears and is claimed to be unlimited. Religion, in this sense, can provide the ultimate promise of a source that will never run out. Individuals who represent, embody, and communicate this energy in ways that enliven the imagination and emotions of followers can galvanize and motivate moral communities. What struck us about megachurches is that they speak about these churches and their leaders in intimate and tender terms—it's not about dogma or a theology as much as it is about the charisma of their pastors and the intimate nature of the truth that has brought them home. Congregants spoke in reverent terms: "He speaks to my heart," "I feel like he knows me," "He has a pastor's heart," "It's never dull," "I never fall asleep," "It doesn't feel like church," "It's applicable to me."

And here Collins's *interaction ritual chain theory* serves both to specify the pattern of religious experience as well as to broaden how the interactive ritual process forms the very essence of human social interactions. Religion is a functional expression of what all humans do.[11] Humans are, in Collins's terms, *energy seekers,* or *emotional energy desirers.* It all begins with a desire, a willingness, and motivation to focus on something that is of interest. But this focus is always in relation to others—there is a *co-presence,* whether real (as in other human participants) or perceived—or an observation that others seek the same object. Humans want to be with other "desiring" people. You see this on *Dancing with the Stars* when the camera focuses on the audience looking at the dancers; this co-presence enables one to see and feel inspired and to be moved with, in, and toward other people. This co-presence is often accompanied by a charismatic leader, who functions as an *emotional charging agent* that is at once both the object of focus and the source of desire. At other times, the leader facilitates a focus on other objects of interest, symbolic or material. Co-presence, in essence, triggers the flux and current of stimulation: people feel the co-presence of other seekers and an emotional charge is instigated, perhaps by the leader or by music. Stimulation builds, even to a crescendo, or what Collins calls a "threshold for shared mood."[12] And sometimes there is a peak, a collective effervescence where the air is palpably filled with contagious fervor, and something more takes over—everyone knows it—it is "in the air." Some interpret this energy as deliverance, others enlightenment, some are satiated in the moment, and some are moved to act, but all are moved to think and feel more deeply. All people who experience this want to make it happen again and again.

How Academics Might Read This Book

Finally, why is it challenging for us, as academics, to come to grips with a desire for the ultimate in the religious sense? Why are emotions and the affective desires in our bodies so sublimated in our lives and in our approaches to this subject matter? Why is there such a deep and inherent distrust of the kind of passion and ecstatic joy found in religion? It seems to me a piece of this goes back to Durkheim's *homo duplex*—as academics, who are often secularists, we struggle with the dual nature of our beings. As Durkheim describes, "In brief, this duality corresponds to the double existence that we

---

[11] Randall Collins, *Interaction Ritual Chains* (Princeton, NJ: Princeton University Press, 2004).
[12] Collins, *Interaction Ritual Chains*, 147.

lead concurrently: the one purely individual and rooted in our organisms, the other social and nothing but an extension of society."[13]

Academics are deeply dedicated to their own exploration of what they study and the need to understand and explain it. At the same time, they are committed to a sense of discovering the truth of their subject matter, and a deep aversion to anything that would force them to submit to anything that is bigger than themselves. In this sense religion is a bridge too far: it not only demands they submit to forces that are above and beyond them, but also that they give over control. Religion is at the far end of our ability to construct society, while being an exhibition of the very core of what it means to be human. It is no wonder then that religion becomes something that secular elites resist and often reject as a form of coercion. In fact, for many academics, it constitutes a menacing political force that is often considered a source of totalitarianism.

But desire is also in us as academics. Our argument is that we should be more aware of it in ourselves and more comfortable with the fact that our desires, too, are socially constructed. That we, too, are all mimetic desirers—we can't stop this, but we can be aware of it. As Jonathan Haidt has said, in the academic world, we are mostly WEIRD—"white, educated, industrial, rich and democratic."[14] And I would add secular. Our desires, while rooted in our human nature by virtue of our evolutionary heritage, are also determined and shaped by our culture, and we as selves are constructed through them as we negotiate the world. Some would say we do this with a rather large bias, that rationality is the only way to make decisions. Many might argue that that, too, is ex post facto reasoning. We've been taught, or we have caught the idea, that rationality is the only way to measure one's worth. This book allows WEIRDS to rethink and evaluate their prejudices about American megachurches and encourages them to deconstruct their own antipathy toward ecstatic desire—to rethink their own personal relation to the far side of *homo duplex*—one's own personal desires and interests on the one hand, and the interests and desires of the socially constructed world of religion on the other. In this way, we invite the many skeptics of American megachurches to take a tour of this strange social and religious beast—allowing it to interpret them, even as they will necessarily interpret it.

[13] Émile Durkheim, "The Dualism of Human Nature and Its Social Conditions," in *Émile Durkheim, 1858–1917*, edited by Kurt H. Wolff (Columbus: Ohio State University Press, 1964 [1914]), 337.
[14] Jonathan Haidt, *The Righteous Mind: Why Good People Are Divided by Politics and Religion* (New York: Random House, 2012), 112.

ACKNOWLEDGMENTS

W E WOULD LIKE to thank Steven Pfaff, Marion Goldman, Jason Wollschleger, and anonymous reviewers for their valuable feedback on earlier drafts. The data used in this paper was generously funded and collected by Leadership Network, Dallas, Texas (www.leadnet.org). We would like to thank Leadership Network, Dr. Warren Bird of Leadership Network, and Dr. Scott Thumma of Hartford Seminary's Hartford Institute for Religion Research (www.hartsem.edu) for making the data available to us. This research was partly funded through a grant from the Society for the Scientific Study of Religion.

PART I | Desire Is the Heart
of Religion

I N PART I WE make the case that desire for emotional energy is at the
heart of religion. Humans seek emotional energy, and this energy is the
drug or force that catalyzes sociality. This force feeds humans' fundamental
needs—not only for energy, but also for the emotional satisfaction of joining
with others, all the while remaining oneself. This sums up the problem of
homo duplex: humans desire to be independent, masters of their own universe, sui generis individuals, but they desperately need to do this in and
through others. In the process of achieving this cooperation, affective energy
is produced, which penetrates and swirls between bodies creating, quite literally, a drug-like experience—an experience that has, in one form or another,
sustained humans in groups across time and tradition.

The ligaments that construct this social matrix are the rituals that humans
use to initiate and then re-member this magical, or shall we say *sacred*, solidarity. When these experiences reach peak intensity, they are typically one
of the highlights of a person's life, a "high," if you will, that ties them to
something larger than themselves and helps sustain them in times of isolation and differentiation. This desire to be simultaneously one with others
and one with self, when met, is an explosive combination of joy, emotion,
and ecstasy. This is not singular to religion; in this book, we argue that religious systems, and the powerful myths and social dynamics that characterize
them, are par excellence the *key* deliverers of these experiences throughout
human history. And we further argue that in our current historical moment,

Protestant megachurches[1] are enormously successful in making this experience available and possible for human beings.

When a megachurch informant exclaimed, "I feel like I'm high on God," it made us wonder, at first, "Is this a drug trip, or some phony form of manipulation? Are these people so easily controlled? Is this something we should expose as a kind of pyramid scheme?" Of course, we are very aware of the dark side of megachurches, and we will address that in Part III of this book. We will also speak to the many scandals that punctuate the history and present of megachurches. There is little doubt that in any complex, humanly constructed social form, especially those with hierarchical power structures, scandal is rife, and manipulation is not uncommon. But, in general, that is not our thesis. We are after something much bigger than simply exposing corruption. We argue that religion is one of the chief forms that humans use to cooperate and to flourish. To put it boldly, the megachurch experience is a drug that works. And we don't mean this as a problem but as a solution to *homo duplex* and to the need to cooperate beyond kinship. As Howard Becker argued, getting high on marijuana is not merely a physiological state, but a social phenomenon; in order to experience pleasure from marijuana use, one must go through a social learning process, or in Randall Collins's terms, an interaction ritual.[2] A spiritual high is no different; we trace the ritual process that leads to these ecstatic experiences in Part I.

In Part I we will argue that this drug of emotional energy and sociality facilitates human flourishing. We then parse the problem of human cooperation and show how Durkheim's theory of *homo duplex* is solved through rituals of religion. Along the way, we present our own theory of how people are drawn to participate and invest in certain rituals; we call this the *embodied choice theory,* and it is in large part based on the insights of Collins's interaction ritual chains theory.[3] Here we argue that rituals are the forms by which humans seek emotional energy and create solidarity and community. In this section, we give our full definition of religion. We then argue that megachurches create a solution to the questions, issues, and dilemmas that all humans must face. We end Part I with a short review on how megachurches are an (almost) American original. That is, despite the roots of Calvinism in America's religious DNA, the true source of the spread of Christian faith has been the emotional energy of revivalist preaching, which Jonathan Edwards,

[1] Megachurches are defined as Protestant congregations with weekly worship attendance of 2,000 or more adults and children.
[2] Howard S. Becker, "Becoming a Marihuana User," *American Journal of Sociology* 59, no. 3 (1953): 235–242.
[3] Randall Collins, *Interaction Ritual Chains* (Princeton, NJ: Princeton University Press, 2004).

in deliberate and complex prose, called "Religious Affections."[4] William James manifested and explored this idea in *The Varieties of Religious Experience*.[5] We argue that religion is human experience in its most intense form, used to solve a core set of human quandaries.

Scholars might object to our title's claim that megachurches *won* America and suggest that other groups such as Mormons and Muslims have also seen great growth over the past few decades. We, of course, acknowledge the growth, shifts, and development of other forms of religion in America. However, our argument here is not only about the relative growth of religious groups; it is also, and more significantly, about *power, energy, influence, and cultural ethos.* Megachurches—including their theology, social perspectives, and visual aesthetic—have developed a powerful feedback loop in the wider American culture. The origin of this feedback loop is clear: megachurches eschewed traditional religious ritual forms and architectural aesthetics in favor of mainstream American symbols and structural elements inspired by the American ethos (e.g., the democratization of the clergy and church architecture). However, a strong and pervasive feedback loop has gradually developed in which megachurches have begun to exert their own power and influence back onto American culture. One need only look so far as to google "megachurches and Trump" to see a lively conversation about power and influence in American culture.

Some readers may contend that we overreach. But we argue that for too long, both the study of megachurches and the study of religion more generally have not claimed their power to illumine the core forms and forces that humans use to generate identity, community, and solidarity. Again, this is not to overlook the scandals and failures of megachurches. But that is not the point. We want to understand the nature of human beings as they seek the energy of rituals that sustain themselves and their communities. So, we ask our readers, and particularly our WEIRDS, to give us time and attention as we lay out our theoretical case in Part I, and then, in Part II, to observe how we work through our interpretation and analysis of our extensive data on the twelve nationally representative megachurches that we studied. We believe you, our readers, will not be disappointed, even if you disagree. The latter is welcome but we also ask for forbearance, long enough for the power of our argument to reveal that this is not just about megachurches, but about every one of us as we struggle to create moral communities in which individuals can flourish and be sustained.

---

[4] Jonathan Edwards, *The Works of Jonathan Edwards, Volume 2: Religious Affections*, edited by John E. Smith (New Haven, CT: Yale University Press, 2009).
[5] William James, *The Varieties of Religious Experience: A Study in Human Nature* (New York: Penguin Books, 1982).

CHAPTER 1 | Megachurch: The Drug
That Works

IN 1994, CHARLES Colson called megachurches the "Hot Tub Religion."[1] Colson, of Watergate fame, served as Richard Nixon's special counsel, and in 1974 pleaded guilty to obstruction of justice. Colson sought to redeem himself by creating a global ministry, called Prison Fellowship International. Even famous evangelicals have been suspicious of American megachurches; as we've said, rightfully so. And yet, as we also know, they are becoming *the* way that most American Christians are "doing" church these days. The largest 10% of churches account for more than 50% of all American churchgoers.[2] Megachurches give no signs of slowing down in terms of growth and influence. In the United States, the number of megachurches increased from 350 in 1990 to over 1,600 in 2011, and there is no indication that the trend will abate.[3] Even after surpassing an average weekly attendance of 2,000, megachurches continue to multiply at an average rate of 5% a year.[4] Thus, we don't see these forms as a fad, but as the way Americans "do" religion.

---

[1] Charles Colson, *The Body: Being Light in Darkness* (Nashville, TN: W. Pub Group, 1994).
[2] Scott Thumma and Dave Travis, *Beyond the Megachurch Myths* (San Francisco: Jossey-Bass, 2007).
[3] Scott Thumma and Warren Bird, "A New Decade of Megachurches: 2011 Profile of Large Attendance Churches in the United States," Hartford Institute for Religion Research, 2011, accessed December 13, 2017 (http://www.hartfordinstitute.org/megachurch/megachurch-2011-summary-report.htm).
[4] Scott Thumma and Warren Bird, "Recent Shifts in America's Largest Protestant Churches: Megachurches 2015 Report," Hartford Institute for Religion Research, 2015, accessed December 13, 2017 (http://hirr.hartsem.edu/megachurch/2015_Megachurches_Report.pdf).

Megachurches have been widely criticized for being like religious Disneylands, offering cheap entertainment devoid of any spiritual or moral value.[5] However, we argue that the megachurch is not some passing fancy, a Walmart experience, or even an Amazon.com form of instant gratification, but an embodied total life system. They are far from a passing drug experience, but can provide a sustainable form of spiritual enhancement and community (even if fraught with the potential for corruption) that may very well be what saves American church life from its steady decline. We now know that American churches, including mainline and evangelical Protestant denominations, are not the exception to European secularization but seem, more recently, to be following in Europe's familiar church decline.[6] The scandals of the last generation, and the new identification of evangelicalism with the Trump administration, have done evangelical Christianity no favors in the eyes of millennials and their children. So, in that sense, it appears that our WEIRDS readers may have a point—these trends signal the failure of religious forms as a sustaining life system for many Americans. Yet the data also shows that the practice of prayer, and the enduring need to seek some spiritual direction, remains alive and as vibrant as ever.[7] As Randall Collins reminds us, "A secular world means, not the disappearance of religion but the loss of religious monopoly over rituals."[8] We argue that belief is not the key to understanding religion per se. The true pull of faith and the attraction of ritual are the emotional energy that comes vis-à-vis ritual. This includes not only rituals provided by religious organizations, but also other sources especially among cultural elites, such as mindfulness apps like Calm and Headspace,[9] or even new millennial groups, such as the Liturgists,[10] who

[5] Rodney Stark, *What Americans Really Believe* (Waco, TX: Baylor University Press, 2008), 45.

[6] Mark Chaves, *American Religion: Contemporary Trends*, 2nd edition (Princeton, NJ: Princeton University Press, 2017); David Voas and Mark Chaves, "Is the United States a Counterexample to the Secularization Thesis?," *American Journal of Sociology* 12, no. 1 (2016): 1517–1556.

[7] According to Kosmin et al. (2009), of US adults who identify as having no religious affiliation, only 7% of them do not believe in God. Barry Kosmin et al., "American Nones: The Profile of the No Religion Population, A Report Based on the American Religious Identification Survey 2008," Trinity College Digital Repository, accessed December 11, 2017 (http://commons.trincoll.edu/aris/files/2011/08/NONES_08.pdf). In Cragun et al.'s (2012) study, only 56% of those who identified as atheist stated that they did not believe in God. Ryan Cragun et al., "On the Receiving End: Discrimination toward the Non-religious in the United States," *Journal of Contemporary Religion* 27 (2012): 105–127.

[8] Randall Collins, "The Micro-sociology of Religion: Religious Practices, Collective and Individual," Association of Religion Data Archives, Guiding Paper, 2010, accessed December 13, 2017 (http://www.thearda.com/rrh/papers/guidingpapers.asp), 6.

[9] Calm (smartphone app), accessed January 18, 2018 (https://www.calm.com/); Headspace (smartphone app), accessed December 13, 2017 (https://www.headspace.com/).

[10] The Liturgists, accessed December 13, 2017 (http://www.theliturgists.com/).

gather in large audiences to form and perform their own liturgies of meaning and purpose, even as they say they are a skeptic-friendly seeker group.

Rob Bell, a former evangelical megachurch pastor, whom the senior author wrote about in *Rob Bell and the New American Christianity*,[11] left his Grand Rapids, Michigan, megachurch for fairer weather in Los Angeles. He continues to be very active in his "ministry" online and travels around the country and globe speaking on his newest book, *What Is the Bible?*,[12] which details his "postmodern" interpretations of scripture. The Holy Spirit is no longer claimed as the source of these interpretations—Bell is now more apt to thank what he calls "the universe." This form of naming the ultimate derives its connotations from more acceptable New Age denotations, but a similar sort of emotional energy is created in the spiritual rituals of his speaking events. Indeed, it's striking; having witnessed Bell in his mega-church setting, I noticed that not much has changed as he has translated himself into New Age contexts, other than the way he names the ultimate to which he points. The emotional energy is there, though there are differences, which we will get to in time. Again, New Age spirituality, or any alternative forms of mysticism, have been a part of American religion from the very beginning. There is nothing new about it. William James's *Varieties* included many forms that make today's "gurus" look tame in comparison.[13]

We argue, in fact, that scholars focus too much on belief in our understanding of religion, in large part because WEIRDS are those who do the most analysis of religion, who teach religion in colleges, universities, and postgraduate contexts. The senior author attended a Christian seminary and was always surprised that his seminary instructors focused almost entirely on belief and theology—the rationalization of faith and the ways to either deconstruct it or respond to critiques from the cultural despisers of religion.[14] This tendency to focus on the rationalization of belief seems to be a symptom of our age. And thus, when megachurches and other more emotionally focused forms of religion take off, there is a tendency to say a great deal about their beliefs, and often, how superficial or simplistic they are. There is some

[11] James K. Wellman, Jr., *Rob Bell and the New American Christianity* (Nashville, TN: Abingdon Press, 2012).

[12] See Rob Bell, *What Is the Bible? How an Ancient Library of Poems, Letters, and Stories Can Transform the Way You Think and Feel about Everything* (New York: HarperOne, 2017).

[13] Lee Eric Schmidt, *Restless Souls: The Making of American Spirituality* (New York: HarperCollins, 2005); Jeff Wilson, *Mindful America: The Mutual Transformation of Buddhist Meditation and American Culture* (New York: Oxford, 2014).

[14] Friedrich Schleiermacher, *On Religion: Speeches to Its Cultured Despisers*, translated by John Oman (New York: Harper & Brothers, 1958).

truth to this, but what is missed in this analysis are the emotional dynamics and energies within these institutions and movements.

And indeed, as we turn our attention to ritual and emotional energy as the prime movers of social action, we also turn back to Émile Durkheim's contribution to the study of religious movements. In our own study, we not only turn back the page, but we follow it through, using Randall Collins's work on interaction ritual chains,[15] an update of the Durkheimian tradition, deeply influenced as well by Erving Goffman's work on interaction rituals.[16] Collins's "radical attention to micro-sociology" partners with the "radical empiricism" tradition in religious studies[17] to take seriously the nature of human behavior at its most core level. It looks at behaviors through the lens of humans' feelings, affects, and emotions as they interact and deal with religious forms. "Religion" is often said to come from the Latin *religare*, which means "to bind";[18] therefore, we show that what happens on the micro level during religious ritual, both empirically and affectively, binds and marks the human body. We further argue that religion is always already in the body, a material-discursive "intra-action,"[19] if you will, and not some sort of rational assent to a theological proposition.

As the senior author described in the Preface, the force that took his body over was not something that he called up in his mind, but a movement in his limbs, an affect and energy that moved his body to reach out for the pastor's hand. Indeed, he had no thought of doing that action before the feeling quite literally took over his body, much like a rogue wave hitting him unexpectedly on an ocean beach. Boom—suddenly pushed out of position, he had to recalibrate based on a force and energy coming from deep inside him calling him to stand up and walk down.

Collins is aware of the problem of process and causation on the micro level: what comes first in any ritual action? Clearly, a theological interpretation of a religious experience is relative to the content and context of one's culture. We tend to "catch" what is "in the air" of our cultural context. This means that even when we know the verbal language and bodily motions for whatever is "expressed" in a culture, to "catch" it there must be an affectual

---

[15] Randall Collins, *Interaction Ritual Chains* (Princeton, NJ: Princeton University Press, 2004).

[16] Erving Goffman, *Interaction Ritual: Essays on Face-to-Face Behavior* (New York: Anchor, 1967).

[17] William James, *Essays in Radical Empiricism* (Lincoln: University of Nebraska Press, 1996); Nancy Frankenberry, *Religion and Radical Empiricism* (Albany: State University of New York Press, 1987).

[18] Sarah F. Hoyt, "The Etymology of Religion," *American Oriental Society* 32, no. 2 (1912): 126–129.

[19] See Karen Barad, *Meeting the Universe Halfway: Quantum Physics and the Entanglement of Matter and Meaning* (Durham, NC: Duke University Press, 2007). Barad coined the neologism "intra-action" to denote the co-constitution of subject and object, in which no separately existing entities—bodies, religions, ideas—precede a causal relation.

or emotional spark loaded in the language, which prompts a physiological change that connects the expression and the cultural code. Collins is deeply aware of this dilemma:

> In this chicken-and-egg problem, the causal primacy is with the ritual action; to put this in theological language, the human experience of God is prior and fundamental to theology and belief. Theologians and story-tellers did not create God (and the historical variety of spirits), although once the ritual-based experiences of religious emotion exist, intellectual networks place their interpretations upon these experiences. But interaction rituals always occur in an on-going chain, with prior IRs creating a heritage of symbols that feed into and provide the focus of attention for the next IR in the chain. Thus there is an ongoing feedback loop between cultural ideas of religious realities and the emotional experiences arising from ritual practice, which shape each other on an ongoing basis. But beliefs are the weaker part of the chain, and they die when the ritual practice fails to support them.[20]

Here Collins argues that humans, in some mysterious way, can have an experience of "God" before they develop a belief in a "being" called God. In fact, the sequence of these phenomena is not quite clear—whether the emotion of ritual experience comes before specific thought patterns is hard to decipher. And indeed, we aren't making claims here about the etiology of religious rituals—evidence belies this question. We are arguing that interaction ritual chains of religious groups are a powerful force in religion. As to the first cause of religion, it is an open question; scholars have developed many theories, some more plausible than others. For example, Roy Rappaport's *Ritual and Religion in the Making of Humanity* argues that from the earliest *Homo sapiens*, ritualized practices had a solidarity-building effect, helping humans develop networks of trust, thereby fortifying early human communities and promoting safety from both internal and external threats.[21] Thus, according to Rappaport, rituals emerged, persisted, and were passed down because of their effectiveness in helping construct safe places to sleep and viable child care conditions. This seems rather intuitive—how else would communities create trust and be able to flourish except with rituals of trust and fidelity? One can imagine that the emotional energy coming from these communities underscored the ultimate power of these rituals. How these rituals were

[20] Collins, "The Micro-sociology of Religion."
[21] Roy Rappaport, *Ritual and Religion in the Making of Humanity* (Cambridge: Cambridge University Press, 1999).

created is not clear, but the effect was a flourishing community with the energy to bond together and protect one another.

Symbolic language and the development of stories, beliefs, and doctrines extend across human history, from early caves covered in handprints[22] to the red-splotched screens in one megachurch, symbolizing sinful human blood that could only be "cleansed" by the innocent blood of Jesus. These collections of images and the "heritage of symbols" reified in megachurches are part of our study. Indeed, in our work on megachurches we see a similar enumeration of symbols and ritual actions that collect over time, which accompany the manifestation of ritual forms. Our megachurches did not arise in a vacuum. As we will show, there is a collection of symbols and ideologies that are at play in the twelve megachurches we studied, contributing to and helping shape their aesthetics, doctrines, and theologies. They are a culmination of multiple American lineages: the musical choices,[23] the aesthetics of the buildings (which feel like malls, schools, or theaters, but noticeably *not* cathedrals), and the conservative political undercurrent that remains despite cultural changes based on local and national shifts across time. In short, there is a heritage of symbols that guides and helps renew the emotional energy in these services of worship.

Beliefs do remain an important part of the ritual process and the emotional energy it creates in megachurches. We, however, reframe how to talk about beliefs: we use Antonio Damasio's *somatic marker hypothesis* to contextualize beliefs into a ritual system, because it is through interaction rituals, we argue, that beliefs gain their force and resilience.[24] The somatic marker hypothesis proposes that prior experiences and behaviors have varying degrees of affective valence and salience. These qualities become attached to experiences and the symbols, beliefs, and behaviors associated with them, creating a physiological signal—a somatic marker—of the original feeling that was experienced. As Damasio argues, "Somatic markers are a special instance of feelings . . . [that] have been connected, by learning, to predicted future outcomes and certain scenarios."[25] Thus, when making decisions, the materiality of the body "remembers" the feelings attached to prior experiences through these somatic markers, thereby helping people make decisions

[22] See Reza Aslan's book *God: A Human History* (New York: Penguin Random House, 2017).

[23] April Stace, *Secular Music, Sacred Space: Evangelical Worship and Popular Music* (Lanham, MD: Lexington Books, 2017).

[24] Antonio Damasio, *Descartes' Error: Emotion, Reason and the Human Brain* (New York: Penguin Books, 1994).

[25] Damasio, *Descartes' Error*, 174.

regarding what types of behaviors to engage in. In at least this way, decision making involves affective systems.

We argue that it is in and through ritual experiences that somatic markers become attached to beliefs and symbols. In addition, literature in the cognitive science of religion suggests that some beliefs—those characterized by "minimally counterintuitive ideas"—are remembered, shared, and spread throughout space and time more readily than other beliefs.[26] We argue that this is at least partly because such minimally counterintuitive ideas resonate with our affective structures more readily than other ideas and are thus more likely to be associated with strong somatic markers.[27] Minimally counterintuitive beliefs are those that are counterintuitive enough to grab your attention (like time travel or an omniscient spirit) but not *so* counterintuitive that they become confusing or disorienting (like the uncertainty principle of quantum mechanics, the space–time continuum, or Christian apophatic and mystical theology). Presenting God as a Father who is like an unconditionally loving human parent *except that He is omniscient, can hear your thoughts, and shifts reality in your favor* is a quintessential example of a minimally counterintuitive idea. In addition, we regularly witnessed, throughout our interviews with megachurch members and during participant observation, how compelling the belief that "only the innocent blood of Jesus" can overcome the sin and stain of our "guilty blood" was for attendees. The notion that blood must be shed in the wake of wrongdoings seems to be a pervasive cultural schema, if not an intuitive or instinctual moral impulse.[28] However, Jesus's presence in the story is notably *counterintuitive*—that God would send God's own son to be an innocent, sinless sacrificial lamb. Not only that, but this blood, *Jesus's blood* "from above," embodies counterintuitive strength—it not only pays for sin, but it creates a "capital" that miraculously overcomes and pays the price for all human sins until the end of time. This idea sustains the premise that not only one sin, but *all* human sin, can be made innocent by one human's blood. Because Jesus is God, human sin can be "atoned for." Jesus is called

---

[26] For an important conversation on the merits and problems with current formulations of minimal counterintuitiveness (MCI) theory, see, Benjamin Grant Purzycki and Aiyana K. Willard, "MCI theory: a critical discussion," *Religion, Brain & Behavior* 6, 3 (2016): 207–248. Among other things, Purzycki and Willard point to the importance of *ritual contexts*, in addition to cognitive architecture, for the spread of ideas.

[27] See also, Pascal Boyer and Charles Ramble, "Cognitive Templates for Religious Concepts: Cross-Cultural Evidence for Recall of Counter-intuitive Representations," *Cognitive Science* 25 (2001): 535–564. See also Robert N. McCauley, *Why Religion Is Natural and Science Is Not* (New York: Oxford University Press, 2011); and Justin L. Barrett, *Why Would Anyone Believe in God?* (New York: AltaMira, 2004).

[28] Purzycki and Willard compare *counter-schematic* and *counterintuitive* concepts. Purzycki and Willard, "MCI theory."

"our substitute"; Jesus pays "our penalty"; Jesus achieves victory over death; Jesus has the "merit" to overcome our human debt; Jesus is the example for his followers, and anyone who comes after him should sacrifice themselves for him and others.[29]

These minimally counterintuitive combinations serve as powerful invitations to megachurch members, as they note their inability to conquer sin, to experience the power of Jesus. The One who became human and took on the limits of the human body, and *yet*, lived into a promise that by entering the human experience, this One—Jesus, "sent from God, born of God"—can redeem human sin and deliver the promise of redemption and restoration of full humanity for those who follow him. Thus, symbols and stories of religious traditions matter: they spark attention, become filled with and surrounded by emotional energy through ritual, and, in the process, acquire the ability to reframe human experience—and in the Christian tradition, *redeem* the human condition. So, in this way, attention to beliefs is critically important for understanding not only how a religion is structured, but also for understanding how deeply it impacts the emotions of those who follow it. This counterintuitive notion of a supernatural agent, who is "fully human and fully God," and who, by dying, renews and redeems humanity, is not *so* counterintuitive that it confounds or repulses belief. Rather, there *are* important elements of Jesus's story that feel familiar and intuitive, allowing the counterintuitive aspects to grab attention and provide hope in the present and for the future.

So, although our focus is on practices and behavior, we argue that it is important to show how ideas and beliefs can be powerful motivators and sparks of emotional energy. Collins downplays beliefs, and we appreciate this move as an important reaction *against* the traditional focus on beliefs within religious studies. But it would be incorrect to swing the pendulum back too far, to claim that belief structures have no effect on religious movements or groups; beliefs remain essential to the process of generating religious forms of human energy because some beliefs are more likely to catch and hold attention and affective force and to trigger somatic markers in people. So, in conjunction with the representational and performative meaning making that symbols participate in, megachurch symbols and theology are also in this embodied way an integral part of the puzzle.

But the beliefs themselves are not sufficient. Consider that smaller evangelical churches often have the same minimally counterintuitive beliefs

[29] Derek Rishmawy, "Calvin's Multi-faceted Atonement," *The Gospel Coalition*, 2015, accessed December 13, 2017 (https://www.thegospelcoalition.org/article/calvins-multi-faceted-atonement/).

regarding a personal God and the redeeming blood of Jesus that are preached in megachurches. And yet they remain small, not even approaching the megachurch threshold of 2,000 Sunday attendees. We argue that megachurches, by creating more powerful affective experiences, generate stronger somatic markers, not only for the movements and sensory stimuli connected to the ritual, but also for the symbols, beliefs, and people connected to the emotional energy aroused during the ritual. The symbols and beliefs (which can function as symbols), having been absorbed by the bodies of the attendees, continue to encourage further participation in the ritual and reinvigorate elements of the experience itself. The minimally counterintuitive beliefs are therefore important primarily through their connection to the rituals that attach somatic markers to them. Thus, as Collins argues, beliefs on their own "die when the ritual practice fails to support them," but they become energized and vital for connecting group members to each other through successful energy-inducing rituals.

R. W. Connell's concept of "body-reflexive practices" is helpful here in understanding the dynamics of ritual. He argues that the body is vital for understanding social forces beyond simply as objects carrying symbolic meaning, which is usually the limit to which social theory considers the physical body. "As Turner observed in *The Body and Society*," Connell explains, "bodies went missing a long time ago from social theory. Social theory for the most part still operates in the universe created by Descartes, with a sharp split between the knowing, reasoning mind and the mechanical, unreasoning body."[30] The notion of "body-reflexive practices," however, breaks this trend and understands bodies as "sharing in social agency, in generating and shaping courses of social conduct."[31] Just as we found in our exploration of people's reactions to and experiences in megachurch rituals, for Connell, bodily arousal and social interaction are one integrated complex process instead of two separate mechanisms. They are intimately woven together with constant feedback loops: the social world exerting influence on the body and the body pushing and affecting social action and the affective milieu of social space. "This is not simply a matter of social meanings or categories being imposed on [bodies], though these meanings and categories are vital to what happens. The body-reflexive practice calls them into play, while the bodily experience—[for example] a startling joy—energizes the circuit."[32]

[30] R. W. Connell, *Masculinities*, 2nd edition (Berkeley: University of California Press, 2005 [1995]), 59–60. See also Bryan Turner, *The Body and Society* (Oxford: Blackwell, 1984).
[31] Connell, *Masculinities*, 60.
[32] Connell, *Masculinities*, 62.

Our argument is simple and to the point: *megachurches understand the importance of these body-reflexive practices*. They have mastered the social ritual methods of charging their congregations with emotional energy and embodied cognitive markers that stimulate intense loyalty and a desire to come back repeatedly to get recharged. Megachurches are like drug dealers offering members and nonmembers alike their next hit. They have perfected ways to produce and mark human experience so that it is consistently re-produced and creates a positive and life-sustaining energy. Ritual life is critical but so are the ideas that capture attention, channel the emotional energy, and rally loyalty and motivation to keep coming back for more. We have suggested that megachurches are doing something quite dramatic by creating emotionally powerful rituals. This is no small feat. And the energy they create is sustaining because attendees interpret it as supernatural presence and action.

CHAPTER 2 | The Problem of Cooperation and
Homo Duplex

S CHOLARS HAVE ARGUED that the conditions that make religion possible (in fact, some would say *inevitable*)[1] are the result of natural selection
both on the local, individual level (e.g., behaviors and beliefs) and on the sociocultural level (e.g., social movements). Biological language about natural
selection and evolution may seem antithetical to a discussion of such a socially
constructed cultural phenomenon as religion, but as Vicky Kirby insists, the
social *is* natural.[2] Culture is *not* different in kind from "nature." Sociality and
its diverse proliferation of cultural manifestations are an inextricable part of
human nature. Feminist theorist Elizabeth Grosz advocates for a rescue of
Darwinian evolutionary theory from the grip of contemporary habits of reductionism and determinacy, arguing that the dynamism of Darwin's theory
actually has much to offer in collaboration with humanist and constructivist
approaches to human experience. "Darwin's work offers a subtle and complex critique of both essentialism and teleology," Grosz explains. "It provides
a dynamic and open-ended understanding of the intermingling of history
and biology . . . and a complex account of the movements of difference,

---

[1] Jonathan H. Turner, Alexandra Maryanski, Anders Klostergaard Petersen, and Armin W. Geertz, *The Emergence and Evolution of Religion by Means of Natural Selection* (New York: Routledge, 2018), 2.
[2] Vicky Kirby, "Natural Convers(at)ions: Or, What If Culture Was Really Nature All Along?" in *Material Feminisms*, edited by Stacy Alaimo and Susan Hekman, 214–236 (Bloomington: Indiana University Press, 2008).

bifurcation, and becoming that characterize all forms of life."[3] Too often evolution, and therefore also the bodies it produces, is understood in static deterministic terms, but that is a fundamental misunderstanding of how organic material constantly moves, grows, morphs, adapts, and lives over time. Moreover, evolutionary heritage aside, empirical insights into the way that human minds, bodies, and groups operate on a day-to-day level have time and time again shown that nature and culture cannot be understood as separate or distinct from each other, and certainly not as dichotomous or in opposition to one another.

We argue that religion, along with other forms of creativity, innovation, performance, affective experience, and aesthetics, is a natural and fully embodied human phenomenon. So, far from "reducing" religion to biological causes, we seek to enhance current understandings of sociological approaches to religion. And so it is with this understanding that we approach notions of the bio-cultural evolution of religious thoughts, feelings, and behavior.

With this in mind, we ask are there pieces of the evolutionary story of human becoming that can help us understand the ways in which religious forms emerge and function? In addition to person-level traits such as the ability to conceptualize other worlds, the neurological tendency toward altered states of consciousness, and the ability to cooperate, the complex and imbricated processes of natural selection appear to have favored *groups* and *social structures* that enabled strangers to cooperate and that promoted human sociality. These groups had a competitive advantage in terms of success and survival compared to groups that did not collaborate.[4] Religious systems likely played a key role in this process by promoting beliefs and practices that engendered cooperation and encouraged human sociality;[5] this implies religion may have played a key role in the survival and evolution of the human species. For example, self-sacrificial and moral intentions and behavior were nurtured in the context of cooperative groups that managed to exalt the wellbeing of the *group* and, importantly, the symbol of the group, above and beyond each individual's wellbeing. Our emotional systems appear to instill a genuine motivation to help others with actions that might ignore our own

---

[3] Elizabeth Grosz, "Darwin and Feminism: Preliminary Investigations for a Possible Alliance," in *Material Feminisms*, edited by Stacy Alaimo and Susan Hekman, 23–51 (Bloomington: Indiana University Press, 2008), 28.

[4] Michael Mesterton-Gibbons and Lee Alan Dugatkin, "Cooperation among Unrelated Individuals: Evolutionary Factors," *Quarterly Review of Biology* 67 (1992): 267–281.

[5] Richard Sosis and Eric R. Bressler, "Cooperation and Commune Longevity: A Test of the Costly Signaling Theory of Religion," *Cross-Cultural Research* 37 (2003): 211–239; Quentin D. Atkinson and Pierrick Bourrat, "Beliefs about God, the Afterlife and Morality Support the Role of Supernatural Policing in Human Cooperation," *Evolution & Human Behavior* 32 (2011): 41–49.

self-interest, even at the cost of our lives, in order to help the group or important others. This and other features coalesce to form an orientation to the world that is often supported and legitimated by intuitions about supernatural beings; when this orientation is taken up by culture and given shape and structure, what tends to result is a religion. So, not only increased levels of sociality, but also the social structures that ascribe meaning to social desires and urges, were vital in the survival and flourishing of the human species. For more on the evolutionary process, see Appendix B.

Indeed, this is interpreted as one of the core messages of St. Paul, the early organizer of the Christian church: "Bear one another's burdens, and in this way you will fulfill the law of Christ" (Galatians 6:2, NRSVA). Paul encouraged the Galatian community, which was riddled with strife between early Jewish and Gentile followers of Jesus—they were asking, do the uncircumcised (Gentiles) need to get circumcised to be "in" the body of Christ? Paul argued that the identity of the Christian is not a matter of who has the "right" marking, but rather who, like Christ, gives his body for others. Paul ends the letter to the Galatians by saying, "From now on, let no one make trouble for me; for I carry the marks of Jesus branded on my body" (Galatians 6.17, NRSVA). That is, for Christians, it is not what they have, but what they give away that creates their identification with Christ. Paul is arguing that leaders are not those who possess "more" but those who give all for others. It is one of the signal moments in the early Christian community—leadership must be marked by self-sacrifice. And this dilemma plagues all human communities: when selfish behavior trumps selflessness in leadership, community erodes and chaos ensues. Christianity and other religious groups revolutionize the requirements for community and for social cooperation—the expectations could not be higher. And so, with the evolution of human *sociality,* successful religious groups contribute to solving the problem of cooperation by encouraging, and in some cases demanding, human self-sacrifice—an ultimate form of sociality.

As we have argued from the beginning, Durkheim's description of human nature as *homo duplex* is at the heart of our understanding of why religions function so well to orient cooperation and provide community in human groups. In a fundamental way, Durkheim's description of the profane and the sacred is captured in the movement from our existential and individual isolation to a group that interacts and cooperates. This movement from the individual to the social group is neither smooth nor automatic, but to survive we must cooperate, and the movement to cooperation is experienced as both a challenge and a gift. A gift, precisely because it means our survival; and this movement is facilitated by emotion; it creates collective effervescence, which human beings have interpreted as the sacred throughout history.[6] As we mentioned in the Preface, humans must solve the problem of *homo duplex* continuously. We have already argued that rituals—including but not limited to religious rituals—are the processes by which this is achieved. Religions, at least up until the modern period, have been an essential, and perhaps the most effective strategy for facilitating cooperation through their ability to generate affective and emotional energy within and between participants.

As Durkheim makes clear, the union of individual and society is never a one-way movement; each is "penetrated" by the other. Thus there is no pure "individual," nor is the individual erased when she enters society—the two share measures of each:

> Although sociology is defined as the science of societies, it cannot, in reality, deal with the human groups that are the immediate object of its investigation without eventually touching on the individual who is the basic element of which these groups are composed. For society can exist only if it penetrates the consciousness of individuals and fashions it in "its image and resemblance." We can say, therefore, with assurance and without being excessively dogmatic, that a great number of our mental states, including some of the most important ones, are of social origin. In this case, then, it is the whole that, in a large measure, produces the part; consequently, it is impossible to attempt to explain the whole without explaining the part—without explaining, at least, the part as a result of the whole.[7]

But Durkheim takes this dynamic further: not only is the person saturated by their social reality, but the "passions and egoistic tendencies" of the individual and the demands of the collective remain in constant tension. "Therefore," Durkheim continues, "society cannot be formed or maintained without our being required to make perpetual and costly sacrifices. Because society surpasses us, it obliges us to surpass ourselves."[8] However, we take issue with Durkheim's supposition that humans are by *nature* egotistical, and only by virtue of *culture* social and moral.[9] Rather, we assert that *both* aspects

---

[6] Émile Durkheim, "The Dualism of Human Nature and Its Social Conditions," in *Essays on Sociology and Philosophy*, edited by Kurt H. Wolff, 325–339 (Columbus: Ohio State University Press, 1964 [1914]).

[7] Durkheim, "The Dualism of Human Nature and Its Social Conditions," 325.

[8] Durkheim, "The Dualism of Human Nature and Its Social Conditions," 338.

[9] Durkheim inconsistently discusses *homo duplex*. In some works, he seems to indicate that humans are by nature egoistical and become moral through culture, but in other places he suggests that egoism and individualism reflect the cultural context. See Jonathan S. Fish, *"Homo Duplex* Revisited: A Defense of Émile Durkheim's Theory of the Moral Self," *Journal of Classical Sociology* 13 (2013): 338–358.

of our human nature are biologically and culturally rooted. Neither can be extracted from nor reduced to either biology or culture. Social desires are part of our evolutionary heritage, along with egocentric desires. These two dueling impulses are in dynamic interaction with each other. We argue, then, for a more complicated understanding of *homo duplex*, which includes the recognition that there is *no clean distinction in the biological and cultural origins of self or society*—each is deeply entangled with the other.

Importantly, we claim that megachurches are remarkable in that they juggle these goals smoothly and effectively. Indeed, we will show that they develop the self and society in ways that support both sides of Durkheim's polarity. Through energizing rituals, megachurch participants experience intense energy that fills each individual with a powerful sense of personal satisfaction. However, this satiation of *individuals'* desire can only be attained in the context of *group* rituals, thus requiring social participation and thereby supporting and integrating both sides of *homo duplex*. To be sure, megachurches create rituals and opportunities to discipline and increase self-control, selflessness, cooperation, generosity, and a desire to care for others. However, one of the most dynamic marks of these churches is the focus on the other side of *homo duplex*—the need to *exert the ego*—this is evident in the way megachurches uplift the uniqueness of each individual, highlight the importance of using personal spiritual gift(s), focus on personal salvation, and have their sights set on the mission for each individual to become a better person and experience more fulfillment and love. However, a person's *self* is only "real" and "special" if it becomes manifest within the body of Christ. Christ's body *is the church* and exists to serve the wider community, both locally and globally. This presentation and call to exert the ego works well within the megachurch model because empowerment of the individual always has the goal of serving the other: the church, the "body of Christ." Therefore, it is argued that when one is acting in one's gifts, one is witnessing to the work of God in the individual; in other words, exerting the ego is framed as a way of witnessing to the work of Christ in oneself—presented as an act of one's sacred duty.

It is often said by those outside megachurches that members are self-centered, self-involved, and obsessed with their own salvation, but we have also found a deep strain of nurturing one's individual gifts for the sake of family, friends, the church, and the wider community. In one sense, we argue that megachurches offer an effective solution to the individualism that Durkheim was concerned about in late nineteenth-century French and European culture, which focused on valuing the individual above anyone else: "This cult of man has for its first dogma the autonomy of reason and for its first rite freedom of thought."[10] Durkheim goes on to say that "if [individualism] does not serve something which exists beyond it, it is not merely useless; it becomes dangerous."[11] Again, what we will show is an intense push by megachurch leadership to develop individuals' gifts and desires as the critical mode and mechanism to serve each other along with their national and global communities.

In addition, megachurches must deal squarely with the issue of free-riders, those who would consume what the organization produces without contributing to its production.[12] That is, megachurches promote member involvement and seek to nurture local leadership, but they also put a great deal of effort and resources into attracting new visitors who contribute little in the short term. Such visitors and low-commitment attendees are necessary for the church to maintain and grow its large size. In this way, large size and the presence of free-riders are interrelated, and by necessity create a classic problem of collective action:[13] in larger groups, many will choose to free-ride if given the chance. And we see this in megachurches. Longtime megachurch researchers Scott Thumma and Dave Travis explain that megachurches have more free-riders than other churches partly because they make a specific effort to attract and recruit new visitors, seekers, and marginal attendees.[14] This strategy requires that megachurches simultaneously satisfy the religious preferences of what we call low-cost attendees—or free-riders—*as well as* create high-cost opportunities for committed members who take up lay leadership roles. Attention to these dual priorities results in more devoted lay leadership and larger numbers of attendees who facilitate the "feeling," identified by megachurch members, that "this is the place where people want to be." The argument, and the opportunity, is that free-riders actually *benefit* megachurches, because by helping the church appear more successful and thus stimulating greater amounts of emotional energy, they entice still greater numbers of potential attendees. We argue then that there is a *free-rider benefit* for megachurches. Counterintuitively, by attracting free-riders, megachurches create a halo effect of interest precisely because humans are

[10] Émile Durkheim, "Individualism, and the Intellectuals," in *Durkheim on Religion: A Selection of Readings with Bibliographies and Introductory Remarks*, edited by William S. F. Pickering (Cambridge: James Clarke & Co., 2011 [1975]), 65.

[11] Durkheim, "Individualism, and the Intellectuals," 70.

[12] For example, attending church services and never donating any money to the congregation.

[13] Individuals have an incentive to free-ride off the contributions of others (i.e., consume goods/services without contributing to their production), but if everyone does this there will be no collective goods and services to consume.

[14] Scott Thumma and Dave Travis, *Beyond Megachurch Myths: What We Can Learn from America's Largest Churches* (San Francisco: Jossey-Bass, 2007).

energized by each other's presence, while also offering members a chance to share the faith with newcomers. This enhances the *buzz* of the crowd, or what Collins calls *co-presence*, which generates energy within the crowd and enthusiasm among loyal members and leaders who *are* willing to give themselves to the church financially and organizationally.

This dynamic of loyal members and the presence of newcomers must be maintained, otherwise decline can take place. While visiting one of the megachurches in our study, the senior author noted the potential pairing of diminishing energy and diminishing numbers. A sanctuary that was built to house 6,000 members had "only" 1,500 attendees at their main service. As I looked around, I sensed the forced enthusiasm from the worship service leaders, who seemed to be feeling the need to be enthused, but also wondering where everyone was as they looked out on a vast cavern of empty seats. I could feel the emotional energy drain from the church, particularly when the youth pastor stepped up to preach. His weak public speaking skills combined with his own forced enthusiasm made me squirm in my cozy seat. I began to wonder when the service would end.

In all these churches, there must be a balance between engaged members, new attendees who are "checking the church out," and those "inquiring" about getting involved. It is a dynamic equation that may result in church decline if, for too long, attendees begin to wonder, "Where is everyone?" As we saw in another one of our megachurch sites, when a pastor was forced to leave after a sexual and financial scandal, the church quickly folded since there was no one left with sufficient charisma to attract newcomers or maintain and nurture leadership. Fewer newcomers quite literally *drain* the church of energy with devastating results, financially and to the long-term health of the church.

So, in fact, free-riders are necessary for megachurches, which are less harmed by them than smaller churches because of their numbers. That is, they have enough core committed members to handle large numbers of free-riders.[15] These megachurches need new visitors to continue creating the buzz of interest and growth, and the hope is that visitors will eventually become interested and engaged. The question then is: How did megachurches survive long enough with free-riders to gain sufficient members such that free-riders don't undermine their success? One answer is that they may have had fewer

[15] Larger, heterogeneous groups are more likely to engage in collective action because they are more likely to have a core critical mass of very interested participants. See Pamela E. Oliver and Gerald Marwell, "The Paradox of Group Size in Collective Action: A Theory of the Critical Mass. II," *American Sociological Review* 53 (1988): 1–8.

free-riders when they founded the church.[16] Because most megachurches grow quickly,[17] likely due to a combination of energized services and a charismatic leader, they may rapidly move to a condition in which free-riders are beneficial, one in which free-riders feel welcome and free to move to more committed roles in the organization when ready.

We return, therefore, to our core thesis: we argue that humans are continuously driven to solve the problem of *homo duplex*, and that this is precisely what leads us to both our greatest heights of cooperation across kinship, country, and ethnicity, and some of our worst instincts, including tribalism, racism, nationalism, and even global climate extinction. The latter is motivated by the desire to control and dominate resources for one's own nation and group. In all these cases, the evolutionary process has stumbled upon a solution: the evolution of *ultra*-sociality and the nurturing and development of social affects and emotions in the context of community.

Our bold claim is that religion is *the most effective method of facilitating human cooperation, and that megachurches are particularly successful in doing so*. In analyzing our qualitative and quantitative data of twelve nationally representative megachurches, we went through multiple stages of trying to categorize the experiences of members in megachurches. (See Appendix A for more information on our data and methodology.) But what became clear is that we had to accept, despite our own early misgivings, the tremendous energy, joy, and excitement that megachurch members experience in their churches. After an initial failed attempt at categorizing the data, during which we overlooked the emotional power of these churches, we finally took the affective emotional energy of the members' expressions seriously. That is, an emotional desire is quenched in these churches, which mobilizes a process and dynamic reproduction of socialization that demands self-sacrifice for the sake of the group.

Our task then is to further differentiate these processes. We tell that story; give it a social structure; and explain both why it works so well and how megachurches speak to human sociality and encourage fellowship beyond kinship, while creating sources of goodwill and gladness in the hearts of their members.

---

[16] Smaller congregations tend to have fewer free-riders. See Rodney Stark and Roger Finke, *Acts of Faith: Explaining the Human Side of Religion* (Berkeley: University of California Press, 2000).

[17] Scott Thumma and Warren Bird, "Recent Shifts in America's Largest Protestant Churches: Megachurches 2015 Report," Hartford Institute for Religion Research, 2015, accessed December 13, 2017 (http://hirr.hartsem.edu/megachurch/2015_Megachurches_Report.pdf).

CHAPTER 3

Interaction Rituals and Embodied
Choice Theory

Reason is and ought only to be the slave of the passions.
—David Hume, *A Treatise of Human Nature*[1]

God is like a drug, a high, can't wait for the next hit.
—Megachurch attendee

I T IS WITH some irony that we turn to a Scottish Enlightenment philos-
opher, who was an atheist, to begin our central theory chapter for a book
about how churchgoers get "high on God." Given the obsession with reason
and rationality that characterized the Enlightenment, it may surprise some to
learn that one of its greatest philosophers, David Hume, poked through the
arrogance of the claim that human beings are first and foremost rationalists
in their thinking and doing. Hume skewers this high estimate and indeed
flips the notion on its head in a way that WEIRDS certainly might disdain.
In many ways we, as authors of this text, took years to come to our own
conclusions that initially were neither obvious nor apparent to us during our
first take on American megachurches. After going over the data, and even
writing articles using the data, in the early stages of researching this book,
we did not see the full reality of what was happening in these churches. Early

[1] David Hume, *A Treatise of Human Nature*, edited by David Fate Norton and Mary J. Norton
(Oxford: Oxford University Press, 2000), 2.3.3.4.

on, we thought we'd show their superficiality and their biases, and the way they anesthetize churchgoers from reality. But then, as we went over the data and continued attending megachurch services, we began to realize that these are very successful human groups, developing communities that enjoy forms of ecstatic worship, nurture families in positive and joy-filled habits of service and mutual care, and reach out into their communities to offer care, love, and forgiveness as well as food, shelter, and medical relief to those in great need both near and far.

Our temptation was to go the way of the cultured despisers of religious experience and, claiming the moral and epistemological high ground, demonstrate that we were superior both morally and rationally to megachurch members. But in time, we began to see that this "we" was formed in the biases of our own thinking—we had become slaves to our "passions" and prejudices. And, it is always so. One of the traditions in sociology of religion, rational choice theory, is quite explicit in its enactment of this arrogance. In fact, finally, and thankfully, its heyday within the sociology of religion is beginning to pass because of too many misalignments between prediction and practice.[2] This is not to say that we don't think about what we feel, but that what we feel in our bodies is not separate from what we think in our heads, and that our reasoning and rationalizations are mostly ex post facto, because reason is, more than we know, a servant of our passions and affections.[3]

So in the process of coming to our "senses," in a quite visceral manner, we come to our megachurch data with theory formed by this revolution in thinking, and a wakeup call to examine and beware of our senses. Thus, the senior author's experience of the "altar call" described in the Preface, and the revolutionary notion that it is and always has been our senses that form the impressions, and which only later begin to rationalize as our thoughts, that move us to act and believe what we do. This book charts our journey into what we call the theory of "embodied choice."

Embodied choice theory suggests that people make choices (consciously or unconsciously) based on the needs, demands, and desires of their complex human experience: they make choices that will increase their emotional energy; that will expand their access and acceptance into helpful coalitions and mating markets; and that will enhance their political and social capital.

---

[2] Steve Bruce, *Choice and Religion: A Critique of Rational Choice Theory* (Oxford: Oxford University Press, 1999); Stephen Sharot, "Beyond Christianity: A Critique of the Rational Choice Theory of Religion from a Weberian and Comparative Religions Perspective," *Sociology of Religion* 63 (2002): 427–454; Colin Jerolmack and Douglas Porpora, "Religion, Rationality, and Experience: A Response to the New Rational Choice Theory of Religion," *Sociological Theory* 22 (2004): 140–160.

[3] See, for example, Damasio, *Descartes' Error.*

Inclinations toward these human success strategies are driven by cognitive systems that rely *heavily* upon information that comes from the body's affective systems, including somatic markers attached to prior experiences. Humean sentiments lead in judgment. Megachurches work by meeting the emotional needs of humans. And human beings, as we show in the interpretation of our data, make embodied choices of movement, expression, affiliation, and creativity, and only in the aftermath of these experiences do they consciously rationalize these choices. In a constant feedback loop, conscious thoughts, representations (including of the bodily processes), and appraisals take on integral roles in the continuous production and management of affective valence and tone of experience.

While we use Collins's theory of interaction ritual chains[4] to describe the process by which humans experience, consume, and produce emotional energy, we add our twist by arguing that these processes are integral to the nature of what it means to be human. That is, humans are *homo duplex*: both absorbed and sometimes hobbled by their selfish needs and interests, but also yearning, whether consciously or not, to be a part of a greater whole. These impulses are always deeply entangled, since even our selfish desires are socially constructed and our social interests are deeply motivated by egocentric desires. Durkheim's explanation of this multifarious web in human nature is nearly mystical, but it also, we believe, gets at the tragic edge that stalks the human condition across time and tradition: our successes are intermingled with remarkable chaos and tragedy. We are a species whose desires can be noble but are often tripped by deep inner conflicts that put us at odds with others, whether other groups, religions, nations, or, in the end, with our environment. Durkheim meditates on the inner-conflicted nature of these entangled human drives:

> The body is an integral part of the material universe, as it is made known to us by sensory experience; the abode of the soul is elsewhere, and the soul tends ceaselessly to return to it. The abode is the world of the sacred. Therefore, the soul is invested with a dignity that has always been denied the body, which is considered essentially profane, and it inspires those feelings that are everywhere reserved for that which is divine. It is made up of the same substance as are the sacred beings: it differs from them only in degree. A belief that is as universal and permanent as this cannot be purely illusory. There must be something in man that gives rise to this feeling that his nature is

---

[4] Collins, *Interaction Ritual Chains*.

dual, a feeling that men in all known civilizations have experienced. Psychological analysis has, in fact, confirmed the existence of his duality: it finds it at the very heart of our inner life.[5]

Our theory of embodied choice dovetails with Collins's work on the processual ingredients for rituals that are critical for the way human beings create emotional energy. The first is bodily assembly. As we've shown all along, megachurches are nothing if not places where bodily assembly is critical to the energy and sense that *something is about to happen*. Certainly, when a megachurch venue is packed, the energy in the room "feels" full. At these events, expectation is in the air; in fact, sometimes pastors, like any good entertainer, make the people wait, coming in just a tad late. In so doing, anticipation builds, and the emotional energy in the auditorium, is, as they say, *lit*. Crowds give the feeling of anticipation that something is happening, and that you don't want to miss it. Since our bodies are co-created with social and symbolic meaning, it is a natural response for humans to find their emotions elevated and expectations increased as they gather for an event.

Collins's second processual ingredient is *barriers excluding outsiders*. That is, emotional energy is normally heightened in the context where barriers exclude what are perceived as "outsiders." These barriers reduce distractions, facilitating the sense that what's happening *here* is all that matters, and enhancing the feeling of an engaged in-group. As humans, we have a sense that if some place is off limits, it must hold something worth seeing and experiencing. What is unique about megachurches is that there is nearly none of these typical barriers. Indeed, wherever we visited a megachurch as part of our research—including many of the churches in the sample and many more beyond those—the message communicated was always "you are welcome." No matter the venue, people were welcome, overflow spaces were available, no one was left out. Indeed, in the two churches that were African American, and another that was Hispanic, we were struck by the fact, that even when we were virtually the only white people in the room, the welcome was intense and overwhelming.

Instead of physical or cultural barriers, however, there were affective barriers. The only barrier we experienced, in both our studying and attending these churches, is that one must, for full inclusion, pledge one's faith in Jesus Christ and pledge to support the church monetarily in one's service to the community. Of course, in addition, while the door may be open to all who want to come, it is also true that in nearly every megachurch we studied, there

---

[5] Durkheim, "Dualism of Human Nature," 326.

is discouragement or condemnation of LGBTQ relationships and the refusal to perform same-sex marriages. So, for LGBTQ folks and their allies, these barriers are high and the "costs" are often, though not always, insurmountable. That being said, even in these more conservative environments change is stirring, and some contemporary evangelical megachurches are slowly becoming more inclusive on LGBTQ rights. Indeed, one of the surprises about megachurches is that there is a wider diversity of positions on these more controversial issues. And even in churches where same-sex marriage is not celebrated, we've interviewed same-sex couples who attend and feel welcome even if their marriages are not. Perhaps if there is anything that excludes outsiders, it is the sense of whether one can feel the affective and emotional pull of the services. And to be sure, without meaning to, this can be either an attraction or a form of repulsion—that is, there are certainly those who find this kind of intense emotional energy problematic.

Collins's third processual ingredient is critical to the process of feeling in or out—a *shared emotional mood.* Indeed, if one doesn't feel the sense of the crowd or doesn't share the emotion of the group, a situation can quickly become excruciating, and those who are self-conscious quickly head for the exits. But for those who sense that this is *their place and these are their people,* there is almost nothing quite like participating in an ecstatic group in which you feel the emotions of inclusion and like-mindedness. As one megachurch goer explained, "The movement of the Holy Spirit goes through the crowd like a football team doing a wave. I could look up in the balcony and see it pass, and the people doing it. Hundreds get saved." Indeed, in one megachurch we attended, the pastor would hold up his Bible and then move it across the large sanctuary, and everywhere he would go, a wave of folks would rise and then sit as the Bible passed. It created enormous energy across the crowd and as the pastor's Bible hovered over large swaths of people, the crowd became giddy as the wave initiated them in the reading of the scripture.

The fourth and final processual ingredient is a *mutual focus of attention.* As Collins summarizes, "At peak moments, the pattern tends to be jointly shared among all participants: in high solidarity moments, bodies touch, eyes are aligned in the same direction, movements are rhythmically synchronized."[6] As if on cue, Collins describes the power of worship services in megachurches in which bodies are aligned, often moving, in rhythm with one another, to the song, and then with heads pointed forward, as the pastor begins to preach. Megachurch pastors are invariably charismatic figures,

[6] Collins, *Interaction Ritual Chains,* 135.

whom Collins calls *energy stars*. They take center stage and, as we will show in Part II, become the key focus of attention that is critical to their churches' growth. There is really no way to overestimate the megachurch pastor's impact on the vitality of these churches. In one case, as senior author, I visited the site of a megachurch, where a former, longstanding charismatic pastor had been relieved of his duties a year earlier due to his confession of having had sexual relations outside his marriage. A new and much younger pastor had been called to the church. I visited to see how the church was faring; it was clear that the new pastor didn't have the same charisma. The sanctuary, built for 8,000, had curtains cutting the stadium in half, and the energy of the place felt depressed at best. I met the new pastor afterward, and my main reaction to him was that he was looking for reassurance. He was a dynamic young man, but had stepped into shoes that he could not fill, and the experience seemed to drain him of energy—his emotional tone was depleted. I felt it and walked away feeling sad for him. This is not what one finds in energy stars.

Collins is correct: the emotional energy of these communal assemblies is critical to how they thrive, survive, and even die. If one could create an emotional energy meter, one would literally sense and see the energy ebb and flow both during the service and over the life of the church. In the senior author's course on Religion and Culture, I taught Collins's *Interaction Ritual Chains* and his theory of emotional energy. I gave students the opportunity to visit religious settings to test the theory and to observe religious rituals. I gave a wide range of options at multiple religions' worship sites. One student visited and wrote a paper about a megachurch worship service without knowing that I had also attended the same service. The student observed a strong flow of energy in the service, and as the service moved through group singing and announcements, the student wrote about its high energy. But when the pastor stood up to preach, my student observed that she was an assistant, rather than the senior pastor. The student observed with a kind of clinical precision that the energy in the room quickly faded, and it only reappeared when the singing continued. This student had no experience with this church and was new to any kind of religious setting, so she wasn't drawing on experience, but only on what she saw as the "energy flow" in the auditorium. Thus, her paper reflected the precarious nature of these institutions. On the one hand, megachurches provide enormous joy and satisfaction to attendees who need and want their desires met. But the precarious nature of this bargain depends so much on the health and genius of the energy stars.

We argue that Collins's treatment of emotional energy is undeveloped, amorphous, and undifferentiated. This may be in part because he wanted to create a generalizable variable. To be sure, in a later article with Jorg Rossel, Collins admits that the concept of emotional energy is "fuzzy" and needs "further specification."[7] They state that "emotional energy is central to motivating social interactions and attachment to social symbols, but more work is needed to connect this dimension to the varieties of emotions that are subjectively experienced and socially expressed."[8] Collins describes emotional energy (EE) like a type of capital, similar in some ways to social, cultural, or human capital. These forms of capital (including EE) are all described in the singular but they are made up of a variety of different things (i.e., they are the stock of social, cultural, or human assets and value) and people (or groups) have different levels of them. Collins describes EE as a "feeling of confidence, courage to take action, [and] boldness in taking initiative"[9] and in other places he offers other emotional examples of EE, such as joy, awe, or anger. His lack of a clear definition undercuts his ability to measure what it is, how it arrives, and what makes it fluctuate.

We argue that EE is essentially *an individual's stock of residual affective states,* interpreted consciously as varying emotions. Unlike other types of capital that tend to be more stable and quantifiable, EE is dynamic and constantly in flux. If humans had an EE index meter, we'd see a pulse that is continuously changing. For one hypothesis about the biological underpinnings of EE, see Appendix B.

Our definition of EE intentionally distinguishes between "affective states" and emotion. *Affect* is experiential and embodied; it is not dependent on conscious or linguistic processes to exert its influence. *Emotions* are the conceptual and performative schemas that help individuals understand, interpret, and communicate their affective states; they are cognitively and culturally contingent. Different cultures have distinct emotional labels for similar affects.[10] Collins, like other sociologists, does not distinguish between affect and emotion. But he does describe EE manifesting as different emotions. In this way, affects are interpreted as different emotions making up the stock of EE capital.

[7] Jorg Rossel and Randall Collins, "Conflict Theory and Interaction Rituals: The Microfoundations of Conflict Theory," in *Handbook of Sociological Theory,* edited by Jonathan H. Turner, 509–532 (New York: Springer, 2001), 527.

[8] Rossel and Collins, 515.

[9] Collins, *Interaction Ritual Chains,* 39.

[10] This conceptualization of affect and emotion is reflected in Lisa Feldman Barrett's work. See Lisa Feldman Barrett, *How Emotions Are Made: The Secret Life of the Brain* (New York: Houghton Mifflin Harcourt, 2017).

In the context of megachurches, we argue that EE manifests in response to the following six realms of affective desire that motivate people to engage in megachurch rituals and activities:

1. a *sense of belonging and welcome*—megachurches attempt to decrease barriers to entry and go out of their way to welcome newcomers;

2. a *sense of awe and sensory stimulation*—the church services, and sometimes the buildings themselves, facilitate what we call a "wow" factor, a feeling, which megachurch attendees expressed on many occasions, that *this* is the place to be;

3. what we call a *reliable leader*—a charismatic figure who creates warmth, welcome, and trust in members such that he—and it is always a *he* in our sample of twelve megachurches—not only speaks the "truth," but embodies, sometimes quite literally, the "skin" of Jesus;

4. a feeling of *deliverance*, experienced as a sense of wanting, or longing, or desperate hunger to escape loneliness, sin, or depression that typically occurs in moments of what is traditionally called the "altar call" (described in the Preface) for those who want to "accept Jesus" and be saved;

5. a new *purpose,* which a person typically received as a relief from this longing, often with regard to a new identity "in Christ" and the charge to "be one's best self," along with the "call to serve" one's community or city; and finally,

6. a process of *re-membering*—our term for an experience many attendees described—which centers on participation in *small groups*, a structural element that is universal in the megachurches and evangelical churches we have studied.

Re-membering is a process of reifying each person's membership in the church, "the body of Christ," and "remembering"—whether being reminded of the pastor's message, a scripture lesson, or the need to confess and be held "accountable to other brothers and sisters." Re-membering involves celebrating the simple act of hospitality, the sharing of stories, the breaking of bread, and the joy of community and family. It is a time to share joy, laughter, and burdens with others in intimate human fellowship.

The megachurch ritual cycle that functions to address each of these six desires became, after much discussion and debate among us as authors, the "core" of the book, which we explain in Part II. The arc of desire revolves around these six core needs, each of which we are argue is intentionally engaged in these megachurches. Meeting each of these six desires requires forms of EE that are produced within the ritual space; the desires are enacted, practiced, and fulfilled through a ritual process with *six stages* that constitute the "arc" of vitality in megachurches. This arc is the desire for EE being met through ritual practices that create and sustain emotional energy, what Collins calls a "morally suffused" energy that often creates confidence and joy.[11] As we will observe and analyze, the "joy" at times was overwhelming and clearly sustaining to these members; as the title of our book says, they felt "high on God." Since this EE is pleasurable and sought out, but can only be attained in groups, it facilitates cooperation among strangers and gives this cooperation a moral rationale, making it a sacred action. EE satisfies people's individual desires while merging them with the collective in ways that are challenging and rewarding, and, in megachurches, without great costs, at least for most visitors; and even for those most involved the benefits of service and participation far outweigh the price to participate.

> *Our hypothesis: Megachurches provide remarkably successful interaction rituals because they are particularly good at generating the processual ingredients and meeting the six core affective desires of participants. We argue that religion is an astonishingly effective solution to the problem of cooperation and homo duplex, and that megachurches are a prime example of religion doing what religion does best: binding people together in cooperative moral communities held together by cohesive, affective interaction ritual chains.*

This leads us to a matter that has haunted us for some time: considering our work on megachurches, how would we define religion in a way that reflects the core of how megachurch members enact and experience spiritual desire?

---

[11] Collins, *Interaction Ritual Chains*, 39.

CHAPTER 4 | Defining Religion: Sacred Moral
Communities

D URKHEIM ARGUES THAT human beings need, more than anything
else, to be engaged in and supported by a community. For most of
human history, this community has been led by priests, shamans, or other
types of intermediaries that connect the community to that which is ultimate, that which is sacred. Now, we can argue the relative purity and trans-
parency of these priests and shamans, but this really isn't a question of purity
of intention or action. Religious figures of the past and present have always
had a mixed moral record of intentions and motives. It is more a question
of what these sacred figures did and now do for their respective cultures
that matters. What Durkheim is arguing is that all human groups have
sought to create a sacred moral community. From the cave-dwellers to the
Egyptians, from the Romans to the Muslims, from the indigenous priests in
South America to the Mormon priests on Salt Lake—each in their own way
sought to manifest sacred energy to the people, to sustain an organization
that would serve the needs of the whole. Humans, even in the age of the
Enlightenment, much less in our more secular time, still seek to construct
a sacred canopy. As Peter Berger argued, "Man does not have a given relationship to the world. He must ongoingly establish a relationship with it."[1]
Thus, our initial definition of religion is apt: *Religion is the socially enacted
desire for the ultimate that binds a group into a moral community.* Secular groups

[1] Peter Berger, *The Sacred Canopy* (New York: Doubleday, 1967), 5.

and secular governments seek to harness a common good, where everyone is tended to within one's borders; where the elderly have care, and parents can educate their children, and young men and women can grow up to work and make families. Once put in this light, the fierce fights we have between religion and the secular seem more like fights to prove the sacred nature of one's group. And even here, the adequacy of secularism, as a form that can sustain a moral community, remains up in the air. Do secular communities create a vibrant and robust enough vision of humanity to maintain an ultimate sense of purpose and coherence? Is secularism strong and vigorous enough to sustain a civilizational canopy? Can it and will it provide purpose and reason against the threat of suffering and death? We don't know. For now, we argue that religion will remain with us for the long term. Humans, who are riddled by doubt and driven by the fear of death, seek both fulfillment in our own sense of identity and ways to interact with their communities, both the one and the many. And so, analyzing our megachurch data made us rethink our older definitions of religion. We then came up with this definition that will be our guide for this book:

> Religion is (1) a social enactment of a desire for the ultimate. It is (2) embodied in ritual practices; (3) described by systems of symbols and beliefs; (4) developed in communal settings, and often institutionally legitimated. (5) Religion interacts and negotiates with powers and forces that are experienced as within and beyond the self and group. (6) This power or force is most often referred to as god/spirit or gods/spirits. (7) The affective experience of ritual and the symbolic, and social boundaries constructed in rites, mobilize group identity and bind the group into a moral community. Last, (8) these moral communities produce networks of solidarity, and carry the potential for tension and, more rarely, conflict and violence within and between groups.

Religion is from the Latin *religare,* which means "to bind." Religion, in the context of the megachurch, binds one's desires to an ultimate—whether to fellow megachurch members, the charismatic pastor, or the mission of the church. These commitments are first and foremost social enactments. None of our desires, or our fears for that matter, come out of nowhere. Each family and tribe, each culture and country, has certain desires and anxieties that percolate up to frame hearts and minds. We are not born free. But we are born into families and groups in which our desires and ultimate values are socially constructed, though by no means determined. Nonetheless, as Durkheim argues, we need forms and structures that shape our rituals and practices, and guide and determine what we pursue and avoid. In the modern world of the West, our desires are fashioned for money, prestige, possessions, and power.

Desires are framed and forged through and with the rituals and aims that cultures create and uphold. And from these cultural resources, symbols are built and beliefs are manufactured by what we learn in our early books, in our schools and through our families. Our communal life vibrates with certain ideas and ideals that shape our institutions, educationally, socially, and, in our present time, electronically. And sometimes, religions, as clusters of beliefs, doctrines, and rituals, shape where we place our value, our hopes, and our aspirations. Whether our religions become powerful to us often depends on our parents, our communities, and the leaders who guide and shape who we want to become. In the religious realm, we begin to conceptualize these powers and forces that are within and beyond us as spirit(s) and god(s). But even in the secular realm, the spiritual often becomes a power or presence that is less personal and organized, but remains a power to which many of us—or, we would argue, all of us—must respond. At one point or another, we ask the question, what is ultimate to us? And it can be quite small in shape and content, but humans want to be connected to what they love and what they experience as sacred.

Through all sorts of symbolic and social forms, rites of different kinds mobilize group identities and bind individuals together into moral communities. When nations are under threat, whether from within or from without, a nation's *civil religion is tapped and used to create solidarity.*[2] We are bound, even in our postmodern electronic communities, to a moral and sacred community of people with whom we agree, and for whom we will fight when necessary. And these communities produce forms of solidarity and potential tension as various others come and go, critiquing and coopting what we think, until there is a time at which we say we can go no further. And it is at these times that there is conflict and, more rarely, violence. But we would argue, even atheists are believers, when it comes to mobilizing against the other. Religion is a way to understand the human condition as a total way of life from birth to death, from solidarity to war, from the profane to the sacred. We are all inevitably caught up in webs of ultimate desire. Religion, we argue, is the distinctively human way to negotiate this terrain and to come to grips with the kind of sacred, moral community we want to be and become as human beings.

One might ask, what about God? Well, this, too, is a question that our ancient texts invite and indeed command us to negotiate, accept, and embrace.

---

[2] Robert Bellah, "Civil Religion in America," *Daedalus* 96 (1967): 1–21. See Philip Gorski's update of these ideas in *American Covenant: A History of Civil Religion from the Puritans to the Present* (Princeton, NJ: Princeton University Press, 2017).

On this matter, we are not writing theology, we are thinking about how the religious rituals in megachurches satisfy and inspire members to create moral communities. The task, then, of this book is to make that as clear as can be. But also, to argue that no one can avoid the human task of creating a sacred, moral community. So, this book is one way to understand how humans come to grips with this undertaking, and how they solve what Durkheim says we all must face: that we are *homo duplex*, selves that need to be separate and set apart, but also connected to sacred communities. It is an enormously complex task, and we invite our readers to think about it for themselves even as we show how it works for megachurch members.

| Megachurch: An American Original (Almost)

M ANY ASSUME THAT megachurches are a new phenomenon and an American invention; in this chapter, we show that neither assumption is true, and argue that megachurches have been an inevitable aspect of the Christian faith from the beginning. That is, the Christian faith's primary modus operandi from the start was to translate the faith into wider publics and cultures—to seek to infiltrate other languages, cultures, and one social system after another. It is in the early language of the faith that Christ is in all, for all, and through all, and when Christians came together they were called the "body of Christ." This body made each person essential but only as they were a part of the church, a part of Christ's body. In this sense, we circle back to Durkheim's potent phrase *homo duplex*; this faith responded to the need to glorify and harmonize the one and the many and to bring them into one society, one church, one large megachurch:

> The ideas and sentiments that are elaborated by a collectivity, whatever it may be, are invested by reason of their origin with an ascendancy and an authority that cause the particular individuals who think them and believe in them to represent them in the form of moral forces that dominate and sustain them. When these ideals move our wills, we feel that we are being led, directed, and carried along by singular

energies that, manifestly, do not come from us but are imposed on us from the outside.[1]

Thus, the phenomenon of Christianity was responding to a deeper human need and the movement within humanity to solve the dilemma of our duplicity, our dual natures. Humans must confront this dilemma, both our need to be uniquely ourselves and to be in harmony with the *socis*, a larger and thus sacred community of faith.

Again, this book plays on this theme that megachurches are responses to deep human needs and demands; they are not aberrations, but a part of our longer bio-social-cultural heritage that pushes us toward greater wholes, sacred communities, even as we struggle to maintain our individuality. And so, as we inquire into the origins of megachurches, we begin, with tongue in cheek, a review on how megachurches are an "almost" American original. Indeed, we argue that megachurches have always been a part of the Christian tradition, from the early cathedrals of the Catholic tradition to the great Eastern Orthodox basilica of Constantinople. The latter was built in 537 C.E. and called *Sancta Sophia* in Latin and *Hagia Sophia* in Greek; the basilica is one of the great structures in human history. Built for the Eastern Orthodox patriarch, it was conquered and temporarily converted into a Roman Catholic cathedral from 1204 to 1261, and then later, in 1453, remade again by the Ottoman Turkish Empire into an Islamic mosque celebrating the conquest of Constantinople. It remained a sacred canopy for the Muslim world, and now is a museum in secular Turkey, which may be changing even as we write this book.

We argue that megachurches are human constructions that are natural manifestations of the human need to sacralize our communities in a wider communal setting and to use architecture and human organizations to meet these deep needs. David E. Eagle rightfully historicizes the megachurch[2] as something not new to the modern world at all. Eagle finds their origins in the sixteenth century: megachurches were plotted as products of French Huguenot and Calvinist reformation with their deep commitment to preaching and "hearing" the word. And by hearing, this meant constructing buildings with one functional purpose in mind: the process of preaching and teaching the gospel to as many people as possible. This brand of "bigness" grew out of a transatlantic passion for focusing on the proclamation of the scripture and the preaching of the Bible. Such a focus on word is hardly a

[1] Durkheim, "Dualism of Human Nature," 335.
[2] David E. Eagle, "Historicizing the Megachurch," *Journal of Social History* 48 (2015): 589–604.

modern phenomenon, but indigenous to Christian scriptures themselves and no less modern than the great Jewish convert, the Apostle Paul. Paul, by his own overweening ambition, sought to create a movement from an obscure teacher and healer—Jesus—whom he never met in the flesh but who utterly captivated his soul. A polymath of his time, Paul traveled the known world of his period, and translated this "gospel" into cultures far afield from his Jewish roots. And Paul's method, as he spoke to the empire of his day—Rome—was the preaching of the word. In his famous letter to the Romans, Paul argued, "So then faith *comes* by *hearing*, and *hearing* by the word of God" (Romans 10:17, NKJV). The Christian tradition, unique among the Western monotheistic traditions, has an abiding and structural demand to translate this "word" into each culture and its own language. Paul's stunning confidence can only be imagined in his eccentric and supercilious testimony in Athens:

> Some said, "What does this babbler want to say?" Others said, "He seems to be a proclaimer of foreign divinities." (This was because he was telling the good news about Jesus and the resurrection.) So they took him and brought him to the Areopagus and asked him, "May we know what this new teaching is that you are presenting? It sounds rather strange to us, so we would like to know what it means." Now all the Athenians and the foreigners living there would spend their time in nothing but telling or hearing something new.
>
> Then Paul stood in front of the Areopagus and said, "Athenians, I see how extremely religious you are in every way. For as I went through the city and looked carefully at the objects of your worship, I found among them an altar with the inscription, 'To an unknown god.' What therefore you worship as unknown, this I proclaim to you." (Acts 17:18-23, NRSV)

Paul fashioned the religion of Christianity as a missionary faith that inspired followers thereafter to imitate and make it a religion able to speak in any context, using the words and conventions of that place to make clear to all cultures, that this faith answered the fundamental urge and need in human beings—something that Durkheim penetrates with his analysis, "Once the group has dissolved and the social communion has done its work, the individuals carry away within themselves these great religious, moral, and intellectual conceptions that societies draw from their very hearts during their periods of greatest creativity."[3]

---

[3] Durkheim, "Dualism of Human Nature," 336.

Humans carry within themselves this need to overcome the one and the many, the space in between self and other, person and community, a space that erupts and disrupts the human consciousness that must be resolved. And it is in response to this deep human conundrum, we argue, that the Christian faith has sought to answer the bell. Paul's ability to accommodate each culture charted the roadmap of how future apostles and Christian entrepreneurs would navigate their own ways in foreign cultures. And this only picked up speed with the Reformation—a revolution that joined wider trends in the modernization of Western civilizations to discover, dominate, and trade with other cultures and thus to learn the language of the other. Of course, this was a secularizing process, but also a progression that Protestantism adopted and took advantage of. Neither Judaism nor Islam aimed at this same type of accommodation, and each in its own way has struggled to fully adapt to modernity. But even as Christianity, in both its Protestant and Catholic forms, has had to change, it has also paid a price for these accommodations. So, this history of the megachurch has deep roots in the origins of the faith, as well as showing how forms of the Christian church protested, adapted to, and produced modern forms of culture, democracy, and modernity.

Indeed, with the Reformation, Martin Luther and John Calvin broke from the hierarchical structures of the day, seeking to purify and release the power of the faith for the sake of bringing a decontaminated gospel and the scriptures, translated into the common languages of the day, to the people. Once released from their authority structures, as the sociologist David Martin has argued, Protestantism became positively related to globalization.[4] And with its emphasis on inward reflection and demand for personal commitment, Protestantism exploded in forms no longer controlled by ecclesiastical authorities, molding identities that were portable and relatively durable. It created communities that braced individuals against the utilitarian calculations of modernity; it made the formation of democracy a plausible way to organize states; it empowered individuals (sometimes even women) to think entrepreneurially in terms of religion, culture, and economy; it developed an egalitarian and democratic perspective and polity, which has been guided by charismatic leadership, both in and outside the church; and it has used the expressive and affective tendencies of the premodern world in the embodiment of new sects, including the rise of Pentecostalism and its many forms of megachurches that now have spread across the world.[5] Thus,

---

[4] David Martin, *On Secularization: Towards a Revised General Theory* (Burlington, VT: Ashgate, 2005).
[5] Donald Miller and Tetsunao Yamamori, *Global Pentecostalism: The New Face of Christian Engagement* (Berkeley: University of California Press, 2007). Scott L. Thumma and Warren Bird, "Megafaith for the Megacity: The Global Megachurch Phenomenon," in *The Changing World Religion Map: Sacred Places,*

Protestantism (in all its forms) extends the Anglo-American movement of modernity, using the principles of voluntarism and taking advantage of open religious and political markets. As we will see, it followed the trail of early Methodism that empowered and disciplined the poor, creating communities of accountability, internalizing the Protestant ethic, and giving them a voice and a rising standard of living.

Of course, we are also aware that along with the benefits there were costs to these incursions into the world: the further secularization of the faith in the prosperity gospel and the occasional exploitation by charismatic charlatans. Indeed, these "darker" aspects to the faith will be the subject of Part III. For now, we examine the critical stages of the development of the megachurch over the last 400 years, the peculiar dimension of this faith, and how and in what ways megachurches have been predictable products of this development. We will then end with an estimation of the current American religious market, and how it bodes well for megachurches and what that means for the future of megachurches in America.

Transatlantic Formations of the Megachurch

As Eagle points out, one of the earliest versions of the modern megachurch emerged in France:

> The edict of Nantes (1598) granted Protestants in France the right to legally build and organize churches. Already by 1601, Protestants began dreaming big. The Huguenot architect Jacques Perret provides a dramatic example. In his 1601 book, *Des fortification et artifices, architecture et perspective*, he draws up plans for an idealized Protestant temple. . . . It held nearly 10,000 people on its main floor. . . . The preacher stood close to the center of the nearly square building to maximize the ability of worshippers to hear the sermon.[6]

What is critical here is that these buildings are no longer conceived of as sacramental locations, set apart from the secular—a longstanding notion in Lutheran and Catholic theology—but are now used for multiple purposes. "The church" no longer refers to a building, but to the people—a radical idea that Perret announced in a slogan posted outside his temple: "The Christian

Identities, Practices and Politics, edited by Stanley D. Brunn (New York: Springer Dordrecht, 2015), 2331–2352.

[6] Eagle, "Historicizing the Megachurch," 592.

Children of God are his true temple."[7] Again, the translation of the message of faith moved into the broader world of secular culture and politics, the sacred bleeding into the secular and the secular partnering with the sacred. Protestantism upends the neat categories and prepares the way for perforated boundaries between the sacred and profane that become the pattern that marks the religious life of modernity, as well as beginning to challenge the very notion of separating the sacred and the profane. As we have argued, this mixing has been a part of the Christian message from the beginning, in the ministry of Jesus who continually broke boundaries of gender, ethnicity, and religion, as well as with Paul, who translated the words of the messiah into the world and language of the Gentiles. Again, megachurches in this sense become agents that have trespassed boundaries in the Christian religion from the beginning.

This desire to break out of what Paul called the "old wineskins" marks a Protestant movement away from the traditional forms of the Catholic past, galvanized by Calvinist roots transferred into the American religious and cultural DNA. Thus, separated from the traditions and bureaucracy of Catholic rites and rituals, the emotional energy of revivalist preachers spread the Christian faith across the North Atlantic, beginning with the English Wesley brothers, whose very denomination's name—Methodism—followed function: small groups devoted to Christian fellowship, prayer, and the work of invading every sector of society with the good news of Jesus Christ and the transformation for the sake of every aspect of life.

Parallel with the Wesleyan project, America's first great theologian, Jonathan Edwards (1703–1758), hewed a more precise and rational form of revivalism. Edwards was an unlikely vessel of renewal. He spoke in deliberate and academic language. His beautiful but complex prose adumbrated an intricate and probing theology of faith. And in his most famous book, he adjudicated the question of authentic conversion—it was called *Religious Affections*.[8] As Edwards asserts, "From hence it clearly and certainly appears, that great part of true religion consists in the affections. For love is not only one of the affections, but it is the first and chief of the affections, and the fountain of all the affections."[9] But Edwards explains that there are twelve signs that appear to be indicators of true religion, and further, twelve more signs that are sure marks of these holy affections. This book was written after

[7] Eagle, "Historicizing the Megachurch," 592.
[8] Jonathan Edwards, *Religious Affections* (Vancouver: Eremitical Press, 2009 [1746]).
[9] Edwards, *Religious Affections*, 13.

one of the early revivals of the Great Awakening in his own church, which, as fate would have it, included the conversion of his wife, Sarah.

Indeed, Edwards was one of the great expositors of the scriptures, deeply influenced and educated in natural philosophy as well as the liberal arts of his time. He was well acquainted with the growing development of science, both speculative and empirical. He took this keen eye into the religious and spiritual development of the Christian soul. For Edwards, this was no simple or easy path, but a demanding one in both mind and heart to discern human affections so that one would not be fooled in seeking and being saved in Christ. At the heart of this "sweet" knowledge of God was a light that created both holy affections and holiness of act and spirit. Edwards's powerful and intense preaching helped to inaugurate the First Great Awakening in American religious history. However, his power to persuade was not so much in the tone or tenor of his preaching, but in his verbal acuity to press the purity of the faith, and seek commitment on the deepest and most profound basis.

One of Edwards's most important sermons was called "A Divine and Supernatural Light, Immediately Imparted to the Soul by the Spirit of God, Shown to Be Both Scriptural and Rational Doctrine." In it, Edwards judiciously and juridically makes the case that the "heart" and affections are the primary vehicles by which true discipleship is determined—but his case is made not by conjuring great emotion, but through precise rational arguments that seek to persuade listeners to convert to a true and unambiguous affection for God in Christ:

> This light, and this only, has its fruit in a universal holiness of life. No merely notional or speculative understanding of the doctrines of religion will ever bring to this. But this light, as it reaches the bottom of the heart, and changes the nature, so it will effectually dispose to a universal obedience. It shows God's worthiness to be obeyed and served. It draws forth the heart in a sincere love to God, which is the only principle of a true, gracious, and universal obedience; and it convinces of the reality of those glorious rewards that God has promised to them that obey him.[10]

Edwards was convinced that by rational argument the "spirits" could be tested so that the followers of Christ could be found pure and uncontaminated by the world.

---

[10] Jonathan Edwards, "A Divine and Supernatural Light, Immediately Imparted to the Soul by the Spirit of God, Shown to Be Both Scriptural and Rational Doctrine," 1734, accessed January 9, 2018, (https://www.monergism.com/thethreshold/articles/onsite/edwards_light.html).

In reading Edwards's sermons one is struck by their careful logic and rationality. But at their core was Edwards's determination to instill and reveal the purity of his hearers' hearts. He believed that God's spirit would woo their hearts to a guiding commitment to Jesus Christ. And this was neither easy nor pleasant for himself or his listeners. The relentless pressure Edwards put on his congregants to continually demonstrate signs of true piety came to a head in the late 1740s when Edwards reversed a long-held practice of opening communion to nonbelievers. He began to demand an explicit expression of faith in Christ before a person would be allowed to receive communion.

Edwards's congregation lost patience with his demands. In 1751, he was overwhelmingly voted out of his own church and ended up preaching at a small, obscure set of mission churches, including a tiny Native American mission in 1751. In 1757, in recognition of his theological brilliance and his leadership, Edwards was called to be president of the College of New Jersey, later Princeton University. But before he could take office, he died on March 22, 1758, of a fever following a smallpox inoculation. And while his own life and career ended in defeat, his legacy and focus on the affective nature of faith became one of the foremost contributions to American religion.

Indeed, it is often said that the main contenders in American Protestantism have been the rational theology of the Puritans and the more emotional intensity of Pietism; or, in more contemporary vernacular, the battle between the mind and emotion. But as we have argued, not only is this a false dichotomy, but it doesn't hold up empirically. Religion is always a matter of affect, as we will show, but the main events in culture, across time and traditions, have always been the movement between the soul and society. And as Durkheim describes, this has always been a complicated and taxing give-and-take process in which mutual sacrifices are demanded:

> In fact, however, society has its own nature, and, consequently, its requirements are quite different from those of our nature as individuals: the interests of the whole are not necessarily those of the part. Therefore, society cannot be formed or maintained without our being required to make perpetual and costly sacrifices. Because society surpasses us, it obliges us to surpass ourselves; and to surpass itself, a being must, to some degree, depart from its nature—a departure that does not take place without causing more or less painful tensions.[11]

As we will argue, there is no better place to show this give-and-take but in the study of Christian congregations—in the slow and tedious observation of

[11] Durkheim, "Dualism of Human Nature," 333.

church members working out this divide within themselves as they become members of megachurches. On the ground, in the pew, from the perspective of congregational studies, and in American history, this is where one finds the taxing and emotional capacity of humans seeking to negotiate the costly demands of "society," "church," and "faith" amid fellow believers and religious leaders as they work out their own salvation. Thus, while congregational studies may seem prosaic and even mundane, we argue that it is precisely in these "pews" (or stadium seats, as some megachurches would have it) that we see how human beings labor to negotiate the tedious demands of society and the passion in their own souls to be themselves even as they are members of a group. In this sense, we claim that it is in these strange megachurch laboratories where we find what human beings are really doing when they claim to "work out *your* salvation in fear and trembling" (after Philippians 2:12).

This verse, which by the way is in Paul's advice to the congregants in Philippi at the first Christian church established in Europe, is once again encouraging and warning against internal conflict in the Philippian community. To be sure, conflict and tensions are a hallmark of the faith, and yet another example of the powerful forces demanding costly sacrifices and the promise of benefits as humans wrestle in the interstices of the self and other, the soul and the community. One of the fundamental themes in Pauline literature is how the Apostle must constantly persuade and intercede in and to his churches as they struggle to overcome internecine conflict.

And it is ever the case in Jonathan Edwards's time. For those coming after Edwards, the argument between mind and emotion becomes even clearer. George Whitefield, in partnership and some tension with the pietism of the Wesley brothers, won the day in both numbers and influence. Some, and here we mean Protestant elites, have claimed that the contemporary movement toward emotion and affection is new, but we think it has always been a primary way Americans have responded to faith. Nowhere is this more powerfully understood than in the life and times of George Whitefield (1714–1770). Whitefield, an Anglican cleric of British roots, was seven years younger than the Wesleys and Edwards but refused to bow to their authority. Whitefield became an itinerant revivalist par excellence. He was a friend of Benjamin Franklin, a fellow self-promoter and entrepreneur. Whitefield hired a publicist to advertise his preaching; he edited his own journals, and used the theatrical arts to sway his audiences to cry and moan.[12] Whitefield preached in fields and city streets in the heyday of the First Great Awakening, able to

---

[12] Frank Lambert's study of Whitefield's masterful use of modern media, *"Pedlar in Divinity": George Whitefield and the Transatlantic Revivals 1737–1770* (Princeton, NJ: Princeton University Press, 1994).

be heard by outdoor crowds of more than 30,000. He became a celebrity in the United Kingdom and in British North America. In fact, he is often said to be a figure who honed and unified the British North American identity, bringing a rough-and-tumble population to tears of repentance while listening to his stories from scripture and his moving descriptions of the need to convert.[13]

Thomas Kidd, an historian of this period of American evangelical history, suggests that a fifth ingredient be added to the classic four-part definition of evangelicalism given by David Bebbington (conversion, activism, Biblicism, and crucicentrism): the ministry of the Holy Spirit.[14] We agree, and argue that the work of affect and emotion is always the primary power that leaders and groups use to activate change and mobilize individuals into organizations. Once again, without this we miss the wider context for understanding the development of not only religion, but the culture of human communities—there is no momentum to groups without deep emotional energy, and there is no organizational structure without combining the emotion to wider social alliances, and in this case churches and religious councils. Whitefield's ability to touch human emotion and motivate decisions for faith framed the American identity as affective, democratic, and self-righteous, and encouraged both a purity of heart and a sense of self-made community.[15] Whitefield is the quintessential exemplar of what many have sought to become: stars in the world of American megachurches, melding a community that would generate the drive for success in every aspect of life.

Whitefield went to great lengths not only to build up his fame but also to smooth and accentuate the characteristics that were communicated to the public. Whitefield sought converts, and he used every method to effect conversion and to build and polish his authority as a revival preacher. In his diaries, he recreated scenes from his life, and much of what biographers have of him are his edited retellings. As one of the main progenitors of the American identity, Whitefield was pragmatic, prone both to entertain as he sought conviction and to make much of himself even as he was preaching conversion to Jesus Christ.

[13] Jerome Dean Mahaffey, *The Accidental Revolutionary: George Whitefield and the Creation of America* (Waco, TX: Baylor University Press, 2011).

[14] Thomas S. Kidd, *George Whitefield: America's Spiritual Founding Father* (New Haven, CT: Yale University Press, 2014), 36.

[15] Thomas S. Kidd, *George Whitefield: America's Spiritual Founding Father* (New Haven, CT: Yale University Press, Reprint edition, August 9, 2016).

In shaping his image, Whitefield was deeply practical and duplicitous—intent on success at all costs. He was an early critic of slavery, but when it became more convenient he not only advocated for slavery in order to keep his South Carolina plantation running, but also became a slave owner. Whitefield wanted to help the poor and the downtrodden, so he built the Georgian Orphan House. The orphanage "proved" his faith—even as he was illegally bringing slaves to Georgia two years before slavery became legal in that state. Thus, his good deeds were built in the 1750s on the backs of slaves that he used to run his plantation and orphan home.[16]

To be sure, Whitefield evangelized his slaves, thus justifying his ownership in his mind. This moral relativism spotlights an undercurrent in evangelicalism that, in the name of conversion, many immoral acts could be justified as believers professed to build a larger agenda for revival. This structural injustice has often been rationalized by personalizing issues—slave owners justified themselves by converting or showing compassion to their slaves. North Atlantic evangelicals, at least regarding slavery, had a mixed record at best, particularly on the American side.[17] And we see this tendency among evangelicals both in Whitefield's period and our own. All can be saved, but some may pay the price of inequality before they reach heaven. Personal faith in Christ often became a way to void one's conscience.

None of this is surprising, as we will see when we look at church scandals in Part III of this book. When they succeed, megachurches and the success of the their pastor bristle with a kind of goodness, but when they fail, victims pile up. And so it was with figures from early American Christianity. It remains true, however, that Whitefield's legacy is one of creating unity out of a disparate and motley British American population that, partly due to Whitefield's intense belief in Christ and his powerful push for sanctity, created a collective sensibility rooted in the Calvinist drive for independence out of which an American character was born.

We need to continually go back to this idea that the Christian faith translated and penetrated enormously diverse contexts to reimagine a religious and cultural unity that few could have described or predicted would emerge within these early colonies. The impress of the gospel to make oneself a slave to Christ for the sake of the kingdom of God mutated within this motley mosaic of British American community—a community that included

<hr/>

[16] Jessica Parr takes a more topical approach in *Inventing George Whitefield: Race, Revivalism, and the Making of a Religious Icon* (Jackson: University Press of Mississippi, 2015).
[17] Mark A. Smith, *How Culture Has Trumped Religion in American Politics* (Chicago: University of Chicago Press, 2015).

a mix of early American enlightenment figures such as Franklin who dreamed of a new experiment in a Christian, democratic, and independent polity. There are many who paid the price for this American experiment, so we are in no way justifying colonialism or, indeed, the genocide of the early indigenous peoples of the Americas. However, we are arguing that these megachurches and their leadership have deep connections to those who have gone before them in American history and culture.

Perhaps the most famous of the era's English evangelicals was the non-conformist Charles Haddon Spurgeon. His Metropolitan Tabernacle in London attracted thousands and could hold 6,000 listeners. It also founded and ran an orphanage and an alms house. Spurgeon became an inspiration for D. L. Moody, the American revivalist of the late 1900s. They were cut from similar class backgrounds; neither was college-educated, but both were self-made entrepreneurs—again, a common quality of megachurch leaders. They inspired and encouraged many evangelical leaders in the American setting to simply begin preaching if they felt the call and had a gift. And for Spurgeon, the call and the gift were both palpable. Spurgeon's charisma made him willing to move outside of conventions—he was never ordained. Spurgeon took a strong stand against slavery, following in the footsteps of most British evangelicals of that time. His sermons attacking slavery were burned by his fellow Baptists in America. Spurgeon called slavery the "foulest blot" that "may have to be washed out by blood."[18]

American Charles Grandison Finney (1792–1875) was, like Spurgeon, another renowned preacher of the Second Great Awakening (1790–1840). He was an ordained Presbyterian but struggled with many of the doctrines. He ended up in New York City and founded one of the great evangelical and activist churches of the nineteenth century, the Broadway Tabernacle. The church was very much in the genre of the megachurch tradition—it could seat 2,400 but accommodate 4,000. Finney was radical, and not only on slavery. At the Tabernacle, he hosted "contemporary debates on women's rights, abolition, and prohibition; and the building housed an extensive ministry to the poor."[19] Finney eventually moved on to become the second president of Oberlin College. Oberlin was the first college to accept women and black students; it participated in support of the Underground Railroad, and it actively resisted the Fugitive Slave Act.

---

[18] Larry J. Michael, *Spurgeon on Leadership: Key Insights for Christian Leaders from the Prince of Preachers* (Grand Rapids, MI: Kregel Publications, 2010).
[19] Eagle, "Historicizing the Megachurch," 595.

Finney combined an intense evangelical faith with a deep egalitarian conviction that no one was above sin nor outside the call of Christ. Finney's *Lectures on Revivals of Religion,* published in 1835, were a sober and calculated method on how to convict sinners. As Finney suggested, revival "is not a miracle." He continued,

It is not a miracle according to another definition of the term miracle—something above the powers of nature. There is nothing in religion beyond the ordinary powers of nature. It consists entirely in the right exercise of the powers of nature. It is just that, and nothing else. When mankind become religious, they are not enabled to put forth exertions which they were before unable to put forth. They only exert the powers they had before in a different way, and use them for the glory of God.[20]

Finney, who was trained in the law, did not seek to convert by emotion, at least in the sense of using the promise of salvation as a goad to conversion. He was far more apt to preach in a way to "evangelize" Christians to the truth of the gospel, to reinvigorate faith, and in this case to make "backsliding" Christians do the right thing. Thus, his *Lectures on Revival* were aimed at Christians who had grown "cold" in the heart and had lost the zeal for faith in action. The lectures were a ruthless estimation of how one had sinned and how one must repent. Finney gave no room for avoiding the judgment of God on sin, for pretension of goodness, or for any equivocation about one's duty to judge oneself and to ask for forgiveness and mercy. Finney demanded moral exertion, full and sober evaluation of one's moral failures; he abjured original sin as a doctrine not worthy of God. At the end of his life, he believed that Christians could achieve moral perfection and freedom from sin in Christ. We might imagine him as forerunner of the "strenuous mood" in the moral philosophy of William James.[21]

And to be sure, this bears on the notion in the American character of the nineteenth century that human effort is critical to human transformation. Finney was less sanguine about human efforts, but there is in his work the seeds of what came later in the thinking of megachurch pastors and Christian authors in the twentieth and twenty-first centuries—with effort and practice in the faith, one could do all things. Some could argue these claims to self-improvement, despite their resolute soberness, are the

[20] Charles G. Finney, *Lectures on Revivals of Religion* (CreateSpace, 2015), 7.
[21] William James, "The Moral Philosophy and the Moral Life," in *The Will to Believe and Other Essays in Popular Philosophy: Human Immortality* (New York: Dover Publications, 1956).

seeds of the twentieth-century prosperity gospel. The self-help movement, after all, is a relentless sermon on self-improvement. This is not far from the work of Norman Vincent Peale, the twentieth-century megachurch pastor, who promoted positive thinking and the importance of unyielding self-improvement.

Russell H. Conwell (1843–1925) stands out as an exemplar and bridge between the late Puritans and ascetic Protestants of the mid-nineteenth century and the prosperity gospel types of the twentieth century. Conwell's work as preacher and purveyor of what we now call "positive thinking" both evokes and extends the Protestant evocation of the human potential movement. Conwell came out of military service in the Civil War writing biographies of generals in the Civil War, before he sought education for the ministry. All during this time, he developed ideas about how to create growth via the transformation of one's attitude. His success as a speaker and preacher enabled him to build the Baptist Temple in 1891 in Philadelphia. He encouraged and inspired the mainline Philadelphians to dream big about not only what they could do for themselves but for others. He became a master speaker in how to transform one's life. Conwell attracted and preached to thousands at his Temple, but also moved beyond the church to nurture education, and was pivotal in starting what would become Temple College, and later Temple University. Conwell was Temple's first president.

The Baptist Temple has all the earmarks of what later megachurches would include: facilities for youth such as bowling alleys, sprawling auditoriums, and exquisite music. And indeed, Conwell became most famous for his startling "Acres of Diamonds" speech, which he is said to have performed 6,152 times. He explained that the inspiration for the speech came during an 1869 trip to the Middle East, during which he spoke with an Arab guide who told Conwell the story of a man who wanted to get wealthy and thus sold his property. But soon afterward, the man learned that diamonds had been discovered on the land that he had sold, which made his buyer rich. The theme that Conwell drew from this story was that one must "make hay" where one lived. What you have and what you are can make you rich if you begin to exercise your God-given talents and direct them, as he claims God commands, toward making money. Listening to the Acres of Diamonds speech performed by a professional actor today, one can still hear the way it resonates with so many of the themes proclaimed by twentieth-century prosperity gospel preachers.

Conwell tells one story after another of men who had sold their home or property only to have the buyer come in and discover that "wealth" was somehow right under their nose, and that—in New Testament parlance— they would get rich if they had "eyes to see it." It is one of those positive thinking cues that, if followed, gives everyone hope that if one uses one's own resources, money will follow. And Conwell is not shy about saying this precisely: "Money is power." In fact, it is the "duty" of each of his listeners "to get rich . . . to get money."[22] Conwell met the most obvious counterarguments to his rather prosaic advice, and responded simply, "Think if you had the money you could endow the Temple college." That is, money is a resource for doing good. He often told a tale of a little girl with "57 cents," who gave it to him as a contribution to the down payment on the new temple he sought to build. She had heard his vision and immediately started saving to give to the campaign; she died tragically, but left this prosaic small sum of money, 57 cents, to help toward the building of the Temple. The seeds of this gift, he said, made its construction possible.

One of the more illuminating moments in the speech is Conwell's retelling of a story about a Temple University seminarian who condemned Reverend Conwell's preaching on the importance of making money. "Money," he insisted to Conwell, "is the root of all evil."[23] Conwell, without skipping a beat, asks the seminarian to give him the full verse from the scripture, 1 Timothy 6:10, and Conwell corrects him saying, "It is the *love* of money that is the root of all evil." Conwell is correct, of course, but the arguments on these matters are so much more complex than a matter of judging whether one loves the money that one seeks. This ambiguity and all the variations on this theme are brilliantly exposed in Kate Bowler's *Blessed: A History of the American Prosperity Gospel*.[24] Bowler's volume is a comprehensive study on the enormous growth and power of prosperity gospel churches in the twentieth and twenty-first centuries.

The overlap between the prosperity philosophy and the rise of American capitalism is a long and strange journey, but they are surely joined at the hip. Industrial capitalism fueled wealth in the early cities, like New York and Philadelphia—home to Conwell—and monopoly capitalism was just beginning to change the landscape of American cities at the turn of the twentieth century. To be sure, for Conwell, there was an open and hungry market of young people, eager to learn how to discover diamonds in their own backyard. Conwell used tried-and-true methods, telling story after story of individuals who found wealth by developing their own resources and using it to serve many, including, not coincidentally, the story of his own effort to build his extravagant church facilities and to begin a college that would

[22] Russell Herman Conwell, *Acres of Diamonds* (New York: Cosimo Classics, 2008 [1890]), 22, 20.

[23] Conwell, *Acres of Diamonds*, 25.

[24] Kate Bowler, *Blessed: A History of the American Prosperity Gospel* (Oxford: Oxford University Press, 2013).

serve and inspire young men and women. Conwell's early students were from the "working class," taking night courses to advance themselves, and were dubbed "night owls" at that time. "Owls" became the nickname for students at the college that became Temple University.

What is remarkable about Conwell's actual speech is how familiar it sounds in our day and age. Joel Osteen, pastor of the Houston megachurch Lakewood Church, surely could have given this speech. But Conwell is not naïve. He had seen the worst of what men could do to each other in the Civil War. He had put himself through college and training for ministry. In a certain sense, he was the self-made man that he dreamed he could become. He also clearly had his share of charisma, to which people in the moneyed classes of his time responded, but also the kind of inspiring story that fueled working-class dreams of everyone having the chance to get ahead. And this is important: a part of what megachurches have given the public is a dream—one big enough to inspire, based not so much on class or sophistication, but rather on what one can do for oneself, and the promise that there is a place at what some Christians have come to call the *banquet table of abundance*.

Now this ethic of ambition is most certainly a transvaluation of the *early* Christian community of sacrifice and martyrdom. But by the turn of the nineteenth century, the American value of self-made success had penetrated and merged with Christian values and culture. Christian language overlaid and validated this ideology, providing anyone with the fuel to make money and to stamp one's life with "blessings." As skeptics and cultural despisers, some academics have cynically downplayed and skewered this kind of ideology as the work of the exploitive class, fooling the uneducated classes to pine for dreams few will meet. And yet we see this process of human development and inspiration for self-improvement as a critical part of what it means to be an American. It is precisely immigrants and refugees who have often taken the most advantage of this spirit of self-improvement. As we will see, Pentecostalism, a product of the early twentieth century, created an ecclesiology of upward mobility for the masses, not only in this country but around the world. Again, cynicism may soothe the academic need to portray others as fools or as puppets in a "rich man's" game, but in truth, megachurches have been one of the ways in which the lower and middle classes have improved their lives, morally and even economically. Again, megachurch pastors, as we will show in Part III, have had their share of liars, cheats, and some who have exploited their "flock," but this does not mean that all or even most pastors have gone down the road.

There is hardly a better synecdoche of this process than the life and times of Aimee Semple McPherson. In all its basic features, McPherson's story is par excellence one that exemplifies the pattern that we've seen through this history. She was born in a farmhouse in Oxford County, Ontario, in a rural area halfway between Detroit and Toronto. She was raised in the Salvation Army, an international disaster-relief and humanitarian-aid nonprofit, one based on military discipline to help those in need. The organization arose out of the Holiness movement, so not far from the tradition of Pentecostalism that McPherson turned to in her ministerial career.

McPherson is described from early on as a performer, someone who had a flair and charisma that became apparent almost immediately as soon as she entered the public square. In her late teens, she attended a Pentecostal revival meeting and met Robert Semple. She fell in love, as she seemed to do on a regular basis, and converted to Pentecostalism, following her husband to China where he contracted malaria and died. Aimee retuned to the United States, had her first child, and continued in ministry with her mother in New York. There she met her second husband, Harold McPherson; he, too, was an itinerant preacher, and in time, Aimee recognized a deep calling to preach that had clearly been there from the beginning; her husband could see her enormous talent and encouraged her. They lived out of a "Gospel Car," moving from one revival to the next. Her husband, however, wanted a more stable life; he filed for a divorce, and Aimee and her mother continued their revival ministries, driving from one city to the next and leaving her husband behind. By 1918, Aimee and her mother ended up in Los Angeles and began to dream about settling down and creating a permanent ministry. With Aimee's entrepreneurial vision and her mother's business savvy, they raised enough money to build the Angelus Temple, her "home" and her ministry for the next twenty-one years until her death in 1944.[25]

In so many ways, Aimee's story is a rags-to-riches one, from obscurity to international celebrity, and like those of many megachurch stars, it is full of drama, success, tragedy, and redemption. What's critical here is that so much of it is based not just on the charisma of the preacher, but also the tenor of the times. Aimee's story is arresting in part because, as a woman, she faced cultural and structural issues that discouraged her leadership, even though in the Pentecostal denominations, women were technically allowed to preach. Therefore, her celebrity was rare, and built on the radical and ingenious talents she honed along the way. Eventually, her skills and abilities were finally recognized for what they were—extraordinary. Charisma is a socially constructed quality, and the times, context, and person melded together in

---

[25] See Matthew Avery Sutton's biography for a comprehensive analysis, *Aimee Semple McPherson and the Resurrection of Christian America* (Cambridge, MA: Harvard University Press, 2009).

Aimee to create a sensation all its own. Over the nearly twenty-one years of her crusade Aimee ministered to millions. According to records, in the first seven years alone, Angelus Temple received 40 million visitors, and her radio ministry went out to many more. This was an extraordinary event and person, made an even more powerful and poignant example by the fact that she was a woman. Along with her revival ministries she had a continuous and ongoing charitable service center modeled on the Salvation Army; it gave out food, blankets, and clothing, and is said to have served more than 1.5 million during the Great Depression.

Aimee's ministry was hampered by various organizational and personal scandals across its two decades of work. Her popularity went up and down, but she never quit. In every respect, she became a model to many of the revival teachers and prosperity gospel preachers over the last century. In a public sense, her scandals were as memorable as her ministerial triumphs, but in terms of conversions and healings that were claimed in her name, we should not underestimate the full impact of what they meant on those she touched.

We would argue that this is one of the areas that is understudied in the field of the sociology of religion—what are the positive and life-giving aspects of these ministries? We simply don't study these kinds of effects, at least not with any frequency. What we catch in the mainstream are the stories of scandals and defeats. So, in that sense, this book takes a different path, for in our study of the six different features of desire found in our megachurch data, we analyze how the process works, and to a large extent we look at "success." And what do we mean by success? We mean rituals that "work" in people's lives. Rituals that attract large numbers of both committed members and spiritual seekers, which bond them to one another, and engage them in life-giving stories and experiences. These rituals create communities in which people are encouraged and held accountable to what we see as generally life-giving forms of human solidarity.

This, then, is a different story, not one of simply reducing megachurches to dependent variables, but one seeking to understand them as sites for the creation and enactment of a desire to know more about a God whom they believe calls them to care for one another and invites them into a loving and forgiving intimate relationship with that same God—a force for good that they believe calls them to acts of love, justice, and peace, and encourages a fellowship of loving care and forgiveness, both between neighbors and extended toward whatever strangers may enter these voluntary communities of faith.

But before we drift too far into the sunny side of the megachurch movement, it's apt and stunningly contemporaneous to meditate on one more example from recent history, which lifts up the fact that the dramatic success of megachurches has had a remarkable impact in our present time, while highlighting the shadow side of our own success-driven American present. Norman Vincent Peale was the longtime megachurch pastor of the Marble Collegiate Church in New York City from 1932 to 1986. Peale was enormously successful, but attained his greatest fame from his best-selling book, *The Power of Positive Thinking*.[26] The book, published in 1952, sold more than 2 million copies in its first five years. Peale's fame grew, and the story is joined by a significant family in US history—Fred Trump's New York clan. A successful New York real estate developer, Fred was the father of President Donald Trump. Fred Trump read Peale's book early on and then began to attend Marble Collegiate with his family on a regular basis. The father, like the son, found in Peale a kindred soul, who believed in positive thinking at any cost, enabling one to succeed no matter the price. Donald J. Trump on more than one occasion has said that Peale had a tremendous effect on him and his success. Trump attended the church off and on, and was married at Peale's church for his first wedding.[27] Trump, in fact, noted that Peale's philosophy "saved" him on multiple occasions, including during his bankruptcy in the late 2000s. And during a difficult time in his presidential bid, Trump recalled that Peale was one of the "greatest speakers" he ever heard.[28]

Gwenda Blair, the author of two biographies of the Trump family and President Trump himself, argued that Peale's philosophy fit hand in glove into Trump's life and business strategy:

> "Believe in yourself!" Peale's book begins. "Have faith in your abilities!" [Peale] then outlines 10 rules to overcome "inadequacy attitudes" and "build up confidence in your powers." Rule one: "formulate and staple indelibly on your mind a mental picture of yourself as succeeding," "hold this picture tenaciously," and always refer to it "no matter how badly things seem to be going at the moment."
>
> Subsequent rules tell the reader to avoid "fear thoughts," "never think of yourself as failing," summon up a positive thought whenever "a negative thought concerning your personal powers comes to mind,"

[26] Norman Vincent Peale, *The Power of Positive Thinking* (New York: Fireside, 2003 [1952]).
[27] Gwenda Blair is author of *The Trumps: Three Generations of Builders and a Presidential Candidate* (New York: Simon & Schuster, 2001) and *Donald Trump: The Candidate* (New York: Simon & Schuster, 2007).
[28] Gwenda Blair, "How Norman Vincent Peale Taught Donald Trump to Worship Himself," Politico, 2015, accessed January 16, 2018 (https://www.politico.com/magazine/story/2015/10/donald-trump-2016-norman-vincent-peale-213220).

"depreciate every so-called obstacle," and "make a true estimate of your own ability, then raise it 10 per cent."[29]

It is indeed advice that trains one to maintain a positive picture of one's success regardless of circumstance and how one feels about one's life. The advice creates an *erasure of self-doubt,* and any thoughts or notions of one's inadequacies or weaknesses. It is a program for freeing one of self-doubt, self-reproach, and, not the least, the Christian notion of repentance—a theme central to the ministry of Jesus Christ, who taught but one prayer, the Lord's Prayer, which at the center, teaches followers to say, "forgive us our sins and we forgive those who sin against us." By all means necessary self-doubt and self-reproach are overcome in the name of keeping one's "best self" in mind. This advice is at the heart of Joel Osteen's ministry, the Houston megachurch superstar, who continually reminds the millions who follow him at his church and online across the world.[30]

Journalist Timothy Noah wrote an essay in the fall of 2016, "Tilting at Windmills: The Futility of Trying to Normalize Trump . . . Dale Carnegie versus Norman Vincent Peale." Noah, of course, did not know that Trump would go on to win the presidency, but he, like many, became fascinated with Trump's ability to stay "sunny" even in the worst of circumstances, whether being sued by literally hundreds of institutions, or being slashed and burned on the presidential campaign trail. Noah explained Trump's ability to remain positive no matter the circumstance as a direct result of Peale's philosophy and preaching. Noah compares Dale Carnegie's 1936 *How to Win Friends and Influence People* and Peale's best-selling *Power of Positive Thinking*. In Carnegie's book, there is a self-reflective refrain that encourages instances of "strategic apologies,"[31] whereas in Peale's book on positive thinking, "apologize" only appears twice, and in each case about what Peale identified as a distraction.[32]

It has become a theme in President Trump's years in office that whatever goes wrong is either not his fault or really another way in which opportunities are created for him and the country to "win." As Trump has made consistently clear, he does not apologize, and if someone "hits me, we're

[29] Gwenda Blair, "How Norman Vincent Peale."

[30] Joel Osteen, *Understanding Your Value,* accessed January 16, 2018 (https://www.joelosteen.com/Pages/Article.aspx?articleid=6465).

[31] Dale Carnegie, *How to Win Friends and Influence People* (New York: Gallery Books; original published 1936, this version, 1999), 127–134.

[32] Timothy Noah, "Tilting at Windmills: The Futility of Trying to Normalize Trump . . . Dale Carnegie versus Norman Vincent Peale," *Washington Monthly* (2016), accessed January 16, 2018 (https://washingtonmonthly.com/magazine/septemberoctober-2016/tilting-at-windmills-3/).

gonna hit them ten times harder."[33] In this sense, Trump sees apology as a sign of weakness and a way that undercuts his vision of winning. Trump sees himself as "winning" and without fault. In no way is this to say that Norman Vincent Peale is the source of President Trump's capacity to avoid blame or his ability to seek revenge, but it is hard not to wonder: Perhaps what is touted as one of the greatest aspects of megachurches—the positive thinking and upbeat spirit—is part of, or at least functions to mask, the megachurches' dark shadow? And as we will see in Part III, an inability to be self-reflective or self-critical is one of the fundamental faults for megachurches that have slipped into scandal. That is, ego, the charisma of the pastor, or in Trump's case, his success as businessman and president, becomes the absolute focus of attention. Americans are well suited for this focus on winning; it helps them to ignore bad circumstances and their own faults and weaknesses. Certainly, this is part of what we saw in Russell Conwell's Acres of Diamonds speech: "make money and get rich." For many reasons, not all attributable to positive thinking, Americans have made this philosophy work for them. The power of positive thinking is not a problem if it motivates and helps one to overcome distractions or defeats. But if it causes one to ignore outside forces signaling the need to change course, then the egocentricity of *homo duplex* becomes a whirling vortex of denial, pain, and destruction.

Megachurch pastors often prove to be brilliant exemplars of the potential for ego to destroy success. This happened in Seattle, Washington, to Mark Driscoll, the charismatic founder of Mars Hill Church in Seattle, which the three of us witnessed close at hand. In the late 1990s Driscoll's ministry exploded in success. He grew a megachurch in less than ten years, but through his own hubris and unethical behavior, it imploded quite literally overnight. In Driscoll's path, he left a wide swath of victims and abused people, to whom he never apologized.[34] So, yes, the megachurch story is one that tracks the rise of those addicted to success, in the vein of Joel Osteen, a Gatsby-like figure in the tradition of F. Scott Fitzgerald, as well as nearly Shakespearean tragic collapses, where hubris can and does cause enormous pain. And that is a part of the American story, as well as the stories of global megachurches, with the rise and fall of megachurches that are more like

[33] Fox News Insider, "Trump Warns GOPers: 'Anybody Who Hits Me, We're Gonna Hit 10 Times Harder,'" *Fox News* (2015), accessed January 29, 2018 (http://insider.foxnews.com/2015/11/03/donald-trump-warns-republican-candidates-about-using-negative-ads-against-him).
[34] Warren Throckmorton's blog is the most thorough and comprehensive history of the collapse and fall of Mark Driscoll's church; it is also thorough in tracking how Driscoll has "spun" this past: http://www.patheos.com/blogs/warrenthrockmorton/2017/04/09/mark-driscoll-spins-the-end-of-mars-hill-church/.

cities unto themselves than neighborhood churches.[35] Again, these stories of scandal do not discount the good that these churches have done, but they do underscore how tumultuous and desperate the need is for humans to negotiate the pull of the self and the need for community. Megachurches are ideal laboratories to investigate the twists and turns within this crucible of self and society. However, before we examine the dark sides of this dynamic, we investigate why and how, when done well, megachurches can create flourishing human communities.

Durkheim, at the end of his essay "Dualism of Human Nature," is not sanguine about us resolving the ongoing fracture between the self and society, the one and the many, the individual and the community. Each node builds its own world, but that world is somehow incomplete, and we struggle to find a place where the two meet and find some sense of reconciliation. Durkheim is not optimistic that a time of peaceful coexistence is on the horizon. He argues, "Since the role of the social being in our single selves will grow ever more important as history moves ahead, it is wholly improbable that there will ever be an era in which man is required to resist himself to a lesser degree, an era in which he can live a life that is easier and less full of tension. To the contrary, all evidence compels us to expect our effort in the struggle between the two beings within us to increase with the growth of civilization."[36]

It is important to be thinking of megachurches in our current moment. Few institutions are created in our culture that bring groups together to serve a common purpose or seek unity across our distinctions. However, here we are, studying a movement that claims its purpose is to serve a God whose main message is reconciliation in the person of Jesus Christ. In that sense, it is a fascinating experiment in overcoming *homo duplex*. We are not suggesting that megachurches are the answer, but we recognize them as an experiment in repairing the breach that Durkheim argues is a permanent aspect of our nature. This study of megachurches gives us one way that religious organizations are trying to reconcile the divisions within each person. As we will see, there is some success in it, but we also know that where there is light, there

[35] Harry Farley, "Singapore Megachurch Scandal: Pastor Barred from Running Any Charity Ever," *Christianity Today* (2017), accessed January 29, 2018 (https://www.christiantoday.com/article/singapore.megachurch.scandal.pastor.barred.from.running.any.charity.ever/109594.htm); Ruth Moon, "Founder of World's Largest Megachurch Convicted of Embezzling $12 Million," *Christianity Today* (2014), accessed January 29, 2018 (http://www.christianitytoday.com/news/2014/february/founder-of-worlds-largest-megachurch-convicted-cho-yoido.html).
[36] Durkheim, "Dualism of Human Nature," 339.

is always a shadow. And so, Part III will show the shadow of this attempt at light, a dilemma that Durkheim argued will never be resolved.

American Church Culture Today

A dynamic interplay and tension between continuity and change has always characterized both American religion and Christianity. The aim of this section is to give the reader a contemporary and ground-level sense of what has happened and what is happening in American Christian churches, as well as a feel for how megachurches have grown and changed the American landscape. In recent decades, we have seen dramatic shifts in our religious climate, including the decline of the Protestant mainline, the growth of American evangelicalism—highlighted in the explosive expansion of megachurches— and the rise of those who either claim no religion or practice spirituality without religion. As the religious landscape transforms beneath our feet, we are faced with this question: Has something fundamentally changed in how American Christians experience and express their faith?

We propose to think about American religious history from the perspective of local churches and their congregational histories. This is not typically done in the study of American religion.[37] We think that is a grave mistake, since most religion takes place at this level, in the basements of small and big churches. In one sense these details are thought to be mundane or inconsequential—not very exciting or illuminating. We beg to differ. Our investigation asks if the micro trends and everyday events in a congregation have anything to teach those of us who think and write about American religious history. We answer this in part by examining how American religion has changed over the last century. With this more recent historical foundation, we offer evidence from our written histories and ethnographic studies drawn from research done on dozens of congregations. The evidence sheds light on the hidden undercurrents of social and cultural transformations that have created broader changes in the American religious landscape.

Mark Chaves's 2011 book, *American Religion: Contemporary Trends*,[38] offers an overview of American religious trends during the last hundred years. The continuities are what we might expect: belief in God, frequency of prayer,

---

[37] For notable exceptions, see, for example, Nancy Ammerman, *Congregation and Community* (New Brunswick, NJ: Rutgers University Press, 1997) and T. M. Luhrmann, *When God Talks Back: Understanding the American Evangelical Relationship with God* (New York: Vintage Books, 2012).

[38] Mark Chaves, *American Religion: Contemporary Trends* (Princeton, NJ: Princeton University Press, 2011).

church attendance, and belief in heaven and hell, but the changes are what really stand out. He cites that in 1957 only 3% of Americans would mark "no religion" on a survey; by 2008, 17% did,[39] and by 2014, 23% of adults self-identified as "religiously unaffiliated."[40] Further, 91% of Americans in 1924 agreed that Christianity was the only true religion, whereas only 41% made the same claim in 2008.[41] Even more striking is the fact that two-thirds of contemporary Americans say that a religion besides their own might offer a true way to God.[42] Meanwhile about a third of Americans are "born again" and more than one in five claim no religion,[43]

The new Pew Study on the American Religious Landscape[44] shows a continuing and relatively dramatic decline in religious activity nearly across the board. Roman Catholics have lost nearly a fifth of their membership, down to 20% of the American population; more dramatic is the nearly 25% decline in mainline Protestants since the Pew study in 2007. This, combined with the significant movement upward among the unaffiliated, from 16% to nearly 23% of the American population, tells a grim story, at least in terms of total numbers of American Christians. The country has dropped from being nearly 79% Christian to 71% in only seven years. This is even more dramatic considering that a third of the millennial generation is no longer affiliated with any faith. Thus, if one is considering the future, the millennial generation seems to foretell a US population that is losing interest in and loyalty to the Christian faith.

Tellingly, the unaffiliated, including about a third of Americans under thirty, still believe in some sort of divinity and profess being "spiritual," but they are not seeking a religion. They are happy without one.[45] Today, *not* believing in God is a live option; that is, there are fewer social and cultural pressures toward faith, much less toward church attendance. Moreover, not practicing a religion is more common than ever, even among those who do believe in God—and these believers are less certain that their own beliefs comprise the one true faith. In other words, we are entering a time in which

[39] Chaves, *American Religion,* 19.
[40] Pew Research Center, "U.S. Public Becoming Less Religious," full report on the *2014 Religious Landscape Study,* November 3, 2015, (http://www.pewforum.org/2015/11/03/u-s-public-becoming-less-religious/).
[41] Chaves, *American Religion,* 27.
[42] Pew Research Center, "U.S. Public Becoming Less Religious," 62.
[43] Chaves, *American Religion,* 6; Pew Research Center, "U.S. Public Becoming Less Religious," 19.
[44] Pew Research Center: Religion and Public Life, *America's Changing Religious Landscape,* May 12, 2015, accessed January 9, 2018 (http://www.pewforum.org/2015/05/12/americas-changing-religious-landscape/).
[45] The Pew Forum on Religion & Public Life, *"Nones" on the Rise,* October 9, 2012, accessed January 9, 2018 (http://www.pewforum.org/Unaffiliated/nones-on-the-rise.aspx).

religion is up for grabs, the guard rails have been torn down, and there is no one who has the capacity or the will to tell us, collectively, how to do religion or how to manage our faith.

What do these shifts mean for American Christian subcultures, and what might they portend for American Christianity in the future? Some have called this a *liquid modernity*,[46] and we think this is accurate, but we don't think there is less faith; even those who have no religion tend to believe in God. As we have signaled throughout Part I, the desire to move from our own personal perspective into a relation with the other, whether a community or a god, remains—the same dual nature knocking at our doors and demanding to be solved. But the shift is real.

Chapter 6 narrates how these shifts have occurred through the study of local churches and congregations, and finally how megachurches have come to offer options for those on the search. But even here the certainty of the past is no longer as important; megachurches offer a moving island of plausibility to twenty-first-century seekers who wonder if there is a place to find oneself in relation to God, Jesus, and one another. The last century gives us a unique window into the radical transformation of how Christians have done faith, how church has become an option instead of a requirement, how spirituality is the air we breathe, and how megachurches offer a unique island of plausibility for faith, for joy, and for community.

[46] Zygmunt Bauman, *Liquid Modernity* (Cambridge: Polity Press, 2000). Bauman announces the move away from a "heavy" and "solid," hardware-focused modernity to a "light" and "liquid," software-based modernity.

CHAPTER 6 | Congregations in a Time
of Change

H OW DO CONGREGATIONAL studies illumine the trends in American
religious belief over the past hundred-plus years?[1] The senior author's
book, *The Gold Coast Church and the Ghetto: Christ and Culture in Mainline
Protestantism*,[2] traced the momentous changes in the twentieth century
through the lens of Fourth Presbyterian Church in Chicago. Fourth Church,
as insiders usually call it, today serves more than 5,000 adults in a congregation generally considered liberal Protestant. According to the data, liberal
Protestant megachurches are rare. Thus, this is a counterexample of liberal
Protestant decline and an interesting church to think about in a book on evangelical megachurches. Thanks to Fourth Presbyterian's voluminous archives,
the senior author excavated the complex history of the city of Chicago from
the perspective of a leading liberal, mainline Protestant church. I argued that
there were specific transformative moments in Fourth Presbyterian's history
that illumine the wider changes in American religion.

We pick up the story of Fourth Presbyterian Church at a time when
it was in the mainstream of early twentieth-century evangelical mainline
Protestantism. John Timothy Stone, its pastor from 1908 to 1928 and a

[1] Part of this chapter is reprinted and adapted with permission from James K. Wellman, Jr., "Turning
Word into Flesh: Congregational History as American Religious History," *Journal of Presbyterian History*
91, no. 2, Copyright [2013], Presbyterian Historical Society.
[2] James K. Wellman, Jr., *The Gold Coast Church and the Ghetto: Christ and Culture in Mainline Protestantism*
(Urbana: University of Illinois Press, 1999).

dynamic leader in the denomination, forged a growing and influential congregation. He was an evangelical Presbyterian, a person of repute in the wider church (a moderator of the denomination in 1913–1914), a friend of Woodrow Wilson, and a strongly evangelical Christian who started an underground young men's ministry with the ambitious goal of evangelizing young businessmen in the Near North Side of downtown Chicago. He built a large ministry, with 2,000 to 3,000 attending in the 1910s, along with a strong missional enterprise—churchgoers gave more than $500,000 each year for overseas mission purposes alone. Elite young Protestants sacrificed their privilege to go overseas in mission to China; in fact, one of Chicago's fairest sons, a young man from an elite family and Yale graduate, died in China within two months of his overseas mission; his obituary made front-page news in the Chicago newspapers.

One of Stone's elders, Henry Crowell, chair of Quaker Oats, not only supported global missions, but also pushed his company into international markets—presaging American influence overseas, as well as accelerating the American understanding of the globe, which, as David Hollinger has argued, had profound reciprocal effects on American culture and politics.[3] After the war, and in reaction to the modernist/fundamentalist Protestant controversies, Crowell broke with Fourth Presbyterian and became a leader and central donor and funder of the Moody Bible Institute. Crowell, a strident Biblicist, left his substantial wealth to the Moody Bible Institute with the proviso that the Institute would maintain an evangelical and conservative set of doctrines in perpetuity.

The modernist/fundamentalist controversy in the mainline denomination and the US Presbyterian Church forced a split between liberals and moderates on the one hand, and theological conservatives on the other. The overall controversy was a long time coming, but it reached its zenith in the 1910s, and in the early 1920s forced Presbyterians to take sides on the issue of core doctrines. The conservatives and fundamentalists demanded that the Bible be interpreted as the inspired and inerrant word from God—they upheld the virgin birth of Christ, the belief that Christ's death was necessary for the atonement of sins, the bodily resurrection of Jesus, and the historical reality of Jesus's miracles.

A presenting issue in much of this debate was the argument over the Darwinian theory of evolution. Most liberals either accepted evolution or at least thought it a valid option. Conservatives and those who would become

---

[3] See David A. Hollinger, *Protestants Abroad: How Missionaries Tried to Change the World but Changed America* (Princeton, NJ: Princeton University Press, 2017).

fundamentalists found the new science abhorrent and a sure way to undercut the authenticity and authority of the Bible. Much of what happened in twentieth-century Protestantism drew on these debates; sides were taken, and denominations were split between modernists and fundamentalists. Today, not all evangelicals are fundamentalists, and not all liberals believe in evolution, but the general split still holds and the two American Christianities have gone their separate ways. Most of the megachurches that we studied are on the conservative side of this theological spectrum, with some exceptions.

Generally, liberal Protestants uphold the freedom of individuals to think for themselves on issues, so there is more latitude on doctrine. But while evangelicals may quietly demur on some doctrines, in general they hold a high view on the authority and inerrancy of scripture, though fewer might call themselves fundamentalist. Thus, there is much more fluidity on these issues and doctrines than many think. We learned never to take someone's view on these matters for granted—we found many exceptions to the rule in our megachurch members.

The senior author wrote the book on the Fourth Presbyterian Church, covering each of the four long pastorates of the twentieth century. John Timothy Stone, an evangelical Christian, served in the 1910s and 1920s, a time when his church was becoming more moderate theologically. Before the war, Stone had built a church with the kind of certainty and muscularity that befitted someone entrenched in privilege. Stone's status and the church's finances facilitated his ability to rally Chicago elites to invest in an evangelical mission, joining a broader turn-of-the-century movement to Christianize the world. As noted, in the 1910s, Fourth Presbyterian sent many to serve as missionaries, often to China and India, and ensured this mission was thoroughly embedded in American culture and politics. Stone was nationally known as one of President Wilson's trusted confidants. He supported the First World War generally as a cheerleader and also as a chaplain for American military bases. He worked tirelessly, speaking nearly every night of the week to troops in training. In the postwar period, however, everything changed.[4] The ghastly nature of the war put the lie to the glory of fighting for the country and undercut the whole notion that its purpose was to spread faith and democracy.

[4] See my article with S. R. Thompson, in which we trace the interaction and transformation of American Christianity and US foreign policy during this period: James K. Wellman, Jr., and S. R. Thompson, "From the Social Gospel to Neoconservativism: Religion and U.S. Foreign Policy," *Interdisciplinary Journal of Research on Religion* 7, no. 6 (2011): 1–41 (http://www.religjournal.com/articles/2011.php).

Isolation became the theme for this interwar period. Stone's ministry did not fail after the war, but his vision no longer rallied his congregation. By the time he retired from Fourth Presbyterian in 1928 his dreams were much diminished, and when he took up the presidency of McCormick Seminary, his ambitious building plans for it were torpedoed by the economic shock of the Great Depression. More generally, mainline Protestantism declined, and the Depression hampered growth and mission efforts among evangelical churches as well.

As the United States pulled back from its international engagements, the Protestant elite turned away from faith and mission work. Rev. Harrison Ray Anderson, Stone's successor, could not reignite the same level of commitment to missions that had characterized Fourth Presbyterian during the heyday of Stone's pastorate. Furthermore, a second major change in American religion came in the 1960s. For the first half of the twentieth century, Fourth Presbyterian attracted the elite of Chicago and influenced wider social movements in the city. But as the Rev. Elam Davies took the helm in 1961, this began to change. While Davies's Welsh brogue and talent for oratory drew large crowds to the church, the broader social movements of the 1960s overshadowed both his leadership and the church's willingness to engage American culture.

Early in his tenure, even as Davies retired Fourth Presbyterian's antiquated pew rental system, he condemned local antiwar protests and largely ignored the civil rights movement. His engagement with issues of urban poverty and the racialized ghettoes of Chicago came late. Fourth Presbyterian did eventually build apartment units for low-income families and created a strong tutoring program for residents of the nearby Cabrini-Green public housing development. But Davies failed to preach against the building of public housing that segregated African Americans on the west side of the Dan Ryan Expressway. Chicago's downtown, called the Loop, became a haven for white privilege, surrounded by what came to be known as the *second ghetto,* which moved black Chicagoans away from the downtown elite.[5] Furthermore, by the end of Davies's tenure, Fourth Presbyterian no longer attracted Chicago leaders nor had much of a voice in the political issues of the city. In 1985, Rev. John Buchanan's ministry acknowledged this shift. No longer was there a direct line, as Davies had once bragged, between the pastor and the mayor. Rather, the church became only one of many instruments for promoting community service throughout the city.

[5] See Arnold R. Hirsch's *Making the Second Ghetto: Race and Housing in Chicago, 1940–1960* (Chicago: University of Chicago Press, 1998).

To describe Buchanan's era I used the phrase "lay liberal Christian."[6] These were Christians who lived their lives not by rules and doctrines, but by a generalized sense of transcendence and love for self and neighbor. Ensconced in a position of economic and social power, they felt no tension with their environment. They no longer looked to convert others; in fact they accepted and bragged about their pluralism, fully at home with their decentered status. As a result, mainline Protestants forsook loyalty to any one denomination or to any single religious subculture. In particular, parents no longer demanded or expected that their children should attend church—a trend that ensured that their youth would drift away from church as well. As Hoge, Johnson, and Luidens described in their 1994 *Vanishing Boundaries: The Religion of Mainline Protestant Baby Boomers*, these trends created a flaccid and benign theological identity, which led inexorably to the continuing deterioration and weakening of the Protestant mainline denominations.[7]

At the time when I published the book, I argued that Fourth Presbyterian was a counterexample of this decline, and its continued vitality made the point; however, its inability to attract power brokers, to challenge city business, or to send young people out in mission to the world illustrated a religious body fully accommodated to their upper-middle-class milieu. To be sure, the church embraced its socially progressive identity, supporting LGBTQ ordination and same-sex marriage. In 2012, its church rolls boasted 5,000 members, but attendance was far smaller. With Buchanan's retirement, Sunday attendance declined to 1,200 congregants at the several services. In 2014, the Fourth Church called their first woman to be pastor of the church, the Rev. Shannon Kershner. Kershner, a southern Presbyterian, has a dynamic personality and fits the lay liberal ethos of Fourth Presbyterian—she is comfortable with "doubts" and is clear that Christianity is not the "only way." Or, as she says, "No, God's not a Christian. I mean, we are . . . For me, the Christian tradition is the way to understand God and my relationship with the world and other humans. . . . But I'm not about to say what God can and cannot do in other ways and with other spiritual experiences."[8] For Kershner, Christianity is one way among many paths to truth. As an

---

[6] The phrase comes from Dean R. Hoge, Benton Johnson, and Donald A. Luidens, *Vanishing Boundaries: The Religion of Mainline Protestant Baby Boomers* (Louisville, KY: Westminster/John Knox Press, 1994). Nancy T. Ammerman explores a similar trend in her essay, "Golden Rule Christianity: Lived Religion in the American Mainstream," in *Lived Religion in America: Toward a History of Practice*, edited by David D. Hall (Princeton, NJ: Princeton University Press, 1997).

[7] Hoge, Johnson, and Luidens, *Vanishing Boundaries*.

[8] Robert Herguth, "Prominent Presbyterian Pastor: 'God's Not a Christian . . . We Are,'" *Chicago Sun-Times*, March 7, 2018 (https://chicago.suntimes.com/chicago-politics/prominent-presbyterian-pastor-gods-not-a-christian-we-are/).

egalitarian and liberal Protestant, she was critical of Donald Trump's behavior leading up to the 2016 presidential election, and more generally willing to make her case for a moderate, left-leaning social and cultural vision.

Fourth Presbyterian's current leaders do not expect the church to lead the city or for its pastors to be talking with mayors or the president. They *do* want intellectually, theologically, and morally gripping sermons; a worship service with professional-quality liturgy and music; facilities that provide space for young families; and outreach programs that offer tutoring and social services. The church that once led the city and influenced a nation now constitutes an upper-middle-class enclave, with neither the ambition nor the energy to change the world, much less a city.

When I moved to Seattle in 1997, I intended to follow my study of Fourth Presbyterian with a similar analysis of churches on the West Coast. I assumed I would be able to track down an even greater number of thriving, mainline liberal churches in a part of the country known for its liberal politics and culture. To my surprise, I was wrong. I could only identify a few vibrant, liberal churches that were managing to grow. In the process of looking, however, I came across a veritable cavalcade of prospering evangelical churches in the heart of the Pacific Northwest. Indeed, in 1999 and 2001, the evangelical Luis Palau Ministries in Portland and Seattle led two of the largest public gatherings in the Pacific Northwest. Evangelical churches had not only gained a foothold in the region, they had nearly doubled in size, while mainline congregations had declined by more than half since the 1980s.[9]

I published these findings in my 2008 monograph, *Evangelical vs. Liberal: The Clash of Christian Cultures in the Pacific Northwest.*[10] I examined twelve vital, liberal congregations and twenty-four thriving evangelical churches. My criteria for the "vital liberal" churches were simply churches that were not failing and that had either grown or maintained their membership and budget for at least the previous three years. The liberal church membership averaged 280 members and the congregations averaged $500,000 in their annual budgets, giving less than 10% of their funds to mission. The sample of twenty-four evangelical churches, on the other hand, included churches that had nearly doubled in size over a five-year period, averaging $2 million annual budgets and 13% in annual mission giving. While most of the liberal churches had no active missionaries, the evangelical congregations

[9] See "Religious Congregations and Membership Study," which shows the Protestant mainline held nearly 11% of Washington State's population in 1980, and only 4.58% in 2010, while evangelicals had grown to more than 12% compared to 8% in 1980. Accessed January 15, 2012 (http://www.rcms2010.org/).
[10] James K. Wellman, Jr., *Evangelical vs. Liberal: The Clash of Christian Cultures in the Pacific Northwest* (New York: Oxford University Press, 2008).

averaged nearly ten permanent international missionaries with many more individuals and small groups committing to short-term mission work.

But the most stunning difference between evangelical and liberal churches was in the kind of social service churches offered to their communities. In the process of doing the research, we interviewed nearly 150 liberal lay members and clergy and nearly 300 evangelical laypeople and ministers. Through coding this data, it became clear to me that evangelical churches did much more than liberal churches in day-to-day social service for their communities. In nearly every evangelical interview there were reports of individuals and groups serving those in need—a trend that was much less common in the liberal congregations. If they spoke about service, liberals mentioned LGBTQ rights or urban homelessness, but they rarely spoke about engaging in direct service for others. While liberals often belonged to formal, service-oriented community groups, evangelicals were overwhelmingly doing work for others in small, informal neighborhood groups.

It became apparent that researchers are not aware of evangelical service in large part because evangelicals do most of their service through informal networks. In one case, a group of evangelical retirees gathered once a week to paint houses for the elderly in their various neighborhoods. Because of the format of their service, there were few points of contact with local service organizations. On the other hand, liberals spoke a great deal, in abstract terms, about caring for the poor, particularly for the homeless and sexual minorities, but they rarely mentioned concrete, direct service to others.

Eight of the twenty-four evangelical churches in my *Evangelical vs. Liberal* study were megachurches. At that time, I would have said that megachurches are a relatively new phenomenon in the American religious landscape. And while it's true that megachurches emerged in the public imagination in the wake of cultural changes of the 1960s, as we've seen they are not "new" at all. Further, the number of megachurches has exploded since the 1970s and has steadily increased since. Between 1990 and 2000, the total number of megachurches in the United States increased from 350 to over 600. Today there are more than 1,600 and there is no indication that the trend is slowing.[11] In fact, while the median congregation size of an American church is about seventy-five active members, more than 50% of all churchgoers attend the largest 10% of churches in America. Based on a large sample of qualitative and quantitative surveys (originally executed by the Leadership Network) and our own observations of megachurch services, Part

[11] Scott Thumma and Warren Bird, "Recent Shifts in America's Largest Protestant Churches: Megachurches 2015 Report," The Leadership Network and Hartford Research Institute, The Beck Group, 2015.

II examines how megachurch members experience and evaluate their lives in these institutions.

Lessons from American Religious History

CULTURE CONTROLS CHURCHES

Even when Fourth Presbyterian was in its heyday, it was captive to the tastes and attitudes of Protestant elites. Woodrow Wilson's attempt to create a League of Nations was the last great experiment in a social gospel for the world. It failed miserably, and Wilson died in despair. The First World War led the world not toward peace, but to an interregnum of isolation and mutual distrust, which eventually created a worldwide economic depression that paved the way for the Second World War. Churches were largely absent from the interwar dialogue over war and peace, and larger forces undercut any hope for a Christian message of reconciliation, whether in Europe or in America.

After the Second World War, the Protestant mainline found itself muted and muddled, and evangelical churches came to the fore, pushing themselves into American politics via the elections of Ronald Reagan and George W. Bush. But in these cases, little of their moral and social agenda moved forward. American culture, as well as its military and economic interests, paid little attention to either the Religious Right or the diminishing Christian Left. Social inequality skyrocketed. Militarism was in full bloom. And America became notorious as the reigning world empire, loathed by many even as it trumpeted peace following the collapse of the Soviet Union. But churches were not players in these movements, either from the right or the left. Churches, to a considerable degree, were creatures of the culture; power and economic interests led the way, and churches followed, either as cheerleaders or as timid critics. We argue that megachurches are no different; even though they may claim moral superiority, they have largely (and successfully) adapted to the current cultural climate.

EMOTION OVER MIND

As we've mentioned before, American Protestantism has always shifted back and forth between the values of the Puritans and Pietists or, in more contemporary vernacular, the mind and emotion. From the perspective of theologians this may be true, but on the ground, in the pew, from the perspective of congregational studies and American history, the true winner has always been the emotional capacity of a religious culture. Even in Jonathan Edwards's time, the question was about the authenticity of religious affection, and the revivalists, George Whitefield and the pietism of the Wesleys, won the day— both in numbers and in influence. Some, and here we mean Protestant elites, have claimed that the contemporary movement toward emotion and affection is new, but we have shown that it has always been a primary way that Americans have responded to faith. In the senior author's studies, the movement toward churches that evoke an expressive response has been telling. Americans want to feel something, whether it is a sense of connection, the ecstasy of Christian contemporary worship, or that "feeling for the ultimate" that is the legacy of Friedrich Schleiermacher's liberal theology.[12]

This emphasis on affective experience extends into the realm of megachurches. Megachurch goers are interested not so much in the cognitive claims made—right beliefs or orthodox theology—but in a powerful, affective experience of the divine. Recent research on the physiology of emotion shows that thought without emotion—that is, without affective triggers— is not only powerless but ineffective. In other words, our ability to reason is hampered unless there is an affective and emotional driver behind it.[13] People cannot and do not make decisions based on logic or reason alone— thought and emotion merge, such that human beings, empirically, function in this matrix of emotion and mind. The trumpeting of correct dogma and the diminishing of emotion's importance in church life and practice has been one of the primary failings of mainline Protestants. It is the reason that Protestant mainline pastors, equipped with a graduate education in theology and ministry, are often powerless in the face of charismatic megachurch pastors who know this obvious truth: if people are not emotionally engaged in their religious life, practice and belief dissipate and disappear. In Part II, we show *how* megachurches meet the desires of their attendees and provide them with rewarding affective experiences.

LEADERSHIP COUNTS

American religious history illustrates the importance of charismatic leaders from Jonathan Edwards to Aimee Semple McPherson. Typically, the Protestant mainline sees this kind of charisma as a "problem," but when its

---

[12] See Friedrich Schleiermacher and Richard Crouter, *On Religion: Speeches to Its Cultured Despisers* (New York: Cambridge University Press, 1996 [1899]).
[13] See Antonio Damasio, *Descartes' Error: Emotion, Reason, and the Human Brain* (New York: Penguin Books, 1994).

congregational members are asked about the reasons for their attendance, growing churches are almost always focused on individual pastors. While doing research at Fourth Presbyterian Church, I found that when members were asked about the church, the first thing they said was how much they loved John Buchanan. The same was true, historically, about Fourth Presbyterian's previous pastors, Stone, Anderson, and Davies.

A successful charismatic leader is not merely an emotional virtuoso, but someone who is expertly aware of the integration of mind, body, and emotion and who can engage others because they understand the crisis of the moment, use their tradition (religious and otherwise) to answer this problem, and employ engaging and structured ways to show others how to overcome the challenges of the day. This can come from introverted or extroverted leadership, from highly emotional and dryly intellectual individuals. But it always engages the listeners' heads and hearts, minds and emotions, and gives them hope to overcome the challenges of the day. In Part II, we explore the charisma of megachurch senior pastors.

CONGREGATIONS TELL THE STORY

To study religious people, we must study where and how they congregate— their narratives, interpretations, and meanings—and this tells the vital story of American religious history. To generalize about churches and organizations without having listened to and experienced what goes on in these churches is to ignore the actual day-to-day factors that make American religion live and die. What happens in churches can only be studied by talking to congregants and by listening to leaders. Having done this kind of research, we know how and why the Protestant mainline is failing and how and why American megachurches are succeeding. Culture, emotion, and dynamic leadership skills count and make all the difference in these churches. And in the twenty-first century, megachurches have exploded and now dominate the American religious marketplace. We now show how megachurches conquered America.

PART II

Pistons of Desire and Power: Cracking the Megachurch Code

We understand even less how these two worlds which are wholly opposite,
and which, consequently, should repulse and exclude each other, tend,
nevertheless, to unite and interpenetrate in such a way as to produce
the mixed and contradictory being that is man; for it seems that their
antagonism should keep them apart and make their union impossible.[1]

—Émile Durkheim

A S WE'VE SEEN, megachurches are an expression emerging from the imbrication of modern religious, political, aesthetic, and consumer cultures that has been a long time coming. That is, they are a direct manifestation of creative energy and are a constantly evolving response to the felt needs of their communities. The best and the brightest of these megachurch stars have realized that whenever things become too comfortable, too stable, too predictable, the jig is up. And, as we have said, the union of self and society is unstable and forever in some tension, which, as Durkheim reminds us, reflects the very nature of the human condition. The contradictory

---

[1] Émile Durkheim, "Dualism of Human Nature," 333.

and paradoxical nature of megachurches comes through in figures like the Canadian evangelical pastor Bruxy Cavey. Cavey started the Meeting House megachurch in Toronto, Ontario, and named the engine of his church vision, *The End of Religion*.[2] Cavey grew an 8,000-person megachurch based on the principle of "wrecking religion," that religion was not the building of a temple or structure to which one bowed, but the nurture of a radical way of life, living out the grace and peace of Jesus's life of reconciliation. And while this seems revolutionary or new, it is neither. When we turn to Jesus's ministry, for instance in Matthew 15, we see the same world-shattering language in the stories of what Jesus said to the religious of his own day:

> Then [Jesus] called the crowd to him and said to them, "Listen and understand: it is not what goes into the mouth that defiles a person, but it is what comes out of the mouth that defiles." Then the disciples approached and said to him, "Do you know that the Pharisees took offense when they heard what you said?" Jesus answered, "Every plant that my heavenly Father has not planted will be uprooted. Let them alone; they are blind guides of the blind. And if one blind person guides another, both will fall into a pit." But Peter said to him, "Explain this parable to us." Then he said, "Are you also still without understanding? Do you not see that whatever goes into the mouth enters the stomach, and goes out into the sewer? But what comes out of the mouth proceeds from the heart, and this is what defiles. For out of the heart come evil intentions, murder, adultery, fornication, theft, false witness, slander. These are what defile a person, but to eat with unwashed hands does not defile."

Jesus outraged the religious authorities of his own time, breaking the restraints on tradition that had put some in power and stifled the original spirit of the tradition. Cavey does the same in the Canadian setting, a liberal and secular culture: butting up against nearly every traditional norm of "Christian" behavior in his church rituals, wrecking religion to save faith, with the motto: "the church for people not into church." Cavey, while a smooth-talking and brilliant orator, is no Hollywood savant; he is a frumpy, long-haired, earrings-wearing man, who looks more harried than handsome. In a remarkably similar claim to Cavey's, Rob Bell, the pastor who founded and ran a 10,000-member megachurch in Grand Rapids, Michigan, walked away from the church he built at its height, arguing a similar point: let us

---

[2] Bruce Cavey, *The End of Religion: Encountering the Subversive Spirituality of Jesus* (Colorado Springs, CO: NavPress, 2007).

save "the beautiful Jesus" so that the gospel can be lived out in action of love and justice. I summed up the ministry of Rob Bell in my book that told his story:

> The gospel can't be protected; neither can it be destroyed or confiscated. In Bell's vision, it is always and forever revealing itself in actions of charity whether inside or outside the church. No one owns charity or the revelation of Jesus Christ. He maintains, however, that it can be distorted by dogma and obscured by those who seek to own it. He desires to witness to what he calls "the beautiful Jesus" who comes to announce the kingdom of God—where charity lives, forgiveness is practiced, and the outsider is welcomed because the outsider is the one in whom Christ dwells eternally.
>
> The genius of Bell's message and the truth of this beautiful Jesus becomes real only when Jesus is enfleshed in acts of charity and compassion. While Christian belief is that Jesus was incarnated in flesh, this belief is all too often debated and argued to the point where tribes form, enemies are made, and the very basis of the revelation is defeated. This is precisely what Bell warns his followers against in his last Mars Hill sermon: "Beware of those who take the flesh and want to turn it back into words."[3]

We are making the claim that this is one of the core elements of the human condition, that the two worlds of the sacred and the profane are forever in tension with one another, and this pull is sometimes resolved for a while in churches, in which human beings can flourish and experience the kind of ecstasy that we will analyze in Part II. Then, in Part III, where we uncover the dark side of megachurches, we show the devastation that arises when the tensions collide and the beauty of charisma collides head-on with either corruption or egotism—a process sparing no one. As Durkheim so brilliantly diagnoses, humans are destined for this endless agony; individuals and groups find and join with what they experience as an ultimate partner, only to discover the pairing is fated to collapse of its own weight. But before we see the wreckage, we will crack the code of the power and desire in megachurches by analyzing how six affective human desires are met and satiated in the process of interaction ritual chains in megachurch worship services.

Our approach, then, reflects slowly evolving trends in both sociology and in the study of religion toward increased attention to the body. While many

[3] James K. Wellman, Jr., *Rob Bell and the New American Christianity* (Nashville, TN: Abingdon Press, 2012), 154.

critical cultural theorists have explored the representational and performative aspects of embodiment for cultural production and social life, the body's role as a "religious strategy" has received very little attention.[4] John Bartkowski argues that scholarship on the body tends to fall into two camps: "Rival perspectives . . . either privilege the deterministic effects of culture on the body (best exemplified in Foucault's [1979] "docile bodies" thesis), or treat the body as an extremely malleable tool in the crafting of identity (as found in Butler's [1989] exposition of embodied "performance" as improvisational theater)."[5] Kathy Davis explains that while these approaches have been and continue to be important and valuable, they avoid addressing the actual *materiality* of the body. So, while there is excellent theorizing about the cultural meanings attached to bodies and the power structures built around bodily manipulation and control, these theories may ignore or dismiss the material body as a sort of "coat rack." Linda Nicholson explains: "Here the body is viewed as a type of rack upon which differing cultural artifacts, specifically those of personality and behavior, are thrown or superimposed."[6] However, more recent scholarship on embodiment has begun to integrate insights about the dynamics, activities, and presence of biological bodies.

Inspired by the work of new materialists and material feminists, we understand the biological materiality of the body to be "more than a passive social construction . . . rather, [it is] an agentic force that interacts with and changes the other elements in the mix."[7] In our theoretical approach, attention to and consideration of the agency of the material elements of the body—its cells, muscles, neurotransmitters, hormones, beating hearts, and moving limbs—in no way detracts from the importance and mutual centrality of social and representational accounts of embodiment. These lenses on embodiment, we aim to show, need not be in competition, but rather can be combined and intertwined to reveal the co-constructed network of feedback loops that characterizes our psycho-bio-social-cultural embodiment,

[4] John P. Bartkowski, "Faithfully Embodied: Religious Identity and the Body," *disClosure: A Journal of Social Theory* 14, no. 4 (2005): 8–37. See also John P. Bartkowski, *The Promise Keepers: Servants, Soldiers, and Godly Men* (New Brunswick, NJ: Rutgers University Press, 2004).

[5] Bartkowski, "Faithfully Embodied," 10.

[6] Linda Nicholson, "Interpreting Gender," *Signs* 20, no. 1 (1994): 79–105. See also the discussion in Kathy Davis, ed., *Embodied Practices: Feminist Perspectives on the Body* (London: SAGE Publications, 1997).

[7] Stacy Alaimo and Susan Hekman, "Introduction: Emerging Models of Materiality in Feminist Theory," in *Material Feminisms*, edited by Stacy Alaimo and Susan Heckman, 1–19 (Bloomington: Indiana University Press, 2008), 7. For more on new materialism and material feminisms, see, e.g., Stacy Alaimo and Susan Hekman, eds., *Material Feminisms* (Bloomington: Indiana University Press, 2008); Diana Coole and Samantha Frost, eds., *New Materialisms: Ontology, Agency, and Politics* (Durham, NC: Duke University Press, 2010); and Victoria Pitts-Taylor, ed., *Mattering: Feminism, Science, and Materialism* (New York: New York University Press, 2016).

leading to a more comprehensive understanding of such complex and multi-dimensional phenomena as religious experience.

That said, without claiming that the six affective desires that we uncovered in our data and will investigate here are universally experienced in the same way by all people, we do detect consistent patterns of their emergence and manifestation in megachurch attendees. We suggest that the six desires are complex but traceable bio-social-cultural phenomena, formed and enacted in and through both the "body" of the social group and the individual bodies of each participant. The affective desires are an emergent property of the convergence of humans' biological and cultural heritages—meaning that the desires are shaped both by American culture, social dynamics, and power structures *and* by the materiality of the physical body.

CHAPTER 7 | The Micro-sociology of Interaction
Rituals within Megachurches

IN THIS BOOK, we are working out of a paradigm of micro-sociology, using Randall Collins's work on *interaction ritual chains* to understand how *emotional energy* is produced and flows in megachurches.[1] Collins's contribution challenges postmodern theory in its description of how meaning is constructed in human beings but also, more importantly, in human groups. As opposed to a macro system of global capital hegemony or a framework of power that uses social controls to determine and shape human desire and activity, Collins argues—we think convincingly—that a micro-sociology of group interactions provides a more plausible explanation of how and why megachurches function with such success. Having used Pierre Bourdieu's theory and work in the past, we frequently found it impossible to explain how his abstract concept of *habitus* could shape and form human beings, much less human communities.[2] *Habitus* is abstract and gives no real mechanism for how one might describe or illumine the actions of human beings as they were concretely acting and believing in their everyday lives. Collins's work is pragmatic and more empirical. It is informed by recent research on human emotion and evolutionary theory to make sense of how humans actually manage and negotiate their daily social and cultural interactions.

[1] Randall Collins, *Interaction Ritual Chains* (Princeton, NJ: Princeton University Press, 2004).
[2] Pierre Bourdieu, *The Logic of Practice* (Cambridge: Polity Press, 1990); James K. Wellman, Jr., *The Gold Coast Church and the Ghetto: Christ and Culture in Mainline Protestantism* (Urbana: University of Illinois Press, 1999).

Collins's approach fits well with our emphasis on radical empiricism, reflected in the thinking of William James,[3] which examines how humans function in their actual circumstances, emotions, and events on the ground; thus, our aim is to examine *the experience of bodies and emotions as they enact religiosity and are a part of megachurches.* We ask the question that many of our readers might ask: Are the people in this study lying about the reasons that they were involved in these churches? Are they practicing a form of false consciousness, only participating in these churches because they are prisoners of a capitalist economy that inflames a desire to consume even when it comes to church? This is a real question, and we deliberate on it in Part III of this book. For now, however, we first listen to megachurch members, taking their own explanations seriously, and put them in a theoretical model that not only accepts their explanations but analyzes them in such a way that illumines the data, which we argue would predict what might happen if others experienced these churches.

To accomplish this, we draw on focus groups and interviews as well as survey data. See Appendix A for further description of our data and method. Focus groups are a particularly useful method for studying interaction ritual chains, as responses typically have a "chain-like" feel to them in which participants engage and build off the responses of others. The performative element of focus groups—where respondents seek to convey the intensity and power of their experiences—aligns well with our study, as it encourages participants to provide rich accounts of their spiritual experiences and essentially relive them through their account to the group.[4]

Furthermore, applying and extending Collins's work to our data, we are able to analyze and explain what moved megachurch members to become involved in these churches. We argue that neither the seduction of postmodern capitalism alone, nor pure rational choice, leads our megachurch members to engage. Rather, what attracts members to these churches is a process of interaction ritual chains that produce and evoke deep desires as well as the emotional energy created by collective effervescence. We suggest that rational choice does come into play, but only after humans first experience the affective pull of these megachurches. That is, the emotion and energy of megachurch practices are in the body before they are adjudicated in the mind. And the overwhelming affective experience is so positive that rational choice is an ex post facto rationalization of just how good it feels to be in these

---

[3] William James, *Essays in Radical Empiricism* (Lincoln: University of Nebraska Press, 1996); Nancy Frankenberry, *Religion and Radical Empiricism* (Albany: State University of New York Press, 1987).
[4] We thank an anonymous reviewer for this insightful point.

institutions and often, a review of the extraordinary benefits that accrue to these individuals and their families. Affect, we argue, dominates their initial experience and produces a desire to be involved. Affect clearly leads, though a reflective choice follows. Thus, our *embodied choice theory* drives our theorizing as an explanation for what we discovered. We argue that it is an embodied movement of experience that produces a choice and desire to participate in these megachurches. To be sure, the emotional energy convinces folks that the benefits of these churches far outweigh the costs—thus, rational choice is used to calculate a commitment to these churches, but emotional energy, created by the arc of activities that megachurches provide, drives our megachurch members into intense and satisfying relationships with their churches. The interaction ritual produces emotional energy through the micro-sociological interactions within megachurches, all the while stimulating a collective effervescence in these congregations that draws so many to them. We will crack the code of these megachurches and provide a close-hand description and theory of how they achieve such overwhelming success.

In our research, having analyzed and considered all the data, we enumerate six core desires that these megachurches evoke and meet:

1. Members feel *acceptance* immediately, which creates a feeling of *belonging*.
2. They experience a deep sense of *spiritual energy and stimulation,* in the music and the atmosphere, which we name the *"wow" factor*.
3. They identify a *reliable leader*, describing the megachurch pastors in terms of their *charismatic leadership*.
4. They feel the exhilaration of *deliverance* and the promise of *certainty* produced by the altar calls or when megachurch members describe "hundreds" coming down to "accept Jesus."
5. They experience a sense of personal *purpose* in discovering their "gifts," which they use in *service* to the church as well as in their communities.
6. Their participation in small groups, which we define as a *re-membering process* (both as a prompt and confirming an affiliation) linked to the Sunday experience, gives members a bridge between their weekly worship services—creating, as we argue, a deep sense of *solidarity,* which we know becomes for many of our informants their extended primary community.

The six chapters that follow in Part II, therefore, tell the story of the megachurch worship service as a matrix within which these six desires are met; how megachurch members are charged; how the cycles of emotional energy are produced; and the process by which collective effervescence creates an overwhelming connection of megachurch members to God, one another, their pastor, and their communities. We connect this as well to Collins's four ritual ingredients of *co-presence, a shared mood, a mutual focus of attention,* and *barriers to outsiders.* Collins argues that these are "ingredients," not "determinant[s] . . . because a situation is an emergent property. A situation is not merely the result of the individual who comes into it, nor even of a combination of individuals (although it is that, too). Situations have laws or processes of their own; and that is what [interaction ritual] theory is about."[5] These ingredients produce what Collins outlines as ritual outcomes:

1. group solidarity in megachurch membership;
2. emotional energy in individuals—an energy that sustains participation;
3. symbols of social relationship or sacred objects (often charismatic pastors); and
4. standards of morality, ways in which megachurches pronounce rules and regulations for the moral lives of their members.[6]

For an overview of what is to come in our discussion of the Megachurch Ritual Cycle, see Figure 7.1.

As we narrate and define Collins's interaction ritual structure, we will briefly outline the ways the six desires are addressed in a chronological manner within megachurches. This is only a model and, to be sure, in actual practice, affect and emotional energy flows throughout megachurches are going to be particular to each person and each instance. Therefore, even though there is a clear chronology to the megachurch ritual cycle, the notion that affect flows in an organized chronological manner should be interpreted loosely—each experience that approximates this model is a variation on a theme. Therefore, we will show how the affective desires are evoked and addressed in overlapping and synchronic ways, which reinforces the power of the collective effervescence of these churches.

Megachurches are total life systems in that they seek to produce an experience that is all-enveloping, beginning with the ritual process of *co-presence.* From websites, architecture, and aesthetic branding, to an ultra-friendly church welcome team, to evangelism and outreach, entering a megachurch is in many ways like coming into a womb—a total system that seeks to communicate that "you" belong and that "you" are accepted. We know from our data that the experience can be quite electric, and that it leads to a feeling of

[5] Collins, *Interaction Ritual Chains,* 5.
[6] Collins, *Interaction Ritual Chains.*

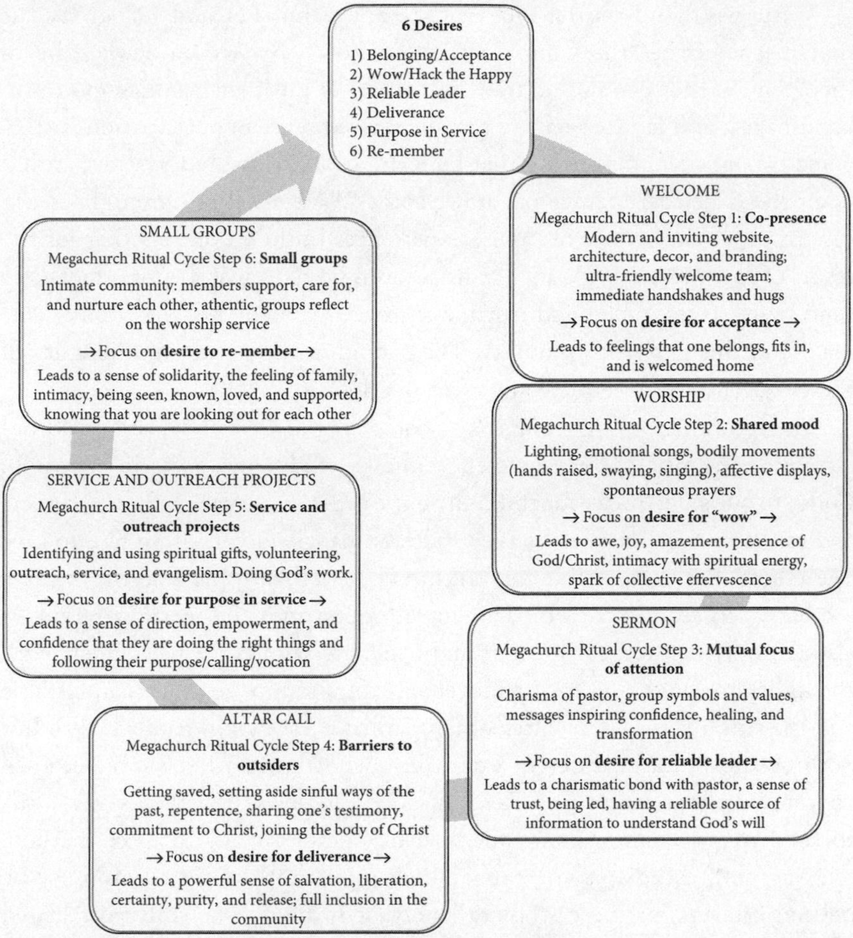

6 Desires

1) Belonging/Acceptance
2) Wow/Hack the Happy
3) Reliable Leader
4) Deliverance
5) Purpose in Service
6) Re-member

WELCOME

Megachurch Ritual Cycle Step 1: **Co-presence**

Modern and inviting website, architecture, decor, and branding; ultra-friendly welcome team; immediate handshakes and hugs

→ Focus on **desire for acceptance** →

Leads to feelings that one belongs, fits in, and is welcomed home

WORSHIP

Megachurch Ritual Cycle Step 2: **Shared mood**

Lighting, emotional songs, bodily movements (hands raised, swaying, singing), affective displays, spontaneous prayers

→ Focus on **desire for "wow"** →

Leads to awe, joy, amazement, presence of God/Christ, intimacy with spiritual energy, spark of collective effervescence

SERMON

Megachurch Ritual Cycle Step 3: **Mutual focus of attention**

Charisma of pastor, group symbols and values, messages inspiring confidence, healing, and transformation

→ Focus on **desire for reliable leader** →

Leads to a charismatic bond with pastor, a sense of trust, being led, having a reliable source of information to understand God's will

SMALL GROUPS

Megachurch Ritual Cycle Step 6: **Small groups**

Intimate community: members support, care for, and nurture each other, athentic, groups reflect on the worship service

→ Focus on **desire to re-member** →

Leads to a sense of solidarity, the feeling of family, intimacy, being seen, known, loved, and supported, knowing that you are looking out for each other

SERVICE AND OUTREACH PROJECTS

Megachurch Ritual Cycle Step 5: **Service and outreach projects**

Identifying and using spiritual gifts, volunteering, outreach, service, and evangelism. Doing God's work.

→ Focus on **desire for purpose in service** →

Leads to a sense of direction, empowerment, and confidence that they are doing the right things and following their purpose/calling/vocation

ALTAR CALL

Megachurch Ritual Cycle Step 4: **Barriers to outsiders**

Getting saved, setting aside sinful ways of the past, repentence, sharing one's testimony, commitment to Christ, joining the body of Christ

→ Focus on **desire for deliverance** →

Leads to a powerful sense of salvation, liberation, certainty, purity, and release; full inclusion in the community

FIGURE 7.1. Overview of the Megachurch Ritual Cycle

Although the ritual cycle is patterned, the ebbs and flows of desire and emotional energy are much more fluid and unruly. For each step, one of the six affective desires is highlighted as a primary focus; however, in reality the entire cycle is involved in creating and maintaining the affective pulse that meets each desire. Any and all of the six desires may be expressed and addressed at any time throughout the cycle, even if there is a focus on one during each step.

being comfortable, accepted, loved, and welcomed. Upon entering, people don't feel judged or looked down upon or conspicuous. They feel like they really "fit in." Normally, it is an overwhelming and jarring moment for many, to enter a huge venue, to realize that they may not know anyone, other than those who may have invited them. At that moment then, the "need" to be accepted is at its most intense, and so for megachurches, the entrance, the first impression, becomes a critical moment in determining whether newcomers stay or leave.

What we found during our visits to megachurches and in our data is that megachurches think intensely about how to welcome newcomers to their venues; they choose and train volunteers to greet with smiles and warm handshakes, and labor to ensure that an excited sense of anticipation is triggered by signs and messaging that both direct and reassure the stranger that he or she is neither strange nor unwelcome. As we will see throughout our discussion of the six desires, these experiences build on one another for the result of turning participants to Christ, and, perhaps just as importantly, to bind them to the group and institution, making them feel that this is *their* place and this is *their* community. The thoughtfulness and intentionality of these churches is remarkable and often overlooked.

The second ritual ingredient is a shared mood. Of course, the mood has already been initiated by a greeter, who also guides and gives information. Coffee to one side, a place for children on the other, information for newcomers and for those who know what they want, and a friendly, smiling face to give one a sense that in these churches the mood is, well, "happy," and the greeters are happy to see newcomers. This introduction into the worship service is also an "opportunity" for greeters and ushers to familiarize newcomers with the lighting, songs, and bodily movements of worship. Seats are comfortable and the singing is upbeat, often accompanied by swaying, hands raised, but nothing substantially different from what one would find at a subdued rock concert—at least not at first. Leaders voice and show that they want "you" to be there, welcoming newcomers with announcements directed at those who are new, and displaying the vitality and warmth of the community by offering prayers for those who are lonely or in need. The collective shared mood is one that speaks volumes not just about the desire to make one feel accepted, but also to suggest that this is a place where the moment of "wow" is experienced: people feel and express joy and want to share that mood of uplift with one another, or as one newcomer exclaimed, "I watched the Holy Spirit [move] like people doing the wave at a football game . . . hundreds got saved!" In other words, the intentionality and focus that goes into creating a viable co-presence intensifies and initiates a shared mood, and this is only the beginning of what's coming.

Collins's third ingredient in the ritual process is a *mutual focus of attention*. This comes through via singers and song leaders, but the key focus is on the pastor or lead teacher, who is almost always male. Through both the music and the preaching, a desperate need is expressed, in that each person is, in some form, found wanting, a sinner. The minister is clear that he, too, stands in judgment, which is quickly followed by the sense that while he's human and has many flaws, he also knows that in Christ, the solution is found, that new life is available, that anyone can claim this life, and that the whole world is offered this free gift of grace. In other words, the worship service messaging emphasizes and creates a sense of need, which is immediately followed by the redemptive inspiration that there is a way out—that relief is within reach, that one can be *delivered* and that there is a *solution.* Thus the leader, who relates to you and knows where you have been, also offers you a way out, a solution to the grip of sin, creating access to God, the Father who knows you, forgives you, and wants more than anything else to save you. So, the focus of attention is the charismatic leader, the *reliable leader*, who, while human, has found a way through to the Father who will never fail, the Father who is not like one's earthly father, but who will forgive, release, and send you out into the world a new woman, a new man, delivered and guided into a new life in Christ.

These churches, in one form or another, create altar call settings, and here, after the buildup to the sense that one has a need—a need that can be remedied—the time for decision comes. There is relief from the despair of being separated from God the Father and it is through His Son, Jesus, who died and made the path open and free to the Father. This sense of deliverance ripples through these congregations, and without making it explicit creates a *barrier to outsiders.* That is, all are welcome, but the true inner circle belongs to the saved, to those who have responded to the call to conversion. This is a powerful process, by which one is welcomed, loved, accepted, called out in one's sin, and offered a free pass to the "reliable Father." From here one is invited to go up to "touch" the pastor, who wants to heal and accept you into deliverance from sin and separation. The movement of deliverance is a moment of liberation, of entrance into Christ, of purification, of being in the community of faith. The barriers to outsiders are real, though the constant hope and invitation is that you, too, just like those you have witnessed, can come and be saved.

What follows are two interaction ritual links that highlight Collins's emphasis on the importance of understanding interaction rituals as existing in *chains*. In megachurches, worship is never understood as a once-a-week Sunday event. The invitation and expectation are not only to enter "into Christ" but also to enter into community, to mark oneself as a member of the family, and to discover your strengths and purpose to serve others. The identity of evangelical Christians is inextricable from the call to serve the world in the name of Christ—to be Christ's body, his hands and feet, within their communities and throughout the world. This process, then, is one in which one not only takes on a new identity "in Christ," but one's gifts are identified for the sake of serving the community and one's neighbor. Members are invited and encouraged to participate in service projects aimed at enacting the character and work of Christ within the wider community and world. As the "body of Christ," one is challenged to serve, give, and spread the word. This has the dual effect of filling participants with a sense of purpose and direction, while signaling to themselves and the rest of the group their devotion and loyalty to the gospel message and the church community.

Last, the megachurch model is designed as a total life system, and in the process of accepting God's grace, one is invited into small groups that underscore, develop, and reinforce one's new identity and that further solidify membership and commitment to the church. Small groups and opportunities to serve are vital ingredients for the *megachurch model* because they function to *enact* and *mobilize* what is learned (group symbols) and gained (emotional energy) during the worship service. These links channel and solidify the fleeting nature of these experiences into transformed, cohesive personal *identities* and a vibrant, cooperative *community* (including subcommunities and small groups) that permeate the rest of their lives, both individually and communally. They also, in a pragmatic sense, create a bridge from Sunday to Sunday to keep the fire burning throughout the week.

Of course, both of these chain links—service projects and small groups— are interaction rituals in and of themselves, even as they contribute to the larger chain initiated in the worship service. Our focus on these elements emphasizes the importance of what sociologists Edward Lawler, Shane Thye, and Jeongkoo Yoon call the *micro-to-macro process*. They extend Lawler and Yoon's *relational cohesion theory* to explain how social interactions that include joint tasks, shared responsibility, and social unit attributions can accumulate to transform a network of individuals and pairs of individuals into a cohesive, centralized group. That group, in turn, becomes an object of commitment, loyalty, and immense positive affect.[7] "In an individualized world," they explain, "group ties are self-generated from the bottom up. That is, they develop and are sustained through repeated social interactions that take place around joint tasks or activities, promoted and framed by the group unit . . . [that] involve *affective sentiments* about the group itself."[8] This is directly related to Durkheim's *homo duplex*: "How do individualized, privatized actors create and sustain affectively meaningful social ties to social units—relations, groups,

[7] Edward J. Lawler and Jeongkoo Yoon, "Commitment in Exchange Relations," *American Sociological Review* 61, no. 1 (1996): 89–108; Edward J. Lawler, Shane R. Thye, and Jeongkoo Yoon, *Social Commitments in a Depersonalized World* (New York: Russell Sage Foundation, 2009); Edward J. Lawler, Shane R. Thye, and Jeongkoo Yoon, "Emotions and Group Ties in Social Exchange," in *Handbook of the Sociology of Emotions: Volume II*, edited by Jane E. Stets and Jonathan H. Turner, 77–101 (Dordrecht: Springer, 2014).
[8] Lawler, Thye, and Yoon, "Emotions and Group Ties," 79.

organizations, communities, and nations?"[9] The answer: the micro-to-macro process. Megachurches—including each interaction during the worship services, small-group meetings, and outreach social service activities—are complex collections of micro units that facilitate and enact macro impulses of devotion to the larger group. Through this process, individuals' commitment expands to motivate them not only to service for the church, but service for its surrounding community, the state or nation, and even the world with the "life-changing" and "world-transforming" power of the message of Jesus Christ. And here, it is not only a big-picture view that one is called to, but a *process* by which members are invited to first "discover their gifts," then "develop their gifts," and ultimately to be called to "use their gifts" on behalf of Christ and others to reach out and heal the world. Thus, as we have suggested all along, this micro-to-macro project resonates with a way to solve the tension Durkheim outlines in *homo duplex*: one is in between, caught halfway between the self and the world, and the individual needs to be deeply invested in both, even at the same time. Megachurches understand that model and create a system that functions to do both—develop individuals in their gifts, as well as to bind these folks together in a community, small and large, in which they find rest, strength, co-presence, a shared mood, tools to develop oneself, and opportunities to help and serve the world. The genius of these institutions is that they meet individuals' needs but also maintain a focus on their communal context. And when they serve, they do so in ways that use individual gifts that serve the person and the megachurch community, as well as the wider community and the greater global community.

[9] Lawler, Thye, and Yoon, "Emotions and Group Ties," 78.

CHAPTER 8 | Desire for Acceptance
and Belonging

" IMMEDIATELY WHEN WE walked in, I felt the love and the family closeness that I had never felt in the church that I grew up in."[1] We, too, as investigators, felt the same shock of welcome when we visited these churches. On one cold, blustery Sunday morning, two of us walked into a megachurch. The building was a transformed two-story business building, nondescript, a part of a commercial real estate hub of businesses with names that give no clue to their purpose. As we walked toward the building, the rain fell, and out of the glass doors came two smiling twenty-somethings with hot coffee and an umbrella to save us from the rain and cold as we walked in. We were then met with greetings inside, and a table with more smiles and people asking how they can help. We felt, well, welcomed. And then turning to look around, we saw a separate glassed room, with friendly young adults greeting families with young kids. With signs that were clear and evident marking rooms for each grade and type, we thought, "Well, this is delightful and organized, what a plan!" And the greetings weren't overboard, just enough to say, "Welcome, we're glad you're here." Now, not every megachurch we visited and examined in this study had this same over-the-top sense of unreserved love, but it was a piece of this puzzle that became clear and present. Megachurches, despite their secularity and lack of obvious

---

[1] Part of this chapter is reprinted and adapted with permission from James K. Wellman, Jr., Katie E. Corcoran, and Kate Stockly-Meyerdirk, "'God Is Like a Drug . . .': Explaining Interaction Rituals in American Megachurches," *Sociological Forum* 29 (2014): 650–672. Copyright [2014] by Wiley.

signs of being a "church," know how to make people feel that they are accepted and welcomed. A megachurch attendee described it in this way:

> I say it is the littlest big church you'll ever go to. Because you come here and you feel the community and it doesn't feel like you're just another face. I mean I think the first time we came here we must have greeted by 10 or 15 different people. It was crazy. It was just like, like yeah I'm feeling okay. We're like new. New face. Because you feel safe. You feel so loved in this place that it's just safe to step out. You don't feel like you're taking a risk to step out and service. Because so many people do it and they loved you from the moment you walked in that door, they have just loved on you. And the moment you walk back out again, I mean they just, they love you. And so, it's you want to give back whatever you can because you feel so loved in this place.

With the characteristics we have identified, in many ways one might think that these megachurches have read Randall Collins's book *Interaction Ritual Chains*! The data we analyzed provided us a veritable bouquet of points that produced the ritual ingredients Collins described. Follow along in Figure 8.1, which summarizes the elements of this first step in the megachurch ritual cycle.

First is *bodily assembly*, which allows individuals to watch the emotions of others as they engage in the same ritual. A minimum requirement for this is bodily *co-presence*. As one megachurch member reflected: "So I came in and sat down and I mean, I just started crying, I said, 'I have come home. This is so different from what I thought it was going to be.' So friendly and everybody was so warm and for a big church I was just amazed by it, I just couldn't wrap my mind around it. So that first Sunday I said, 'Okay, being Baptist isn't so bad.'"

Indeed, as the senior member of the team I went into one of our two black megachurches, where my wife and I were the only white people in the sanctuary. We were immediately greeted as if we were long-lost friends, and then they reached out to us afterward, inquiring whether we were visitors. Not only was it friendly, but there was a gripping sense of urgency in the singing and the ritual life, and the preaching made you want to be with these people. One of the highlights was the testimony of a young black man, a former drug user and dope dealer who had struggled with homelessness, and who had been "saved" by the church ministry. He had recently found his gift in his voice. He was invited to sing. He opened his mouth and the church began to devolve into a delirium of joy—the sheer volume and velvet quality of his voice was overwhelming. The congregation responded with deep adoration

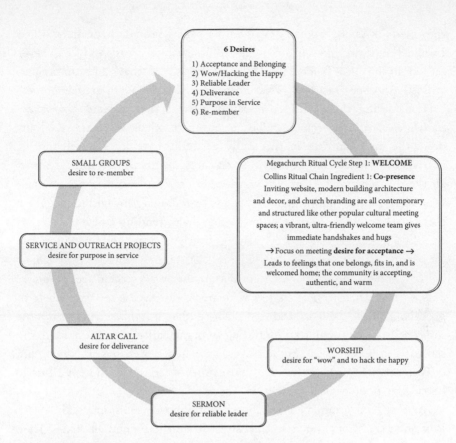

FIGURE 8.1. Megachurch Ritual Cycle Step 1: Welcome

and adulation. Further on, adding to the moment, it was also "graduate Sunday," and every graduate, from junior high school up to graduate school students, came up—I counted fifty-eight individuals. Each was interviewed to tell what they had done, and then congratulated with flowers and an ovation. All of this created a shared mood between my wife and I and the rest of the congregation. As we were leaving in our car, we were breathless with the joy of their service and its clear relevance to the lives of those in the church, and the immediacy of their acceptance and care for each other and for us.

We know as sociologists that humans have a natural fear of being shunned and are often anxious when walking into a new place, especially as a minority. There is always a lurking sense that one could be spurned or ignored, which makes any disapproval deeply aversive—thus, on the contrary, when people are greeted with such delight, the pleasure of approval and the relief of that fear is not only deeply appealing, but highly affectively motivates them to repeat interactions during which they have felt welcomed, accepted, and that they belong. As one woman described her experience emphatically: "When I walked in, it was like I had come home. It absolutely was. And I had never set foot in this place before. The Holy Spirit was here, that's all I can say, and still is." Another concurred: "I have never felt so welcome in my whole life."

Considering this, Collins's ritual ingredient that expects *barriers excluding outsiders* may sound and be opposite to what we found. And indeed, the megachurches in this study generally have lower levels of this ingredient, particularly in terms of cultural membership capital. Across all the megachurches, there was a strong desire to attract new people (i.e., "outsiders") and a commitment to doing so by removing any obstacles to their participation. These churches acknowledge that attending a new church, especially a large one, can be intimidating, overwhelming, and uncomfortable for newcomers. Part of this is due to a lack of congregational knowledge, or cultural capital; humans want information that makes them feel comfortable, such as when services start, what happens during the services, where to go, whom to ask for help, and so on. These knowledge barriers can inhibit someone from coming into the building from the parking lot or even into the sanctuary from the foyer. Successful megachurches' websites, therefore, are consistently updated and artfully done as they reach out to those with little knowledge to describe what they are about to experience.

And indeed, compared to churches from the mainline and liberal Protestant tradition, evangelical websites are startlingly new and fresh. They seek to be "relevant," especially to a younger demographic. To be sure, this is not only intentional but successful. The senior author visited a megachurch that is literally fifteen minutes from his house, in the middle of Seattle, an urban residential area. One might expect to find a middle-aged to elderly clientele, but in fact, young people and young families dominate the demographic. The pastor is a dynamic forty-nine-year-old man, with a quick wit and a sharp sense of how to speak to the needs of his congregation. He is neither hip nor handsome, but he preaches a Bible-based and relevant message that clearly makes young people flock to the church. To be sure, these churches have intentionally created a welcoming, nonintimidating ethos designed to provide the requisite congregational knowledge to make the transition from the "outside" to participation in the ritual as seamless and easy as possible. A megachurch lay leader said: "We're very intentional about making you feel welcome."

And indeed, in remembering their first visit to the megachurch, many respondents described how important it was that they were greeted and welcomed upon entering the building and, in some cases, the parking lot. One respondent described how she "was really very intimidated" and that the "very warm and welcoming" greeters eased her intimidation and made her feel more comfortable. Because she "know[s] how important it is [for visitors] to have that warm welcome," she is now a greeter herself who specifically looks "for those intimidated people." Another respondent, recalling her first visit, mentioned how she debated whether to even go because she "didn't know anybody there," but that once she arrived, she was greeted immediately upon exiting her car and was handed a welcome bulletin with congregational information. She said the greeters will "keep you, make you come on in and by the time you got in at least ten people had said something to you by the time you made it to the hospitality desk, by the time you made it to your seat they made sure you were welcome." Two respondents noted that on their first visit, they arrived at the wrong time, but were immediately helped by a greeter. Greeters "come and they shake your hands and say, 'Do you need anything? Do you want a coffee? Are you new here? We will show you where to go, how to sit.' And they will find you a spot even." This helps reduce the uncertainty and uneasiness of new visitors, who initially lack important congregational cultural capital but are quickly brought up to speed.

For most megachurches, individuals are welcomed "as they are," however they are dressed. A mother and new member described how her previous church required one "to wear your Sunday best," which was difficult for her children. One of the things that stood out the most to her about the megachurch was that people could wear whatever they wanted and that her son could "wear his jeans." Others mentioned the benefit of being able to go to church in regular clothes—"shorts, flip flops, whatever"—and highlighted how this made visitors, including homeless individuals, feel comfortable attending. This atmosphere also makes congregants feel more comfortable inviting others to come to church, because they know the people they invite will be accepted and welcomed with open arms regardless of their appearance.

In addition to easing congregational knowledge and clothing barriers, these churches also intentionally seek to eliminate or reduce any knowledge obstacles to participation in the ritual, such as having to know a liturgy, songs, or prayers. A respondent identified how the structure of the church "is such that you're comfortable with it, you know? There's not a lot of liturgy and repetition and things that you don't know are coming." Nearly all the megachurches display the lyrics of songs on large screens at the front of the church, so that individuals can participate without prior knowledge of the songs and without having to know how to use a hymnal. The music tends to be upbeat, loud, contemporary, and reminiscent of a rock concert, although a few of the megachurches also offered a more traditional service. This allows individuals to draw on cultural capital they already have from participating in the secular world, rather than requiring specific denominational knowledge or subcultural membership capital.

Not having formal liturgies tied to specific denominations allows the megachurches to appeal to individuals from diverse backgrounds. One church noted a transition from a more formal liturgy (i.e., clergy wore robes, and traditional songs associated with their denomination were sung) to a more informal worship service designed to appeal to "folks who come from different traditions" (i.e., clergy dressed casually and contemporary songs were sung). Respondents from one megachurch noted that their "loose" connection to Lutheranism—that is, using contemporary music and forms rather than more formal liturgy—made their church "user-friendly," "welcoming," and "refreshing." Attendees often described the "authenticity" that accompanies the leaving behind of traditional ritual elements.[2] The respondents identified that everyone, including newcomers and people from diverse backgrounds, engaging in worship together contributes to its authenticity. In this way, barriers to outsiders in the form of cultural membership capital are viewed as ostentatious and rote "pomp and circumstance."

The intentional attempt to reduce cultural membership requirements (i.e., congregational and denominational knowledge) demonstrates that these churches are seeking to remove barriers to outsiders and facilitate newcomers' participation in the church. While Collins identifies excluding outsiders as a means of increasing collective effervescence, he also notes that collective effervescence can be amplified when there are more individuals participating in a ritual.[3] The megachurches in this study are effective at increasing the number of ritual participants, thereby creating a larger-scale shared mood. Thus, the lack of barriers to participation does not detract from the ritual, but contributes to it.[4]

Generally, pastors in mainline denominational churches are more likely than their megachurch counterparts to wear a robe and stole, congregants are more likely to sing contemplative hymns to organ music, and the sanctuary will probably have an altar and stained-glass windows. "Meaning seekers," who have little to no experience in churches, and who are trying to make sense of the contemporary world, often find formalism uncomfortable or dreary. The aesthetic of a megachurch is exemplified by pastors

[2] Kimon Howland Sargeant. *Seeker Churches: Promoting Traditional Religion in a Nontraditional Way* (New Brunswick, NJ: Rutgers University Press, 2000).

[3] Collins, *Interaction Ritual Chains*.

[4] G. A. Pritchard, *Willow Creek Seeker Services: Evaluating a New Way of Doing Church* (Grand Rapids, MI: Baker Books, 1996); Wade Clark Roof, *A Generation of Seekers: The Spiritual Journeys of the Baby Boom Generation* (San Francisco: Harper San Francisco, 1994).

who typically wear casual, often stylish street clothes, and members who are informal, even apt to bring coffee or food with them into the sanctuary. Megachurch sanctuaries typically look more like a gym or a warehouse with contemporary lighting and a stage. Lights are low and words for the worship music are projected on the screen at the front. A young or modern person is likely to feel more comfortable and inspired singing along with a band than thumbing through a hymnal, with the expectation to simultaneously read music and sing words. In addition, leaders in megachurches are often young, attractive, charismatic, energetic, and relatable. In an effort to appear fresh and different, affiliations to traditional denomination are often downplayed; for example, Nancy Martin noted how, at one point, Safe Harbor Baptist Church (affiliated with the Southern Baptist Convention) removed the words "Safe" and "Baptist Church" from their roadside sign and Sunday bulletins, opting instead to advertise as, simply, "Harbor."[5] Martin explains that "a short, easy-to-remember name is a key part of successful branding . . . leaders at the church frame this as an important part of being inviting to newcomers, to nonbelievers and fallen away Christians."[6]

The intention is to strip away, or "de-churchify,"[7] the aspects of traditional religion that might make newcomers—or what Bill Hybels called "unchurched Harrys"[8]—feel uncomfortable or inhibited. And the sense that these venues aren't "church" lowers expectations, or at least renders former experience less relevant, so that when the "magic" begins, expectations are often shattered, and the joy of it is overwhelming: "When you walk in the doors [of the church], you are so taken out of church . . . you lose the bigness because you don't feel like you're at church. You feel like you walked into someone's living room, you've walked into the mall, you've walked into whatever feels comfortable for you. I mean . . . you walk in and your whole perception of walking into a church, a big church or a small church, is obliterated." Here, megachurches are playing on expectations: church is *typically not warm and welcoming, it is stiff and uncomfortable.* But in this place, you are *at home and welcome, not because you look right or are acting right, but because you are here.* In the Christian sense of the word, this is *grace,* or *unconditional acceptance,* which is one of the prime movers of human joy: that one has found somewhere where they know that they are *at home, or at least a place that feels*

[5] Nancy Martin, "Small Groups in Big Churches" (Unpublished PhD Dissertation: University of Arizona, 2007), 123.
[6] Martin, "Small Groups in Big Churches," 123.
[7] Martin, "Small Groups in Big Churches," 124.
[8] Pritchard, *Willow Creek Seeker Services.*

like home should feel—marking the human body with the ability to let down barriers to be open to what is coming.

This comes to an even deeper sensibility that, as one of the megachurch members exclaimed, acceptance reflects an *intense commitment* to meeting folks where they are no matter the issue:

> Nothing scares us. Yeah, nothing scares us. Everything has been born out of need, you know, I mean it's really, we just felt needs and try and . . . [Interviewer: You mean you have deviant attenders?] People who need Jesus come to this church. I was going to say I think that that little subtitle for [our church] . . . is *come as you are and you will be loved*. And there is a reflection of that mentality, for sure in our ministries and in lots of other ministries that people are giving them a little more permission to be real I would say. And that's what's happening. That's where some for our ministries, you know, flow out of that. You know, just kind of commissioned to actual struggle and be honest. I hear a lot of that.
>
> [Another focus group member]: To have a problem without being a problem is what he's saying. God has made them holy but the rest of their problems that are in their life. We have people come to us on the crisis side that say that other churches just don't talk about this.

One can sense the pride here, that there seems to be nothing and no one that is *not accepted*, at least in many of these churches—a willingness to be a place where all are truly welcome, where those who are, in the words of Christian scripture, "the least, the lost and last" are not only welcomed but embraced (Matthew 25:40) (NIV). We sensed this effort toward radical acceptance in the megachurches that we visited, but the words of megachurch members overflowed with a deep rush of grace from which they derived a sense of relief and joy.

Secular Venues for the Sacred

Justin Wilford has suggested that one of the reasons that the unique ritual style found in megachurches—at once secular and welcoming— has seen such extreme success is its ability to present a "counterstrategy" against post-Christian secularity. He shows that megachurches, as a post-modern, postsuburban phenomenon, succeed by "effectively enacting and representing—that is, performing—secular, everyday *places* in such a way that they become religiously meaningful."[9] Rather than constructing a

9 Justin Wilford, "Purpose Driven Place: Saddleback Church and the Postsuburban Transformation of

"sacred space" away, *separate,* from the mundane, profane world, the megachurch style creates an atmosphere that is, strikingly secular and casual,
but then *infuses* the secular, fragmented reality with profound meaning. As
Wilford elaborates:

> Members of Saddleback in south Orange County related feelings of
> absence, loss, and emptiness in their stories ("testimonies" in evangel-
> ical parlance) about becoming Christians and members of Saddleback.
> Of course, these are old themes in Protestant narratives of salvation.
> But for Saddleback members they were experienced in terms of an ab-
> sence not of salvation, grace or God's love, but of social orientation.
> The terms "aimless," "lost," or "disconnected," and explanations like
> "I didn't know where I was going in life," and "I needed something to
> center my life on," were elaborations on one of Saddleback's signature
> themes: purpose.[10]

Contrary to stereotypes surrounding megachurches, our analysis of the data
found that, although the megachurches maintain conservative "fundamentalist" theologies and lean to the right on social issues, usually supporting
a Republican agenda, very rarely were these issues discussed in the church.
Megachurches, to grow and meet their needs, keep things in the middle range
of evangelical theology and normative claims. There is very little explicit
talk of culture war issues (abortion, same-sex marriage, etc.) even though
the church's official position is known. Therefore, more than searching for
a specific brand of theology, members and seekers alike seem to be acting
on their desires for comfort, belonging, and purpose when they walk into a
worship space that is as secular as the spaces they experience all week long.
The genius of the megachurch is that it is precisely in the secular where the
sacred life moves and has its being—again, a bubbling up of the offer of grace
coming up from within, rather than necessarily being forced or coerced into
a religious regime.

   This also tracks back to one of our core arguments in the history of the
megachurch movement: megachurches both embody the world (i.e., secularity) and bring out the sacred at the heart of the secular. This is a point
made by Peter Berger, the preeminent sociologist of religion, in an essay

American Evangelicalism" (Unpublished PhD Dissertation: University of California, Los Angeles), 2–3,
emphasis his. Justin Wilford, *Sacred Subdivisions: The Postsuburban Transformation of American Evangelicalism*
(New York: New York University Press, 2012).

[10] Justin Wilford, *Sacred Subdivisions: The Postsuburban Transformation of American Evangelicalism*
(New York: New York University Press, 2012), p. 12.

he wrote not long before he died, "Further Thoughts on Religion and Modernity."[11] Berger, starting with Jose Casanova's phrase, "all institutions have correlates in consciousness," argues that there is a "default secular discourse [that] co-exists with a plurality of religious discourses, both in society and in consciousness."[12] And here we circle back and assert, as we did earlier, that the Christian tradition has within it a secular center from the very beginning of the tradition. We see this in Jesus's words, which disrupted Jewish piety, arguing that it is not "what goes into a person that makes a person unclean, it is what comes out of a person's mouth that makes them clean" (Matthew 15:11). Jesus, as a prophetic Jew, claims that it is what comes from one's soul that makes one righteous rather than obedience to externals. In this challenge to Jewish orthodoxy, Jesus revolutionized time and space—all time and space is and can be made sacred. The sacred, rather than being the exclusive possession of the Temple and the religious, is open to all who internalize the ethic and spirit of grace and truth. Berger's claim that all institutions have correlates in consciousness suggests a plausible case can be made that megachurches, while experienced by many as intrinsically secular, become sacred as their members embody acts of acceptance, grace, and reconciliation. In that sense, as a surprise to many—even those that attend these churches—megachurches become sacred centers. Indeed, many of our secular friends, and even our liberal (and conservative) Christian friends, have asked: "How can anything good come from a megachurch?" We ourselves have asked this question, and even those coming to these churches, who experience their secular nature, ask similar questions. But that is precisely the argument: embodied acts of grace and acceptance are the source of the sacred in the secular. Faith is always "new" in actions of love and mercy. New, because it is always breaking out from within secular space to reorient and ignite an experience of the sacred from within the human spirit. The very secularity of the megachurch is the mystery of Christian consciousness once again making new wine in an old wineskin. This is the potentially revelatory nature of Christian piety that always surprises, because it always comes from within the secular nature of societies—beginning with the radical nature of its founding figure, Jesus of Nazareth. Jesus first disrupted religious forms to call his followers to a life of embodied grace, truth, and love. In that sense, this "new life" is always a surprise both to scholars and those who experience it in the pews, or in the case of megachurches, in the plastic chairs or plush seats of megachurch auditoriums.

[11] Peter L. Berger, "Further Thoughts on Religion and Modernity" *Society* 49 (2012): 313–316.
[12] Berger, "Further Thoughts on Religion and Modernity," 336.

| Desire for Wow, or Hacking
the Happy

I T IS EASY to be cynical about megachurches, and, as authors, we came
into this book with that temptation, particularly when it came to the
overwhelming sense of joy that we read and witnessed.[1] But the truth is that
as we have continued to do the research and dig into the data, we've found
that megachurches find a way to "hack the happy" within their members.
And so our task is to express, describe, and explain this joy in analytic language, and to analyze how megachurches pull off this powerful combination
of deep joy and ecstasy. The data shows that megachurch members are overwhelmingly "in love" with megachurch worship. There is an overpowering
"wow" factor in their self-reports about worship; 92% of senior pastors say
that their worship is a place where "God is experienced and where they have
a good time." We came to think of megachurch services as *fields of wonder* that
energize and synchronize human bodies and feelings with remarkable acuity.
And, as researchers, we had to take our time to orient ourselves to the reality
of the power of these services. There were times that the saccharine nature of
the music and lyrics was very hard for us to take. As one megachurch member
described, the song "How He Loves" is one of her favorites, with verses like,

> He is jealous for me, Loves like a hurricane, I am a tree,
> Bending beneath the weight of his wind and mercy.

[1] Part of this chapter is reprinted and adapted with permission from James K. Wellman, Jr., Katie E.
Corcoran, and Kate Stockly-Meyerdirk, "'God Is Like a Drug . . .': Explaining Interaction Rituals in
American Megachurches," *Sociological Forum* 29 (2014): 650–672. Copyright [2014] by Wiley.

When all of a sudden, I am unaware of these afflictions
    eclipsed by glory,
And I realize just how beautiful You are,
And how great Your affections are for me.

This song, produced and sung by the David Crowder Band and one of the most popular in its genre, precisely communicates both the ferocity of God's love and how penetrating this love is for each person in these megachurches. While it may be too much for outsiders, for insiders the power and impact of this music is overwhelming. For one megachurch member, the songs at first seemed over the top—coming from a more traditional, liturgical background, he found the ultra-emotive singing "crazy":

> We had a neighbor that invited us to this church. And my wife fell in love with it right away. I was born and raised Catholic and so my first meeting, or my first service here, I sat way in the back. And the music was very good based upon, you know, my experience with it now. But I was just like this is crazy. You know, people have their arms up in the air. I was like, well, thanks for inviting me but see you later.

But as time went on, he later explained, just as his wife "fell in love with the church," he too became fully engaged. For outsiders, looking in on these activities, especially secularists, it has the feel of a soft-rock concert, something that is purely manufactured. From research on these churches, all of it is produced to derive the kind of reactions that we heard from our respondents.[2] Insider studies of the music of these churches shows how intricate and intentional the music is in creating "the high" that is intended, and how the coordination of songs pushes human bodies toward the "wow" that most in the community say they experience.

The senior author had his own moments that were stunning. At one point, while I was doing research at a highly ethnically, racially, and socioeconomically integrated megachurch, in the midst of music that "rocked" the service, everyone was standing and dancing. The reality of white and black and brown young people, mixed together, swaying and lifting their arms to the music in worship, reminded me of what Martin Luther King, Jr. called the foretaste of the kingdom of God,[3] where all are one in harmony.

[2] Kevin L. McElmurry, "Alone/Together: The Production of Religious Culture in a Church for the Unchurched" (Unpublished Dissertation: University of Missouri, 2009).

[3] Be Scofield, "King's God: The Unknown Faith of Dr. Martin Luther King, Jr.," *Medium*, October 13, 2017, accessed February 4, 2018 (https://medium.com/@bescofield/kings-god-the-unknown-faith-of-dr-martin-luther-king-jr-2009-869537387ebb).

Differences exist, but they blend, synchronize, and harmonize in a wider vision of rich and poor, black and white, insiders and outsiders, all in one great company of solidarity—a truly holy communion. This picture came to my mind as I witnessed (and participated in) what looked like the commonwealth of humanity reconciled and in wonder of one another. For all my critical faculties, I thought this was truly remarkable considering that, with Americans' chronic habit of separating and segmenting, King's words still ring true: "Sunday morning is the most segregated hour of the week."[4] In at least two of our megachurches, this was not true—we encountered a true mix of Americans of all colors, ethnicities, and classes.

Rhythmic Entrainment and Emotional Energy

The large auditoriums of the megachurches usually have cameras that survey the audience and project their images on large screens, which makes it seem, at least, that not only is something happening in these venues, but that people *want* to be here, they *enjoy* being here, and they anticipate that *something* is going to happen here. Collins describes how "there is a palpable difference between being in an establishment where there are lots of people and one that is nearly empty."[5] Crowds facilitate "more tacit interaction," "give a sense of social atmosphere," and make participants feel like they are "where the action is."[6] With 2,000 or more people present, megachurch worship services have the added energetic benefits of a large crowd, which creates its own sense of anticipation. Now this puts enormous pressure on megachurch leadership to create the "crowd"—this is done by using lights, curtains, and various forms of stage setting that make all the difference, but empty seats are, in a visceral sense, veritable kryptonite to the atmosphere and "charge" of the megachurch "juice," if you will. Thus, there is enormous pressure to bring more people in and keep them there, to make the experience both comfortable and "amazing," and to "fill" the auditoriums with a sense of "anticipation" and "wonder." One can only imagine how much pressure this puts on those who organize these venues. But numbers and crowds count in terms of the feeling of *presence, and the sense of an assembly*—this is the place where everyone

[4] See, both for verification of segregation and that it may be declining, Michael Lipka, "Many U.S. Congregations Are Still Racially Segregated, but Things Are Changing," Pew Research Center, December 8, 2014, accessed February 4, 2018 (http://www.pewresearch.org/fact-tank/2014/12/08/many-u-s-congregations-are-still-racially-segregated-but-things-are-changing-2/).
[5] Collins, *Interaction Ritual Chains*, 82.
[6] Collins, *Interaction Ritual Chains*, 82.

is and everyone wants to be. So, organizationally, as researchers we were often impressed by the ability of these churches to manage expectations, to create the atmosphere that *marked human bodies* with expectation and hope that this is a place where something was and is happening. Figure 9.1 summarizes the elements of this vital second step in the Megachurch Ritual Cycle.

Successful ritual interaction, as Collins makes clear, always involves a mutual focus of attention and a shared mood that interacts dynamically to create cumulative effects. These steps for a successful ritual are initiated naturally as the church service begins. Usually, in megachurches, there are three to five songs at the beginning of the service to get congregants in a worshipful mood and to initiate mutual *entrainment*. A band or choir leads these songs from the stage, which directs and focuses the attendees' devotion. The stimulation of emotion comes by way of the lyrics of songs that are emotionally charged, often setting up a need (sinfulness) and presenting a solution (Jesus's blood). The music is loud and emotive, and it is customary (and sometimes

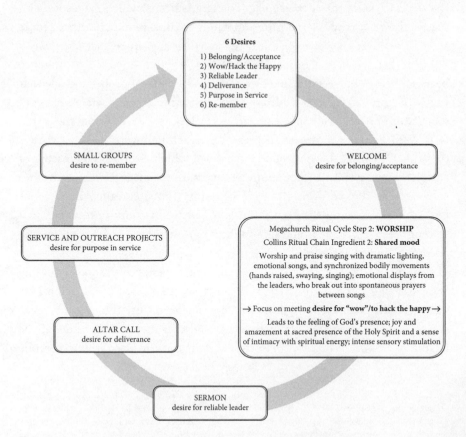

FIGURE 9.1. Megachurch Ritual Cycle Step 2: Worship

prompted by the worship leaders) for people to raise their hands, close their eyes, and even rock back and forth to the music, representing a bodily commitment to emotional participation and the kind of entrainment that we saw repeatedly.

Rather than a contemplative or inward-seeking exercise, the musical worship time is often an outward expression of praise and the sharing of joy—a time for generating *collective effervescence*. In fact, "contagious" was commonly used to describe worship. This portion of the megachurch service is bursting with what we have coined a *connectic* experience: a multisensory mélange of sensory input. One man described how he and his wife "were kind of blown away by the theatrical set. [. . .] It touches every modality that we have. And so it was kind of [like] 'Whoa.'" The singing and music are vital components of attendees' emotional experiences: "It's the singing: you enjoy it. [. . .] an hour and a half goes by and it's like we're done, can't we hear some more?" Some respondents were so touched by the musical worship that they cried: "The worship was so powerful that I was in hysterical tears the entire time. I couldn't even sing."

The *collective effervescence* evoked during the worship service is intensified by the fact that there are thousands of people contributing to it, a result of having few barriers to ritual participation, as described in Chapter 8. Cameras scan the audience and project images of people worshiping, raising their hands with closed eyes, crying, singing, or smiling. Seeing individuals around oneself (or a close-up shot of someone on the projection screen) facilitates the recognition of a shared experience and mood, which contributes to the growing sense that *something is happening*. Respondents noted how powerful it was for the entire congregation to be engaged fully in the worship: "The singers can stop singing. [. . .] You can stop the music and that place will *still* be vibrating because the whole congregation is singing." One participant said, "There is just nothing more powerful than when 10,000 or 11,000 people [are] singing at one time." One couple confessed that the musical worship was even more influential than the pastor in their initial attraction to the church. The husband started, "His message didn't bring [us] in. [. . .] When everybody's up there singing, you hear everyone singing—"

"You want to sing!" his wife finished his sentence eagerly.

Another respondent noted how during this time, people are "standing up and excited"—they are "into it" so it feels very "alive." It was common for respondents to describe the emotional energy produced by the worship as "huge" or "unreal" or to use expressions like "wow" or "whoa."

The production of high levels of *emotional energy* is clearly demonstrated in the interviews, which are permeated with words conveying emotions and senses. Individuals described their megachurch experience with emotive and sensory terms, such as (word frequencies): loving (385), feeling (680), amazing (81), awesome (43), exciting (51), wow (56), crying (29), touching (38), and feeding (56). The worship and sermon combined to create a powerful emotional experience for attendees, who described this experience in vivid and ecstatic ways—as a high, a drug, a feeling, energy, life, the Holy Spirit, and so on. One respondent expressed how the music energizes him: "I love coming here to a concert every Sunday. It's the bomb. [. . .] It just energizes you that you never know who is going to be there." Similarly, another said, "And we loved it [the worship service] because of the energy and it just recharges us." One man raved about the effective preaching of his pastor and how it "opens you up" to God, such that "God's love [communicated through the sermons] becomes [. . .] such a drug that you can't wait to come get your next hit." One interviewee compared the preaching from the pastors to youth camps. He explained, "You'd go to these youth camps and you would come back just so jacked up and then [. . .] you'd get back to the church [i.e., his previous church] and it's already pulling you back down, but this was the first church [i.e., the megachurch] that we ever walked into where I felt like I did coming out of those camps. And that was every Sunday."

A female interviewee in another focus group responded by describing the feeling of being "jacked up" as a "spiritual high." Many respondents identified *needing* the experience and used sensory terms such as "hunger," "thirst," "being fed," and "feeling" to describe it. Indeed, the lively and powerful singing and music are important for attracting individuals and keeping them in the church. Many survey respondents identified the worship style and music of the megachurch as highly influential for why they joined and remain at the megachurch. Out of a scale from 1 (*not at all*) to 5 (*a lot*), roughly 61% of respondents gave the worship style a 4 or 5 ranking as influencing their decision to join, and roughly 80% gave a ranking of 4 or 5 for it influencing their decision to stay. Additionally, 45% and 62% of respondents gave a response of 4 or higher for how influential the music and arts were for why they joined and continue to stay respectively. One attendee described how the singing and music keep individuals coming to the church, including herself: "I think this [the worship and music] is why it hits people right away. So they don't want to miss the singing and worship and see all these people enjoying this." Many respondents concurred.

Emotion, Persuasion, and Contagion

As Durkheim explained, humans, as they enter a sacred space, experience their "vital energies . . . hyper-excited, the passions more intense, the sensations more powerful; there are indeed some that are produced only at this moment. Man does not recognize himself; he feels somehow transformed and in consequence transforms his surroundings."[7] In this sense, there is nothing new in the way humans are persuaded and experience transformation: "Aristotle refers to the emotional mode as 'putting the audience into a certain frame of mind'. . . . Psychologist Kari Edwards observed from her experiments that 'affect means of persuasion' were more effective than 'cognitive means of persuasion.' The most successful forms of persuasion influence the audience's emotions."[8] And there is little doubt that the "wow" factor of these services is meant to do one thing: to persuade and penetrate human bodies with the kind of joy that allows them to "soften" and be prepared for persuasion. Some suggest that this emotional orientation is new or a factor of recent American history, but we would argue that this is how it has always worked. So, when it is said that this is a discovery of the modern age, we think this is simply the way humans have always experienced the *numen*, the sense that they are in the presence of something "bigger than themselves." Thus, it is not a surprise to us that "the Gallup organization found that nearly six out of ten Americans believe that God communicates to them through their internal feelings."[9]

And persuasion is the point of creating emotion in these moments. As Pritchard argues, for megachurch members, emotion is "a means to understand truth"; it is not merely about conveying "information about God" but about facilitating people's experiences with God.[10] Emotions can be used for persuasion in three ways. The first is to remove hostility—facilitating laughter is particularly good for accomplishing this.[11] The second is to create a mood that makes the person more susceptible to the speaker.[12] And "the third function of emotion is to energize the audience's support of the speaker's proposal by linking it with the emotional desires of the audience."[13]

---

[7] Durkheim, *Elementary Forms of Religious Life*, 424.

[8] G. A. Pritchard, *Willow Creek Seeker Services: Evaluating a New Way of Doing Church* (Grand Rapids, MI: Baker Books, 1996). See also Kari Edwards, "The Interplay of Affect and Cognition in Attitude Formation and Change," *Journal of Personality and Social Psychology* 59, no. 2 (1990): 202–216.

[9] Pritchard, *Willow Creek Seeker Services*, 109.

[10] Pritchard, *Willow Creek Seeker Services*, 111.

[11] Pritchard, *Willow Creek Seeker Services*, 112.

[12] Pritchard, *Willow Creek Seeker Services*, 112.

[13] Pritchard, *Willow Creek Seeker Services*, 112, partially citing Robert Oliver, *The Psychology of Persuasive Speech* (New York: Longmans, Green and Co., 1942), 215.

Megachurches understand the importance of emotion not only for persuasion, but for creating an energizing feeling of joy and anticipation: "Of all the senses, music plays to the emotions with the least interference. It is not tied to emotional life; it is emotional life. . . . The sound of the megachurch is, however, not the music of the pipe organ, the hymnal, and the robed choir. It is the sound of the FM radio, contemporary, changeable, tuneful, and, best of all, simple, sing-alongable. And there is a lot of it. Almost half of a typical service is music."[14] And this is all combined with spectacular screens that create a karaoke Christianity for the audience to sing along to flawlessly.

Kevin McElmurry, a sociologist who worked with the worship team in a megachurch while he was doing his dissertation on this church, entitled his thesis, "Alone/Together."[15] McElmurry, a musician himself, described his own experience working with the worship team, revealing in intimate detail the lengths they went to in order to produce an experience that would attract, transform, and influence the typical unbeliever, particularly men, or what they called the "lone Texas cowboy." McElmurry's church, in particular, had a "heart" for men. Of course, not all megachurches are focused on a specific gender, but many are, partly because men make up only 40% of the typical megachurch membership.[16] And catching the attention of men is critical. Men, at least in evangelical theology, are most often the decision makers for their family in terms of the children and how time is spent; thus, it is paramount to reach them. McElmurry explains, from his own perspective, that he admired the energy that these churches invested and the lengths they went to trying to attract and keep men: "the incredible investment in music represented by River Chapel's production equipment, cultivation of talented musicians, and attention to the tiniest of sonic detail is to me quite captivating. This investment is also expressed non-materially in their fundamental commitment to the idea that producing excellent music is a means for reaching the unchurched seeker and connecting him with god."[17]

Indeed, McElmurry readily admitted that he loved working with such sophisticated musical equipment. Megachurches, he said, were some of the most "well equipped venues for the production of live music anywhere."[18]

---

[14] James B. Twitchell, *Branded Nation: The Marketing of Megachurch, College Inc., and Museumworld* (New York: Simon & Schuster, 2004), 85.

[15] McElmurry, "Alone/Together."

[16] According to Thumma and Bird's 2008 survey of North American megachurches, 100% of the senior pastors in their study were male. See Scott Thumma and Warren Bird, "Survey of North America's Largest Churches 2008," Hartford Institute for Religion Research, 2008, accessed February 5, 2018 (http://www.hartfordinstitute.org/megachurch/megastoday2008detaileddata.pdf).

[17] McElmurry, "Alone/Together," 47.

[18] McElmurry, "Alone/Together," 132.

And while McElmurry did not share the specific type of Christian evangelical theology that was expressed in the staff meetings or from the pulpit, nonetheless, he said that "during the time I spent there, I often felt like one [of them]"[19] In other words, even as a sociologist, deeply trained in the arts of ethnography and the sophistication of music making, he *felt* like he belonged, or at least he could imagine participating in the belief system held up by the church he was serving and studying. Thus, even for skeptics, and people trained in the "business" of music, the power of the worship generated at least a simulacrum of piety that "felt" real and emotionally enticing. And this was the whole point of the preparation in these worship services, to "attract," catch," and "convince" the unchurched and "lonely" men in the auditorium that they too could find a "safe place" to be welcomed into the joy of "discipleship" in Jesus Christ. The length and detail covered in this process is relentless and unending in its focus on every facet of the worship process: "Almost every moment of the weekend worship ritual at River Chapel is planned, scripted, and rehearsed weeks in advance with the explicit intention of providing a 'safe space' where the skeptical postmodern seeker could potentially experience a personal connection to god the very first time one walks through the door."[20]

And here, "postmodern" is not so much an identification of a new epistemology in academic parlance, but more a description of what consumers want and expect in contemporary culture—that is, excellence in presentation and style of music and oratory, *and* an *authenticity* of emotion in how one communicates about any subject. Moreover, in the context of being able to listen to anyone they want on podcast or online, preachers must attain a high level to "catch" the ears of would-be converts. And megachurches are keenly aware of how careful and sophisticated their "consumers" are in terms of erudition and tastes. McElmurry describes the "*Up/Down/Up* narrative" of the sonic pattern embodied in the worship music, which functions to prepare megachurch participants to be emotionally open and prepared to hear the word: "It is a worship practiced in a mode that I have characterized as Alone/ Together. This relatively passive, potentially anonymous, potentially temporary, low stakes, low obligation mode seems to resonate with interpretations of changes in many voluntary organizations."[21] That is, it is critical for newcomers, and especially for men, to avoid the experience of being forced, or being personally identified, or somehow feeling a sense of compulsion to

---

[19] McElmurry, "Alone/Together," 61.
[20] McElmurry, "Alone/Together," 143.
[21] McElmurry, "Alone/Together," 148.

respond. Creating this megachurch mood is no small accomplishment: both open and enticing, low key and attractive, soft sell and yet life changing, this conjunction of *no big deal*, side by side with the invitation to a life-changing commitment, is the tightrope that many of these megachurches seek and achieve.

But the results from this intricate dance of worship are worth it. The aesthetic and mood are meant to relax and open the hearer to the possibility that there is something in the message that is "bigger" than oneself, something that can transform one's life, making it better even amid the hazards of this life without discounting who one is, all the while offering a life-transforming and world-changing opportunity. And to be sure, all along, the music is a critical factor that "softens the heart," interests the mind, and "opens" the listener to a new word of life. As one newcomer from McElmurry's study revealed:

> I entered with stress from the day and in a generally bad mood due to some work situations. The praise songs opened my spirit and put a smile on my face. During the talk I was really kind of zoned in and emotionless. I was soaking in the points and following everything but not really connecting until the point was made that Jesus took the bread and wine to the disciples and they were amazed that the highest being was now being sacrificed for the lowest. This caused me to reflect on how negative I can be and miss all the blessings that are in my life. Before I was hurried and self-focused (what can I do to make my life better and look better), and annoyed by "distractions" (kids, dog, traffic). Now I have forgotten about all the little stuff from the day. I relaxed my mind and heart and focused on the message and the music. *Then God sort of took over my mind.* I am thankful for my wife, kids, and opportunities at work. As long as I am responsible to the best of my ability I do not need to worry. He has a plan that will provide and get us through. It may not be my plan, but it will work. I am excited about tomorrow and going home to see my kids tonight.[22]

Here we see the full complexity that megachurches know what they are dealing with in getting those in their churches to experience the life in Christ that is liberating and exhilarating—it is seeking to surprise them with joy amidst their life's complexity, fully realizing that they need to meet their

---

[22] McElmurry, "Alone/Together," 162.

personal needs even as they are trying to negotiate the convolutions of their lives "in the world."

Katie Corcoran captures the contagion in these services, where people may be "alone," but the presence and co-presence of their megachurch members is a deeply affective and effective way of socializing those who are "outsiders" to experience the emotion of the insiders, to be close and witness another who is caught up in a "moment." This witnessing of another acts again as a *significant bodily marker* that is one of the most powerful connectors that creates and communicates the power of *numen* in the megachurch experience:

> The bodily assembly of people is necessary to create a situation in which ritual participants can be affected by the presence and emotional experiences of others. Emotions are often contagious; like viruses they can spread, such that the emotions of individuals around each other tend to converge (Hatfield et al., 1994; Barsade, 2002; Hendriks and Vingerhoets, 2006; Hennig-Thurau et al., 2006; Hareli and Rafaeli, 2008). When an individual observes the emotional states of others, this can automatically and unconsciously activate them in the observer (de Waal, 2008). This process is facilitated by similarity and social closeness, which makes it easier for the observer to identify with the object thereby enhancing the "subject's matching motor and autonomic responses" (de Waal, 2008: 286).[23]

We can then understand why megachurches do so much outreach and expend so much effort in getting the "unchurched" into their venues: they know that the joy and the "wow" of their services can only be experienced in person, as the crowd and its emotion create its own sense of urgency that something is happening here that happens nowhere else.

Gerardo Martí's recent work on "The Global Phenomenon of Hillsong Church" is again a reminder and a confirmation of the sonic power of joy and ecstasy that comes out of these megachurch experiences.[24] Not long ago, the senior author visited New York City and witnessed firsthand one of the Hillsong Church satellites there. This church plant, nested on the tenth floor of a downtown skyscraper, in terms of power, excitement, quality, and visual dalliance, left me breathless. Having understood the dynamics of every aspect of their work, my viscera were tainted by my mind, which was analyzing

[23] Katie E. Corcoran, "Thinkers and Feelers: Emotion and Giving," *Social Science Research* 52 (2015): 686–700.
[24] Gerardo Martí, "Editor's Note: The Global Phenomenon of Hillsong Church: An Initial Assessment," *Sociology of Religion* 78 (2018): 377–386.

every move of the singers and band members on the stage. My analytic lens acted as an antiseptic to the aural and visual feast. Nonetheless, the four lead singers, each with magnetic musical abilities, took turns bathing us in their tonal virtuosity—and it was not only their young voices that soothed and uplifted, but each represented a different global continental culture and ethnicity, so that anyone in the audience might have a chance of identifying with those upfront. The brilliance of the way they would figure a song, like a wave that would just keep coming, made it all not only memorable but simply resplendent—young, beautiful voices ostensibly taken up by the divinity of their message, each giving the feeling of uplift and majesty—communicating that all is possible, all is available, all can be done for you and with you. The dynamic and youthful head pastor, who was not preaching that day, was there to call for the offering. He proceeded to give a mini-sermon on how the church can and should buy this building and be a permanent fixture in the city. His offhand figure was something in the $50 million range. Made breathless by the music, my breath came out during the offering sermon; I admired his chutzpah, but thought, "Well, I wish we could have been done after the musical number, I would have walked away on air."

As Martí sums it up, Hillsong is one of the leaders in the worship "wow" factor in megachurches, appealing not only to middle-class Americans, but indeed to urbanites, to the hip, to Hollywood, to the very top levels of sophisticated modern culture:

> Moreover, the social quality of worship allows cosmopolitan urbanites to become part of a larger group. However anonymous a person may be, they are part of this group, this family, and this house. Even the shape of the music—the power ballad, the war cry—provides individuals a basis for individualized action in the world apart from the group, resourcing the enactment of a strategic religious identity (see Martí 2017; Martí and Ganiel 2014). Hillsong music also provides a sonic religious identity, one that is portable and reproducible, whose aesthetics are mimicked with readily available instruments using recordings and YouTube videos as a guide, such that immersion in the tribe is accessible in more and more places, and, via digital reproduction, can be relived again and again.[25]

---

[25] Martí, "Editor's Note," 382; Gerardo Martí, "New Concepts for New Dynamics: Generating Theory for the Study of Religious Innovation and Social Change," *Journal for the Scientific Study of Religion* 56, no. 2 (2017): 157–172; Gerardo Martí and Gladys Ganiel, *The Deconstructed Church: Understanding Emerging Christianity* (New York: Oxford University Press, 2014).

And despite some of "our" skepticism about these "ballads," and "war cries," megachurches use music to rev up emotion, to prepare their hearers to *experience* what they call the *word of God*, a word that comes by way of the "wow" factor, no less.

Preparing for the Word

As McElmurry has shown, music and the fields of wonder that they create can open humans up to receive.[26] And worship—from the tone and tenor of the music to the fluctuation of lighting, to the way slides and images rotate, all invite participants "to be fed," in the language of evangelicalism. That is, one is led to a "womb-like" or "alone-together" position, such that the human body is unlocked and less defensive, and the mind is free to receive what is coming in the sermon. As one megachurch member from our study described:

> I was just, the Holy Spirit was just there and I couldn't, I didn't know what was wrong with me that I couldn't control myself and I was feeling very embarrassed but just had never felt that way in years. And then, I mean at [name of other church] they didn't have worship, really. So, I was really needy. So, they teach Bible, but they don't, you know. And the Lord just, you know, softened my heart with it.

Creating the "need to feed" response, in fact, is the point of worship. People, without worship, have their defenses up and their critical faculties in place, and are not ready "to receive the word," "to feed on Jesus," "to let the spirit make me new." This sense of the "wow" is readying each worshipper to receive the word, the good news, "to feed on Christ." And this is the "spirituality of hunger" that many megachurch members speak to:

> And spiritually, that draws me, I'm more and more hungry. You know, you want more, and He gives you more. If you're obedient and when you're hanging out with people that are going through the same thing, it's much more powerful.
>
> This is where I go. This is where I worship. This is where I get fed spiritually. This is where my needs are met physically. I feel good. I want to be here. I want more.

---

[26] McElmurry, "Alone/Together."

On Wanting More

We end by suggesting, à la Durkheim, that this lush combination of being fed individually, and suffused in the love and communion of the crowd, cannot last. As Durkheim suggests,

> The result is that we are never completely in accord with ourselves for we cannot follow one of our two natures without causing the other to suffer. Our joys can never be pure; there is always some pain mixed with them; for we cannot simultaneously satisfy the two beings that are within us. It is this disagreement, this perpetual division against ourselves, that produces both our grandeur and our misery: our misery because we are thus condemned to live in suffering; and our grandeur because it is this division that distinguishes us from all other beings.[27]

Humans are, as Durkheim makes clear, filled with the desire to both meet their individual needs and to connect with that which is larger than themselves. And megachurch worship rocks to that same pendulum, creating a worship that is *alone/together*—that appeals to the deepest needs of the self for ecstasy and joy, as well as preparing the hearer to be open to that which is beyond the momentary ecstatic high. The word that is coming is no nursery lullaby, however. It is a word that will say, in the end, that the individual alone is not enough, that there is a call to something higher. This call will ask the hearer to leave behind the immediacy of the "wow" factor for something larger, something bigger, something more urgent—a commitment to something larger than the self. And this strange paradox is at the center of the Christian tradition: "Then Jesus told his disciples, 'If anyone would come after me, let him deny himself and take up his cross and follow me. For whoever would save his life will lose it, but whoever loses his life for my sake will find it. For what will it profit a man if he gains the whole world and forfeits his soul? Or what shall a man give in return for his soul?'" (Matthew 16:24–26). Throughout Jesus's ministry, early followers would turn away, because the path ahead became too difficult, costing too much. And Jesus, instead of wooing them on, simply walks away; he begs no one to follow him because he knows how difficult the path will be.

And so this paradox is in the tradition, but it is also in human nature: there is no path that does not demand sacrifice, there is no final

---

[27] Émile Durkheim, "The Dualism of Human Nature and Its Social Conditions," in *Essays on Sociology and Philosophy*, edited by Kurt H. Wolff, 325–339 (Columbus: Ohio State University Press, 1964 [1914]), 329.

resting position, whether in the self or in the community that marks the end of the journey. Durkheim points to this paradox at the heart of human nature. Even the highest and most spiritual paths have their paradoxical endings—and so the "wow," which ushers one to the leader, promises a new challenge, as we will see.

| Desire for a Reliable Leader

Yes, and the words come out of him {senior pastor}; he is so open to the Holy
Spirit speaking through him that it always touches, I mean everybody gets
something right (motioning to her heart) here from the message. And so that, God
is love, the Holy Spirit is love. And so, when you feel that connection, you just
feel loved. You just know that God is just so thick here.

—Megachurch attendee

MEGACHURCH PASTORS HAVE rarely been studied in terms of charismatic leadership.[1] We do so in this book, but framed within the
larger story of megachurch culture and the cycle of desire that we have developed in our theory of megachurch success. And in megachurches, for those
who attend, *their desire and the force of feeling, the zenith of emotional energy*, is
squarely centered on the head pastor. The muscle memory of the megachurch
is exercised around the extraordinary nature of the pastor. They are the *en-*
ergy star. Nearly 90% of the growth in these larger churches comes during

[1] For exceptions see Katie E. Corcoran and James K. Wellman, Jr., "'People Forget He's Human': Charismatic Leadership in Institutionalized Religion," *Sociology of Religion* 77 (2016): 309–333; and James K. Wellman, Jr., *Rob Bell and the New American Christianity* (Nashville, TN: Abingdon Press, 2012). Part of this chapter is reprinted and adapted with permission from Katie E. Corcoran and James K. Wellman, Jr., "'People Forget He's Human': Charismatic Leadership in Institutionalized Religion," *Sociology of Religion* 77 (2016): 309–333, Copyright [2016], Oxford University Press. Also, from *Rob Bell and the New American Christianity*, by James K. Wellman, Jr., © 2012 Abingdon Press. Used by permission, all rights reserved.

the tenure of the pastors that we studied. He—it *is* always a *he*, at least in our sample—is generally around forty-eight years old, with race reflecting the dominant character of the congregation. Most pastors have a graduate education and are six feet in height. More than any other single variable, the megachurch pastor facilitates, directs, and dominates Collins's "mutual focus of attention." The pastor is both the central figure around which most activities, and in some sense the lives of individuals, revolve, and the mouthpiece for the explicit articulation of the values, beliefs, morals, and symbols that will define the group.

This was tangibly the case in my experience with Rob Bell, the former megachurch pastor at Mars Hill Church in Grand Rapids, Michigan.[2] In interviewing him and becoming a "friend" of sorts, I sensed the awe of his "audience." That is, wherever I was with Bell, whether in his home or out in public or at a performance, Bell was not only the focus of attention but was the center of attention, and if the conversation moved away from him, he would move away from it.

In my work on Bell,[3] I used Lady Gaga's "Teeth" lyrics from *The Fame Monster* (2009) to illustrate this fixation on charismatic figures: "Got no salvation / Got no religion . . . Tell me something that'll save me / I need a man who makes me alright . . . My religion is you." Lady Gaga, the queen of pop, made a splash with the *Fame Monster* EP, harking back to 1970s glam rock, skewering fashion show runways. She exposed the charisma of mega-celebrities strutting their stuff, and, without stretching too much, pierced the "charismatic bond" that is so potent with the megachurch pastors in our study, and certainly with Rob Bell.

For charismatic figures, either you are with them or you're not. I watched this swing back and forth, as people fell in and out of love with Bell. And so it is with all charismatic megachurch pastors; for those who are "in love," he becomes the focus of attention, but when affection wanes, tension between expectation and reality elicits instability and doubt. Lady Gaga goes to the heart of what many distrust about pastoral leaders who perfectly mirror the feelings and thoughts of their hearers and then channel what their hearers want to find in themselves: "Show me your teeth," she sings, "My religion is you." Hers is an attack on figures that play proxy to the hopes and dreams of generations searching for the answer to their problems—a way to pierce through the persona of those who pledge to lead people to the Promised Land. But that is the point; charismatic figures are proxy figures who are

---

[2] Wellman, *Rob Bell and the New American Christianity.*
[3] Wellman, *Rob Bell and the New American Christianity.*

experts at "impression management, segregation versus contact."[4] That is, these figures become objects of reverence, as well as points of envy, but they are careful not to get too close because that might break the spell—thus, the need to negotiate distance. We heard in many of the responses of our megachurch members that the pastor seemed so "shy in public" or that the pastor rarely "mingles" with members, but then this lack of contact is quickly rationalized: "Well, of course, there is just too many of us for him to be in contact." So, the gift is to manage the impressions of those who "buzz" around these pastors, to keep folks close but not too close, aware of the pastor's humanness but not too aware of their "real" lives.

Bell evokes these same feelings on all sides and effortlessly exemplifies the charismatic bond that is central to this story.[5] In *Rain,* his inaugural twelve-minute film of the twenty-four-film set *Nooma* collection, which marked the real beginning of his charismatic rise, Bell's classic collection of traits is on display. The setting is a Bell family vacation in the deep woods. Bell starts on an early walk with his one-year-old son, Trace. The scene is one of bucolic bliss with an edgy, moody guitar playing in the background—set against a cloudless sky. Bell opens with a wondering statement: "Do you ever have those moments? If you could just freeze them . . . just so beautiful." And instantly the observer tumbles into this timeless moment of a dad and his son on an early-morning walk. As they round the lake there is a twist in the story: clouds move in, and Bell narrates, "It starts to rain. It always rains, doesn't it?"

On cue, Bell tells the biblical story of Jesus and his kingdom. Bell recounts the parable of the wise and foolish builders—one who builds his life on sand and another on rock (Matthew 7:24–27). When the rains and the storms come, the first is destroyed and the second stands. The person who has built his life on sand has "rejected Jesus's teachings," says Bell, but the one who built her life on the rock, and has "come to follow Jesus," will withstand any storms that come—and they will always come.

In the film, the rain comes slowly at first, and then begins to pour. Bell takes Trace off his back and puts him close to his chest. And as the rain envelops them, Trace is wailing at the top of his lungs. Bell bundles his son to his chest, and coos with deep passion, "I love you buddy, we're going to make it, Dad knows the way home. We're going to make it." Immediately, Bell's

---

[4] Lorne L. Dawson, "Crises of Charismatic Legitimacy and Violent Behavior in New Religious Movements," in *Cults, Religion & Violence*, edited by D. G. Bromley and J. G. Melton, 80–101 (Cambridge: University of Cambridge Press, 2002).

[5] Wellman, *Rob Bell and the New American Christianity.*

narration smoothly moves to a discussion of the Psalms, where God's people cry out repeatedly to God, who promises that he will listen. Bell explains, "There is this false and twisted idea in the church that God is looking for people who have no problems . . . The essence of salvation is admitting, 'I don't have it all together.' Jesus says, 'I'm not looking for the healthy but the sick.'" The listener's vulnerability is touched and tapped as the way in, and the way through.

Like the father in the story of the prodigal son, Bell models here the relationship between God and humanity: God hears the cry of the vulnerable one, and the Father will listen. The Father comforts the lost, and the Father knows the way home. Bell ends the film with this benediction, "Now may you when you're soaking wet, when you're confused, may you cry out, and may the creator of the universe hold you tight and may you hear him say, 'I love you buddy, Dad knows the way home, we're going to make it.'"

The film evokes wildly contrasting emotions of bliss, terror, intimacy, fear, being lost, and being found. It promises comfort even amid terrible distress. All of this is combined with a message that in Christ, the lost and confused believer who builds her life on the rock is still held in God's hands, close to God's heart. It's a remarkable debut of Bell's ability to engage the viewer, the listener, and the follower on so many different levels. Artistically, it is noteworthy because the complexity of emotion is communicated in a short film. The visuals and the musical score, along with Bell's voice, tone, and intonation, effortlessly arouse the feelings of the moment in which the viewer sees a transparent portrayal of what a good father will do during the reality of life's catastrophes. Fatefully, the filming for *Rain* was done on 9/11. One of the producers recalled the experience of shooting on such a tumultuous day: "Filming started the morning of September 11, 2001. The towers were down, and we didn't know if there was going to be a government by nightfall because the Pentagon was on fire. We didn't know if we should keep going or not."[6] The charismatic bond builds on a social crisis and a talented leader who can communicate the thoughts and feelings of followers and can offer, in word and in action, a way out.

The charismatic leader is the one who shows the way even amid the most tragic and dire circumstances. And here we touch again on this deep desire in human beings for a reliable leader, one who knows the way even in the chaos of life. Indeed, the desire for a reliable and able leader dominates all the responses in our study. Megachurch members *want and need* to admire their

---

[6] Interview with Bell associate by author, November 19, 2011.

leaders, which in turn gives them joy and certitude that all is well, and that they and the church are moving in the right direction.

Charles Lindholm describes the relationship as a "compulsive, inexplicable emotional tie linking a group of followers together in adulation of the leader, or tying the lover to the beloved, which is commonly symbolized in the imagery of charisma."[7] And it's true that the power of this relationship can endure enormous strains that would typically wreck nearly any relationship. We will see examples of the loyalty of megachurch members when we examine megachurch scandals in Part III. The senior author studied, interviewed, and supervised graduate students who did research on Mars Hill Church in Seattle. The pastor, Mark Driscoll, in many ways captured a whole generation of young Seattleites and many across the country, as he managed to be the focus of attention for young "rebel" Christians from 1997 until 2014, the year of his Seattle ministry's demise. What amazed many of us who witnessed this slow train wreck was his ability to maintain the loyalty of followers, as they rationalized and justified his immoral and abusive behavior.

Perhaps more than anything, the ability of "followers" to withstand and put up with the "bad behavior" of charismatic figures is a testament to the power charisma has over its followers. It underlines the need and desire for figures who "have the answer," who can anticipate the longings and desires of the hearts of their followers, and creatively and linguistically respond to followers in a way that lets them know they are known and understood, and that there is an answer.

And no less a figure than Jesus himself, as a charismatic figure, knew how to create a scene, goad a question, and answer it, all in a matter of one short interaction. In Jesus's interface with the woman at the well, he meets at the top of the day, something no rabbi would do, and talks to someone outside his tribe, something rabbis had traditionally refused. She is a woman of some disrepute, and yet he engages her; she is a woman with self-assurance equal to Jesus, and yet Jesus digs beneath her self-possession and reveals her deeper desires. It is a masterwork in charismatic leadership: exposing, naming her deep longing, and answering it all in a short, revolutionary détente with a woman, a Samaritan—someone who is a doubly excluded outsider in the traditional boundaries of Jewish culture.

Now Jesus learned that the Pharisees had heard that he was gaining and baptizing more disciples than John—although in fact it was not

[7] Charles Lindholm, *Charisma* (Cambridge: Basil Blackwell, 1990).

Jesus who baptized, but his disciples. So he left Judea and went back once more to Galilee.

Now he had to go through Samaria. So he came to a town in Samaria called Sychar, near the plot of ground Jacob had given to his son Joseph. Jacob's well was there, and Jesus, tired as he was from the journey, sat down by the well. It was about noon.

When a Samaritan woman came to draw water, Jesus said to her, "Will you give me a drink?" (His disciples had gone into the town to buy food.)

The Samaritan woman said to him, "You are a Jew and I am a Samaritan woman. How can you ask me for a drink?" (For Jews do not associate with Samaritans.)

Jesus answered her, "If you knew the gift of God and who it is that asks you for a drink, you would have asked him and he would have given you living water."

"Sir," the woman said, "you have nothing to draw with and the well is deep. Where can you get this living water? Are you greater than our father Jacob, who gave us the well and drank from it himself, as did also his sons and his livestock?"

Jesus answered, "Everyone who drinks this water will be thirsty again, but whoever drinks the water I give them will never thirst. Indeed, the water I give them will become in them a spring of water welling up to eternal life."

The woman said to him, "Sir, give me this water so that I won't get thirsty and have to keep coming here to draw water."

He told her, "Go, call your husband and come back."

"I have no husband," she replied.

Jesus said to her, "You are right when you say you have no husband. The fact is, you have had five husbands, and the man you now have is not your husband. What you have just said is quite true."

"Sir," the woman said, "I can see that you are a prophet. Our ancestors worshiped on this mountain, but you Jews claim that the place where we must worship is in Jerusalem."

"Woman," Jesus replied, "believe me, a time is coming when you will worship the Father neither on this mountain nor in Jerusalem. You Samaritans worship what you do

not know; we worship what we do know, for salvation is
from the Jews. Yet a time is coming and has now come
when the true worshipers will worship the Father in the
Spirit and in truth, for they are the kind of worshipers
the Father seeks. God is spirit, and his worshipers must
worship in the Spirit and in truth."
The woman said, "I know that Messiah" (called Christ) "is
coming. When he comes, he will explain everything to us."
Then Jesus declared, "I, the one speaking to you—I am he."
(John 4:1–26, NIV)

In a matter of one short interaction, Jesus revolutionizes what it means to be
a Jew, a man, a dominant group; this act has extraordinary consequences and
revolutionary results for his life and ministry. Jesus, as the focus of attention,
draws the woman in, and engages her at the deepest level of her need, evoking
a desire and hope that surely was yawning in her and perhaps even deeper in
the human spirit—a desire to be known, to be called forth. This "foreign"
woman is recognized, made known, put on the level of the "chosen" people;
she is worthy of care and concern, And, of course, the larger story is that all
people, no matter their origin or background, can find living water. For this
new teaching argues that "salvation" is now open to all. Jesus evokes this revolutionary charismatic bond across time and traditions; even those with no religion or another religion find in Jesus deep admiration. Jesus, like few before
and after him, sees the other, speaks to the other, and wants to free the other.

As Lorne Dawson explains, charismatic leaders tend to be "more emotionally expressive" and equipped with superior rhetorical and impression
management skills.[8] Thinking of Jesus in these terms is the ultimate under-
statement, but it reminds us that megachurch pastors are following in *these
footsteps,* trying to explicate, explore, and illumine what this figure, Jesus,
means to their megachurch members. This is no easy road to follow, but
when it happens, it is like lightning hitting the ground; the dazzling display
of charisma draws thousands to it, expecting that they too might be plugged
in. But like a megachurch pastor, Jesus quickly disappears. Managing time
with and time away from followers is critical; like a great dance, he knows
when to move close and when to push away—managing energy and exposure, and knowing when absence makes the relationship stronger.[9]

[8] Dawson, "Crises of Charismatic Legitimacy," 82.
[9] A recent study showed that distance actually increases care in intimate relationships: Stephen Coleman,
"Book Review: The Digital Difference: Media Technology and the Theory of Communication Effects,"
Journal of Communication 67 (2017): E7–E8.

As Dawson further explicates, there is a reason that these figures are so mysterious and, in many ways, mercurial: "If too many people have too much contact with the leaders, their human frailties may show through. Such exposure undermines the element of mastery and exaggeration essential to sustaining the tales of wonder, compassion, and extraordinary accomplishment commonly used to establish the aura of special authority around these leaders."[10] And this exaggeration of the goodness and ability of these megachurches percolates throughout the interviews with members in the churches. Even when a pastor can't visit physically, he is there by a simple phone call, and for most this was enough. And, of course, for a small number of members this was *not enough*, and often led to their leaving these churches. Nevertheless, for most the fact that the pastor can even reach out at all, by phone, becomes one more sign of his immense compassion. Thus, his lack of being available becomes a sign that when he can reach out, even in a generic phone call, it is even more potent—this paradox of the pastors' lack of availability combined with a small gesture creates an enormous reservoir of goodwill and even bliss within these churches. A megachurch attendee said: "He blesses me to no end and I love that in him. He said so many things. He's such a courageous speaker and not only that, if you've got some kind of problem or death or something or another and he maybe don't get to you, but he'll call you on the phone and you know what he'll say? Let me bless you right now before we start and he blesses you on the phone. When you hear his voice, you feel relieved. He's just that good. He's good. He is good and I love everything that he does."

Thus, there is a quality around these pastors, which not only exaggerates their goodness and their ability to meet the needs of the congregations, but creates a bank of trust that bubbles up as a fount of blessing and relief despite their lack of close presence. And this quality of trust is not only experienced as a feeling, but produces real effects. See Figure 10.1 for a summary of the role of the powerful effects that a charismatic pastor can have on the Megachurch Ritual Cycle.

We're reminded of Matthew 14:34–36, in which people came to Jesus for healing: "When they had crossed over, they landed at Gennesaret. And when the men of that place recognized Jesus, they sent word to all the surrounding country. People brought all their sick to him and begged him to let the sick just touch the edge of his cloak, and all who touched it were healed"

[10] Lorne L. Dawson, *Comprehending Cults: The Sociology of New Religious Movements* (Toronto, Ontario: Oxford University Press, 1998), 143.

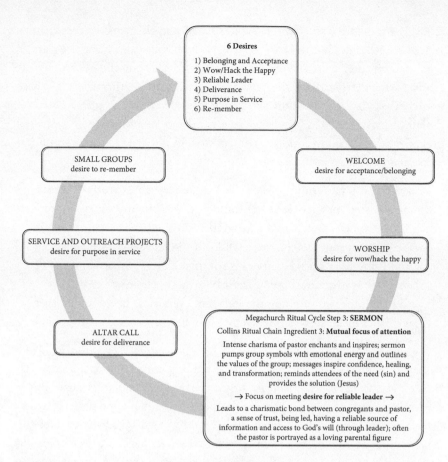

6 Desires

1) Belonging and Acceptance
2) Wow/Hack the Happy
3) Reliable Leader
4) Deliverance
5) Purpose in Service
6) Re-member

SMALL GROUPS
desire to re-member

WELCOME
desire for acceptance/belonging

SERVICE AND OUTREACH PROJECTS
desire for purpose in service

WORSHIP
desire for wow/hack the happy

ALTAR CALL
desire for deliverance

Megachurch Ritual Cycle Step 3: **SERMON**

Collins Ritual Chain Ingredient 3: **Mutual focus of attention**

Intense charisma of pastor enchants and inspires; sermon pumps group symbols with emotional energy and outlines the values of the group; messages inspire confidence, healing, and transformation; reminds attendees of the need (sin) and provides the solution (Jesus)

→ Focus on meeting **desire for reliable leader** →

Leads to a charismatic bond between congregants and pastor, a sense of trust, being led, having a reliable source of information and access to God's will (through leader); often the pastor is portrayed as a loving parental figure

FIGURE 10.1. Megachurch Ritual Cycle Step 3: Sermon

(Matthew 14:34–36). Megachurch members recall a similar sense of healing that comes from the very fact that their pastor embodies this sense of charismatic gifting, in which his very presence creates not only a sense of trust but a potential for healing—as one young man recalled:

> Number one, I feel like I can trust him. The place we were at before the pastor was very trustworthy and he always said I think we grew from maybe 700 people to 4,000. And he said he always wanted to be a pastor that you can touch him. You can feel him. You know he's real. And even though this place is a little big, you can't physically touch him but you can feel like you can touch him because you know enough about him. And his, what he talks about is very real and you can associate with it. But it's so, there's no barrier in my way from getting the word. But then when he delivers the word, he gives the illustrations, and he backs it up with the scripture.

Thus, the presence of the pastor inspires trust, and this trust creates the potential for healing, and the basis of this is the connection that these pastors have to scripture, to the Word, not only the Bible, but the Word, who is Christ, which gives them the power. It is no wonder that most of these churches practice in one form or another the idea that the scripture is the "infallible Word of God," and that this word can be and must be delivered and "fed" to the congregation, by the pastor, in a way that they can understand and be certain about it:

> And then you have [him] preach . . . I mean it was just truth. It wasn't a sugar-coated message. It wasn't some guy, you know, wanting to start a church to be a preacher so he started a church for his own terms. It was a guy you could tell he was fearful if he didn't do this, we obviously would bring him down because this was his calling. Just straight out of the Bible but in a way, you don't hear how most people say it. You knew the Holy Spirit was speaking through him every time he got up on that stage. So, I mean then all the people, just people getting involved and people getting fired up.

Collins explains that energy stars generate and propagate emotional energy first by their ability to *empathize with and elevate* the problems and dilemmas of their hearers, but second by offering them a deep *experience* of hope and possibility that these dilemmas are not the end, but the beginning of a new journey into release, relief, and redemption. Humans, at whatever level, generally seek solutions that can bring liberation. And this release recognizes that there is someone who knows what they are going through, has been where they are, and knows the way through. In this sense megachurch pastors are a source of empathy and relief and the possibility of a future hope.

Megachurch Pastors as Flawed Vessels

Sociological research on charisma tends to underscore how charisma is a social, dynamic, and interactive process by which individuals come to perceive certain qualities of a person as extraordinary and worthy of authority.[11] Because charisma rests in the social relationship, this relationship can be undermined by behaviors that deviate from the perceived extraordinary qualities of the

[11] Lorne L. Dawson, "Psychopathologies and the Attribution of Charisma: A Critical Introduction to the Psychology of Charisma and Explanation of Violence in New Religious Movements," *Nova Religio: The Journal of Alternative and Emergent Religions* 10 (2006): 3–28.

leader, which often leads to charismatic disenchantment—that is, the withdrawal of the charismatic bond.[12] More recently, Paul Joosse proposed that ordinary behaviors, not just moral deviance, can lead to charismatic disenchantment as they can damage perceptions of the leader's extraordinariness.[13]

We disagree. In fact, our take on the charismatic leaders in our research is that there is less conflict between the extraordinary and ordinary qualities of the charismatic leader, and followers can be attracted to both. A megachurch attendee described the senior pastor as: "no different than you and I. That's what we love about him." Charismatic leaders in megachurches do not have to worry about backstage encounters with followers or discussing their ordinary life, because being ordinary can be a part of their charisma. *We propose that extraordinary and ordinary qualities both can contribute to the establishment of a charismatic bond between megachurch pastors and attendees.*

In the research literature about New Religious Movements (NRMs), the power and distinctiveness of charisma is marked as a key trait of charismatic leadership. Often, within these groups, the bond between leaders and followers is tight and contained within limited numbers. On the contrary, megachurch pastors can maintain their charisma even though the group is large. What we found, in distinction from the NRM leaders whose vulnerability is downplayed, is that megachurch pastors are elevated as uniquely gifted persons to deliver the good news of Jesus Christ, but this gift does not demand that the leader be either perfect or superhuman. Indeed, it is precisely because they are "vulnerable" and "human" in their leadership styles that these pastors are extolled.

The model of charismatic leadership no doubt idealizes the megachurch leader, but it is precisely because they are fallible (and admit their weaknesses) that they become walking models of Christian leadership. A megachurch attendee said: "The first person we ran into was [the pastor] and I still make fun of him. He was a walking reincarnation of Christ. Just, he'd walk up to you and just shake your hand and put his arm around you, not knowing him and all of a sudden, Jesus was just like overflowing out of this guy's pores. You don't get that in any other church." And in some sense the uniqueness of this

[12] Robert W. Balch, "Charisma and Corruption in the Love Family: Toward a Theory of Corruption in Charismatic Cults," in *Sex, Lies, and Sanctity: Religion and Deviance in Contemporary North America*, Vol. 5, edited by M. J. Neitz and M. S. Goldman, 155–179 (Greenwich, CT: JAI Press, 1995); Janet Jacobs, *Divine Disenchantment: Deconverting from New Religions* (Bloomington: Indiana University Press, 1989); Paul Joosse, "The Presentation of the Charismatic Self in Everyday Life: Reflections on a Canadian New Religious Movement," *Sociology of Religion* 73 (2012): 174–199.

[13] Joosse, "The Presentation of the Charismatic Self in Everyday Life."

form of Christian charisma finds the seeds for this paradox of perfection and limits in the Christian tradition itself.

The Apostle Paul, who we've suggested is a model of the early Christian megachurch pastor, gives an extraordinary enunciation of his own limited nature, which he clearly wanted expunged. And, as Paul says in the Second Letter to the Corinthians:

> Therefore, in order to keep me from becoming conceited, I was given a thorn in my flesh, a messenger of Satan, to torment me. Three times I pleaded with the Lord to take it away from me. But he [Jesus] said to me, "My grace is sufficient for you, for my power is made perfect in weakness." Therefore, I will boast all the more gladly about my weaknesses, so that Christ's power may rest on me. That is why, for Christ's sake, I delight in weaknesses, in insults, in hardships, in persecutions, in difficulties. For when I am weak, then I am strong. (2 Corinthians 12:7b–10)

It's important to remember that Paul never met the historical person of Jesus in the flesh; Paul only speaks of him as a "risen" figure, who is now Lord of all. Paul, just before this passage, speaks of a man (presumably himself) who had been "caught up to paradise and heard inexpressible things, things that no one is permitted to tell. I will boast about a man like that, but I will not boast about myself, except about my weaknesses" (2 Corinthians 12:4– 5). But this theme is crucial in the megachurch mentality: weakness and the recognition of one's human frailties, rather than being marks of one's illegitimacy, become, in part, the way megachurch pastors legitimate their pastoral identities—in some ways they *must be wounded healers*, empowered to preach but only in and through their fragile natures.

We argue that Paul's messages and experiences become deeply significant for Jesus's followers. And, as we've said, Paul is the prime exemplar of a disciple of Jesus. Paul is not divine, and his weakness, rather than disqualifying him, acts as a paradoxical stamp of legitimacy—the representative of Christ is the one made perfect in weakness.[14] Now certainly Jesus himself portrays this charism, that beauty can come from death—Jesus's resurrection is the sign and symbol of the Christian faith, and in him, death is overcome. But for Paul, the model of leadership is set for those who come after him. Christ's messengers are not those who boast, but those who are strong even in their weakness. This leadership model is precisely the paradox

---

[14] This is distinct from charismatic leaders in NRMs, who typically attempt to avoid showing weakness and instead emphasize their perceived superhuman qualities. For example, see Dawson, *Comprehending Cults*.

we find in megachurches. It is what lay people expect from their leaders, that their weakness (sin) is admitted, confessed, repented, and forgiven—a process by which their strength is transmitted. As another megachurch member emphasized their pastor's genuineness:

> The word that comes to me is "authenticity." I think that the people who come here try to be authentic with each other and they've, I've messed up. I mean [our pastor] from the pulpit will say I cheated on an exam and I got caught and my fiancée found out and confronted [me]. I mean he's not hiding; he's not trying to be like I'm the perfect pastor. And if you're like me, you can go to Heaven. He's just saying you know what—I messed up this week or whatever. I think authenticity is really key.

And as we will show, megachurch pastors embody a combination that is quite unique, reflecting the Christian tradition that leaders are charismatic but human, down to earth, and deeply practical but also *heavenly minded, flawed* but willing to be vulnerable, as St. Paul says, "For when I am weak, I am strong" (2 Corinthians 12:10).

Megachurch Pastors as Energy Stars

"You don't get that in any other church." A megachurch member made an analogy between his senior pastor and the Energizer Bunny, stating that he is always on top of whatever God asks of him: "[Senior pastor] is totally led by the Holy Spirit. If God is telling him this is what we need to do, then he's all on it. He's like that bunny, that bunny that goes like that." Another described her senior pastor as constantly working and wondered how, as a person, he could do everything he does without being drained: "I'm thinking when do you [the senior pastor] sleep? [. . .] I'm drained on Sundays [. . .] and I can imagine if it's draining for me what it is for him, he's doing it [the sermon] three times." She then answered her own questions: "When a person is anointed and appointed by God, the Holy Ghost is going to take over. You know you are not going to be operating [on] your own strength and your own endurance. [. . .] You know you're not ordinary, you're extraordinary." She suggests that the senior pastor's ability to do what seems superhuman is through supernatural intervention, which gives him the strength and endurance he otherwise would not have. And of course, this amplification not only makes the pastor seem larger than life, but also creates distance from him that is natural when often there are thousands of people who attend. So of course there is no personal time for the pastor and his parishioner. Thus, he works endlessly as well as operating on energy that comes from the Spirit.

Moreover, as we have seen, large majorities of megachurch members describe their senior pastors' preaching as exceptional. One member mentioned that his senior pastor is "the best preacher I've ever heard and I've been listening to preaching for sixty-five years." Another church member similarly exclaimed the senior pastor's gifted preaching: "He's always been very relevant and he's always been very biblical, and good at articulating anything he's trying to say." They continue, "And not too many people are gifted like that," again identifying the pastor not only as exceptional but rare. Similarly, another megachurch member said, "[The senior pastor's sermons are] just straight out of the Bible but in a way you don't hear most people say it. You knew the Holy Spirit was speaking through him every time he got up on that stage." Here the megachurch member is highlighting how his senior pastor's biblical sermons are not the same as what "most people say," because he believes God is speaking through his pastor. Others described their senior pastor's "gift of wisdom" as expressed in his sermons as supernatural or as providing a "divine look into the world." The megachurch pastor's preaching ability is one of his most valued capacities, and, for some, a divinely inspired ability. This is consistent with past research that emphasizes the superior rhetorical skills of megachurch pastors, but also a charismatic gifting that is almost always called "rare" and "extraordinary."[15]

While the descriptions of the senior pastor were permeated by perceptions of his extraordinary, divinely given qualities, he was also described in more ordinary, human terms. These descriptions provide the other side of the charismatic bond. The megachurch pastors are not only charismatic in their gifting but also in the perception that they are deeply grounded and humble, because they know the source of their talent; they also know that they are flawed, and many megachurch members admire the humility of their pastors as much as their brilliance. This complex combination is part and parcel of the Christian tradition and a deeply attractive characteristic in leadership. People find themselves inspired, drawn to, and captivated by leaders who are at once extraordinarily gifted and able to poke fun at themselves.

[15] Dawson, "Crises of Charismatic Legitimacy"; Wellman, *Rob Bell and the New American Christianity*; Ann R. Wilner, *The Spellbinders: Charismatic Political Leadership* (New Haven, CT: Yale University Press, 1984).

The Megachurch Pastor as Human

More than a third of megachurch members who discussed their senior pastor described him as human in some way without being prompted (see Appendix A for information on the data and coding procedures). We were struck by the number of comments that *explicitly* attempted to convey the humanity of the senior pastor. In fact, we think this is a critical aspect of the charismatic bond, which both elicits awe at the pastor's gifting, and simultaneous relief that the pastor is human, too, just like us. One megachurch member said, "People forget he's human. He's human, he's just like you and I." Another continued, "He's no different than you and I. That's what we love about him," and still another confirmed. "Yeah. Absolutely, love that about him." Some respondents described their senior pastor's human characteristics, such as being "shy," "introverted," "sensitive," and even "stingy." Several members noted that although their senior pastor is in a position of authority, he is just like everyone else and treats others as his equal. One noted how the senior pastor never "preaches down" to them and brings his "real-life" stories into his sermons, which communicates that he is "no different from us." Another mentioned how the senior pastor incorporates his typical, human activities into his sermons: "The average person, Christian or however you want to put it, we watch movies, we listen to music, we read our Bibles [. . .]. A lot of people have a balance and [senior pastor's name] shows to have that balance because he can just incorporate it into the service. But you don't hear other pastors talking about [how] they watched a certain movie or they listen to certain music [. . .]."

Similarly, another said, with a sense of pride, that their pastor is a "normal person" and that his use of everyday human activities teaches "you that you can be a human being [. . .] enjoy life and be saved." In fact, the megachurch pastor's ability to talk to the attendees as equals and provide relatable stories and illustrations were two of the main qualities respondents praised about their pastor's sermons.

Almost half of all references to the senior pastor's human side extolled his ability to speak to them on their level, like average human beings, without talking down to them. Several members noted that whereas other pastors "use big words" that not everyone understands, their senior pastor "doesn't try to use big words or stuff." He doesn't try to "tell you how intelligent he is over you," but he keeps "it simple so everybody can understand it." For instance, a woman described how the senior pastor's sermon sounds like "you are having a regular conversation. It's not like *oh thou art*, it's more like I'm trying to make my point, [. . .] because he has this way of like taking movies and associating it [*sic*] in a Christian way." Members from nearly every megachurch in the study constantly praised the accessibility of their pastor's preaching, repeatedly testifying that "even a child could understand" his message. One interviewee recalled an interaction with an older member of the congregation illustrating this: "But when she heard him [the pastor], she was 97 at that time, she said, 'If I'm 97, and [my] great-great-grandchild was sitting there, he's 3, and here's my daughter, and she's in her 30s, [and] we all can understand what he's saying, then that is the man you all need.'" Another noted that if the senior pastor did use a big word, he defined it and then would "joke [about it] and say this is to let y'all know I done had [*sic*] some education." The senior pastor's ability to talk to the audience as a normal human being with accessible, easy-to-understand everyday examples and humor appealed to the attendees and helped them identify with him and his sermon.

Nearly half of all references to the senior pastor as human emphasized how the pastor was relatable and his messages were relevant to their lives. A member mentioned that the senior pastor "breaks it down. He gives examples. He just pulls in everything, sports, [and] media." Another identified how the sermons touch on situations in which people are able to relate: "No matter where you are, there's probably a scenario for everything you can think." In fact, many megachurch members felt the senior pastor was speaking *directly* to them. For example, one said: "It just really applied to my life. And it was kind of one of those feelings like is [the senior pastor] talking to me? Does he know my story? [. . .] And it's like whoa, he really got to my heart. [. . .] I've just been to eight other churches and none have been able to speak to me in that way." Many respondents were amazed by how the sermons were directly applicable to them as though the senior pastor knew what was going on in their lives and wrote the sermon with them in mind. These pastors are experts at transforming "a historical or mythical ideal from a remote abstraction into an immediate psychological reality," which helps create a connection between them and the attendees.[16]

As we've argued, rather than undermining their charismatic authority as has been suggested in NRM research,[17] identifying their own human frailties,

[16] Manfred F. R. Kets de Vries, "Ties That Bind the Leader and the Led," in *Charismatic Leadership: The Elusive Factor in Organizational Effectiveness*, edited by Jay A. Conger and Rabindra N. Kanungo, 237–252 (San Francisco: Jossey-Bass, 1988), 240–241; see also Dawson, "Crises of Charismatic Legitimacy"; Wilner, *The Spellbinders*.

[17] Dawson, "Crises of Charismatic Legitimacy."

whether it is a performance or not, supports the senior pastor's charisma. This contributes to enhancing the charismatic bond.

Emotion and the Charismatic Bond

A defining characteristic of charismatic authority is an intense emotional bond between the leader and his followers. Roughly a quarter of all comments regarding the megachurch pastor referred to this emotional bond. Trust is a key feature of the charismatic attachment.[18] The pastors' openness about themselves and their lives and their relatability were primary reasons many of these comments gave for describing the senior pastor as trustworthy, authentic, and real. One member mentioned that whereas other pastors often come with a "façade," their senior pastor, by incorporating everyday life experiences into his sermons, "keeps it real," which makes it "easy to just go ahead and accept the message." Remembering his first visit to the church, another recalled that what "struck" him unlike anything he'd experienced in any other church before was the "authenticity in what he [the senior pastor] was saying." Respondents in different churches repeatedly used the word "authentic" to describe their senior pastor. One newcomer to a church said: "I can trust him [the senior pastor]. [. . .] You can feel him. You know he's real. And even though this place is a little big, you can't physically touch him but you can feel like you can touch him because you know enough about him." This quote illustrates how the senior pastor opening up about himself, and allowing his congregants to feel as though they know him, strengthens the charismatic bond. Whereas large group size is often thought to decrease charismatic leaders' ability to form relationships with their followers,[19] by presenting themselves as relatable human beings, megachurch pastors foster identification with their attendees and elicit trust from them. One member even said that he trusts the senior pastor more than any other person alive: "I trust him best I know of any man alive and that comes from just having—observing this giving spirit of his, you know, up close and all [. . .] he's the real deal."

Another component is that the attendees feel emotions expressed by the senior pastor. As Dawson notes, charismatic leaders are often deemed "more emotionally expressive."[20] The respondents identified feeling emotionally

[18] Dawson, "Crises of Charismatic Legitimacy."
[19] Doyle P. Johnson, "Dilemmas of Charismatic Leadership: The Case of the Peoples Temple," *Sociological Analysis* 40 (1979): 315–323.
[20] Dawson, "Crises of Charismatic Legitimacy," 82.

and spiritually connected to the senior pastor and his message. One interviewee exemplifies this sentiment: "[Pastor's name] is so open to the Holy Spirit speaking through him that it always touches, I mean everybody gets something right here from the message. And so that, God is love, the Holy Spirit is love. And so when you feel that connection, you just feel loved." One lay leader recalled a time when she yelled "I love you" to the senior pastor as he walked by and he responded, "I love you more." She further noted how although he "can't get around to everybody, you know that he loves everybody in this church." Doyle P. Johnson identifies how followers may become less "emotionally dependent on the leader" as the group becomes larger and they have less interaction with him.[21] Thus, it is notable, that even in several-thousand-person congregations in which pastors have little direct contact with attendees, roughly 30% of references to the emotional bond with their senior pastor mentioned feeling loved or encouraged by him in spite of the size of the group. For example, a lay leader describes how the senior pastor "tells us all the time how much he loves us. And he's made the statement so many times, 'Hey, I may not know all of you the way that I want to know you, but we have a whole eternity to get to know each other.' [. . .] And that's something great to look forward to." The ability to make attendees feel loved without regular direct contact seems to be a by-product of the pastor's highly relatable sermons. One lay leader notes "feeling loved on through osmosis, [. . .] because the scripture is communicated well [. . . and in] everyday terms."

The senior pastor and his sermons also evoke emotional responses in the attendees. Fifty percent of comments about an emotional bond with the pastor described experiencing some type of emotional response to him or his sermons, such as love, laughter, excitement, and awe. For example, one respondent said, "He blesses me to no end and I love that in him. [. . .] He's such a courageous speaker; transparent; baring his soul. When you hear his voice, you feel relieved. He's just that good. He's good. He's good and I love everything that he does." Attendees were emotionally affected by the words and behaviors of their senior pastor: "When [the senior pastor] stands up there and tells us we pray to God to send us the people that no one else wants. [. . .] How can that not affect you? You know he's our spiritual leader and we believe in him, that's why we're here. You know we love him and we trust him and we want to do what God's told us to do." Here we can see that the emotional connection is bidirectional—the attendees feel love *from* their senior pastor and they in turn feel love *toward* him. One respondent

[21] Johnson, "Dilemmas of Charismatic Leadership," 317.

emphatically declared his positive sentiments toward the senior pastor: "He's on fire. [. . .] He's the shepherd." Others shared similar feelings; another mentioned how the senior pastor has "got a regiment that will follow him off the cliff" and another said that the senior pastor is "revered because he knows his flock [. . . and] connects with people."

While this charismatic bond is not jeopardized by the ordinary qualities of the pastor for megachurch members as in the case of NRMs,[22] there is still a tension between the extraordinary and ordinary sides of the leader. One new member chastised other new members for idolizing their senior pastor, saying, "I love [pastor's name], [. . .] but if we as Christ followers put him on a pedestal and idolize him, God isn't going to be too happy." One member's comments further exemplify this tension: "We've heard from folks, [. . .] we don't want to put him [the pastor] on a pedestal, you know, he's real, he's human, and at the same time, something more than human and he's something, you know, that we put on a pedestal." Another participant in the focus group agreed; yet another noted "it's a tension that's kind of constant." One participant followed up with a question: "How can you not though [i.e., put him on a pedestal]?" To which another responded, "That's exactly right." The same question was repeated and another responded, "It's a real tension." Maintaining a balance between these two sides of charisma—extraordinary and ordinary—is a balancing act that is constant tension for charismatic leaders and for their followers in this study.

Megachurch Pastor as Reliable Leader

Douglas Madsen and Peter Snow, in their analysis of political behavior and leadership, describe the power of the "charismatic bond" between a leader and his or her followers. They argue that the charismatic bond involves a "proxy control" that allows participants to perceive the leader as one who "acts on their behalf." He portrays empathy with the troubles and dilemmas of the followers, can "project knowledge" and understand their needs and emotions, and then offers solutions and models of "self-efficacy" that reassure them and functions to "reduce the stress" of the followers. This process is both dependent on and productive of a sense of the leader's trustworthiness and authority.[23] As is abundantly shown by our data, megachurch pastors

---

[22] Joosse, "The Presentation of the Charismatic Self in Everyday Life."
[23] Douglas Madsen and Peter G. Snow, *The Charismatic Bond: Political Behavior in Time of Crisis* (Cambridge, MA: Harvard University Press, 1991), 5–22.

create an enormous reservoir of goodwill, not only because they are extraordinary at delivering well-organized and interesting sermons, but because they are asking and answering questions and problems that their members are experiencing. Indeed, the pastors normalize the human experience of their members, and they relate to that experience in ways that give their hearers the sense that they, too, have been there, experienced these problems, and by faith and by action have learned, with the help of scripture and Spirit, to overcome and solve these issues.

This is no small achievement, because these megachurch pastors have many things going on at once: they have to relate emotionally to the issues that their members are experiencing, and place this experience in both a personal context and a scriptural domain so that the lessons and solutions for overcoming these issues come not only from their own experience but are filtered through their reading and interpretation of scripture. This is hermeneutical talent because we know that many want to be megachurch pastors, but few in fact make it to the top. And those who do are looked upon as deeply gifted as well as transformed by their sense that they also have been where the listener has been. They understand the perspective of their parishioners, and they are deeply connected in a bond of trust that, while intimate, is also transactional. And a part of what this transaction is preparing listeners for what's to come, that despite their problems and the dilemmas they face, deliverance is possible. The altar call and the time of healing, which generally follow the sermon, create a holding place, in which the uncertainty of their lives, both in their "sin" and in their "sickness," can and will be relieved and healed. Thus, the "talk," "sermon," or "chat" is a long preparation for *the time to receive relief, to make a decision "for Christ," to create a moment of "destiny."* In this way, the drama of one's problems is laid bare, the potential for healing is offered, and now the *certainty of deliverance and relief can come.*

As we suggested all along, the megachurch pastor must deliver the goods—to be vulnerable, but strong, able but familiar with weakness; to be a fellow traveler, but one who knows the way, to be with his followers, but to be their shepherd. This is no small feat. If "he" fails to deliver, the magic comes to an end. We will see this in Part III: when the charismatic bond is broken or simply begins to fade, these churches quickly decline. There is much on the line. As we've noted, most of the growth in these churches happens under the founding pastors, but we have also noticed a time limit to megachurch pastors, when the magic fades, usually lasting twenty years—after which the bond starts fading and the magnetism loses its power, and the show can end. We will examine this process, but in the meantime, Chapter 11 reviews the response to the call of the pastor to the altar. The response, we argue, is the promise of deliverance for megachurch members as they hear the call of the reliable leader.

Desire for Deliverance

Man is man only because he is civilized.[1]
—Émile Durkheim

I F THERE IS a revolutionary moment in these megachurches, it is during the altar calls and services of healing. These moments swell with energy at the emotional peak of the church service. Here, circling back to Durkheim's notion of *homo duplex* that lies at the foundation of our analysis, we argue that humans don't go easily into this civilizing process. The task is tall, and taming their dark side, either by "confessing their sin," in the words of Christian theology, or by "coming to grips with their anomie" in the sociological language that we use requires discipline and submission. This offer and invitation to be "saved" demands much more than a simple cognitive claim or a rational argument. Humans seek out reinvention and intervention on a visceral level—the altar call is a response to a deeply affective invitation to salvation and release for the sake of a "new life," or what Durkheim might call "civilization." And not only must congregants "see it," but they also must "feel it" so that they know that it is "for them."

---

[1] Émile Durkheim, "The Dualism of Human Nature and Its Social Conditions," in *Essays on Sociology and Philosophy*, edited by Kurt H. Wolff, 325–339 (Columbus: Ohio State University Press, 1964 [1914]), 325.

This salvific moment of transformation and healing comes at the height of the megachurch ritual cycle—when the music is at full pitch and the sermon has concluded. The invitation is given—the call to release and liberation takes place when the pitch is true and the words have invited a full emancipation. Our study and interviews depict megachurch members with an interest in and willingness to be cultivated and to come into a "new order of being." But this "coming to Jesus" is more than a cognitive ascent to a logical proposition; it is a profound movement of spirit, affect, and emotion that we witnessed across megachurch members of various demographics (and sometimes even in ourselves). Figure 11.1 highlights a summary of the elements and effects of the altar call in the Megachurch Ritual Cycle.

People from every walk of life come and leave all their "burdens at the altar," which, of course, in these megachurch venues was most often a simple, yet dramatically lit, stage. "Coming to Jesus" is a multilayered

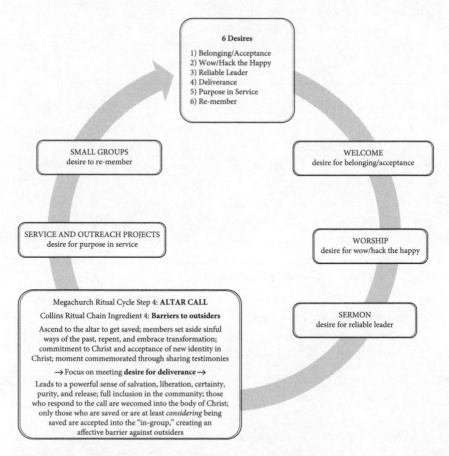

FIGURE 11.1. Megachurch Ritual Cycle Step 4: Altar Call

metamorphosis. For example, this person confesses his process in an uneven, raw, and emotion-filled series of fits and starts:

> And then a lot of people I think feel they have to change their life and they don't want to. So I hear a lot of that. Well I'm still doing this right now. But it's about coming to church, hearing the word, so the Holy Spirit can change [you]. So I think that's what not a lot [of people] want to change . . . [and] the lifestyle. But I was . . . just words can't even explain the Sunday that the pastor had people come up on stage. People actually had weed in church . . . and threw it up on the altar. I just, I just couldn't even believe it. [Another] lady, she was at the altar, went back to her purse, got her purse, got her condoms out of the purse and threw them on the altar. I just couldn't . . . [find] words . . . to explain that. I was just in tears.

The full power of the preaching and the music, as we have recognized, builds up to a veritable dam of affect that is waiting to be released. And while it is not just about those who literally come up for salvation or for healing, it is clearly powerful for those who witness others going forward—it is a tangible way for them to remember their own conversion as well as a way to reconfirm what they believe and what they have gained. The sheer magnitude of feeling in these celebrations is fully embodied and expressed behaviorally: as the songs are played, and many churchgoers lift their hands in praise and prayer, shouting out hallelujah; men and women weep, sometimes audibly; and many, whether voluntarily or involuntarily, convulse in joy, tears, and even laughter.

All of the emotion, music, and invitational preaching are the work of moving people who may know their needs but can't express them, people afraid to show their real emotion, who are embarrassed at how helpless they feel, or even those who want to feel something but can't. All want to overcome inner conflicts and the terror of uncertainty: uncertainty over death or over illness, or over the chaos of their lives, or the terror of helplessness, or simply the terror of being alone; the agony of having done something that cannot be forgiven; the process, as we would say, of managing anomie. And from it all comes the hope of salvation, of redeeming what is torn apart and broken, and of releasing control over one's own destiny. We saw in so many of the megachurch members a need for a new purpose, a new start, a new community, a new set of friends; a place where they could fall apart without embarrassment, but be sure that someone or something was there to put them back together. The altar call creates a tangible space of radical opening to all that is felt and needed, and a dramatic invitation to a new order of life—in the words of the scriptures, a "new way of living."

A Biblical Beginning

Such affectively charged moments of conversion and transformation are not new in the history of the New Testament church and the Christian tradition. We often think that this affective and deeply emotional call to a new life is a contemporary display of emotion. But we argue that it has been in the church from its inception. The earliest character of the New Testament community was one in which all divisions were removed, whether those of language, nationality, or religion—the call of Peter was to a radically transformed life that confronted death and saw it as a pathway to new life, redeemed by Jesus and led by God's spirit. The Book of Acts announces a charismatic community that overcomes all differences, recalling a radical lack of control in which the early disciples appear to be "drunk," speaking in tongues and languages previously unknown to them, and calling back to the prophetic Book of Joel, in which the prophet dreams of a level playing field where all are called, all are welcomed, no matter their gender or station in life. All are invited to this apocalyptic vision foreseen in the prophetic Hebrew scripture, remembering that this *apocalypse* is the great "uncovering," not only of the glory of the Lord, but of the true disposition of all who come and seek healing:

> Then Peter stood up with the Eleven, raised his voice and addressed the crowd: "Fellow Jews and all of you who live in Jerusalem, let me explain this to you; listen carefully to what I say. These people are not drunk, as you suppose. It's only nine in the morning! No, this is what was spoken by the prophet Joel:
> "'In the last days, God says,
>> I will pour out my Spirit on all people.
> Your sons and daughters will prophesy,
>> your young men will see visions,
>> your old men will dream dreams.
> Even on my servants, both men and women,
>> I will pour out my Spirit in those days,
>> and they will prophesy.
> I will show wonders in the heavens above
>> and signs on the earth below,
>> blood and fire and billows of smoke.
> The sun will be turned to darkness
>> and the moon to blood
>> before the coming of the great and glorious day of the Lord.

And everyone who calls
on the name of the Lord will be saved.'

"Fellow Israelites, listen to this: Jesus of Nazareth was a man accredited by God to you by miracles, wonders and signs, which God did among you through him, as you yourselves know. This man was handed over to you by God's deliberate plan and foreknowledge; and you, with the help of wicked men, put him to death by nailing him to the cross. But God raised him from the dead, freeing him from the agony of death, because it was impossible for death to keep its hold on him." (Acts 2:14–24, NIV)

To be sure, this movement comes out of a Jewish landscape. Taking on a prophetic tone, it promises a new way of being, and the leader of the movement is the risen messiah, the Lord Jesus Christ, whose death is not the end of life, but indeed, the beginning of the new age. St. Paul, in his letter to the Galatians, takes the mission to an even more radical level, arguing that Gentiles no longer are subject to the Mosaic law, but indeed, in Christ, "there is neither Jew nor Gentile, neither slave nor free, nor is there male and female, for you are all one in Christ Jesus" (Galatians 3:28, NIV). And for many in the early church, it would be an eschatological age in which the "Spirit is poured out on all of humanity" (Joel 2:28, NIV). So when we witness a megachurch landscape that appears eschatological, where boundaries of class, race, and ethnicity are overcome, this is a reflection of a long tradition in the history of the New Testament church—with precedents reaching back to the Hebrew prophetic traditions. Many tend to think of Protestant affect as a function of recent history, but the truth is that in addition to the energetic and emotionally charged rituals, these suggestions of an unrestricted call are in the roots of not only the early Christian church, but even reach back into the ancient history of Hebrew prophets.

An Unapologetic Call to Conversion

As we noted in Chapter 10, the charisma of megachurch pastors evokes enormous admiration from megachurch members, as well as the desire to change, respond, and convert. These pastors know how to lay out the pain of the human condition and argue that "in Christ" not only is the pain taken away, but one is invited to a new life. Charisma combines a diagnosis of the problem with an answer for solving it. However, the essence of this answer is not an ideology or a worldview, even though those features play a role—the sticking point is the *experience* and *relations* established within which ideology is embedded and granted meaning. Liberation from sin and fear—*salvation*—is marked by a bodily reaction that evokes a deep emotional response. Several respondents experienced bodily affective reactions to their pastor's preaching. For example, one megachurch member recounted, "[Pastor's name] was preaching the word, and then it hit me and I walked up to the altar, collapsed at the altar crying for about 15 to 20 minutes."

After the sermon, it is common to transition into a time of quieter music and reflection. However, this certainly does not imply that the intensity of emotion wanes—quite the opposite. The emotion produced and enhanced by the group experience is turned inward. After the pastor speaks, congregants are encouraged to meditate on his message, to allow the words to sink into their souls, and to open their hearts to change and transformation. This is often the opportunity for the pastor to make an "altar call," during which he encourages congregants to commit their lives to Jesus and accept him as their personal Lord and Savior. This decision involves coming forward to the front of the church and praying with one of the worship leaders. Often, newly saved members will be taken to another room to discuss further details of their salvific decision.

This portion of the service is poignantly marked with heavy sensory pageantry. The collective effervescence in the room is palpable; people report feeling "released," as if they had "walked through the waters but never got wet." When people descend to the front stage to get saved, they often describe feeling "prompted," and even afterward, the "thickness" of their emotional experience of being loved is experienced as redemptive and salvific. The ritual is a potent experience for the entire group. Respondents noted how "amazing" and emotional it was to watch others participate in the altar call: "I grow by watching others transform." Another interviewee describes observing others experience the Holy Spirit during worship: "the movement of the Holy Spirit goes through the crowd like a football team doing a wave. I could look up in the balcony and see it pass, and the people doing it. Hundreds get saved. [. . .] Never seen it in any other church."

Watching others transformed and witnessing their emotion has its own mimetic power altogether. Not only are observers learning how to respond, but they feel a visceral sympathy and often an active desire to be in that place, in that emotional state. In addition to the charm and charisma of the pastor, the accessibility of the message he presents contributes greatly to the success of its reception. It is vital that the pastor's message be arousing, moving, and applicable, but *not* intellectually taxing.[2] Compared to pastors in the more

---

[2] The less marketable liberal or progressive forms of Christian theology tend to recall a legacy of

liberal Protestant traditions, megachurch pastors tend to present a more confident sense of certainty that they have the one and only truth; they offer a vivid and often literal interpretation of the Bible, one strongly accessible and applicable to their listeners' lives.

Comparing Evangelical and Liberal Messaging

Pascal Boyer, a cognitive scientist of religion, argues that the most interesting and influential ideas (and therefore also the most successful god concepts) must resonate with the assumptions and expectations of implicit knowledge, *but also* have attention-demanding counterintuitive aspects.[3] What's critical for listeners in these contexts is that in order to remain relevant, the idea must continue to be *minimally* counterintuitive. While liberal churches emphasize the complexity of biblical interpretations, highlighting the ambiguity of texts and often creating morally abstract principles,[4] megachurches' conservative theology suggests only ideas that are easily accessible for understanding while creating greater fluidity in cognitive management for listeners.

For example, conservative theology anthropomorphizes God, suggesting that "He" is jealous, angry, or pleased. It has been found that "people represent supernatural agents as human-like because the kinds of beings that gods are said to be are only intelligible in relation to the natural ontological category *person*. This incorrigible effect of cognitive constraint dramatically shapes the way people intuitively think about gods."[5] Thus, megachurch theology tends to be easier to understand and conceptualize, providing informal handles that allow the listener's mind to detect agency, particularly in thinking about God. God is given a human-like ability to observe, listen, and act, but in a way that amplifies this ability so that God is both like a human being, and yet goes far beyond human capacities to hear, see, know, act, and respond. In this sense, we argue that the counterintuitive and abstract nature of liberal/progressive theology often arouses a sense of confusion

theology that can be found in nearly all major religious traditions: *apophatic theology*. Apophatic theology emphasizes humans' utter inability to understand the divine, and only speaks of the divine in symbolic, metaphysical terms.

[3] Pascal Boyer and Charles Ramble, "Cognitive Templates for Religious Concepts: Cross-cultural Evidence for Recall of Counter-intuitive Representations," *Cognitive Science* 25 (2001): 535–564.

[4] James K. Wellman, Jr., *Evangelical vs. Liberal: The Clash of Christian Cultures in the Pacific Northwest* (New York: Oxford University Press, 2008).

[5] Todd Tremlin, *Minds and Gods: The Cognitive Foundations of Religion* (Oxford: Oxford University Press, 2006), 112.

or perplexity that the senior author has argued partly explains why liberal theology has lost its power to persuade.[6] On the other hand, conservative God-talk is minimally counterintuitive theology, which evokes a manageable degree of disorientation and intrigue, which both captivates interest and ignites a desire to know this God.

In this sense, we argue that megachurches create *certainty enclaves*. The size of a megachurch, the charisma of the pastor, and the style and organization of megachurches help to protect individuals from the dissonance of "liberal" culture—whether it is the questions and uncertainties it frequently raises, or the discourse and theology within liberal Christian churches.[7] Liberal Protestant church sermons and preachers pride themselves on raising questions and doubts; they often end a sermon in a state of ambiguity. As the senior author has explained, liberal preaching scores high with those trained in liberal Protestant seminaries, but it does not draw crowds of nonspecialists, which represents at least one of the reasons that these traditions are disappearing.[8]

We hypothesize that the size of megachurches creates a *sacred canopy*[9] where doubts are downplayed, and the pastor seeks to create structures of plausibility that allow listeners to negotiate their own doubt in a context of safety, where questions are answered and certainty returns. Moreover, the songs and liturgies of megachurches reinforce the messages of their pastors, so that megachurches become *sanctuaries of certitude*. Within them, it appears everyone is on board with the worldview of the megachurch pastor, as well as the theology of a God who is both in control of creation while deeply and personally interested and involved in every single person's life. This God who made all things, loves all things, knows all things, redeems all things, preserves all things, forgives all sin, and has redeemed all people, creates an enormous reservoir of goodwill, positive feelings, and the hope for a second chance. The idea is that this God "created me and redeemed me," this God will never "leave me or forsake me," this God "knew me in my mother's womb and has a plan for me."[10] This God will never "forsake me or reject me no matter what I do," this God will "forgive and redeem me no matter my sin, in the past or in the future." To imagine this God, then, is to imagine a God that is perfectly reliable, and effortlessly able to bring peace and

[6] See Wellman, *Evangelical vs. Liberal.*
[7] Wellman, *Evangelical vs. Liberal.*
[8] Wellman, *Evangelical vs. Liberal.*
[9] See Peter L. Berger, *Sacred Canopy: Elements of a Sociological Theory of Religion* (Garden City, NY: Doubleday, 1967).
[10] All of these quotes come from snippets of interviews in which megachurch members express the power of the services, and use parts of scripture to explain their faith.

salvation. If we keep this in mind when we are thinking about "the deal" that is made among megachurch pastors, the God they evoke, and megachurch members, we see how beneficial it can become. The cost/benefit analysis of what one must give up in order to obtain a relationship with this God appears very much in the believer's favor. It also puts into focus the sense of joy and relief that comes from members who clearly experience deep relief and satisfaction in their relationships to this God. Indeed, we heard the following and something similar from one megachurch member after another:

> He's working in us every day and He's guiding us. And I can honestly say when I'm prayed for, I'm washed in the Holy Spirit every time. And spiritually, that draws me, I'm more and more hungry. You know, you want more, and He gives you more. If you're obedient and when you're hanging out with people that are going through the same thing, it's much more powerful. And you go out on your own and that leaves you to make all the right decisions to . . . God doesn't want you to be on your own. . . . I read my Bible more and when I do the things He wants me to do, He rewards me every time. I don't know how to explain it.

Of course, this experience of "asking" is a part of this tradition but it is sometimes overlooked, as the focus is frequently oriented toward God, and the greatness of God's love. One megachurch-going woman explained that before coming up to the pastor to seek healing, she said that she remembered the scripture Matthew 7:7, "Ask and it will be given to you." So she came to ask for relief from a breathing problem that had nearly killed her. Later, she said, "I just thought, sometimes as Christians we go about doing good for everyone else, but this time, I thought, 'Why not me?' And so I went up, and I'm not sure I was healed, but the experience was powerful and it made feel like I was worthy of God's love, just like we all are." In going through the transcripts of all the megachurch focus groups, we came across several claims that hinted at miracles of healing based on prayer, but these were usually conditioned by God's promise of peace. There were no outright claims that God had healed anyone, at least not physically. But members certainly claimed that God had brought peace, through forgiveness and a sense of love and presence. As we saw with the woman asking for relief from a breathing problem, she did not confirm that she was healed, even though the request itself brought some peace. Nonetheless, she wasn't deterred by the ambiguity in response to her appeal. She was instead empowered by the *encouragement to make the bid*. In that sense, the *possibility* for a miracle and healing is held onto—and the request a form of peace-giving, even though there seemed to be no actual physical miracle, other than a sense of emotional relief.

We did not come across anyone who was sensitive to the potential cognitive dissonance arising between the claim that God heals, and the fact that while many ask for healing, not much actual physical healing appears to occur. Nonetheless, what does seem to happen during both altar calls and requests for healing is that many megachurch members feel empowered in their agency and encouraged in their relationship to the church and to God. Whether or not physical healing occurs, many who speak positively of these churches experience a renewal of hope, of fellowship with others, and a felt sense of the presence of God in whatever they are facing. The affect and feelings of these megachurch members are overwhelmingly positive and upbeat. It seems that the experience of their worship, the ability to be in the presence of one another, to focus on a supernatural agent that is so much for them—both for their potential and for their healing—fills them with hope and love. The evidence for the latter is overwhelming. Megachurch worship, altar calls, and prayer services for healing create joy and hope.

This description of a prayer service for healing taps this same sense that the power is in the asking, not necessarily in the results. And not only as a witness to a faithful request, but a witness to others of the power of a group that believes and asks with complete assurance. In this case, a group of church members nearly 400 strong came to the hospital to pray for a person who was in critical condition and to witness to their faith:

NEXT SPEAKER: Yeah [pastor's name] said he would like to have a heal[ing], the church, he said church would like to hold a healing for [the patient's name]. And at the hospital they were going to have it outside, they needed his ICU room and it was summer . . .

NEXT SPEAKER: It started thundering . . .

NEXT SPEAKER: Thundering and lightning so as only God could manage it. A security guard came around and said you can move inside. And there were three or four hundred people from the church at that healing service.

INTERVIEWER: Wow.

NEXT SPEAKER: Yeah, it was real amazing.

NEXT SPEAKER: See I work at that hospital and the effect that that had, the just for my coworkers and for, there was a lady being wheeled out. She was being discharged and she heard the music and she said "Take me to where that music is." And she stayed for the service. So it wasn't just for him.

NEXT SPEAKER: For [patient's name].

NEXT SPEAKER: That was for so many others.

NEXT SPEAKER: And so many other people saw God through that service.

The description of the impact of the service of prayer avoided speaking to the actual condition of the patient; instead it focused on the "witness" of the gathering of church members at the hospital. A church member who worked at the hospital mentioned the "power" of the witness of this gathering for healing prayer and communicated that it had drawn many people "to the Lord." And so, again, the healing of the actual patient is not mentioned, but the impact of the gathering is the point of what is called the "witness of faithful asking." So, in the end, it is not really about the physical healing of the patient but about witnessing to the faithfulness of the church—and the affect and energy of a large group of members singing uplifting tones, which drew others to the church by the emotional energy created by the gathered voices. The emphasis, then, is the witness to the energy of the church gathered and outreach to those unchurched, and the hope for healing that signals all things are possible, even if there is no actual healing.

An Unapologetic Invitation

But what we found in many of these churches is that, instead of making the call less demanding, they increasingly requested higher commitment,[11] even while allowing for lower commitment from newcomers. In this way, megachurches create powerful expectations, particularly in the realm of financial giving. And while some do make sacrificial offerings to the church, we often hear members says that each person is asked to use "their talents" in helping the church, so nothing is asked for that the member doesn't already have. And there certainly are enough members to share the load of leadership. Thus, while megachurches demand commitment, this is focused on leadership, and even in these areas, as they would say, "many hands makes for light work." So, while demand is high, the workload is spread out. And this challenging call is actually something that attracts many to these churches, even

---

[11] While they request higher commitment, it is just a request. There are few, if any, sanctions for not engaging in higher levels of commitment. Many respondents applauded the fact that their churches didn't pressure anyone into service, although they encouraged it.

as their size helps spread the burden over larger numbers, so that members hardly ever mention burnout:

> I just kept thinking in our previous church, lukewarm, lukewarm, lukewarm. And then when we got to the [church] it was like this is on fire. The Spirit is on fire here and together like as a group we are just in awe of what God's doing . . . it wasn't anything that we personally did. It was that, that sense of the spirit and just being in awe about what he was doing through this group of people. That is only something that can be attributed to him.

Thus, increased demand, or at least claims of higher demands, tended to attract newcomers, making them believe that their former churches lacked real commitment—indeed, many in these churches actually critiqued low-demand churches, and lauded the type of preaching that demanded a decision and called for higher commitment of membership and resources. But as we've mentioned, the irony is that the structure of the congregation allows, and in some ways encourages, free-riders, while also claiming to have a faith that requires higher levels of commitment. This allows them to have what they perceive as a high-cost faith with few obligations to behave in a high-cost manner. The demanding nature of the pastor's call attracted many to the church:

> I think the thing that has kept me here and caused me to get involved is just the, the boldness and the conviction and just being unashamed about what the gospel says. And just lifting God's word on the high week in and week out . . . the boldness and just preaching the gospel for what it is and not, not sugar-coating it and not being seeker friendly because Sunday morning, it's a time that we gather to lift God's name on high and worship together. And if you're doing that for the praise of other men then it's just in vain. . . .

Indeed, we found that megachurch members were intrigued and deeply impressed that megachurch pastors were willing to offend and call members to account:

> It is offensive. I mean it's in your face and that's what, that's what the scriptures are about and I think that's the first time I've ever been in a situation where I mean you are, you're [addressed] personally from the stage in a way that I've never been addressed before. And you don't have a choice. You have to have an opinion, either one way or another.
> And we deal with it in a way that glorifies God but does not sugar-coat the events surrounding it at all. And it's opinion. It's not

historical . . . let's look at the truth and what the scripture says and what preaching verse by verse does not allow you to do is skirt an issue . . . So it forces you to confront scripture in a way that I personally [never] had to confront before.

As we've mentioned, in many contexts the demanding and unapologetic nature of megachurches tends to be glossed over; prosperity gospel churches tend to get much of the national press. Doubtless, churches like Joel Osteen's Lakewood Church hype a type of gospel message that is oriented toward self-empowerment and the importance of asking for what one needs monetarily as well as in all other areas of life. The power of the prosperity gospel is a part of the American megachurch movement, but we would say the majority of megachurches openly critique it and move in a very different direction, at least in terms of the nationally representative set of churches that we studied and interpreted in this research.

The story of one megachurch member gives a vivid sketch of the kinds of demands these churches want to make on people's lives. In response to a pastor's altar call, a young husband and father came forward (it appears that this wasn't his first time): "I walked up to the altar, collapsed at the altar crying for about 15 to 20 minutes, got up and said, 'All right works this is it. If I'm gonna do this, I'm gonna do it.' So I told my wife, 'I can't be doing the things that I'm doing.'" We don't hear what he has done, but it's clear that the man is struggling with *what he should do and how he can respond.* He went on to say:

> You know, what's my first step. And they told me about boot camp, and I thought that would be the best step for me to go back and get that foundation back. And then while I was involved with that, I joined a [men's] group . . . and that was basically a one-year in-depth comprehensive study, training us up to be Godly men, and that was going great, until about my sixth or seventh month into it, and one thing after another just kept pulling me away where I couldn't go to it anymore and I had to drop out. So, but I'm still . . . I've tried to get involved with various ministries, but the church won't respond.

The man clearly wants to be involved, but he also shows his own growing ambivalence. What would it mean for him to give himself to the ministry? Is the church truly interested in what he feels called to do? And then, the man's own internal dialogue discloses his own uncertainty about giving more time to the church:

> So, that was part of the [. . .] things [that] happened. [. . .] I'm called, I've gone into youth ministry because where that's where

I feel it too, that or security. You know. And I find that both of them, I keep emailing and calling people and nobody will get back to me. So, I just said, then fine, then I'm not going to worry about this anymore. And I don't know if I'm wrong, because I got a brand-new baby and everything in the family, so I still haven't found a job. So, I'm wondering if God just wants me to focus on the family and not worry about it, but then every time we come in here. And [the pastor] starts preaching about, you got to be involved, you got to be involved. So, I'm like . . . I feel bad, I feel guilty, but it's like, what do I do. Do I answer that call and take myself away from my family, or do . . . is my first ministry my family?

One can feel and hear this man's uncertainty. And perhaps he's right; he should concentrate on his child. But the point is that these churches do not flinch—they make demands on those who attend their churches. They both want more people to come to their churches, and they seek from these attendees a deep and broad commitment to the work and service of the church. The pastors in these churches take very seriously the call to Christ. In a certain sense, in a culture that generally wants everything to be ambiguous and open ended, it is a radically and deeply countercultural stance.

And again, this is a part of the Christian tradition. The demands made by Jesus on his disciples are well known: "If anyone comes to me and does not hate father and mother, wife and children, brothers and sisters—yes, even their own life—such a person cannot be my disciple" (Luke 14:26, NIV). So, this kind of demand on followers of Jesus is neither new nor foreign for anyone with a moderately well-informed take on the New Testament. And yet, because it is countercultural and an unusual injunction to hear in contemporary culture, the demanding nature of the call to discipleship can stun those who have never heard this kind of demand before. And to be sure, we did not hear megachurch pastors preaching, "You must follow Christ and leave your wife, parents, and children behind." But we did hear a demand from these churches that something more was expected from those who would come, join, and lead. And in some ways, when we heard the demanding nature of megachurch calls to discipleship, it surprised us. Evangelical churches, and particularly megachurches, are mostly known for what some call a "powder puff gospel," a nondemanding invitation to soteriological bliss. But this is not what we found at these churches. We found churches that were ingenious in their ability to attract people, of all ages and cultures, through the liveliness of their worship and the vividness of their preaching and teaching. But we also found a demanding expectation that, as one pastor expressed it: "When Jesus Christ calls you, each must give their full selves to God and to others." In that sense these are countercultural institutions. It's not what we expected to find, but it added to a long series of surprises in our exploration of what it means to participate in, declare membership in, and respond to the call of American megachurches.

This demand from these megachurches can be seen as a command to follow the path toward self-denial—that is, to deny purely ego-driven desires. And, relative to our theme of *homo duplex*, this is the encouragement to move beyond the self and to embrace the community. Indeed, as we have argued, megachurches encourage and *demand* that their members turn away from their purely selfish ways of being, to give themselves more fully to their communities—the far side of *homo duplex*. And as we will see in Chapter 12, on service, this is a complicated dance in these churches: one is called to both recognize one's gifts but also to use these talents *for the sake of serving one's community.* As we've mentioned, megachurches have found an extraordinary way to both help members see their own talents and to encourage them to use these resources for the sake of others, or—in the language of the megachurch—to serve *the body of Christ.*

Our argument in Chapter 12 is that much of the service to the community is motivated by faith, but it is most often accomplished *anonymously,* which again harkens back to the biblical injunction, "But when you give to the needy, do not let your left hand know what your right hand is doing" (Matthew 6:3, NIV). Thus, the process of knowing one's talents and giving them away is far more complex than it seems, as we will explore next.

| Desire for Purpose in Service

Morality begins with disinterest, with attachment to something other than ourselves.[1]

—Émile Durkheim

Megachurches Are a Miracle

Megachurches, when they work, are like well-oiled machines that create deep reservoirs of joy, acceptance, ecstasy, and a desire not only to be delivered from suffering and uncertainty, but also to share that sense of salvation with others. This movement toward freedom—from burden and sin to the desire to share and care, however, is neither simple nor necessary. So, in religious language, it is a *miracle*. That is, a person who has made mistakes, or "sinned," is willing to admit to it and to believe that a "god" wants to heal his or her sin, forgive it, and redeem it in service and love to others. It is a miracle, considering what we know about human nature. And in social scientific language, it is a long journey, filled with cognitive dissonance, and sometimes understood functionally as a form of *costly signaling*.[2] To form relationships with others, with a group, or a community—all the while cooperating with

---

[1] Émile Durkheim, "The Dualism of Human Nature and Its Social Conditions," in *Essays on Sociology and Philosophy*, ed. Kurt H. Wolff, 325–339 (Columbus: Ohio State University Press, 1964 [1914]), 327.

[2] Costly signaling theory argues that costly signals are evolutionary adaptive strategies that aid in overcoming collective-action problems. Costly signals are behaviors that are costly to individuals due to the price of the action, sanctions, guilt, or the price of deception, and indicate to others through their costliness that one is not a free-rider, but rather a cooperator (i.e., a contributor to the collective good). For this reason, costly signals must be costly to fake, otherwise free-riders would be able to imitate them. Several scholars have argued that certain religious behaviors are costly signals of commitment

this complex system that offers little certainty—is asking a lot of human beings. The promise and the draw of this "hope" is that these megachurches appear to contribute to and enhance levels of happiness, emotional security, and well-being in their members. It appears that, consciously or not, these people aren't *faking it*—the fullness of their joy, their relief, and the apparent profundity of their transformation appears so genuine that *something good* must be occurring.

And indeed, religious groups, and megachurches especially, are uniquely skilled at creating trust among strangers and encouraging non-kinship relationships of confidence and goodwill. But again, we ask the question: What allows strangers to enter these activities that are certainly *not necessary* and yet seem to be enormously beneficial, both to those who are orchestrating the system and those who are absorbing its effects? Again, in the parlance of the social sciences, "Solidarity in a successful interaction ritual is accompanied by momentary bursts of emotional energy or 'charge.' There is a rush of confidence, invincibility, or power."[3] Our data provides powerful support for exactly this—we've seen the impact and the effects of these "bursts of emotional charge" in our research and its findings (see Appendix A for a description of our data and method). The megachurch ritual process encourages strangers to venture into a space in which they often don't know anyone and elicits in them the feeling that they are *home* and *loved*—a state that is remarkable. The entire megachurch ritual process is important for the sustainability of this effect. Right from the start, newcomers' first impressions are that the church is welcoming and full of people who are friendly and helpful. They are drawn in with smiles and hugs from strangers as an orientation to the process and the ritual system begins; and as we have seen, there are several links in this processual ritual chain. The newcomers experience songs and bodily movement rituals that create a sense of gravitas and profundity—sometimes with a tone of deep gratitude, sometimes with bold celebration, and sometimes revealing a desperate sense of yearning. Then,

---

(i.e., behaviors that are so costly to individuals, they would not rationally do them if they were not truly committed). See Eli Berman, "Sect, Subsidy, and Sacrifice: An Economist's View of Ultra-Orthodox Jews," *Quarterly Journal of Economics* 115 (2000), 905–953; and William Irons, "Religion as a Hard-to-Fake Sign of Commitment," in *Evolution and the Capacity for Commitment*, edited by R. Nesse, 292–309 (New York: Russell Sage Foundation, 2001). Extensive volunteering can be considered a costly signal of commitment to the group, as it is unlikely that someone would engage in it, due to its cost, if he or she wasn't a true believer and committed to the group. In this way, service to a megachurch can serve as a costly signal of someone's trustworthiness and commitment to the church.

[3] Meredith Rossner and Mythily Meher, "Emotions in Ritual Theories," in *Handbook of the Sociology of Emotions: Volume II*, edited by Jan E. Stets and Jonathan H. Turner, 199–220 (Dordrecht, Netherlands: Springer Netherlands, 2014), 208.

they hear a masterfully crafted sermon—a sermon that describes a problem that they themselves may be experiencing and then presents scripture that appears to directly answer that very problem. At the very least, the scripture illumines the problem in a way that is surprising, inspirational, hopeful, and redeeming. In the afterglow of the sermon, other people, who also appear to be strangers to one another, find themselves willing to descend to the stage in the "altar call." They are welcomed and blessed by the pastor, then greeted by friendly people who pray with them before ushering them into another room. As the service continues, there are more songs, greetings, and announcements, and finally a hopeful exhortation for the visitors to return. There is a general feeling that all are welcome even if a new person cannot contribute financially and doesn't believe they have anything else to offer. In fact, for visitors who are in trouble or in need, there are often people ready to listen and provide real help for specific problems. Some megachurches are so comprehensive that it seems like no matter what trouble a person has, there are special ministries just for them. From the visitors' (and the researchers') perspective, the system seems to work for most people in the room or auditorium. Many seem to gain a great deal from these encounters and shared ritual experiences; groups of friends appear to emerge, and the leaders maintain an air of friendliness, approachability, and knowledge. And, as we highlighted as of high importance in Chapter 10, the pastor's voice is trustworthy. The songs, sermon, and altar call create an energy that seems to come out of nowhere. It all feels good and *right*. Others, who "know" what is happening, encourage those who are new to return or to go to a small-group meeting corresponding with their interests.

The questions surrounding how to facilitate such powerful experiences, the creation of high levels of emotional energy, are what every megachurch member faces. How do they make everyone feel "at home"? How do they help new potential members trust the leaders? How can they come to trust the people in charge of the children's ministry? In fact, each member must also answer these questions for themselves. How do they know that the pastor is telling the truth? The pastor seems to know a lot about what people are going through, and he gives answers for these dilemmas. But are these problems solved by a religious remedy? What can this god offer someone who doesn't know him? It is said that this god has come to earth in Jesus. Who is this figure, Jesus? Why should anyone trust him? The stories about him make him out to be an incredible human being, but they also say that he is a god, a part of the triune godhead. How can three gods be one? How do people feel so good in this place? And the seats are so comfortable. Is it worth the drive? They seem trustworthy, but is it all really true?

Morality That Transcends and Fulfills the Self

In the Christian scriptures, the Apostle Paul turns his back on his Jewish tradition: he gives up his reputation, his family, and all of his material possessions, and in the end is crucified on an upside-down cross. This man, who many say invented the Christian Church, describes followers of Jesus in this way: "For we are to God the pleasing aroma of Christ among those who are being saved and those who are perishing" (2 Corinthians 2:15, NIV). This is to say, by the time a megachurch member asks the question of whether one should serve in megachurch ministry, a lot has happened to them. They've gone through the gauntlet of questions and issues that we just went through—perhaps not consciously, or in our language, or in this sequence, but in some form or another, doubts and questions have been answered, or if not answered, temporarily shelved. And what is called a "new self" has come into being, or as Paul would have it, "Therefore, if anyone is in Christ, the new creation has come: the old has gone, the new is here" (2 Corinthians 5:17, NIV). And those who regularly attend megachurches have come a long way, not only in their own deliverance from their "sin," addiction, or doubt, but even from many of their own egos—they are freed and released to serve others. And this task of service is deeply attached to the new purpose in their lives. So, when we come to hear them talk about what they do, it is good to remember from where they've come—and so we can perhaps listen to their voices with a new ear for what they are saying. One of the megachurch members describes their experience this way:

> I'm still in the toddler stage as a Christ follower; this is my third year. I feel like God is continually putting me in situations where I have to grow. It's been a wild ride. I grow most in obeying God. My biggest spiritual growth is by serving. Also, [name] helped me, that's where you learn your spiritual gifts and your personality. It helped me accept that this is how God made me to be. Before I found God, I felt like a worthless person. The elder made me feel special and helped me embrace what I'm supposed to do in life.

Thus, these churches are not only in the process of giving their members a desire to serve, but also a purpose for their lives in Christ. In that sense, their whole lives are impacted and shaped by their deliverance into Christ and by their sense of mission. And this mission is not only about service but about discovering their gifts, often articulated through a spiritual-gifts assessment or a strength-finding course. These tools, and in reality the entire ritual process, help members build an identity "in Christ" and teach them how they are "called" to contribute to the community. Thus, this is not just about giving or serving, but about *finding themselves* in their strengths, celebrating their blessings, and encouraging them to use these endowments to help others and to bring more people into the fold. Figure 12.1 provides a summary of the vital role that discovering a sense of purpose and calling in service and outreach projects has in the Megachurch Ritual Cycle.

And this is what we found repeatedly: the genius in megachurch socialization is that it not only encourages service to others, but conceptually roots this service in the good soil of "gifts," or what the tradition calls the *charisms*, or *healings*, given by the Holy Spirit for the "building up of the body of Christ." The socialization process is then an organic *synecdoche*, of how the one relates to and becomes the whole—each piece or person fits into the wider puzzle and is needed for the puzzle to be complete. In that sense, these megachurches create a total system by which newcomers are added into the wider structure, welcomed into the church *body,* socialized, and formed into a

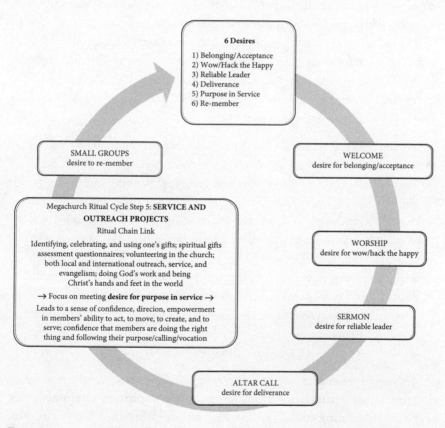

FIGURE 12.1. Megachurch Ritual Cycle Step 5: Service and Outreach Projects

new identity as representative of the organic whole. Their whole lives become an extension of the work of these ministries, giving them a sense of purpose that many have not experienced in their lives. Indeed, as one megachurch member expressed in the preceding quote, she felt "worthless" before her entry into the church.

And here we go back to Durkheim's point made in this chapter's epigraph: "morality" may begin "with detachment," but this is no Kantian *deontological ethic* where the self is sacrificed. Rather, in the language and action of a megachurch member, in order to respond to God's call to continue Christ's ministries, she must identify and explore who she is; she must purify her intentions, discover her gifts, and honor her desire to let those gifts shine. Thus, the *self is not denied so much as fulfilled* in the process of exercising one's gifts in the project of "building up the body of Christ." Once again, the system of the megachurch moves in a logic of *both/and* rather than *either/or*. The language is not about self-denial, but about self-fulfillment as found "in Christ, through Christ, and for Christ." Service to others is then a completion of one's proper role in the body of Christ, which only works as the body is in harmony with itself and with every other aspect of one's life.

The nature of this discipleship, then, is expressed in an intense effort to make one's whole life an expression of their commitment to Christ's *mission* in the world—so that, as this megachurch member describes, every part of life becomes a witness to faith and to the body of Christ—and it is much more than just an exercise in *feeling good*:

> It's learning something. . . . We're not just listening to, oh this is going to make me feel good. Or I can remember this when I don't feel good. But it's, I'm learning something and walking out of church going, did you know that? And being excited. I don't think you get that even like when we do something that's topical. Like walking out of there going, how in our marriage are we displaying Christ's relationship through the church. Like okay. It doesn't just, like, say, oh well you're my husband, I'm supposed to be submissive duh, duh, duh. It's like how is this our testimony and it's real. And I think that sometimes when you just get that okay here's your, here's your three ways and then a joke. I think sometimes you miss the reality of what does it mean to be a Christian and that you are living out a mission.

The language that is often used in these circles is that these are *missional* churches where the message from the pulpit is not for entertainment (we hear her deride the "three stories and a joke" preaching model) but indeed for the task of making one's whole life a mission—the work of Christ in the world. Megachurches truly seek to be an integrated system of thought and action. There is an extraordinary emphasis that the work of preaching is not "head knowledge" that one simply saves up or is entertained by, but rather is to be embodied in ministry to one's family, marriage, and community. This translates, for many in these churches, to a process of being "plugged in," or as one megachurch member describes: "They like to call it equipping or getting trained because they don't want to perpetuate the idea that you go to Sunday school and then you continue to store up all of this knowledge and something without actually ever putting it to use." Knowledge of Christ, then, is for the sake of service to the community vis-à-vis the gifts that Christ has given to each person. Thus, megachurches seek a patterned partnership of the exercise of one's God-given gifts for the sake of Christ's body, the church, so that there becomes an ideal partnership among the needs of the community, the gifts of church members, and the wonder of this pattern of discipleship in Christ.

Early Church Models of Christian Community

As we've mentioned earlier in the book, there is little doubt that even in these megachurches, as Peter Berger has argued, there is *a default secular discourse, which coexists with a plurality of religious discourses.*[4] We've seen it repeatedly in our review of megachurch ministries: members easily shift between the secular discourses of their ordinary lives, and religious discourses, whereby they attempt to more fully integrate the vocabulary and consciousness from their Christian faith. In this way, a biblical orientation echoes in their descriptions of their ministry, which marks how their faith lives *both in society and in consciousness.*[5]

One of the powerful traditions that one hears in the language of purpose and service are the echoes from Paul's First Letter to the Corinthians: "Just as a body, though one, has many parts, but all its many parts form one body, so it is with Christ. For we were all baptized by one Spirit so as to form one body—whether Jews or Gentiles, slave or free—and we were all given the one Spirit to drink. Even so the body is not made up of one part but of many" (1 Corinthians 12:12–14, NIV). Thus, you hear in the discourse of megachurch members this deep sense that each member is not only a spectator and observer of the action, the pastor, the music, and the ministry, but is also called

---

[4] Peter L. Berger, "Further Thoughts on Religion and Modernity," *Society* 49 (2012): 313–316.
[5] Peter L. Berger, "Further Thoughts on Religion and Modernity," 316.

upon to bring his or her gifts into the *body of Christ.* Each one is integrated and necessary for the full functioning of *the body.* This determined sense of need, desire, and gifting marks these churches in which talents are identified and called forth for the sake of the body, for the sake of serving the neighbor, for the sake of the body of Christ. As Paul says, "Now you are the body of Christ, and each one of you is a part of it" (1 Corinthians 12:27, NIV).

And to be sure, these gifts are necessary for the proper functioning of the body, the organization, the organism if you will, in the sense that a body functions only when all the parts are recognized and developed. But then, Paul immediately moves into one of his most well-known scriptures, known even to those outside the church—1 Corinthians 13, the "love chapter." Here, Paul achieves some of the most elevated and grand literary flourishes in Western culture, where he argues:

> If I speak in the tongues of men or of angels, but do not have love, I am only a resounding gong or a clanging cymbal. If I have the gift of prophecy and can fathom all mysteries and all knowledge, and if I have a faith that can move mountains, but do not have love, I am nothing. If I give all I possess to the poor and give over my body to hardship that I may boast, but do not have love, I gain nothing. (1 Corinthians 13:1–3, NIV)

So, in megachurches, there is always this cautionary note, that yes, service and the right use of strengths is critical to the proper functioning of what is called the "body of Christ," but even if all gifts are in motion, and all things are being appropriately used, there is a perception that if there is no love between and within these churches, something goes off the rails. This check and balance, or in the rhetoric of church discipline accountability, must include the discipline of service done in the "spirit" of love. Again, this is a high calling by any standard of morality—not only to do the good, but to do it in the name *and* spirit of love.

Likewise, we heard in many members' descriptions a freedom to fail and freedom to start over. Many of these megachurches, because of their size and the large number of potential volunteers, can afford to give members the latitude to switch between and out of ministries. Indeed, this flexibility and member movement is related to the fact that megachurches are functioning with *scale economies.* There is less fear that ministries could be stalled or undercut by free-riders. In fact, because of the large volunteer pool, megachurches can give members the opportunity to use their gifts in areas of the church where they are most comfortable. Thus, members can avoid burnout or the pressure to do too much, since there is space for freedom to avoid tasks that they either don't want to do or have no ability to do. As a megachurch attendee described:

> And I think that when you have a church this size you've got people who can specialize in certain areas and actually be more efficient and better as a church than just a smaller church where you have to do several different things, you know. I mean we took a group to camp and we had a security team, we had a cook team, we had a media team, you know, and we had, those people they worked hard but they did what they did well and it makes it much easier for everyone else. I think it's kind of contrary to that because there is an economy to scale now.

And because there are so many individuals who are both willing and able, there are more opportunities in which individuals are freed to serve in their areas of interests. Thus they are not only more satisfied doing this work, but more effective and less prone to burnout.

This undoubtedly leads to a touch of arrogance in megachurches; in fact, very often we heard members declare that not only is their church bigger, it is also *better*, precisely because they have more opportunities for service and purpose and there are more individuals with various strengths to fill the gaps and satisfy community needs. And for these reasons, one finds it hard to argue with this logic. One megachurch attendee described it in this way:

> I think it's helped because there are so many more opportunities. No matter what your gifts are, no matter what your focus is, there's an opportunity to use that for God. Where, in a smaller church, there are fewer needs and fewer people to fill them—though we loved getting to know everyone in the church. But in a larger church, yeah the opportunity to actually use your wide range of gifts whether they're in business or whether they're in leadership or administration just expands. Whatever it is, there's an opportunity to plug in here where you don't have that in a small church.

Yet even here there is recognition that something is sacrificed in the process of megachurch ministries in which specialization takes over; members tend to conceptualize it as a cost that they only really get to know people and church members in their own areas of expertise and ministry specialization. Nonetheless, they believe it is a small price to pay, and we heard few or no comments from anyone suggesting that it was time to exit the church or leave in favor of a smaller congregation. We did hear a few comments regarding the downsides of a large church, but even here the sentiment was typically that the benefits outweighed the costs.

Standards of Morality and Sense of Purpose

We are aware that many will maintain the suspicion that megachurches are mostly about puffing up people's egos and encouraging a prosperity gospel. That is, these churches adopt the formula "name it and claim it." There is little doubt that this type of rhetoric is a part of many megachurches, but in our sample of twelve diverse megachurches from across the country we saw very little, if any, of this kind of magical rhetoric or even the idea that the gospel is for wish fulfillment or for easing the conscience of the rich. Indeed, congregants appreciated and praised their pastors' willingness to "offend" the congregants with what they called "truth"—in other words, the unyielding "demands of the gospel" found in the scripture. They were proud that their church and their pastor weren't simply "tickling their ears."

As a symbol of the group, the senior pastor also contributes to the standards of right and wrong approved by the group, giving members a sense of purpose through service and a set of normative standards by which to guide their lives. One man described the message of the megachurch as "unapologetic," explaining that their purpose is to "speak truth" rather than to seek mass appeal: "It's not because [it's] what's hip or what we should be talking about or what's the flavor of the moment. [. . .] It is offensive. I mean it's in your face and [. . .] that's what the scriptures are about."

And indeed, in our research, many interviewees mentioned the importance of the sermons being strongly biblical; this entails an understanding that the Bible stands alone as the source of truth and should be read as a guidebook for life and action—not as something that avoids offense but rather that confronts sin when it is found. As one person said about their pastor, "He preached the word, talked about Christ unashamedly, salvation, sins, those things, and just *did* the Bible." There is much of this very concrete language used to describe how to live one's life. Nonetheless, the focus of the feelings of morality were not on the specific moral content, such as what counts as sin, but rather on the expectation that if one knows the truth (i.e., the Bible), then one should behave accordingly by giving themselves up in service to the church, to their families, and to the community. As one person noted, "Eventually you ought to be [spiritually] mature. [. . .] In other words, you don't have to do this in order to be a Christian, but if you're a Christian, you ought to be doing this."

For this megachurch member, the core of Christian morality—what "one ought to do"—is *service* to God, to others, and to one's family. In describing this morality, a respondent explained that it isn't "so much about evangelism but really reaching out to people because you care," that "it's about going out and finding the homeless people and sharing your lunch with them. You know, that kind of sense of serving them not through your words, [but] through your actions." And here, it is also true that megachurch members were not shy in saying that without the gospel one was lost. But they were also quick to say that they, too, were in need of this grace, and that without Jesus Christ they "could do nothing." So the need for grace was universal, whether as members and leaders in the church—or, as they would say about those outside God's grace, "all have fallen short of the glory of God." They were ready to share that they, too, were "wounded healers" very much aware of their own limitations and shortcomings.

One megachurch member was proud of the fact that her church's vision is "in tune with" the real world and focused on "serving the community." Others described their church as preparing them to serve and allowing them to "love and forgive" their families and to "stand for righteousness" in their communities. One man offered a particularly poignant expression of this view: "If you want to come and observe that's fine. But if you want to be a partner we expect you to live missionally [. . . in order to] make a difference in the city." In this way, attendees' feelings of morality centered on living "missionally" through serving others. The explicit task of evangelizing or "saving souls" was significantly less common. It is not that megachurch members don't want to evangelize, but that there was hesitancy to be explicit about it—perhaps, knowing that most might find this approach unappealing at best, and offensive at worst. To witness to others seems to mean, for megachurch members, *to approach others by an act of compassion, forgiveness, or generosity*.

Perhaps unsurprisingly, the call to service often came from the pulpit, and many respondents were explicit in attributing their "missional" activity to the exhortations of their religious leaders. One person said, "I think there's an emphasis from the pulpit to be missional people." And another said, "If you were listening at all to that sermon today, there were some enormous incisive calls to action for you personally." This characterization of megachurch leaders as focused on service is also supported by the survey data in which roughly 73% of respondents identified their church as encouraging them to serve in the world. Many respondents identified their senior pastor, his sermons, and his example as propelling them to engage in service activities: "When he demonstrates the giving, not just monetarily, but of service, it's hard for us to sit back and say, I don't want to serve tonight." Thus, many participants were prompted to service through calls from the pulpit and the example of their senior pastor.

Across the focus groups, megachurch members emphasized that individuals were never pressured into service, nor were they judged for not participating. They identified that there is "no such thing as a set of rules [. . .] or a legalistic type of standard to abide by." Church members won't "hammer you" for not serving and "if you don't show up at something they're not going to say where were you?" One couple said that "everybody that we met just embraced us, you know, and didn't put any pressure on us to get involved." Instead, individuals are encouraged to serve where God leads them, because they experience a spiritual and emotional desire: "It wasn't serving out of obligation, it was serving because you wanted to do it [. . .] out of love as opposed to out of duty of some sort." Another described how service is about "finding your gifts, wanting people to give [. . . and] to serve because of the joy that they found in doing that." Service is therefore an entirely voluntary activity that many participants engaged in because of the motivational energy gained from the ritual, and the emotional and spiritual benefits derived from the service activity itself. Thus, again, we argue that service is motivated at least as much by what people get out of it as by their desire to witness their faith to others.

Mapping the Megachurch Utopia

As we detailed the actual work and service of megachurches, we slowly became aware that they really made an effort to be like small towns—communities that welcomed all, where every conceivable form of care is given, which includes hospital clinics for "every sinner and sickness." The needs of the many are tended to from birth to death: there is prenatal care, newborn care, childcare, schools, youth sports leagues, afterschool tutoring, college prep help, college-age activities, singles groups, marriage classes, car maintenance facilities, hair salons, job search help, dance classes, fitness classes, recovery resources, medical care, senior living facilities, even a columbarium. For some churches, it seemed as though if you didn't want to, you'd never have to utilize a secular resource again. Whether intentional or not, there seems to be an attempt to create a utopic community that Christians can reside in without fear of impinging secularity.

The church structure wraps each member in community and constant fellowship with like-minded people. We will explore this in even greater depth in Chapter 13, on small groups in megachurches, where community is built and sustained. Because of the size of megachurches, there is enough visible variety to make the community feel vibrant and exciting; but in fact, as far as diversity goes, as delineated in terms of other opinions, lifestyles, or values, there is little to no real diversity. In the vision of Peter Berger, the megachurch provides a sacred canopy with members who, in essence, know the outside world, because most work in it, but choose to live within the constraints and continuities of a world in which one's beliefs are mirrored back to them as good, true, and beautiful. This kind of reinforcement creates a sense of contentment that the world can make sense again. Small-town America can indeed exist, where traditional values of hard work, doing the right thing, and finding people who are like minded is possible. We saw this repeatedly: most sermons avoid controversial topics or alternative ideas; instead they function to set up and maintain plausibility structures of beliefs and actions. They focus on creating and supporting members' sense that the evangelical theology and lifestyle is entirely possible and eminently preferable to all other options—it is what God wants and what the Bible commands. Within megachurches, even when they are in the midst of metropolitan areas, there is at least, in the imagination, *a comfortable small-town atmosphere*, in which one feels that one can trust others, one knows what to expect, and one can be nestled—both physically and ideologically—into this enclave of peace and wellbeing.

There is, however, no doubt that megachurches are clearly committed to community outreach and being "the hands and feet of Christ in the world." This is an embodied experience of giving of oneself—one's energy, time, and labor—for the benefit of the greater body of Christ. For example, Stacy Spencer, senior pastor of New Direction Church in Memphis, Tennessee, which was the number one fastest-growing church in 2012, said, "Our mission is to empower all people through life-changing experiences from the inside out. If it doesn't get out, then we become a stagnant pool that has no life in it." Later he continued, "If we're not helping the poor, then why are our doors open? That's really the heartbeat of who we are."[6] Some churches do have a strong international focus, but it appears that most resources and attention go to local missions, to which most members create and maintain physical and emotional attachment. Members' personal *investment* and physical involvement is vital for the desired effects, which are always threefold. First, pastors teach that service to the community is one of the most important ways that one can serve God, by being God's hands and feet in the world. When talking about the successes and outcomes of the work, they give honor directly to God. The church is said to be *a mere conduit*. For example, members might often say, "God is doing amazing things in this community." Or "God was present—there's really no other way to explain the success of

[6] Stacy Spencer, quoted in Ryan E. C. Hamm, "Outreach Interview: A New Direction, Stacy Spencer," *Outreach Magazine*, Special Issue 2012, 135.

the outreach." Second, outreach projects most often have the dual goal of serving a community need and evangelizing or saving souls. There is often a clear understanding that helping people meet their worldly needs without also attending to their spiritual needs is futile and, ultimately, cruel. At least one of the churches in our study placed a significantly larger emphasis on serving for the sake of evangelism than for the sake of helping people in need. Third, becoming involved in outreach and service-oriented groups and missions has the specific goal of solidifying members' own bonds to the church. This is understood and restated by members and leaders alike—for example, they might say that "members felt more engaged and committed when they became involved in the missions of the church." Even if the sociological theory behind such a statement is not explicitly discussed or understood, the commitment to living out a life of service and purpose generates an enormous amount of energy in these churches. As we've reported, to believe in the gospel is necessary, but to live it out confirms one's belief and solidifies that connection between one's "gifting," one's "purpose," and one's "faith." The bridge of belief, purpose, and service creates a dynamic energy that magnifies how powerful megachurches are in the lives of their members, and it completes the *arc of emotional energy, so that belief is confirmed in action and purpose is confirmed in relation to others*—all of which communicates the energy of the gospel in the world. In this sense, the minister can argue that "Our church not only believes the gospel but lives it out."

Megachurches confirm their own purpose in action. In one of the congregations, the pastor spoke about how "600 volunteers from our church [transformed] a city park." This circle of ministry and service confirmed the power and energy of the gospel to transform members into servants, and to turn their service into a witness to those outside the church. Again, evangelicalism and witness are also connected to the circuit of desire that builds throughout these ritual processes from the first welcome, to the sense of "wow" in the early embrace of new visitors, to the reliability and power of the pastor, to the experience of being delivered from one's own captivity to "sin," to the service one does for others, and then (as we will see in Chapter 13) to the *re-membering* of the church in small-group discipleship communities. Thus, members' participation in these service activities is an indispensable link in the interaction ritual chain that constitutes the dynamism and energy of the megachurch model.

This last goal is *one* of the reasons that local (vs. international) missions are so important. The clear majority of outreach resources are spent on domestic projects rather than on international missions. Some churches have minimal or nearly nonexistent global mission networking; others have a specific focus and delegated funds for global missions, but they almost *always* focus even more on local ministries (with the exception, perhaps, of the megachurches that are closest to mainline Protestantism, which give more attention and money to global issues). For example, Spencer explained, "For us, we start in our own backyard first. There's a lot that needs to be done in our local communities. We don't even have to get on a plane or charter a boat to go and make a difference in the world. We start in our own backyard. If every church could adopt its street, just imagine how much better our communities would be across the nation—if every church got out, made sure the trash was picked up, graffiti was off the walls, kids were tutored, we had neighborhood crime watches."[7]

The number of local community outreach efforts are almost too numerous to name. In fact, in some cases, even the pastors themselves would have a very difficult time listing all of the service activities taken up by their churches because small groups of members are called upon to head up and fund their own service and outreach projects. Occasionally such a group may build on its success and popularity and enter the church leaders' awareness, but often, they stay small and local, though still impactful. If the church is the hands and feet of Jesus in the community, then the small groups are sometimes Jesus's fingers—gripping, digging, building, and pointing to something greater than themselves. One senior pastor explained that about five years after planting his church, the leadership "re-imagined" the point and function of small groups in the church. The names for small groups were changed from "community groups" to "missional communities." And the groups became the organizing agents for much of the church's service work in the community—the groups come up with ideas, organize the resources, and implement the service projects themselves.

However, this is certainly not at all to suggest that there are only a few significant church-wide service effects. In fact, megachurches tend to have an overwhelming amount of service and outreach projects. Such projects are often presented as the *purpose* of these churches. Megachurch members see service opportunities as a primary means to enact their faith, evangelize, and save souls. But there is also always a real sense that serving the community and doing God's work is pleasurable, fulfilling, and truly meaningful for its own sake. For example, after describing his congregations' benevolent actions in the community, Spencer said, "So those kinds of initiatives really give me fuel. When I see the faces and the people—the appreciation of the folks living in our community—that really helps me keep going."[8]

---

[7] Stacy Spencer, quoted in Ryan E. C. Hamm, "Outreach Interview," 143.
[8] Stacy Spencer, quoted in Ryan E. C. Hamm, "Outreach Interview," 140.

It is certainly not unheard of for megachurches to partner with outside community service organizations. For example, one of the megachurches created a 501(c)(3) for the sole purpose of working with existing faith-based community organizations. By harnessing and assessing the resources present in the community, the church could enhance and facilitate others' efforts *and* identify gaps and unmet needs where the church's resources might be the most useful. Therefore, in addition to creating what appear to be fruitful community partnerships, this church also created a summer youth sports camp, a construction company with a training program focused on the dual goals of employment opportunities and affordable housing, and a youth mentorship program focused on the athletic, academic, and spiritual health of young people.

However, we argue that megachurches *primarily* create their own missions, rather than partnering with community ministries or secular missions. They spend the majority of their own resources on their own programming and projects, even if they also encourage partnership with other organizations. We suggest two possible reasons for this strategy: First, megachurches have the resources. They receive large sums from their members and are often looking for ways to spend them. It is much more impressive and more likely to inspire additional donations to show a video of, say, a brand-new senior living complex, housed on the church campus, than to simply report that the money was given to a preexisting organization. That being said, churches employ diverse strategies, and an *inspiring video* may not always focus on outreach. For example, it could focus more on testimonies of addiction recovery within members of the church instead of service in the community. Second, there is excitement in creating something brand new, in seeing a need and tackling it creatively using resources and strategies developed by church members. It is not uncommon for megachurches to adopt a rhetoric that implies an "us against the world" attitude or claims that they have a sort of monopoly on God's presence, as this hyperbole creates its own in-group excitement.

Along the same lines, it makes sense that these megachurches would place a high value on the freedom and *control* afforded when designing and leading their *own* mission rather than joining an existing effort. Such control is appealing to megachurch leaders who may not want to partner with or be socially tied to more liberal social service organizations. Moreover, pastors see service as a tangible and clear claim of the unmistakable and transformational mission to and for others—embodied by each individual member and enacted in every program and service the church makes available.

Megachurch Service: The Other as Ourselves

As we argued at the beginning of this chapter, a successful megachurch is like a well-oiled machine. To be sure, even as the flows of affect and the construction of social symbols are dynamic, contingent, and creative, occasionally even disrupting the best-laid plans of megachurch service engineers, the megachurch model is surprisingly stable and smooth running. It works. While there is certainly some diversity between churches on their implementation of the model, this amounts to variations on a theme—the consistencies are startling. Moreover, it is clear that the people in charge of designing and executing the dynamics of the model know exactly what they're doing. Thousands of people pour through the doors of each megachurch every Sunday to experience and be empowered by the ritual cycle of the megachurch model. Fueled up with affective energy, confidence, and courage to act, participants are emboldened to go into the world to carry out their missions.

The salience of embodiment is rich and multidimensional. The power of the *body* is vital symbolically, performatively, and physiologically. On the socio-biological level, the ritual cycle arouses megachurch participants' bodies in a flush of emotional energy that results in a social fervor imbued and interpreted with meaning. The swell of affective arousal, for many people, regularly evokes what they would call the presence of God and the Holy Spirit.

On the performative level, the Christians' bodies are thrust into the world to *be* the church—to sacrifice, give, and serve the world quite literally as the body of Christ. Megachurch members are urged to take seriously Jesus's command in John 13:35 to show love, and to let everyone know as Jesus explains, "by this everyone will know that you are my disciples." In this way, participants are taught how to be a vessel of goodness and mercy in the world. Not only are they exhorted to control their cravings and desires, but they are also encouraged to comport themselves in such a way that reflects their salvation. For some this may mean a "John 3:16" tattoo or a cross necklace, but for all it means service to Christ and to the church in the world. Each person's body is a representation of the fruits of Christ's compassion, care, and liberation from sin. Each person performs their new identity as a saved child of God.

On the level of social imagination and symbolism, the bodies of the participants unite and meld together, pulsing with a new heartbeat and purpose—the grace and peace of Christ. From a theological and religious perspective, they view themselves as embodying the essence of Jesus Christ, sacrificing and being the arms and legs of the Savior in the world, healing, reconciling, caring, and coming alongside the weak, sick, and vulnerable. At their best, they clearly do a great deal of good, and their members feel enormously energized by the vision and by the mission. Members would call this work a healing ministry of Christ in the world. From a sociological perspective one can interpret these organizations as enormously successful mechanisms that both motivate many to serve and empower these same people to care for those around them. As we've noted, this "missional" lifestyle is a key to megachurches; the message is the mission to heal, care for, and reconcile others to Christ.

We have also argued throughout this chapter that megachurch members buy into this process, and while they are changed by it and persuaded by the need to serve, this service comes from their own desires to fulfill their purpose in the world. In this sense, we contend that from a social service perspective, the mechanism of this care is quite successful in creating the interest and desire to serve. While megachurches are extraordinary in how much service they deliver, this is not a form of disinterested service. Service is performed in part because there is need, but also as a drive to be a witness to Christ—to evangelize and draw others to the mission and ministry of the church. In this sense, it appears self-interested, but megachurch members would argue that attracting others to Christ is the highest and best gift they can give to anyone—inviting a person into a relationship with Jesus Christ. This desire to evangelize others into the body of Christ, into the heart of Christ, is the point and priority of these churches.

Finally, while drawing others in through service, the megachurch system seeks to meet each person's desire for acceptance, for excitement, for a reliable leader, for deliverance from the burden of sin, and for the freedom of hope—all of which stimulates and awakens the need to serve others. It is a powerful arc of energy that acts as a bridge between Sunday celebrations and opportunities to grow more intimate with Christ and with others in their small-group ministries. This is a holistic system, from birth in Christ, to service with and for others, to a lifetime of fellowship and growth with other believers and service to others in need. Megachurches create a whole system that socializes and embodies the ministry of Jesus Christ and continues the ritual cycle by instilling a sense of commitment in attendees who perform needed service for their church and community.

CHAPTER 13 | Desire to Re-member

Since the role of the social being in our single selves will grow ever more important as history moves ahead, it is wholly improbable that there will ever be an era in which man is required to resist himself to a lesser degree, an era in which he can live a life that is easier and less full of tension. To the contrary, all evidence compels us to expect our effort in the struggle between the two beings within us to increase with the growth of civilization.[1]

—Émile Durkheim

Moving from Spectator to Member

The movement from being an isolated individual to a fully socialized being has been the arc of our study across the six desires that we found in our megachurch study.[2] From the thrill of acceptance to the joy of being a part of these churches, our map details how charismatic leaders have led their followers to their deliverance into service, purpose, and now into small groups. Small groups in fact seem to act as midweek pit stops where members get the personalized care and nurturing they need on the way back to the mountaintop experience of their Sunday celebrations. Megachurch members

---

[1] Émile Durkheim, "The Dualism of Human Nature and Its Social Conditions," in *Essays on Sociology and Philosophy*, ed. Kurt H. Wolff, 325–339 (Columbus: Ohio State University Press, 1964 [1914]), 339.

[2] Part of this chapter is reprinted and adapted with permission from James K. Wellman, Jr., *Evangelical vs. Liberal: The Clash of Christian Cultures in the Pacific Northwest*, Copyright [2008], Oxford University Press.

maintain a vibrant emotional energy "high" from week to week, bridged by their support groups, which buoy them over the valley of "secular" life outside the cocoon of Sunday celebrations. And the data seems to warrant this interpretation. The fellowship of megachurches is enormously potent, and our title, *High on God*, is not merely a way to grab attention, but an analytic description of what we found. We are sure that from the outside this all looks too good to be true. And this is precisely why it took us some time to fully understand the power of these churches to capture their followers. When we argue that six desires are being mediated and quenched by these churches, it is an extraordinary sociological claim. But the crowds that are voluntarily attracted to these churches, and the degree of commitment that these churches expect and sustain, is astonishing.

Here we circle back to Collins's theory of interaction ritual chains[3]—we agree with Collins that the energy gained through ritual activity is *not permanent*. Megachurches know this fact, and that is largely why they work so hard to create an enduring sense of acceptance and excitement, and why megachurch pastors *must* deliver. As we will see in Part III, it doesn't take much to bring down these ministries. Dramatic crash-and-burn scenarios are not surprising when so much emotional energy is at play. A pastor who goes rogue, grows old, or fails morally can devastate a megachurch overnight. Thus, to maintain and nurture the wick of desire, so that it remains lit and glowing, is no small achievement. And to keep the desire alive demands total commitment.

One of the primary tasks of the Megachurch Ritual Cycle model is to infuse group symbols, such as the Bible, certain family values, the pastor, and even theological ideas with emotional energy so that they are perceived as of ultimate importance. As we will see, the emotional energy experienced through worship services is only the beginning of the process of gaining purchase on symbolic capital. As Collins describes it, one of the results of emotional energy

> could be regarded as symbolic learning during an encounter, the transfer of symbolic capital through a network, but with one proviso: this is not simply cognitive learning by filling one's memory banks, but acquiring symbols that have a membership significance and an EE [emotional energy] charge. What an individual can "learn" from an encounter that is socially significant is what symbols mean for membership in a particular group; this might take place by

[3] Randall Collins, *Interaction Ritual Chains* (Princeton, NJ: Princeton University Press, 2004).

experiencing the social use of some symbol that one already has some acquaintance with but up until now had not felt its significance.[4]

Thus, translation from the experience of emotional energy to the sense of "owning it" through membership is a process of socialization that megachurches recognize and pursue with total diligence. To get people in the door is one thing, but to make them feel accepted is another; to answer their questions with the sense that Jesus Christ is not only the beginning, but the goal of their lives, takes some practice; and to deliver them from their own sense of inner conflict is yet again no simple matter. Even further, megachurches must inspire members to serve others in the name of Christ, thereby confirming their commitment. Small groups are often not only the glue of community but the individualized nurturing that many need and want. This is not a short-term fling, at least not for those we listened to in these megachurches. They experienced something very profound in their churches that spurred not only the desire to belong, but an affective connection and bond with their faith, with their pastor, and, as we will discuss in this chapter, a desire to connect intimately in smaller community groups. These are familial connections that produce deep ties between strangers and create communities that are clearly life transforming for many who have experienced them. Nearly two-thirds of the megachurch congregants are a part of some group: Bible study, a support group, a service group, or an addiction therapy meeting. And as extraordinary as the worship and music are for these megachurch members, the small groups, in all their variations, often become an end in themselves and frequently become life-saving and life-confirming support networks. Figure 13.1 summarizes the structural and affective elements of small groups that make them so vital in the Megachurch Ritual Cycle.

Our empirical data confirms our observations. Megachurch members leave church services charged with emotional energy, but it drops immediately and the longer individuals go without participating in subsequent events, the more it wanes. To be sure, many members reported how terrible they felt when they missed Sunday services. For instance, one explained, "I didn't miss a Tuesday and Sunday until this week. And I was miserable" and "I hate to miss a Sunday of church because my whole day's off." One woman described how the church service fills her and her husband up, and the emptiness they experience when they miss it: "My husband always says that he needs to come on Sunday. Because it gives him a brand-new feeling for [the] entire week.

---

[4] Collins, *Interaction Ritual Chains*, 153.

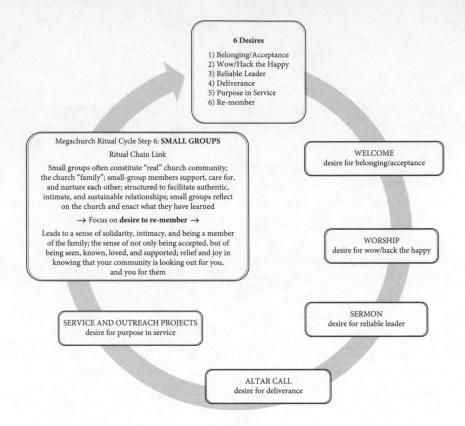

FIGURE 13.1. Megachurch Ritual Cycle Step 6: Small Groups

[. . .] And sometimes when we miss it [. . .], we felt like so empty. [. . .] I know it's crazy to say this, but we really need it. And we are more happy." One member expressed this desire by wishing that he could have the same experience throughout the week: "I would just love to start every work day here for an hour. [. . .] It's just, you leave here so exuberant and then it's on us, I know it is, but it's so easy to get back into that rut." The small-group activities act as pit stops between Sundays. As one member described: "We get poured into from the sermon. [. . .] But during the week we may not get poured into [. . .] and some of the small groups are for us to get poured back into from each other." Another said, "And I can't go just Sunday morning and close the door [. . .] I want relationships throughout the week."

The desire to maintain emotional energy throughout the week led many megachurch members to join small groups, which further develops their attachment to the megachurch and enhances membership feelings of belonging and acceptance. In the words of the participants, these groups help individuals "build relationships with one another in the body of Christ."

They do not put "pressure on you" or "judge" you, but instead are people that one "does life with" and whom you call if you have a problem. Small groups are the "real arms and hands and feet [of the body of Christ] to love and support people." These small groups make the large church feel small: "But I don't consider this a big church because it is broken up into little groups. We're all part of the same ministry and when we see each other it's like a family." Through small groups "you develop relationships and [. . . then] this megachurch becomes just one little small church." Consistently, respondents identified that they felt at home and accepted, that they belonged in the megachurch, which was in large part due to participation in small groups. The survey results showed overwhelmingly that members reported that they have a strong sense of belonging to their megachurch. Small groups are enduring and effective in creating support networks and communities of friends, thereby sustaining loyalty to the group, all the while maintaining the emotional energy generated from the church services.

Too Good to Be True?

And so, for researchers, and surely for readers, the question may come up: What happens when what you are researching is simply too good to be true? This question is not an unfamiliar one for observers of the Christian tradition and history. From the beginning of the tradition, outsiders, as well as those close to Jesus, shared some of these suspicions that the promises of Jesus were mere words. After all, Peter, Jesus's chief disciple, deserted Jesus at his most critical moment. Jesus was crucified between criminals; this was not the death of a hero—or a revolutionary. And yet, his followers knew the promises that Jesus made to them, that he would return, that he would send the "Holy Spirit." And these early Christians would go on to continue to surprise many with their actions of grace and healing to people even outside the community of faith. Indeed, early Christians were looked upon with some awe not only for their community life but for what they did for others, quite often at the cost of their lives. Recent research shows how early Christians instigated care for orphans and refugees, and invented the hospital by starting institutions that cared for those in need, whether Christian or not.[5] This created an overwhelming sense that something new was erupting in the midst of human history.

[5] See Timothy S. Miller, *The Orphans of Byzantium: Child Welfare in the Christian Empire* (Washington,

According to Christian tradition, one of the earliest events that gave hope and marked followers of Jesus with a sense of authenticity occurred during a gathering of Jesus's followers only several weeks after his death. Christians call this time Pentecost, but within the Jewish tradition, which Jesus's disciples observed, it is the Feast of Weeks: a harvest festival, a time to gather and celebrate together in Jerusalem. In this case, the very earliest followers of Jesus were gathered in the same room where they ate their last meal with Jesus before his death. Jesus had told them that although he would die, he would also return and he would see them again.[6]

And so, this sense of suspicion over stories that seem too good to be true has been a part of the Christian tradition from the beginning. As the earliest Christians gathered, they experienced their own very real consternation over the promises of Jesus. We can imagine that when the disciples came together in Jerusalem to wait for their "directions," they gathered perhaps in both hope and suspicion about what was to come. They were not disappointed. The Book of Acts recalls this experience in vivid and eccentric detail:

> When the day of Pentecost came, they were all together in one place. Suddenly a sound like the blowing of a violent wind came from heaven and filled the whole house where they were sitting. They saw what seemed to be tongues of fire that separated and came to rest on each of them. All of them were filled with the Holy Spirit and began to speak in other tongues as the Spirit enabled them.
>
> Now there were staying in Jerusalem God-fearing Jews from every nation under heaven. When they heard this sound, a crowd came together in bewilderment, because each one heard their own language being spoken. Utterly amazed, they asked: "Aren't all these who are speaking Galileans? Then how is it that each of us hears them in our native language? Parthians, Medes and Elamites; residents of Mesopotamia, Judea and Cappadocia, Pontus and Asia, Phrygia and Pamphylia, Egypt and the parts of Libya near Cyrene; visitors from Rome (both Jews and converts to Judaism); Cretans and Arabs—we hear them declaring the wonders of God in our own tongues!" Amazed and perplexed, they asked one another, "What does this mean?"

DC: Catholic University of America Press, 2003); Timothy S. Miller, *The Birth of the Hospital in the Byzantine Empire* (Baltimore: Johns Hopkins University Press, 1985).

[6] Indeed, tradition says that he did return, and even then, Matthew 28:17 (NIV) says, "When they saw him, they worshiped him; but some doubted." The Bible records ambivalence and doubt even in the earliest accounts.

Some, however, made fun of them and said, "They have had too much wine." (Acts 2:1–13, NIV)

To put it bluntly, this was a time of terror for Jesus's followers. Peter, who had denied Christ three times before his death, had now returned to be one of the leaders of this new community, called the "church." Their gathering comes on the heels of Jesus's crucifixion—a death that they wanted to avoid, even though Jesus seemed to welcome it. Most followers were terrified, and many followers of Jesus dispersed. But the core stayed, led by Peter—surprisingly transformed into the earliest spokesperson for the new movement. So, the gathering, after fifty days of waiting, was a time of anticipation, a time of hope that the promise would be fulfilled. And in the telling of the earliest Christian traditions, something did occur. Language was heard coming from Galileans—the Jesus followers—but language that represented the "whole world," that is, every language of the Roman Empire, from the west, the east, the south, and from Rome itself. Something happened that provoked a burst of energy and emotion that had not been seen before, and a new movement was clearly afoot. Peter, a follower of Jesus—an uncertain follower—was now speaking for the movement. Peter quotes the Hebrew prophet Joel, that his vision is now present:

" 'In the last days,' God says,
'I will pour out my Spirit on all people.
Your sons and daughters will prophesy,
your young men will see visions,
your old men will dream dreams.
Even on my servants, both men and women,
I will pour out my Spirit in those days,
and they will prophesy.' " (Acts 2:17–18, NIV)

Scholars of the early church consider Pentecost the beginning of the Christian Church movement. This display of the Holy Spirit enters into the community as a boundary-breaking force; it arrives in a culture and language that can be understood in every corner of the empire, in every dialect and by every gender, calling out a transformative moment in human history by any definition. The energy, the communion—even in cultural and lingual diversity—culminates in a burst of enthusiasm that "outsiders" question as some form of drunkenness. But again, the sense that it is *too good to be true* is not unfamiliar to us as researchers or to readers of our work—the emotional energy and power of megachurches is shocking for many and surely a great surprise to skeptics.

And it is not altogether different from what we find in our own reactions to megachurch members when they talk about their experiences in small groups, and their enthusiasm for their churches—to some extent it is all too good to be true. The energy is overwhelming and surprising: from death springs new life; from what is low, something powerful is coming forth; and from the edges of obscurity, a powerful movement arises. Megachurches fit this bill, in the sense that the power of these organizations is unexpected and their dominance surprises many. And this book, in a sense, is our attempt to answer these questions: What has happened to these people that they desire so deeply to be in communion with one another? What are they doing when they do meet with one another? Why do they seek so often to be in one another's presence? What is the cause of this deep sense of joy that they feel when they talk about their time together? What draws them so profoundly to be so loyal in their commitment to their faith, their church, and their communities?

Invitation to Vulnerability

The conventional wisdom of outsiders about the evangelical tradition generally and megachurches more specifically is that they are doctrinal, rigid, legalistic, and judgmental. In fact, in self-reports from our megachurches it was common for members to say that they felt no sense of judgment in their churches. When asked what attracted them to the church, many commented on the "relational," "dynamic," and "graceful" aspects of their congregations. "Relationship," whether in theological discourse from the megachurch pastor or in the dynamics of their small groups, is a key term for them theologically and ideologically. That is, one's "relationship with Jesus Christ" is what saves, redeems, and empowers one to live, love, and transform one's community. And this "power of relationship" is transferred into congregational life through church fellowship and small-group activities. A key aspect of successful small-group work is trust—a nonjudgmental ethos of acceptance, encouragement, and care. In Rick Warren's best-selling book, *The Purpose Driven Life*,[7] the famous megachurch pastor lays out a sophisticated, in-depth process for developing small groups within Christian congregations—premised on a nonjudgmental though morally accountable process of trust and nurture. The leader (or facilitator) is far from a dictator indoctrinating the Bible into his followers; what he or she does do is facilitate honest sharing

[7] Rick Warren, *The Purpose Driven Life: What on Earth Am I Here for?* (Grand Rapids, MI: Zondervan, 2002).

of members' intimate life experiences in a group setting that is "confidential" but open, morally accountable but "merciful," accepting but ethically "encouraging," fully aware of "human frailty" but expecting the "best" from one another.[8] The power of these groups and the "ethos" that they engender in evangelical megachurch communities is striking. As one megachurch lay leader argued:

> It's very much a turnoff for us to be involved with a legalistic kind of an approach to Christianity, the dos and the don'ts. This is a very grace-oriented congregation without the watering down of church. Stick to good solid biblical foundational truths, but yet allow for sin, we're all going to commit, we're all sinners, we're recovering sinners. And we accept that. We have good solid standards, but we recognize we're all in the same boat together. We just come around people, working with them through the struggles we all have and small-group orientation to get relationships with other people. It's a big church and you get dropped through the cracks and having intimacy in relationships allows you then to practice grace and be a part of people's lives.

These comments resonate with many megachurch members, especially their stress on the importance of truth and the confrontation with sin, but more importantly the insistence that all are a part of the reality of a "fallen world" and that all are in the process of healing through the redemption of Jesus Christ. Pastors and lay leaders constantly mentioned their own vulnerability, perhaps aware of what outsiders might think of them, but they were certainly determined to make the point that their communities were neither legalistic nor rigid. This process of being "convicted" in one's sin was common in most groups. In particular, megachurch men mentioned the "power" of meetings where they could confess their sin:

> At men's retreats people are open to confess areas where they have been struggling in sin and there's a freedom to seek forgiveness. Personally, I have been able to go to our pastor, even as an overseer and tell him areas where I have struggled in sin and the response has not been, get out of here, you're a sinner, it's been, how are we going to work to get this straightened out. And that's been very freeing.

And this sharing of sin was neither superficial nor easy. Multiple megachurch members spoke of the importance of their churches in helping them

---

[8] Warren, *The Purpose Driven Life.*

overcome every form of addiction: drugs, alcohol, and emotional obsessions. Comments such as "Our church seeks to meet every need" were common across the interviews. The group ethos of megachurch congregations in small and large groups supports the identification of sin, its confession and forgiveness, as well as encouraging members to rise above their struggles.

Of course, this acceptance and forgiveness is predicated on the notion of a shared moral standard and a commitment to trying to meet that standard. For example, liberal Protestant church members and leaders condemn evangelicals for their insistence that homosexuality is a sin; but evangelical churches, in response, do not flinch from what they see as a biblically based standard—humans are meant to be in faithful heterosexual marriages and the expression of sexuality is meant for these covenanted relationships. Megachurch members were quick to say that for them, everyone is a sinner, so in that way, they are "no different than homosexuals." Many evangelicals assert that they "Love the sinner and hate the sin." This distinction is, of course, rejected by progressives but central to the group life of the evangelical community. However, it is important to say that there is some diversity of opinion among American evangelicals on this issue—some do argue for the full inclusion and acceptance of LGBTQ individuals.[9] Some even argue for the celebration of diverse sexuality and gender identities as parts of God's creation, and, even more rarely, for the acceptance of same-sex relationships (although this was not the case in any of the churches we studied). We did not come across any LGBTQ individuals who had confessed in evangelical circles that they were in same-sex relationships, but one church had a small blurb on their website advertising a potential new group that sought to have "quiet conversation" with followers of Christ who were personally impacted by the church's stance on human sexuality. However, that same church voted to disaffiliate with its denomination in 2016, rejecting the denomination's decision to "embrace an aggressive political agenda" that included allowing clergy to perform same-sex marriages.

Nonetheless, the vulnerability of evangelicals is a distinct and powerful convention for the megachurch pastors in this study. Indeed, we would argue that megachurches have chosen to move away from more controversial subjects in part because they create controversy and division, and taking a firm stance on them is a "no-win" situation, in which their defensiveness can make them look "small." More to the point, alienating anyone on these more confrontational issues may push away potential members. For megachurches,

[9] David P. Gushee, *Changing Our Minds: Definitive 3rd Edition of the Landmark Call for Inclusion of LGBTQ Christians with Response to Critics* (Canton, MI: Spirit Books, 2017).

alienation, division, and loss of members are significant costs; after all, positive emotional energy is a critical aspect of their ethos of growth and goodwill. In this sense, one could argue that for megachurches, vulnerability is sought and accepted, but certain sins that either go too far or create controversy are, from a cost/benefit analysis, better ignored.

Creating a Marriage Culture

The focus on constructing a space of belonging, intimacy, care, and authentic relationships in the small groups highlights the importance of these virtues in general. Small groups are not only a place where members can "re-member" the transformative power of God's presence in the worship service; they are also a space where the values of the church are solidified and applied to individual lives and identities. Gathering together in the small-group community is an opportunity to gain support for, rehearse, and enact their membership—to re-member—in the community. One of the primary focuses of the small-group structures is *marriage*—seen as not only the glue that holds communities together, but also one of the most vital sites for humans to celebrate their gift of embodiment: sexual intimacy.

There remains controversy over the actual divorce rate in America; on the low side, 40%, and on the high side, 50%.[10] In either case the percentage is high and divorce is often traumatizing, even if it is a matter of escaping from a destructive relationship. In the senior author's book, *Evangelicals vs. Liberals*, I compared the ministries of liberal and evangelical congregations, and one of the stark differences is that liberals rarely talked about marriage, while evangelicals spoke about and worked on marriage on a consistent basis. We found the same dominant attention to marriage in the megachurch ministries that we examined and studied. If anything is true about megachurch culture, it is that it wants and desires to build, sustain, and nurture high-quality marriages. As one megachurch member said, "[The pastor's name] speaks about marriage every single week."

Ironically, the senior author, the day before writing this section, went with his spouse, a therapist herself, to a lecture by John Gottman, sponsored by the Temple De Hirsch Sinai in Seattle. The Gottman Institute, a renowned research-based therapist training organization, is located on the University of Washington campus. Gottman and his colleagues have been studying the

[10] American Psychological Association, *Marriage and Divorce*, accessed March 9, 2018 (http://www.apa.org/topics/divorce/).

reasons couples succeed and fail at marriage for the last forty years. As he said in his lecture, "I like to measure everything and I think we have very good indicators on the variables that create success in marriage and the dynamics that lead to divorce." If anything, Gottman is an enthusiast for marriage and a marriage culture; he believes in it and what it does for the wellbeing of those involved in "happy marriages."[11] Gottman, who wore a kippah at his presentation, was not particularly religious in his language, but he made one thing clear: he wants to help each couple, through scientific observation and results, to "remain committed in a happy marriage," which, as he said, "helps children enormously as they grow up to be adults." He also said that before he and his associates entered the study of marriage, there were no scientific studies that laid out the variables proven to lead to a positive and happy marriage. Gottman then proceeded to speak about the many ways in which his program has helped couples to create, fix, and maintain committed and happy marriages.

We bring this forward to say that from this mental health perspective, there is probably nothing more important than creating a healthy, happy marriage culture for the sake of those who are married and for the sake of the children who are being brought into the world. So, the senior author was always surprised that liberal Protestant pastors and lay people did not seem to take marriage and its health seriously. Evangelicals, as our study indicated, do take marriage culture seriously. And since more than 50% of adults are married, it seems appropriate and critical to nurture and support a marriage culture. This is precisely what we found in the megachurches that we studied. In fact, most of their classes offered were aimed at marriage and family issues, including premarital and marriage counseling, parenting, and childcare classes, with the aim of teaching skills and insights that have "traditionally been the responsibilities of extended families," a megachurch lay-leader noted. Megachurches take on these responsibilities with enormous care. A megachurch lay-leader explained: "So we are educating premarital couples, how many weeks is that? Twenty-eight weeks of premarital a year. And then those couples are paired, those that are going to get married at [our church and by our church pastor] are then matched with what we call a heart-to-heart coach that meets with him four to five times that works through an inventory and helps them address their areas of strength and growth."

Not only do these churches concentrate on preparation for marriage, but they also have separate programs for "repairing" marriage and to help couples

[11] Gottman Institute, accessed March 9, 2018 (https://www.gottman.com/).

who are facing crises of whatever kind: "And then we have a [. . .] marriage restoration ministry and that happens in a small-group focus so we get experience and that's six weeks of follow-up where couples work with coaches who have been restored in their marriage from crisis events such as infidelity, domestic violence, and emotional affairs." In addition to helping couples in their own congregations, they also offer classes to couples outside their churches: "Then we have a number of couples that don't attend our church but there is training for them. So there are four or five churches represented in each class. So we'll probably be helping about 350 people get ready for marriage over each year. And then we reach out to the community, we put it in the paper and we target unchurched couples because there is no one else out there to help them on how to have a great relationship."

Indeed, these ministries aim to be truly comprehensive; for example, they include ministries of restoration for couples in or outside the church:

> And then we have a ministry called [name of ministry] and that's where [name of pastor] will be having a lot of his emphasis go and that's when couples would call and say we are going to get a divorce or we are going to separate and we meet them at that point of Christ where we pair them up with a pastor, a restoration pastor and we assign a professional counselor that helps develop a plan that identifies areas that are creating conflict for the other person such as one spouse might be using pornography, the other spouse may be, you know, abusing alcohol, drugs, maybe domestic violence. So they identify those and then the restoration pastor places them in recovery groups or specific areas of need to change that pattern of behavior and that happens over 10 weeks. And so we give them lots of touches with the pastor, with the counselor and what we call them natural healers, recovery leaders, or lay counseling.

We found this overwhelming focus throughout the megachurches that we studied, promoting a marriage culture, helping prepare couples to be married, enabling them with advice on a positive and healthy marriage life, and then coming alongside many couples who are struggling with a variety of issues that marriages face to help in repair. We saw next to no evidence of judgment or moral finger-waving, but in fact, a great deal of work attempting to prepare, create, and sustain a happy, healthy, and positive marriage culture.

Thinking about megachurches from the perspective of Gottman's work, a secular psychologist with a deep commitment to sustaining couples and marriages, it is a remarkable testament of megachurches to be doing this work, in part because the need, while obvious, seems to be ignored by many liberal organizations, particularly on the left-leaning edge of the Protestant church. And the question is, why? To be sure, liberal congregations support LGBTQ relationships (as does Gottman), and these are important to their ministries—but to be blunt, few attend these congregations, and liberal Protestants continue to decline in numbers and influence. But still, why aren't all churches trying to support and maintain a happy and healthy marriage culture? For liberals, this could include the LGBTQ community. We really don't know the answer to this question, but what we did find in these megachurches is an enormous investment and commitment to a strong, healthy marriage culture, something that the Gottman Institute helps to foster, and which their research shows is a critical factor in maintaining a vibrant and healthy community overall.

Small-Town Cities of Love, Hope, and Support

We've painted megachurches, in some sense, as idyllic worlds of 1950s America. But this isn't altogether true, since the problems of the twenty-first century are deeply intertwined in all of these communities. So, while on the surface it seems that these churches maintain a conventional morality of yesteryear America, they are also deeply committed to taking on the real-world problems of present-day culture. Whether these issues are in the inner cities or in suburbs, megachurches are facing the central issues of our era. To be sure, they typically don't comment at all on larger political issues. And this is somewhat of a shock to outsiders, because the conventional sense is that these churches are breeding grounds for the Christian Right. While members certainly participate in those kinds of organizations, megachurches themselves are not promoting these issues, at least in their public life.

In a certain sense, evangelical megachurches practice a parochial cosmopolitan experience. That is, from one angle of vision, LGBTQ issues are not addressed. Gender transitioning is not addressed. Political candidates aren't supported, at least in any explicit fashion. Instead, megachurches are truly focused on the core issues of salvation; growing each person's character; building communities of happy, healthy marriages and families; and reaching out in service to their communities, serving the needs of the people who are homeless, sick, or hungry, and sometimes also taking this work overseas in similar international service ministries. There is no doubt that for them to share the gospel of Jesus Christ is their core and crucial purpose; there is nothing that is more important than commitment in one's heart to Jesus Christ. And all are invited to this committed relationship. How this faith and purpose is lived out is nurtured in a family-centric way, with care of others, forgiveness toward enemies, and goodwill toward all.

As we have shown, megachurches are sociologically remarkable because they complete a complex ring of desire for many human beings. They make many feel welcome; they give people a sense that something special can and will happen in this place; the pastor dives deep into their psyches to answer the questions that many are facing today, and quite often meet that question with an answer, but also with a request—to commit themselves to Jesus Christ. Deliverance from all things, whether uncertainty, drug addiction, violence, despair, whatever it might be, is offered in this follow-up: Come forward and be delivered, be counseled, be loved by professionals, and cared for by family, those who know what you are going through. And then be ready to be challenged to service, to give one's life and goods for others, in care for the needy, for those who are local and those who are global. And finally, none of this is done in isolation, but in relationship to one's small group, a community of like-minded people who struggle and want to be healed. It truly is a full arc of coming in as an individual and leaving fully embraced in a community of faith and love. Megachurches create powerful communities of love, support, and service, and the emotional energy that sustains this arc of desire is captured and personified in the belief that Jesus Christ is Lord.

Now, of course, all of this can go terribly wrong and become subject to destruction; megachurches are no exception to the rule that power and money corrupt. And, so, we now move to Part III of this book that addresses the dark side of megachurches.

PART III | # The Dark Side of Megachurches: How Some Deceive and Destroy

I N PART III we examine the most troubling side of megachurches: the scandals that arise within these congregations and their impact. Most of the scandals that we studied come from the malfeasance of megachurch senior pastors, and the vast majority of these scandals are sexual in nature, though several also involve financial misdoings and sometimes violent behavior. But in the main, when megachurch pastors abuse their office and power, they are taking sexual advantage of members in their congregations. The abuse is primarily perpetrated against adult women, though a small minority of cases include homosexual relationships or young boys or girls as victims. In the first section of Part III, we theorize a form of *soft patriarchalism* as a way to name this power differential and to explain the relational expectations that we saw in many of the scandals. We contend that the model of soft patriarchalism gives insidious and pervasive power to men and creates opportunities for them to manipulate and ruin the lives of women (and sometimes girls and a small minority of young men) under their pastoral care. These scandals never end well, and they often lead to the implosion of megachurches, where the charismatic bond between the pastor and congregation is irrevocably broken.

In the second section of Part III, we end with an ethical and moral assessment of megachurches. The dominant assessment of megachurches, in both popular culture and in scholarship, is that they tend to be havens of commerce and exploitation, and purveyors of the prosperity gospel. We came into this study with a similar prejudice, feeling that these churches, while wildly successful, were organizations aiming to motivate attendance but in the end became rapacious—stealing their members' time, resources, and even their very identity. The surprise, for us, was that by the time we had thoroughly sifted the data—a wide swath of documents from members and attendees at twelve representative American megachurches, looking at people who were longtime members and leaders, people who were new members, and those that were just visiting—analyzing and re-analyzing it over a five-year period, we found something quite different: wells of goodness, satisfaction, generosity, and inspiration. We have sought to explain how religious organizations have a certain genius at meeting the needs of what Durkheim called *homo duplex*. As organizations, megachurches meet the desire of humans to flourish as individuals and to do so in a group—an equipoise that is rare but deeply satisfying for those to whom the churches speak. Nonetheless, we now examine and illustrate the rare but potent way that megachurches deceive and destroy their members.

CHAPTER 14 | Dissecting Megachurch Scandals

OUR READERS—MANY OF whom are WEIRDS (Western, educated, industrial, rich, democratic, and secular)—if they've made it this far, are probably saying to themselves, what took you so long to get to the scandals and the dark side of these "truly corrupt churches"? And it's a good question. The secular press's core take on megachurches is aptly summarized in this introduction to a story about Bob Cole, the founder and pastor of the 25,000-member Calvary Chapel Fort Lauderdale megachurch. Cole abruptly stepped down in 2014 after multiple accusations of sexual scandal, including an addiction to pornography and charges of child molestation. The news writer begins the article with this generalization:

> Megachurches are often scams. Their owners and preachers become obscenely wealthy and don't have to pay taxes. And a remarkably huge percentage of megachurch leaders become ensnared in ethically dubious (at best) conduct: Ultra-rich Houston pastor Joel Osteen infamously neglected to open his megachurch to Hurricane Harvey victims for days after the storm hit earlier this year.[1]

As noted in the article, the Cole accusations came out on top of the August 2017 story accusing Joel Osteen and his Houston megachurch of a slow response to Hurricane Harvey's victims. Numerous reports emerged about

[1] See Jerry Iannelli, "South Florida's Five Worst Religious Leaders, Including Accused Molester Bob Coy," *Miami New Times*, November 19, 2017, accessed June 24, 2018 (http://www.miaminewtimes.com/news/five-bad-priests-like-florida-megachurch-molester-bob-coy-9839580).

Osteen and whether he needed to delay opening the Lakewood Church because of flooding, or whether he simply postponed it for the sake of convenience. A *Washington Post* story painted an ambiguous picture,[2] but a more informal yet nonetheless revealing video history of Osteen's actions paints a more damning portrait.[3] In any case, Osteen's church did respond eventually with shelter and aid to the victims. Nonetheless, in terms of publicity, megachurches, at least in the press, have been fighting a losing battle.

More locally for us as researchers, the Mars Hill Church in Seattle is a glaring exemplar of megachurch corruption. For more than a decade it was one of the fastest-growing and most-talked-about churches in the nation. It had 15 locations, with more than 260,000 sermon views each week; at its height in 2013, membership stood at 6,489, and weekly attendance at 12,329. Due to controversies involving Pastor Mark Driscoll, including charges of plagiarism, bullying, and financial corruption, attendance declined by two-thirds in 2014. There were attempts to save the church, but Driscoll declined his leadership's "restoration plan" and on October 31, 2014, the lead pastor, Dave Bruskas, announced plans to dissolve the church, effective January 1, 2015.

Studies of Mars Hill are now beginning to emerge, and Jessica Johnson's 2018 book, *Biblical Porn: Affect, Labor, and Pastor Mark Driscoll's Evangelical Empire*,[4] is a brutal and brilliant exposé of the way Driscoll manipulated his congregational empire. Driscoll's corruption toppled a large church, and yet despite his clear financial and administrative malfeasance, he and his spectacular celebrity profile escaped relatively unscathed to Scottsdale, Arizona, to start his next adventure in church planting. Johnson's book is a fascinating exploration of the power of affect, but it also exemplifies the draw of charisma that we discovered in our studies of megachurches; the emotional engagement of these churches is overpowering, for many for the reasons and arguments that we have put forward.

Driscoll's ability to manipulate his flock is legendary. In his last communication to his Mars Hill congregation, instead of a face-to-face conversation, Driscoll chose a thirty-minute video. This coming from a man who regularly exercised a bravado and machismo that rallied and seduced many to his

---

[2] Stephanie Kuzydym and Kristine Phillips, "Joel Osteen Calls Claim He Shut Church Doors on Harvey Victims 'A False Narrative'," *The Washington Post*, August 30, 2017, accessed June 24, 2018 (https://www.washingtonpost.com/news/acts-of-faith/wp/2017/08/29/we-were-never-closed-joel-osteens-houston-megachurch-disputes-claims-it-shut-its-doors/?utm_term=.dedab946e0d4).

[3] See https://www.youtube.com/watch?v=zpCINSEfbUk.

[4] Jessica Johnson, *Biblical Porn: Affect, Labor, and Pastor Mark Driscoll's Evangelical Empire* (Durham, NC: Duke University Press, 2018).

side, both in loyal attendance and millions in donations. So instead of facing his accusers in person, Driscoll addressed his followers on screen. Driscoll started with his tried-and- true origin story of how God gave him Grace, his wife, who *converted* him with her Bible; he told the history of building his church from a small, living room Bible study and then, bathing in his own myth, he exclaimed, "What Jesus has done has far exceeded even what I was praying for or hoping for or dreaming of." Through this boilerplate history, he massaged this fairytale beginning that prefaced his intention to communicate "in a way that is godly," as "a means of loving you and informing you," that he was leaving. These words came out at the same time protests emerged among a multitude of public groups and church members, seeking to personally confront Driscoll's financial malfeasance, abuse of leadership, and large-scale manipulation. Driscoll then claimed in the video that many if not most of the accusations had come from "anonymous" sources. This putative anonymity made it difficult for Driscoll to make what he called "reconciliation." In other words, Driscoll took no responsibility—and from a legal point of view, it was shrewd. He saw the writing on the wall, and he was clearly creating his escape plan.

Nonetheless, Johnson makes this revealing statement about watching Driscoll on live video: "I kept the faith alive until the final minutes of his message." She had hoped that he would take responsibility. In other words, she believed and desired that Driscoll would show some remorse. And then, at the end, instead of any form of mea culpa, Driscoll asked his listeners to pray for the Mars Hill local leaders, who are dealing with so much, that even "at one of our churches, someone is folding up pornography and putting it in our pew Bibles"—thus Johnson's title for her book.[5] In other words, Driscoll painted his accusers as vile and corrupt faultfinders, suggesting that the real problem was their evil activity and their cowardice in not stepping forward. Touché—from there, Mark Driscoll exited. He walked away free and clear to go on to his next venture.

But perhaps what is more revealing than Driscoll's refusal to take responsibility—never admitting to using church international-mission funds to "buy back" his book on marriage to create the illusion that it was a best-seller—was Johnson's reaction. In her book, she states, "Even more disconcertingly, I found myself not only hoping but also believing that he was going to change course and repent of his sin, as he had admonished audiences repeatedly and vehemently to do."[6]

[5] Johnson, *Biblical Porn*, 4.
[6] Johnson, *Biblical Porn*, 2–3.

What this episode shows more than anything else is the power of charisma. Driscoll had become the answer for thousands of young, secular Seattleites, and many beyond, who were yearning for a faith that was sturdy, that could discipline them to follow through on commitments to marriage, their life mission, and their families. Johnson describes Driscoll's ability to create a deep desire and affect—an affect that even pulls in a secular scholar like Johnson. And she is aware of this; in fact she conjectures about her own reaction. Johnson quotes the theorist Brian Massumi: "Thinking through affect is not just reflecting it. It is thought taking the plunge," a process of change that is "the first stirrings of the political, flush with the felt intensities of life."[7] Indeed, charisma has the power to shape desire, to ring the bell of faith, and to turn thought into action that follows through in the social and political worlds. Like the world that Driscoll created, charisma even answers the stirrings of the irreligious heart of a hard-headed social scientist, who despite herself believed in Driscoll's integrity—that he would live the message he preached. We might say, how naïve is that? But as we have shown in this book, the desire to believe in a leader's powers has a strong impact on hearts and minds. Many of us seek the guidance of a leader, someone to give us a desire that we can believe in and inspire in us the will to follow it. And, of course, for many megachurch members, this desire and thought makes a life worth living. Charisma is not always bad or evil by any means. It answers questions that all humans want answered: What should I desire? For what should I give my life? Whom shall I follow and to whom shall I give my ultimate loyalty? Charisma can do great good and it can lead people to great heights. But any good that is as powerful as charisma must be dealt with carefully and with a scrupulous sense of prudence. Megachurches, as we have shown in this book, create powerful answers to the perennial questions that rise in the human heart and in human communities. And, of course, not all charismatic leaders are morally upright or wise, nor are all morally corrupt. In fact, we would argue that most are trying to do the best they can. Some fail. Not all, but the megachurch failures profiled in this section of our book provide a guide and demonstrate when and how things can and do go wrong. It is a warning guide of sorts: not all that shimmers is gold. But equally so, not all that calls us to a powerful vision is a fraud. So our interest and intent is to discern the one from the other.

Some might say that megachurches are prone to scandal. This seems to be a common take in the press, and a general suspicion of many outsiders,

[7] Johnson, *Biblical Porn*, 4; Brian Mussumi, *Politics of Affect* (Cambridge: Polity, 2015), vii, ix.

and it isn't surprising, as cases of megachurch scandals are publicized frequently. In fact, no research shows that megachurches are more prone to scandal than smaller churches. It may be that we are more likely to hear about megachurch scandals because megachurches, due to their size and finances, garner more media attention. On the other hand, it is certainly true that megachurches, because of their resources, create greater temptation for malfeasance, and many megachurches function independently without any denominational oversight. Small congregations with dwindling budgets have little opportunity to commit embezzlement or emotional manipulation, whereas megachurches, with their large budgets and outsized affect, have plenty.

Scott Thumma has shown and argued that the structure of megachurches may lead to an authoritative environment with little accountability that can lead to sexual misconduct and other abuses:

> the organizational structures in place (a successful charismatic leader, with centralized power, few checks and balances, and perhaps inadequate management and leadership training) clearly allow for this possibility (Schaller 1992). The claims of abuse by leadership and a lack of accountability, especially for nondenominational megachurches, are frequent charges heard from former members and external critics. Jack Hyles, minister of the large First Baptist Church of Hammond, Indiana, his son and several staff members have all been accused many times in recent years of sexual and authority abuses. Hyles has denied the allegations; however, they continue to plague his ministry (Elder 1990). Chapel Hill Harvester Church in Atlanta has also had numerous charges of sexual and authority abuse made against its leadership (Thumma 1996a).[8]

Most recently, Bill Hybels, the well-known pastor and, for many, the nominal leader of the American megachurch movement, has become entangled in controversy. In spring 2018 during the height of the #MeToo movement, Hybels stepped down from his pulpit after the *Chicago Tribune* reported multiple

---

[8] Scott Thumma, "Exploring the Megachurch Phenomena: Their Characteristics and Cultural Context," revised excerpt from "The Kingdom, the Power, and the Glory: Megachurches in Modern American Society," doctoral dissertation, Emory University, 1996, accessed January 21, 2018, (http://hirr.hartsem.edu/bookshelf/thumma_article2.html). In the quoted text, Thumma cites Lyle E. Schaller, *The Seven-Day-a-Week Church* (Nashville: Abingdon Press, 1992); Lee Elder, "Allegations Continue to Hound Fundamentalist Hyles," *Christianity Today*, September 24, 1990, 45–46; and Scott Thumma, "Megachurches of Atlanta," in *Religions of Atlanta*, edited by Gary Laderman (Atlanta: Scholars Press, 1996).

"allegations that Hybels made suggestive comments, extended hugs, an un-
wanted kiss and invitations to a staff member to hotel rooms. The newspaper also reported allegations of a consensual affair with a married woman,
and the woman who said she had an affair later retracted her allegations."[9]
Hybels has defended himself for the last several years against allegations of
inappropriate behavior directed at women from his staff. Hybels's defense, in
which he frames himself as the harmless victim, follows a well-worn track
taken by megachurch pastors, arguing that he had innocently put himself in
danger: "[I] placed myself in situations that would be far wiser to avoid. I was
naive . . . I commit to never putting myself in similar situations again."[10]

After Hybels's comments, and the defense by his elders and his handpicked
successors, accusations began to mount and the thin cloak of Hybels's excuses
disintegrated. Indeed, Hybels's denials of wrongdoing, and his own veiled
attacks against the women, were replaced by hurried apologies. Hybels's
successors made mea culpas, knowing that their positions were precarious
at best. Scot McKnight, a leading scholar and evangelical theologian who
followed the case carefully, picked the carcass of the soft patriarchalism as
it buckled under the weight of evidence that utterly undercut the original
denials and prevarications:

> What I do know is this: Bill Hybels and Willow Creek's leadership
> have undone forty years of trust for many. A church that has stood val-
> iantly for women in ministry, that has always stood for Christian grace
> and truth and forgiveness for repenters, that has supported #metoo
> in various places, *that then responds to women as they did to these women*
> unravels the thread Willow has woven for four decades. Many of us
> are asking why Bill Hybels and Willow Creek's pastors and Elders
> slandered the women, calling them liars and colluders, and still refuse
> to offer them apologies. Willow is being undone as we watch, and the
> pastors and Elders are at the center of the unraveling.[11]

Hybels's dramatic plunge betrays a nearly Icarian fall from grace. Hybels, a
hero and exemplar of the American megachurch movement, came too close to

[9] Sarah Pulliam Bailey, "Megachurch Pastor Bill Hybels Resigns from Willow Creek after
Women Allege Misconduct," *Washington Post*, April 11, 2018, accessed June 24, 2018 (https://
www.washingtonpost.com/news/acts-of-faith/wp/2018/04/10/bill-hybels-prominent-megachurch-
pastor-resigns-from-willow-creek-following-allegations/?utm_term=.d48f5c9c2e99).
[10] Bailey, "Megachurch Pastor."
[11] Scot McKnight, "About Willow Creek: What Do I Think?" *Patheos*, June 27, 2018, accessed July
15, 2018 (http://www.patheos.com/blogs/jesuscreed/2018/06/27/about-willow-creek-what-do-i-think/
?platform=hootsuite). Emphasis in original.

the sun, and his wings were not only burned by his failure, but torn from his back. And it's not only the man who fell; it's one of the principal exemplars of the megachurch phenomenon who imploded. Hybels will be seen as an archetypal megachurch pastoral meltdown. At the same time, Hybels's downfall seems as vanilla as they come: a pastor who breached sexual boundaries and abused the women closest to him, even as he seemingly built them up. Hybels betrayed his deepest values.

When Charisma Becomes Destructive

To be sure, it appears that charismatic leadership may increase the likelihood of destructive or scandalous behavior, but we can't say this for sure. We know from Chapter 10 that megachurch pastors tend to be extremely charismatic; they form strong emotional bonds with their attendees. These bonds can be used for their personal gain rather than the benefit of the congregation. Hybels's charisma built a large movement that attracted an enormous following, and from public records it appears that while he may have taken relatively small sums for his salary at Willow Creek, he earned a substantial amount of money from outside consultations and book sales, purchasing a sailboat and a cabin on Lake Michigan.[12]

On the other hand, Rick Warren, the founder and senior pastor of Saddleback Church, exemplifies a much different approach. Warren "paid back" his entire salary to the church; he explained in 2013, "I've been a volunteer Pastor for the last 10 years now. I'm not a professional Pastor, I'm an amateur." Warren explains, "I gave it all back because I didn't want anyone to think that I do what I do because of money. I love Jesus Christ." He continues, "The Bible teaches that we are to love people and use money, but we often get that reversed and you start loving money and using people to get more money. Money is simply a tool to be used for good."[13]

Individuals like Bill Hybels typically have a high degree of emotional intelligence that can be used to influence and control not only their own emotions but also the emotions of others. Their charisma enables them to further their own interests, and we see this in different ways in Hybels and Warren. Warren lives and ministers with integrity; Hybels, not so much.

[12] Michael Frost, "Should a Pastor Ever Own a Private Jet or a Luxury Yacht?," April 23, 2018, accessed June 24, 2018 (https://mikefrost.net/should-a-pastor-ever-own-a-private-jet-or-a-luxury-yacht/).
[13] See Robert Laura, "Pastor Rick Warren Is Well Prepared for a Purpose Driven Retirement," *Forbes*, March 23, 2013, accessed June 24, 2018 (https://www.forbes.com/sites/robertlaura/2013/03/21/pastor-rick-warren-is-practicing-what-he-preaches-and-getting-ready-for-retirement/#7341c6c44dbf).

Nonetheless, charisma generates deep trust from followers and may cause them to ignore the negative qualities in their leader; they may ignore warning signs and instead continue to venerate their leader.[14] This is clearly the case with Hybels, who built up enormous goodwill from his congregation, then used this social capital to attack and destroy the reputation of his accusers. In the end, it did not work—nonetheless, the consequences, as we have seen elsewhere, devastate the life and viability of the churches that they led.

Janet Jacobs describes how charismatic leadership can become abusive and exploitative. She draws on Blau's principle of *least interest*[15] and Emerson's *power dependency theory*[16,17] to explain and understand how charisma becomes destructive. Charismatic leaders have large aggregates of power because they have deep banks of capital (including emotional, spiritual, and sometimes financial) that their followers value and for which there are few close substitutes. While followers depend on the leader for such rewards, the leader has many followers with whom he can have an *emotional exchange relationship,* making him less dependent on any one follower than each is on him. The fact that he has the "least interest" means that he maintains the most power in the relationship:

> The demand for the leader's love is greater and yet it is a limited commodity, allocated sparingly and only to those who are deemed worthy. The value placed on the leader's love is therefore very high, while the value placed on the devotee's love is much less significant because of the availability of this emotional resource among the group members. The inequality of power relations is therefore a function of the emotional exchange.[18]

This surely leads to a cost/benefit analysis by megachurch pastors who know who they must keep happy while pacifying the masses with their simple presence. For those who are outside his intimate circle, the megachurch pastor must act as if he cares for these people, whom he either does not know, or does not have the time to get to know. With charisma and a following, pastors can overpromise and get away with it, since the power and interest

[14] Janet Jacobs, "The Economy of Love in Religious Commitment: The Deconversion of Women from Nontraditional Religious Movements," *Journal for the Scientific Study of Religion* 23 (1984): 155–171.
[15] Peter Blau, *Exchange in Social Life* (New York: Wiley, 1964).
[16] Richard Emerson, "Power Dependence Relations," *American Sociological Review* 27 (1962): 31–41.
[17] Jacobs, "The Economy of Love"; Janet Jacobs, "Deconversion from Religious Movements: An Analysis of Charismatic Bonding and Spiritual Commitment," *Journal for the Scientific Study of Religion* 26 (1987): 294–308.
[18] Jacobs, "The Economy of Love," 168.

in the relationship is so unequal. Church members, as we saw throughout this study, consistently expressed excuses for their pastors: "He is so busy, he doesn't have time to come to the hospital." Megachurch members frequently expressed awe when their pastor greeted them with a casual "Hello," when they know he "could be talking to someone else and has so many more important things to do." They feel lucky just to be in the presence of the leader.

The power of presence and relative closeness to the charismatic leader has a long history, particularly in the Christian tradition. Energy, upon touch, emanates from the religious leader or saint. Power is transferred into the follower or seeker. Jesus himself, when touched, recognizes this energy exchange; he describes it as coming at a cost:

> And there was a woman who had had a discharge of blood for twelve years, and though she had spent all her living on physicians, she could not be healed by anyone. She came up behind him and touched the fringe of his garment, and immediately her discharge of blood ceased. And Jesus said, "Who was it that touched me?" When all denied it, Peter said, "Master, the crowds surround you and are pressing in on you!" But Jesus said, "Someone touched me, for I perceive that power has gone out from me." And when the woman saw that she was not hidden, she came trembling, and falling down before him declared in the presence of all the people why she had touched him, and how she had been immediately healed. And he said to her, "Daughter, your faith has made you well; go in peace." While he was still speaking, someone from the ruler's house came and said, "Your daughter is dead; do not trouble the Teacher any more." But Jesus on hearing this answered him, "Do not fear; only believe, and she will be well."[19]

That is, the charismatic leader, and in this case the megachurch pastor, may well be in a superior position to his followers, but that doesn't mean that there isn't a cost to the leader in his interactions with followers. In the senior author's research on Rob Bell, I attended several of his sermons at Mars Hill Church in Grand Rapids, Michigan. On each occasion, I greeted him following the service. Each service was attended by more than 3,000 people. My biggest takeaway was how exhausted he looked, as if he had been run through a gauntlet of sorts. The cost to charismatic leaders is underestimated, and without making excuses for their misbehaviors, problems arise not only from exhaustion but also from isolation—no one really understands their position.

---

[19] See Luke 8:43–50, English Standard Version Anglicized.

Again, in the case of Bell, in one of our interviews, he described how in his first year of his ministry at Mars Hill, the church exploded in growth, with close to 10,000 people streaming into the services each Sunday. Bell explained that on many occasions, he and his wife looked at each other and said, "What are we going to do?" The toll in those years was enormous. Near the end of my research on Rob Bell, he quit and moved to Los Angeles to start a new career as an independent author and speaker. Later, when I visited him in LA he looked utterly transformed; relieved of the duties of the pastorate, he was free.[20] At the time, I told him what I most missed about his work were his sermons. I, too, wished he was still in the pulpit. I had joined the charismatic bond; like his parishioners, I wanted my needs met. This is precisely the burden that these megachurch pastors continue to carry.

This burden in no way rationalizes the abuse done by megachurch pastors. But we do think the research is lacking on the toll taken by these pastors as they bear and maintain this charismatic bond. The question of whether they should be doing this is another question altogether, but it's clear that many people, myself included, felt the draw, and even secular scholars, as we saw between Jessica Johnson and Driscoll, can feel a pull that seems irresistible. This tendency to seek and be drawn into these charismatic bonds may very well be written into our DNA. Powerful leaders are needed and wanted, and so dissecting and understanding how they work and how they abuse their offices is more important than ever.

Megachurch Scandals and a Theory of Soft Patriarchalism

For all the publicity given to megachurch scandals, there has been surprisingly little research done on the phenomenon. We begin with our theory on sexual abuse, including how it occurs in megachurches and why. To be sure, these kinds of sex scandals are part of a long history of mostly male abuse of subordinates, who are usually women. Janet Jacobs's study of New Religious Movements identified that sexual relations with the movement leader are typically expected. In these movements, intimate contact with the spiritual leader of the group often has been considered a reward.[21] It was not uncommon for women to express a desire for sex with the leader because he personified God, and

---

[20] See James K. Wellman, Jr., *Rob Bell and the New American Christianity* (Nashville, TN: Abingdon Press, 2012).
[21] Jacobs, "The Economy of Love."

union with him was "understood as a union with an ultimate being or reality whose human expression is found in the person of the guru."[22] A sexual relationship with the leader expressed a "desire for spiritual fulfillment."[23] Of course, not all the women felt or experienced these sexual relationships as fulfilling; some felt that they were coerced or manipulated into them. While megachurch pastors are themselves not viewed as god(s), they *are* viewed as divinely inspired, vehicles for God's message, and embodiments of the Holy Spirit who have a special relationship with God. Given this, it is not surprising that some women may desire to have a sexual relationship with the megachurch pastor, who is viewed as close to God, and some may engage in a relationship with the pastor through coercion, due to the principle of least interest.[24] But this entire phenomenon needs to be examined as a part of a longer tradition. Is abuse of women by male religious leadership a "normal" aspect of human communities?

We argue there is a longer tradition of bias at work in both the congregational and scholarly disinterest in pastoral scandals, and the fact that they are dominantly perpetrated by male leaders against female persons. Again, we were struck that no systematic work has been done on megachurch scandals. It is not because these scandals have been hidden or few. We suggest that some of this disinterest is due in part to the taken-for-granted nature of religious patriarchy, perhaps until recently (with some exceptions)[25] and with noted exceptions in liberal Protestant denominations (with the rise of female clergy and elders and a strong level of accountability in clergy selection). There is also some scholarly work and research being done by scholars who work on religious extremism and fundamentalism. Martin Riesebrodt theorized the rise of fundamentalism in the modern period in Muslim and American Protestant traditions as a *patriarchal protest movement*.[26] Riesebrodt argues that the galvanizing motive behind the male backlash against modernity has been a renewed and relentless interest in patriarchal power. Riesebrodt identifies this motive as the root cause of the Iranian Revolution and the

---

[22] Jacobs, "The Economy of Love," 162.

[23] Jacobs, "The Economy of Love," 162.

[24] The female attendees only have one senior pastor, whereas the senior pastor has many female attendees. Thus, the female attendees are more dependent on their senior pastor then he is on them. The senior pastor has the least interest in any particular female attendee, as he has other options, whereas the female attendees have more interest in their senior pastor. See Jacobs, "The Economy of Love" for further description of the principle of least interest in application to religious groups.

[25] For exceptions, see Brenda E. Brasher, *Godly Women: Fundamentalism and Female Power* (New Brunswick, NJ: Rutgers University Press, 1998).

[26] See Martin Riesebrodt, *Pious Passion: The Emergence of Modern Fundamentalism in the United States and Iran* (Berkeley: University of California Press, 1993).

resurgence in the mid-twentieth-century movement of American Protestant Fundamentalism. To be sure, in both cases, strong authoritarian male leadership is paramount, along with pushback against modern views on gender equality in the wake of increasing rights for the LGBTQ community. One can see a similar kind of resurgence among white nationalists in America as well as in select European, Hindu, and Muslim countries like Turkey, India, and Russia.[27] A similarly authoritarian male president has emerged in India as well. In each tradition a strong authoritarian male figure is featured, and the rights of women and minorities are diminished. Likewise, these countries' more traditional and patriarchal religious traditions fall in line behind authoritarian exemplars.

Thus, we might ask why the relative silence on the issue of clergy scandal? Why the tendency to overlook these scandals, particularly within the megachurch literature? As Janet Jacobs reflects and suggests, this is a part of a much longer trajectory of male rights and dominance in family life, and a tradition in which females were, by law and by tradition, subordinate to males. That is, within Western culture, there is a taken-for-granted notion that males should and will be in charge, and that this is "natural." This clearly has contributed to the general tendency to overlook megachurch scandals, or to assume that this is just a part of what happens in these cultures—after all, "men will be men." We suggest that both are true: scandals are both overlooked and ignored. What Jacobs highlights is a longer tradition of Western male dominance and patriarchy that was a deliberate part of the social, sexual, economic, and political movement to re-inscribe a form of patriarchy that could withstand the changing times. She explains,

> Here, the work of Friedrich Engels is both informative and insightful. In his classic groundbreaking text, *The Origin of the Family, Private Property, and the State* (1884), Engels elaborates a theory of male dominance and female subordination from an evolutionary perspective. According to Engels, the shift from a hunter-gatherer culture to an agricultural-based economy based on private property led to a system of power and dominance wherein men gained control over land, tools, and ultimately women and children, whose dependence on male providers left them both vulnerable and powerless. This new economic arrangement gave rise to the patriarchal family, which in turn became the foundation for development of other social institutions such as

---

[27] See Basharat Peer, *A Question of Order: India, Turkey and the Return of the Strongmen* (Columbia Global Reports, 2017) and Timothy Snyder, *The Road to Unfreedom: Russian, Europe and America* (Tim Duggan Books, 2018).

religion and government, which reinforced notions of male supremacy. (Engels 1884)[28]

Jacobs explains that, in this way, contemporary authoritarian movements "reproduce earlier religious cultures in which women are treated as the property of charismatic leaders and as sexual commodities."[29] We argue that this tradition of patriarchy is hardly a thing of the past; power structures that dominate and fuel megachurch culture *depend on* a gender ideology of clear gender/sex distinctions and roles, including female submission to a male leader. However, since this structure has been negotiated and reframed for the twenty-first century so that, while it is still largely reproduced, it has become rationalized and somewhat covert, we might call its manifestation within American megachurches a form of *soft patriarchy*. That is, we have found little evidence of pastors or churches explicitly demanding the subordination of women to men (though we cite some exceptions), or the demand that by right, men have all rights over women. Nonetheless, it is clear from our work that, in addition to patriarchal marriage rhetoric, a vast majority of megachurches are run by men, and most of their boards are dominated by men. Ironically, perhaps, considering Hybels's recent scandal and early retirement, he helped to hire one of the first female lead megachurch pastors—Pastor Heather Larson—to replace him at Willow Creek (of course her leadership was "balanced" by her male co-pastor). And yet a mere four months after Pastor Larson took the helm, her career became one of Hybels's casualties; the trust between the congregation and its leadership had been so severely broken by Hybels's transgressions, and the leadership's mishandling of them, that she resigned.

We are not arguing that there is always a conscious hidden agenda in megachurches where men seek to exploit women, and yet, it still happens— and it has largely gone unexamined by scholars. Why? Again, without suggesting a large-scale conspiracy, it is clear that a patriarchal structure is preferred, reinforced, and expected—and, moreover, it is portrayed as fulfilling a divine plan, even if women's subjugation and men's domination is not made explicit. Thus, although we believe this is a form of soft patriarchy, it is a pervasive patriarchy nonetheless. That is, in most of these churches, women are highly honored, and yet rarely do they seek high levels of leadership or speak about the need for equality in leadership for women, as far as we

---

[28] Janet Jacobs, "Abuse in New Religious Movements: Challenges for the Sociology of Religion," in *Teaching New Religious Movements*, edited by David G. Bromley, 231–244 (New York: Oxford University Press, 2007), 235–236.
[29] Jacobs, "Abuse in New Religious Movements," 237.

have seen. Hence, patriarchy that is soft gives paramount leadership to men without having to boast about it or demand it, or even put it into bylaws. Thus, it can deny any accusations of sexism, making it all the more insidious. And yet, it is assumed and often hinted that male leaders are preferred, and perhaps even necessary, to enable the church and the men themselves to fulfill their purpose.

In addition, and this is not an uncommon argument, it is suggested that male-dominated leadership may keep men interested in church. It solidifies a male presence and may make coming to church feel more comfortable for men who might otherwise be turned off by a female-dominated space. Male pastors can also serve as role models to men, inspiring discipline and leadership in male members—giving them the task and "honor" of leading a church, leading their families, being the "head" of their marriage and family. Thus, a soft patriarchy is presented as a way to manage men's energies, bodies, and desires and enable women to create stable homes, to be protected financially and otherwise, and in the long run to sustain order in the community.

PROBING CONTEMPORARY MEGACHURCH SCANDALS

To research megachurch scandals, we used the Google News search engine, which produced eighty-five pages of results with roughly eight to ten news stories on each. We used the title and abstract description to determine if the article was relevant and, if it was, we included it in our analysis. For each article we collected the source, author, date of publication, website link, church and person/people involved in the scandal, the type of scandal, and whether there was an admission or finding of guilt (see Appendix C for our list of megachurch scandals). We identified fifty-six megachurch scandals discussed in forty-eight articles for the years 2006 to 2017, with nearly all articles published between 2012 and the present. We identified five main types of scandal: (1) sex, (2) finance, (3) violence, (4) drugs or alcohol, and (5) other (all other types, typically representing scandals for which vague descriptions were given such as "moral failings"). Some scandals involved more than one type. In nearly eight out of ten of these scandals the perpetrator or focal actor was the megachurch senior pastor. Again, men dominate these positions—though, of course, in some of these contexts, women either support the abuser or participate in the abuse.[30]

---

[30] Paul Crouch, cofounder of Trinity Broadcasting Network, allegedly gave $425,000 to a man he had sex with to keep him quiet. His wife, Jan Crouch, also helped to cover up the story. See https:// www.christianitytoday.com/ct/2004/septemberweb-only/9-13-11.0.html for a full and fair account of the legal battle.

Sex Scandals

Most megachurch scandals involve sexual abuse, usually perpetrated by a male, senior pastor. Sixty-one percent of the scandals involved sex (34 cases out of 56). Of those, eighteen admitted to the behavior or were found guilty of it in a court of law. We further subdivided sex scandals by subtypes: (a) affairs or inappropriate sexual relationships; (b) criminal sexual relationships involving minors; (c) not informing the police of sexual abuse, attempting to cover it up, or facilitating it in some way; and (d) same-sex relationships. We could not subtype one case due to the vagueness of the description "sexual impurity." Nearly half of these cases were men who had affairs or inappropriate sexual relationships. We give examples of the abuse and map how and why we characterize this as a form of *soft patriarchalism*.

Senior Pastor Mark Connelly of the Mission Community Church—a megachurch in Phoenix, Arizona, with 6,200 regular attendees—resigned after he was forced to admit to having multiple affairs. A *Phoenix New Times* online article, which detailed the accusations and Connelly's resignation, featured a letter from the church's leadership, the Board of Servant Leaders, accepting Connelly's resignation and asking for prayer for him. Connelly had "confessed the affairs" and had resigned. The newspaper article loaded a popular video that Connelly had recently released that featured his call for more "Mighty Men." In the sound-only video, Connelly berates men who fail to "lead their homes." He shouts,

> We have enough of men who give up on the marriage when the going gets tough, we have enough of those men. We have enough men who are too lazy to read the scripture and train up their kids in the knowledge of the Lord, but they have hours to spend in front of fantasy football, video games, television and pornography. We have enough of those men. We need more mighty men. We need men who will valiantly fight for their marriages. We need men who will fight for the hearts of their children. We need mighty men who will courageously lead their families. We need mighty men who will lead the church. We need mighty men who will boldly speak the name of Jesus wherever they go. We need mighty men![31]

Besides the obvious hypocrisy of this video, which came out on January 7, 2014, shortly before Connelly stepped down, it features words from the

---

[31] Matthew Hendley, "Mark Connelly, Phoenix-Area Megachurch Pastor, Resigns over Alleged Affairs," *Phoenix New Times*, January 6, 2014, accessed June 24, 2018 (http://www.phoenixnewtimes.com/news/mark-connelly-phoenix-area-megachurch-pastor-resigns-over-alleged-affairs-6636117).

Board of Servant Leaders. Connelly's call to be mighty men is not the rough sense of patriarchal power that is based on coercion, but instead is a call to men to become servant leaders to their families and children. It is a call to take their families under their guidance and care, and to serve their children with "lovingkindness." So, while Connelly's voice is stern and commanding, the call is to a type of *soft patriarchalism* that does not lead by explicit force, but one that, while voiced with a sense of authority, is supposed to exhibit actions that are oriented toward tender, loving care.

Connelly's servant philosophy comes directly out of a 1960s human potential movement called *servant leadership*.[32] Robert Greenleaf coined the term, and it became influential in multiple social and civic spheres, including corporate leadership. Connelly adapts this philosophy, using it to buffer his soft patriarchalism, which suggest that males become leaders precisely when they become servants. Connelly's form of patriarchy uses the language of a contemporary corporate movement to push men to be the kind of patriarchs that are willing, ultimately, to give their lives for a calling greater than themselves, led by men who follow Christ into their families and into the world as servant leaders. Men become leaders by becoming servants.

This rhetoric of soft patriarchalism, in fact, is derived in part from the early pastoral advice given to the first Christian churches. In Paul's letter to the church at Ephesus, his principal point of mission to Asia Minor, Paul exhorted men to give themselves to their families as Christ gave himself for the church:

> Wives, submit yourselves to your own husbands as you do to the Lord. For the husband is the head of the wife as Christ is the head of the church, his body, of which he is the Savior. Now as the church submits to Christ, so also wives should submit to their husbands in everything. Husbands, love your wives, just as Christ loved the church and gave himself up for her to make her holy, cleansing her by the washing with water through the word, and to present her to himself as a radiant church, without stain or wrinkle or any other blemish, but holy and blameless. In this same way, husbands ought to love their wives as their own bodies. He who loves his wife loves himself. After all, no one ever hated their own body, but they feed and care for their body, just as Christ does the church—for we are members of his body.

[32] Robert Greenleaf came up with the concept of servant leadership partly from reading Herman Hesse's *Journey to the East*. Greenleaf came from the corporate world (AT&T), and corporate leaders like Ken Blanchard and Stephen Covey became leaders within the movement, which spread across many spheres. See https://www.greenleaf.org/what-is-servant-leadership/.

"For this reason a man will leave his father and mother and be united to his wife, and the two will become one flesh." This is a profound mystery—but I am talking about Christ and the church. However, each one of you also must love his wife as he loves himself, and the wife must respect her husband. (Ephesians 5:22–33, NIV)

In Biblical scholarship, there is much dispute over whether this was a Pauline communication, due to the impersonal nature of the letter. Paul had spent considerable time in the city of Ephesus, building the church, and yet, there are no personal words to the church in the letter. Nonetheless, the family ethic described in the letter systematized the dominant Christian family ethic, and aptly portrays the kind of soft patriarchal ethic that we are suggesting. This ethic, while giving headship in families to men, obligates them to a code of self-sacrifice—a husband and father should sacrifice himself for the family as Christ gave himself for the church. Thus, even within a society where the patriarchy was strongly enforced by law, Christian groups had already begun legitimating male dominance with the rhetoric of soft patriarchy.

The Christian family ethic stood out as quite distinct from the Greco-Roman world. Greco-Roman family life featured a *paterfamilias* who as father had absolute rights over his family's life, wealth, and freedom. The father's power, or *patri potestas*, gave him absolute sovereignty in matters of life and death. To be sure, soft patriarchalism seems an improvement over the Greco-Roman family; nonetheless, for many today any type of patriarchy appears as an unwelcome hangover and echo from the 1950s. Either way, evangelicals call men to exhibit an ethic of sacrificial care and love for their wives and children. Male power is expressed in a leadership of self-sacrificial care, and despite the hypocrisy of the megachurch scandals, the core ethic of evangelical Christian family life is one of self-sacrificial lovingkindness.

We are not bringing up this biblical account of marriage and parenting to excuse or rationalize the scandals in the megachurches that we are studying, but simply to trace their historical roots. Whether scripture justifies this behavior is a much disputed question.[33] To be sure, for some, the power imbalance implicit in soft patriarchalism is precisely what opens the door to the abuse. And contemporary evangelicals are not unaware of this problem. In fact, the most famous strategy to overcome the temptation of exploitation for traditional American evangelicals is the Billy Graham Rule. Graham, from the beginning of his ministry, vowed never to be alone in the presence of a

---

[33] See Martin Reisebrodt, *Pious Passions: The Emergence of Modern Fundamentalism in the United States and Iran* (University of California Press, 1998).

woman other than his wife, Ruth. Of course, progressive evangelicals argued that this rule would preclude women from leadership positions, in large part, because of the "weakness" of men. Many progressive evangelicals view this as antiquated, even as the US vice president, Mike Pence, has evoked it as his way to protect himself and the women with whom he works.[34] The irony of this is that one of the signal features of Jesus's ministry was precisely his willingness to talk, serve, and minister to and with women, not only those who were Jews, but also "foreigners" and the despised in his day—both serving them and seeing them as disciples.[35]

And, to be sure, conservative megachurch pastors are not the only ones who instigate these scandals. Our second example comes from what can be called the progressive-evangelical side of the evangelical Protestant movement. Earl Paulk, Jr., a Pentecostal minister from Atlanta, led a 15,000-member megachurch. Although traditional in his evangelical theology, he reached out to African Americans and to the gay community during his tenure as archbishop of the Cathedral of the Holy Spirit at Chapel Hill Harvester Church. Paulk's ministry reached its zenith in the 1990s, with President George H. W. Bush marking him as the one of the "thousand points of light" for his service in racial reconciliation and outreach in the Atlanta area. Nonetheless, complaints of affairs with women followed Paulk throughout his ministry. The truly astounding revelation came in October 2007, when a court-ordered paternity test revealed that he was the father of his brother's son, D. E. Paulk. The latter was a rising star in the ministry, and this revelation not only undercut Paulk's credibility, but torpedoed his church and legacy.

D. E. Paulk had been groomed as the inheritor of the mantle, but this "son" of Earl Paulk went a different direction. Out of the rubble of his "father's" ashes, he diverged from his family's Christian and evangelical roots, and started what he called "The Spirit and Truth Sanctuary." While the organization was styled on the ethos and tactics of evangelical call and response, it is an interfaith religious organization celebrating all faiths as "pathways" to "spirit and truth."[36] While D. E. Paulk recovered his own independent sense

---

[34] See Tish Harrison Warren, "It's Not Billy Graham Rule or Bust," *Christianity Today*, April 27, 2018, accessed July 8, 2018 (https://www.christianitytoday.com/ct/2018/april-web-only/its-not-billy-graham-rule-or-bust.html).

[35] See "Jesus Talks with a Samaritan Woman at the Well," John 4:1–26, and Ben Witherington, *Women in the Ministry of Jesus: A Study of Jesus' Attitudes to Women and Their Roles as Reflected in His Earthly Life* (Cambridge: Cambridge University Press, 1987), 39–41.

[36] See the history and description of Spirit and Truth here: http://www.mytruthsanctuary.com/aboutus_history.html#earlbio.

of his ministry, he failed to duplicate the grandeur of his father's megachurch success. He "only" draws 400 to 600 followers for his interfaith fellowship, a shadow of the tens of thousands his paternal father drew.[37]

Most megachurch scandals involve some form of sexual impropriety— while most relate to allegedly consensual adultery, nearly 20% involve sexual crimes against minors. The egregious nature of these encounters is almost too profane to describe, but the story of Jack A. Schaap, who dominated his region as senior pastor of the 15,000-member First Baptist Church in Hammond, Indiana, captures the true obscenity of these encounters. Schaap admitted to having sex with a minor who attended his church. His "spiritual counseling" with teenagers turned into religious foreplay for the sake of seduction and criminal activity. This action, while horrific in and of itself, was just one aspect of this man's corruption. His preaching often turned sermons into a grotesque foreplay; during one sermon at a youth convention, he demonstrated, quite literally and explicitly, how to "polish the shaft" of the "sword of faith."[38] Schaap, after being found guilty of sex with a minor, sought to blame the victim for his actions, arguing that he should not receive the ten-year minimum prison sentence because his victim aggressively pursued him. In response, federal prosecutors released twenty-three pages of additional details regarding the pastor's abuse.[39] This report included text messages and statements from the victim describing how Schaap used his spiritual authority to justify the abuse: [Schaap said this] "is exactly what Christ desires for us. He wants us to marry + become eternal lovers!"; when the victim asked if it was wrong, "You [Schaap] told me [the victim] that I was sent to you from God; I was his gift to you."[40]

Schaap's abuse of his ministerial privilege is repulsive at best, much less representing what Christians do in the name of Christ. Nonetheless, these scandals aren't uncommon, and often descend quickly into macabre stories of sexual and emotional abuse.

The case of Eddie Long, pastor of the New Birth Missionary Baptist Church in DeKalb County, Georgia, reads like an elaborate seduction liturgy.

---

[37] See John Blake, "How the Ultimate Scandal Saved One Pastor," CNN, March 2015, accessed July 8, 2018 (http://www.cnn.com/interactive/2015/03/living/ultimate-scandal-paulk/).

[38] Schaap's preaching to youth: https://www.youtube.com/watch?v=TroUpQXYkGs.

[39] Schaap's attempt to pass the blame: Bill Dolan, "Ex-megachurch Pastor Blames Underage Victim, Wants Out of Prison," NWI, June 3, 2014, accessed July 8, 2018 (https://www.nwitimes.com/news/local/lake/ex-megachurch-pastor-blames-underage-victim-wants-out-of-prison/article_2ae9324b-eacf-546e-9f73-c12147f5726f.html).

[40] Schaap's record of lies revealed: Suzanne Calulu, "The Delusional Followers of Convicted Felon Jack Schaap," Patheos Blog, November 18, 2013, accessed July 8, 2018 (http://www.patheos.com/blogs/nolongerquivering/2013/11/the-delusional-followers-of-convicted-felon-jack-schaap/).

Long carefully groomed multiple young male sex partners. A sizable percentage of Long's congregation deserted him following the allegations in 2010, but at the funeral for him at his church in 2017, they cheered and spoke of Long as a hero. Long's faithful wife bragged about how proud Long was of the fact that church attendance had rebounded and the "balcony had filled once again." Interviews with the young men whom Long manipulated and groomed, now in their twenties, reveal Long's ingenuity in gaining their trust as well as the pain that he had inflicted. Long prepped these young men and became their "dad," grooming them with gifts, love, and admiration before arguing, finally, that "God wanted us to do [these things]." The young men went from being Long's sons to being his playmates, eventually doing things that were "inappropriate, sexual." One of the young men described his agony in this way: "I no longer trust anyone, people, I just don't trust, it showed me how evil people are."[41] In 2010, Long and his church agreed to an out-of-court settlement with the four young men for being pressured into sexual relationships, the details of which were withheld. Long regained his life and profession as a megachurch pastor; the young men seemed lost at best.

When these behaviors move from manipulation to emotional and sexual abuse, soft patriarchalism moves from a philosophy of leadership to a strategy of abuse. Indeed, nine of the thirty-three sex scandal cases (27%) involved churches or pastors accused of covering up sexual abuse, not informing the police, or being negligent with the hiring and monitoring of employees. The well-known and widely admired Hillsong senior pastor, Brian Houston, was found by an Australian Royal Commission to have failed to notify the police about allegations that his father sexually assaulted children. Houston, upon hearing these allegations, relieved his father of any further ministry to children or youth, though he did not report him to the authorities. It appears that it is common behavior for churches to ignore, bury, or push this information away until it is too late or a victim exposes the crime.[42]

Steve Wingfield, senior pastor of First Christian Church of Florissant near St. Louis, took a six-month sabbatical after he was accused of ignoring warning signs regarding the behavior of one of the church's youth pastors (Brandon Milburn, who has been sentenced to twenty-five years in prison for serial child molestation and sodomy of an eleven-year-old boy). The accusations between

---

[41] See https://www.youtube.com/watch?v=6MEhBY9p1EQ.

[42] See *The Guardian's* excellent reporting on the story: Helen Davidson, "Hillsong's Brian Houston Failed to Report Abuse and Had Conflict of Interest—Royal Commission," *The Guardian*, November 23, 2015, accessed July 8, 2018 (https://www.theguardian.com/australia-news/2015/nov/23/hillsongs-brian-houston-failed-to-report-abuse-and-had-conflict-of-interest-royal-commission).

Wingfield and his accusers were that Wingfield, rather than confronting Milburn and a culture of abuse, instead sued the whistleblowers. He later dropped the suit, and after coming back from his paid sabbatical, became even more stubborn in claiming that he had done everything he could for the sake of protecting the children and youth at his church. When a pastor sues parts of his own congregation, a system of conflict remains and the potential for reconciliation is slim at best. Moreover, Wingfield's actions indicate a strategy to protect a system that has been found to abuse children.[43]

Other megachurch scandals included economic fraud, which characterized 14% of the megachurch scandals. The most salacious and outrageous stories came from overseas, where Senior Pastor Kong Hee, at City Harvest Church in Singapore, was found guilty of using church funds ($50 million) to advance his wife's singing career.[44] In another equally astonishing case, Senior Pastor David Yonggi Cho (founder of the world's largest megachurch) was convicted of embezzling $12 million. It appears that his son, Cho Hee-jun, may have been the true source of the crime, even though Cho used church funds to buy stock from his son's company at triple the market rate. The father took the brunt of the blame for the actions.[45]

Megachurch pastoral violence, while the rarest form of megachurch scandal, was equally egregious. Senior Pastor Creflo Augustus Dollar, Jr., of World Changers Church International at College Park, Georgia, with membership of 30,000 members, was accused of physically assaulting his fifteen-year-old daughter and charged with battery, an action that Dollar denied. The charges were dropped after Dollar agreed to an anger management program.[46] Senior Pastor Thomas Wesley Weeks, Jr., of Global Destiny Christian Community (Washington, DC) was witnessed physically assaulting his wife, "beating, stomping and choking" her—and was later convicted of

---

[43] See the write-up of Pastor Wingfield returning to his church: Danny Wicentowski, "After Six Months Away, Pastor at Center of Church Cover-Up Scandal Returns," *River Front Times*, February 9, 2016, accessed July 8, 2018 (https://www.riverfronttimes.com/newsblog/2016/02/09/after-six-months-away-pastor-at-center-of-church-cover-up-scandal-returns).

[44] The pastor, Kong Hee, continues to claim innocence and asks for prayer. Leah Marie Ann Klett, "Pastor Kong Hee Sentenced to 8 Years in Prison, Admits He Will Face 'Very Difficult Days Ahead,'" *Gospel Herald*, November 20 2015, accessed July 8, 2018 (http://www.gospelherald.com/articles/59943/20151120/city-harvest-church-pastor-kong-hee-saddened-by-length-of-sentence-admits-he-will-face-very-difficult-days-ahead.htm?gclid=EAIaIQobChMI3azkj4KL3AIVEttkCh2M-wY_EAAYASAAEgJ_L_D_BwE).

[45] See Ruth Moon, "Founder of World's Largest Megachurch Convicted of Embezzling $12 Million," *Christianity Today*, February 24, 2014, accessed July 8, 2018 (https://www.christianitytoday.com/news/2014/february/founder-of-worlds-largest-megachurch-convicted-cho-yoido.html).

[46] See the story and Dollar's denial: Steve Almasy, "Megachurch Pastor Creflo Dollar on His Daughter: 'She Was Not Punched,'" CNN, June 10, 2012, accessed July 8, 2018 (http://religion.blogs.cnn.com/2012/06/10/pastor-creflo-dollar-she-was-not-punched/).

aggravated assault. Weeks remarried and returned to full-time ministry.[47] Even when forms of violence are exposed, pastors find ways to revive their ministries—again, a patriarchal culture is willing to forgive and forget certain kinds of dreadful behavior.

We end this section with a reflection and an analysis on same-sex scandals within American evangelical churches. And we note that this behavior may be forgiven, though not forgotten, and pastors rarely rebound once found to have engaged in same-sex behavior. Same-sex relations remain taboo within the majority of American evangelicalism, though with some rare exceptions.[48] The story of Ted Haggard and his New Life Church in Colorado Springs provides a representative case of how evangelicals negotiate these turbulent waters. In 2006, it was revealed that Haggard had been having a sexual affair with a male prostitute.[49] It was a shocking revelation for an evangelical superstar. Haggard dominated the conservative Christian world of that time: pastor of a 14,000-member church, president of the National Association of Evangelicals, and a close relationship to President George W. Bush. It was a catastrophic blow to the name and reputation of the American evangelical church. In the years following Haggard's downfall, he published the story of his recovery, and from public records it seems an accurate tracking of his life.[50] He "confessed" to his wife, Gayle, and they went through a process of reconciliation that Gayle records in a best-selling book.[51] In 2010, Haggard returned to Colorado Springs to start St. James Church, which he pastors today, a much-diminished profile from his earlier self. Haggard now supports legalizing same-sex marriage, as do a third of American evangelicals, though for Haggard, homosexuality remains off limits for Christians.[52] In a sense, it shows the power of the soft patriarchalism that is at the center of American evangelical faith—that is, for most American evangelicals, it is not possible

---

[47] See Encyclopedia.com, "Thomas Weeks III," accessed July 8, 2018 (https://www.encyclopedia.com/education/news-wires-white-papers-and-books/weeks-thomas-iii).

[48] See David Gushee, an evangelical ethicist, *Changing Our Mind: Definitive 3rd Edition of the Landmark Call for Including of LGBTQ Christians with Response to Critics* (Spirit Books, 2017). See also David Gushee's *Following Jesus Out of American Evangelicalism* (Louisville, KY: Westminster John Knox Press, 2017).

[49] See the *New York Times*'s revealing interview with Haggard's "male escort": Deborah Solomon, "The Whistle-Blower," *New York Times Magazine*, June 3, 2007, accessed July 8, 2018 (https://www.nytimes.com/2007/06/03/magazine/03wwln-Q4-t.html).

[50] See http://tedhaggard.com/healing-overview/.

[51] See Gayle Haggard's *Why I Stayed: The Choices I Made in My Darkest Hour* (Carol Stream, IL: Tyndale House, 2010).

[52] See Alex Vandermaas-Peeler, Daniel Cox, Molly Fisch-Friedman, Rob Griffin, and Robert P. Jones, "Emerging Consensus on LGBT Issues: Findings from the 2017 American Values Atlas," PRRI, May 1, 2018, accessed July 8, 2018 (https://www.prri.org/research/emerging-consensus-on-lgbt-issues-findings-from-the-2017-american-values-atlas/).

to be gay and an evangelical Christian. Haggard had to renounce his gay sexual life to be able to return to an evangelical pulpit, and even so, his reputation remains greatly reduced. A soft patriarchalism is one of the primary chastening moral norms of the American evangelical church, and anyone who sins against it faces its disciplining consequences. And to be sure, this ethos and ethic of soft patriarchalism is perhaps *the* critical ethos of what it means to be an evangelical pastor, much less a successful megachurch pastor, in America.

Charismatic senior pastors serve as energy stars, channeling and amplifying emotional energy for their congregations; they act as group symbols in whom congregants place their trust. The megachurch energy star must be an empathic, patriarchal, heterosexual man. Thus, it is no wonder that megachurch pastors who fit this style and ethic can manipulate their congregants' trust and use this emotional bond for their own egoistic purposes. Charisma entails the power to create and destroy communities of faith, and this has been reflected time and again in the megachurches that we have studied. Megachurch charisma acts like a divine elixir that feeds the needs of many who attend the megachurches that we studied, but in a minority of cases this power becomes a tool for some pastors to use and abuse their office. We found where abuse occurs, the churches come apart almost as quickly as they rise. If an equally charismatic leader does not step in, the turnstiles on these massive buildings reverse direction, the money dries up, assistants are let go, and where there was once a buzz, a sense of dread pervades; energy is diffused, and seats are empty. One wonders whether Willow Creek, the grandfather of so many megachurch dreams, is following this same dreary downward spiral.

When Charisma Fails

When Pastor Steve Carter, who had taken on the role of teaching pastor after Bill Hybels's sordid resignation from Willow Creek Community Church, read about the allegations brought against Hybels by his former assistant, Pat Baranowski, he threw up. "I felt like my body was shutting down," he said.[53] After months of supporting and defending Hybels through other allegations, the charismatic bond had finally broken for Carter. His body purged. He then immediately walked home and began drafting his resignation letter. Among

---

[53] Quoted in Emily McFarlan Miller, "Former Willow Creek Pastor Steve Carter Breaks His Silence on Hybels Allegations," *Religion News Service*, September 18, 2018, accessed October 25, 2018 (https://religionnews.com/2018/09/18/former-willow-creek-pastor-steve-carter-breaks-silence-on-hybels-allegations/)

other things, he realized how poorly all of the "leaders" surrounding Hybels had mismanaged the scandal.

Scot McKnight, a New Testament scholar and one of the most influential evangelical scholars and bloggers, attended Willow Creek for ten years. He recently articulated Willow Creek's "autonomy" as the core cause of the devolution of Willow Creek. The independence enabled the church to innovate and change on a dime, but with limited external accountability, McKnight argued such freedom and power is prone to corruption:

> Autonomous churches therefore have *autonomous pastors*, and that means these pastors have *no one to whom they answer other than the Elders/Deacons*. Goodness is beyond needed for such pastors because the temptations of a pastor away from goodness are toward power and toward celebrity. It is not uncommon in autonomous churches with autonomous pastors that Elders or Deacons are "on the side" of the pastor. If goodness is present, no problem; if not, enter problems.[54]

Megachurch pastors, who usually sit outside denominational or ecumenical authoritative bodies, have few guardrails to keep them on track. According to McKnight, without a superabundance of "goodness," megachurch pastors are frequently able to do and be whatever they want, and as we've seen, in a small minority of cases, all hell can break loose. As we have seen repeatedly in our examination of megachurch scandals, these pastors use a form of soft patriarchalism to cover their misbehavior, often rationalizing it theologically, frequently hiding it, and consistently getting away with it. In fact, in many cases, by the time the scandal breaks, the pattern of deception is as disturbing as the original crime. In these cases, it is usually too late—parishioners are hurt and damaged, all trust is lost, and not only does the megachurch lose its charisma, but the cover-up of the scandal accelerates the fall, often pulling the entire superstructure down with it.

As we have noted, trust is key in charismatic relationships, and once trust is broken, the energy star loses his magnetic effect, and the force field of emotional energy becomes the disintegrative vortex of chaos and disorder—as is happening at Willow Creek. A veteran church consultant explained to the senior author in the wake of a scandal at his church, "I've seen this many times, after a scandal half the church stays and defends the pastor, seeking to rebuild the church; the other half lashes out and blames the pastor, half

[54] See Scot McKnight, "Willow: Why the Women Went Public?" *Patheos*, July 9, 2018, accessed July 15, 2018 (http://www.patheos.com/blogs/jesuscreed/2018/07/09/willow-why-the-women-went-public/).

of these folks leave, and the other half stays and make life hell for everyone." In other words, acrimony, fault finding, and the blame game sow discord. And what was once "too good to be true" becomes a forest fire of sadness, recrimination, and regret. The positive sea of emotional energy is replaced by a deluge of negativity, discord, and cynicism.

CHAPTER 15 | Conclusion: Havens of Health or Habitats for the Prosperity Gospel?

A FTER STUDYING THE rise and fall of the megachurch phenomenon, we end with a moral and ethical evaluation of these churches. The dominant assessment of megachurches, in both popular culture and scholarship, is that they tend to be havens of commerce and exploitation, and purveyors of the prosperity gospel. That is, most of these megachurch pastors are in it for the fame and fortune. Perhaps they begin with the genuine intention to serve their people, but in the end they transmute into manipulative marketing agents of their own fame who exploit their parishioners, selling whatever it takes to get the group to make them rich.[1]

And to be truthful, we came into this study with a similar prejudice, feeling that these churches, while wildly successful, were organizations aiming to motivate attendance, but in the end were truly rapacious—taking from their members time, resources, and even their very identity. The surprise, for us, was that after spending five years sifting through and analyzing a wide swath of documents from members in twelve representative American megachurches, looking at people who were long-time members and leaders, those who were new members, and those that were just visiting, we found something quite different. We found wells

[1] See Kate Bowler, *Blessed: A History of the American Prosperity Gospel* (Oxford: Oxford University Press, 2013).

of goodness, satisfaction, generosity, and inspiration. As researchers do, we attempted to get at the truth, as subjective as that might be when it comes to religion and its organizations—realizing all along that the responses of megachurch members, leaders, and visitors were highly subjective and very much based on their emotional reactions to their experiences.

Nonetheless, as we have shown, the genius of these churches, whether always intended or not, was to respond to and meet the deepest needs of their attendees with (1) a spirit of welcome, (2) a sense of deep joy, (3) inspiration from the leader, (4) the possibility of deliverance from regrets and past patterns, (5) the discovery of one's strengths and the sharing of one's weaknesses in fellowship, and finally, (6) the possibility of using one's gifts to serve those in need. These six core human desires became quite clear as we explored the data. And we witnessed that many of these churches transformed neighborhoods and sent missionaries around the country and into the world, bringing relief, medical and otherwise, to domestic and international communities in need.

The senior author, having done intense study of both liberal and evangelical Protestant churches in the past,[2] has consistently found that the common prejudices that outsiders frequently express about members of evangelical churches are often just plain wrong. The prejudices are relatively straightforward—that they are superficial, primarily interested in finding a mate, do not think deeply about their faith, or that they only go to church to feel self-righteous and morally superior. As we have seen in the exposition of the data throughout this book, the six desires that these megachurches meet are profoundly human needs, shaped by culture but reflective of the ways in which humans necessarily develop as individuals and as groups in human cultures. As we discussed early on, we are all *homo duplex*, using Durkheim's felicitous phrase—needing a deep sense of individual validation that is simultaneously reinforced by a human community that nurtures both our individual and social identities. When this happens, as we witnessed time and again in megachurch communities, a sense of *collective effervescence* is experienced. Humans feel and believe they are at the center of the universe, at the right place and right time. It is often what is called a *mountaintop experience,* using evangelical language, a moment of conversion or salvation, a transformative and compelling confirmation of their life's purpose and identity.

In this sense, these megachurches are highly effective and professionalized organizations that have pursued and, we would argue, perfected a response to the deeply human need to be oneself in the presence of another, a community of faith that aligns, affirms, and delineates identity, purpose, and

[2] See James K. Wellman, Jr., *Evangelicals vs. Liberals* (Oxford: Oxford University Press, 2008).

goals. That is, these American megachurches have come up with a way to welcome new people, make them feel that this is a place for them, and invite them into a worship that relates to them and inspires them. They offer polished sermons that are entertaining, uplifting, and inspirational, and that empower listeners to make life-changing decisions that bring them joy, new habits, better relationships, community groups, and a desire to serve their communities and the world. From these mountaintop experiences, megachurch members develop deep and long-lasting friendships and fellowships in which they are motivated to care for others, serve others, and reach out to their neighborhoods and beyond, in charity and goodwill, with a good-news message that they themselves had experienced and cherished.

Megachurches comprise holistic enterprises that not only work well, pragmatically and organizationally, but also achieve the kind of results that any nonprofit, humanitarian organization would envy, whether religious or secular—a robust community that inspires members to love and care, that teaches their children how to be responsible adults, and that motivates members to go out into their communities and into the wider world with charity, grace, and goodwill.

But questions remain, and as we know, not all that shimmers is gold. There are many critics of these churches, both internally in the Christian community and externally in the world of scholarship and nonprofit thinking. And we thought it most interesting to take on in this chapter the common judgment, both among Christian thinkers and those on the outside, that these churches are practitioners of what many call the prosperity gospel. This accusation claims they are essentially the natural outcome of a neoliberal and capitalist enterprise, which reproduces the desires for capital accumulation and market dominance that form the core engine of global hegemony in Western capitalism. As an extension of this question, we will investigate the ways these organizations create and promote a culture of health and wealth. In other words, we'll ask, do these megachurches exist to fleece their members and to support a conservative and capitalist agenda? And even more damning than the health-and-wealth agenda, do these churches, whether implicitly or explicitly, preach the ominous prosperity gospel so loathed by academics and left-leaning critics?

Christianity and Capitalism

The question of whether megachurches are simply a function or confirmation of the Western agenda for global capitalism and worldwide neoliberal economic policies is important and worthwhile, one that has been taken on by internal and external critics of Christianity. One particularly comprehensive, persuasive, and damning critique is found in Daniel M. Bell, Jr.'s *The Economy of Desire: Christianity and Capitalism in a Postmodern World*.[3] Bell's book is also relevant because his chief focus is on human desire. That is, he argues that capitalism and the neoliberal economic order are not simply a system of buying and selling, but a comprehensive system of ordering desires in human beings that introduce and coerce them toward a neoliberal economy. In other words, our desires are disciplined by the market to want certain forms of capital, and we both seek these economic products and produce them because the craving for them has been internalized in our bodies. He explains,

> At its most general level, neoliberal capitalism is about the complete marketization of life. In particular, it is about overcoming the obstacles to and inefficiencies introduced into the market by the Keynesian or welfare-state economics of the previous generation and increasing the integration of the entire globe into the capitalist market. Although it is frequently cast as "anti-government" by both its advocates and proponents, it is in fact fond of a lean, strong state that is "small" with regard to its interference in market processes while nevertheless retaining and even enhancing its strength for the sake of security, particularly in the face of threats to the market.[4]

There is nothing particularly new or controversial here. Most Americans take this type of neoliberalism as the status quo, but that, of course, is the point: we "naturally" assume that markets can most efficiently control the free flow of goods, bringing what most want in the quickest and least costly way to consumers. Nonetheless, the language, too, is critical. We are consumers; we desire something and we want a mechanism that brings us what we want in the most efficient and least costly way to us. Whether this is a book or a church, information or organizations, we consume these products: books tell us what we want, and churches feed our desires and help us to become all that we want to be. We have argued that megachurches are the ecclesiastical institutions that currently do this most precisely and efficiently.

So what is the problem? As Bell suggests, "capitalism is totalizing."[5] It takes every person, action, and product and turns it into something that can be bought and sold. Everything, including our bodies and minds, and in the

---

[3] Daniel M. Bell, Jr., *The Economy of Desire: Christianity and Capitalism in a Postmodern World* (Grand Rapids, MI: Baker Academic, 2012).
[4] Bell, *The Economy of Desire*, 24.
[5] Bell, *The Economy of Desire*, 26.

case of our faith, our religious institutions, can be capitalized—made more efficient, producing greater gains and satisfaction for those that consume them. Again, many will ask, what's the problem here? Isn't life about making things more efficient, even things that we call sacred? And Bell would say, that's precisely the issue—we are so ingrained in the market mentality that everything, including what is most sacred, is capitalized and made efficient to be less costly and more productive. To those who wonder why anyone would even question this line of thinking, Bell responds that this compulsive capitalization is a form of "alienation." Alienation is simply when humans become so caught up in the market that they can no longer distinguish authentic human desires from what the market manipulates them to consume. In plain speak, when all things are capitalized, everything becomes a "thing," something to be bought and sold. But, Bell argues, "theology should be subordinate to economy."[6] He pushes against this capitalization of values: "I am suggesting the opposite: the market economy should be subordinate to theology and so reinforce the virtuous life. For Christians the normative vision of economics should comport with Christian confessions and virtue."[7] And, of course, this begs the question—what are Christian economics? This has a long tradition, which Bell covers—he expertly delineates the ways in which a Christian puts primacy on the intrinsic and unalienable value of the human being as made in the image of God.

To make this distinction, one would say that in Christian terms, humans are sacred and inviolate. That is, humans are sacred and are ends in themselves, not to be discarded, or aborted, or in any way used as a means to an end. They are, to use Kantian ethical terms, ends in themselves. But it is not simply an anthropology of the human; Bell would lay out a Christian economics for the church. What is an economics for the church? *Economy*, from the Greek, is defined as that which describes one's household management. What are the values and principles that form and guide the household—that shape and direct the family of faith, the Christian house, the church? For Bell, this is the central claim for the Christian *oikonomia*—the Christian economy or household. This is the household of God that shapes and defines the desires of the community toward Christian goals. Bell spells out the desires of the Christian household, the economy of God:

[P]eople are for desiring and delighting in God and reflecting God's glory. We are created for friendship, for communion, with God. The

[6] Bell, *The Economy of Desire*, 27.
[7] Bell, *The Economy of Desire*, 27.

Trinity is a communion of love into which we are invited. Of course, this friendship is not merely a matter of me and Jesus. After all, Scripture reminds us we cannot be friends of God if we hate our neighbors (1 John 3:17; 4:20–21) and that redemption involves breaking down the walls of hostility that divide peoples (Eph. 2; Gal. 3:28); hence, the commandments are succinctly summed up in the exhortation that we "love God and neighbor" (Matt. 22:35–40).[8]

From a Christian perspective none of this is surprising or unusual. Of course, this is the Christian calling, to love God, ourselves, and each other; to reach out to neighbors, to care for the orphan, the widow, and the stranger. And here, we ask the question: What might be the problem with making these "Christian desires" consistent with a neoliberal and capitalist enterprise? For Bell, that is the point: Christian ethics are totalizing; they compete against and are in tension with the ethic of the market. The question for capitalism is: How much is it worth? What can one get for this? What's the monetary value of this object or even this person? Once each thing is *capitalized*, the argument goes, persons are *thingified*. Some humans are simply of greater value, and others of less value, and some of no value at all. And in the logic of the market, this makes sense. This distinction clarifies the differences between a neoliberal capitalist desire and the desire within a Christian communion—in the latter, all people, no matter their utility, no matter their value, no matter their ethnicity, no matter their financial potential, no matter their intelligence, national identity, or connections, remain eternally valuable and, by definition, loved by God. In a Christian communion, each person is of eternal value. In a capitalist market, other standards are applied—some humans are more valuable due to intelligence, strength, character, and more malevolently, ethnicity, race, or sexual orientation, depending on the state and circumstance. Acceptance, in a Christian context, is unconditional, and in the capitalist realm, each thing, each person's value is conditioned by calculating their market value.

Most of us don't like to even think in these terms. Of course everyone is valuable, most would say. Humans are not things that can be or should be discarded depending on their value. But in reality, as we can imagine, life is more brutal and more conditional—some humans are discarded, destroyed, or simply seen not to matter. We make decisions about humans based on their relative value. Bell would argue this is the logic of the market; others might argue this is the human community being merciful—some humans, fetuses,

[8] Bell, *The Economy of Desire*, 85.

and so forth should be allowed to die. And more than that, there are others in the Christian community who argue that market values in fact create social and economic conditions that allow for greater numbers of humans to flourish. Michael Novak, the Catholic theologian and thinker, argued for capitalism as compatible with Christianity in *The Spirit of Democratic Capitalism*.[9] Novak makes the case that the triumph of democracy, the free market, and Judeo-Christian values are by far the best combination of values, which have disciplined the West and created more wealth and health than any other culture in human history. Steven Pinker's recent work, *Enlightenment Now: The Case for Reason, Science, Humanism, and Progress*, while agreeing with Novak that progress has occurred, argues that the Enlightenment and secular values are the key factors in undercutting extreme poverty, the dramatic decrease in violence, the rise in literacy and longevity—all of which have set new all-time highs over the last fifty years.[10] Indeed, Pinker is apt to blame religion for many of the problems that continue to plague us, or as he calls them, "outdated mythologies," such as religious terrorism and repressive religious authoritarians. Critics have argued Pinker tends to overlook, rather blithely, the threat of environmental degradation and, more importantly, the threat of nuclear oblivion or the rise of new totalitarian powers seeking global dominance at any cost. In other words, we are not that far from our archaic and premodern habits.[11]

Regardless of these kinds of intellectual intramural conflicts, it would be difficult to argue against the power and progress of modern and capitalist economies. Their ability to transform the world, create mega-cities, and re-create economies nearly overnight is a powerful claim that can and is made. Many are benefiting from the power of modern economies, and not only folks in the developed world; as Pinker shows, a wider spread of economic development has helped peoples the world over. There is little doubt that modern economies must directly deal with climate change, which, at least in part, is a product of modern capitalism. Many argue that the very instruments that helped get us into this dilemma may very well be the ones that help transform our economies toward more sustainable industries. There are signs of change on the horizon, and for the sake of us all, we hope this is where we are all headed.

[9] Michael Novak, *The Spirit of Democratic Capitalism* (Lanham, MD: Madison Books, 1982).

[10] Steven Pinker, *Enlightenment Now: The Case for Reason, Science, Humanism, and Progress* (New York: Viking, 2018).

[11] Samuel Moyn's critique in *The New Republic*: Samuel Moyn, "Hype for the Best: Why Does Steven Pinker Insist That Human Life Is on the Up?" *New Republic*, March 19, 2018, accessed July 15, 2018 (https://newrepublic.com/article/147391/hype-best).

So, what about the Christian church in America? What is the economic philosophy that most follow? What comes to mind is, of course, the prosperity gospel, and many accuse the megachurches of being on the front lines of this movement. But the prevalence of the prosperity gospel isn't really that clear from our data. Our megachurches were certainly motivated toward empowering members to become doers and actors in the world, to serve, empower, and care for those on the outside. There were a few that tilted in the direction of the prosperity gospel, but interestingly, these churches were the two African American megachurches in the study, which were both particularly interested in empowering the entrepreneurial lives of their members. In general, however, the push and motivation in most of the churches was toward helping members find their gifts in order to use them for the sake of one another, their families and community, and the world. All of this was for the sake of service in the name of Jesus Christ. Nonetheless, the prosperity gospel is worth addressing in relation to these issues.

What Is the Prosperity Gospel?

Peter L. Berger, the prolific late sociologist of religion, dominated the American sociology of religion for much of the last half of the twentieth century. Berger had the habit of consistently saying quite plainly what others might be thinking but had not said aloud. Berger was also known as one of those thinkers who, instead of stubbornly sticking to his previous claims, was willing to change his mind if the empirical data convinced him of a new direction. For example, Berger was a strong advocate of the theory of secularization from the 1960s on up to the end of the century, when, through his empirical findings, he found himself shifting toward a new position: while secularization may be the inevitable experience of the West and the developed world, in most of the world, religion had become more important than ever.[12]

Berger hypothesized that global Pentecostalism would soon become the dominant faith of the global south, threatening the status of the Roman Catholic Church, and overwhelming the forms of liberation theology so popular in the 1970s and 1980s. Berger hypothesized that a peculiar form of Weber's Protestant ethic lurked at the heart of this rising global

---

[12] Peter L. Berger, "The Desecularization of the World: A Global Overview," in *The Desecularization of the World: Resurgent Religion and World Politics*, edited by Peter L. Berger (Grand Rapids, MI: Ethics and Public Policy Center and Wm. B. Eerdmans Publishing, 1999), 1–18.

Pentecostalism, not the somber and masochistic ethic of self-denial of the Protestant ethic, but a form of the prosperity gospel that sought not only salvation in the life to come, but also to create churches that served their families, and lifted them above their economic circumstances. The goal was not just to "save" them for the afterlife, but to "better" them in the present world in which they lived. And Berger, who never stopped investigating, writing, and thinking, wrote in 2008 a pithy, and one might say peppery, piece for the late *Books and Culture*, " 'You Can Do It!' Two Cheers for the Prosperity Gospel."[13]

Berger was quite aware that scholars on the right and left despised the prosperity gospel as a parody of faith and a get-rich-quick scheme. As Berger argued, this was not new in the history of Christianity—Roman Catholics long ago honed the craft of collecting coin for the sake of salvation, or in simple terms, church donations as quid pro quo for salvation. Martin Luther upended this profitable manipulation and protested that salvation was not up for sale. But Berger leaves no one off the hook by writing if the conservative prosperity gospel is only a get-rich-quick scheme, then liberation theology, at its core, portrayed the state as the collector of profit and distributor of gain. As Berger would argue, both are, at their hearts, an economic promise, divided only by who gets to control the dollar: on the one hand, the rich capitalist, and on the other, the communist brotherhood. Time has shown that both these schemes had their unique forms of domination:

> It is useful to point out that the materialist distortion of the Christian message is fully shared by the liberation theology of the anti-capitalist left. Only here the material improvement is understood in collective rather than individual terms: put your coin in the collection plate of the revolutionary movement, and the soul of the masses will be freed from the purgatory of capitalist exploitation. Theological suggestion: What is good for the rightist goose is good for the leftist gander.[14]

Berger argues that the gospel relativizes the economic agenda of both the right and left. Berger further claims that the resurrection of Jesus Christ means new life not only for individual believers but for the whole world: all things are "relativized," and all ultimate loyalties must be submitted to the

[13] Peter L. Berger, " 'You Can Do It!' Two Cheers for the Prosperity Gospel," *Books and Culture*, September/October 2008, accessed July 15, 2018 (https://www.booksandculture.com/articles/2008/sepoct/10.14.html).
[14] Berger, " 'You Can Do It!' "

"law of love" in Jesus Christ—who is in all, for all, and through all. Not only is each individual invited into the resurrection, but indeed the whole cosmos is transformed or at least given the hope of transformation because of the death and resurrection of Jesus Christ. It is a world-altering event in history. The Kingdom of God has been inaugurated, in which all things, including the individual and the collective, are reconciled in Christ for the sake of truth, goodness, and beauty. Berger's point is that "all things" are altered, and no realm, whether individual or social, is untouched by the reconciling power of the Kingdom of God, including the realm of the economy.

Berger's Lutheran roots may have tended to separate the realm of spirit from society, but Berger doesn't share this same prejudice. And apropos to our argument, Berger uses the example of a prosperity gospel church that he was studying while in South Africa to make his point. Berger describes the church as a classical Pentecostal and prosperity-oriented megachurch that prioritizes the welfare of the souls in the church, but focuses as well on their economic opportunities. Berger uses Rhema Church, in a suburb outside of Johannesburg, to make his point. The church, while primarily attended by folks from the local townships, included whites from the suburbs. Berger describes a wide mix of Mercedes and BMWs in the parking lot, along with an assortment of more conventional automobiles, as well as very modest transportation—in other words, the congregation had attracted a great swath of people, the poor and the rich, mostly black, but a significant number of whites. One might say, a rather motley gathering of peoples, which the scriptures might call the Kingdom of God: people coming from north and south, east and west, all welcome at this gathering. And then, Berger gives a summation of the message:

> The message from the preacher had two major themes. One: God does not want you to be poor! And two: You can do it! That is, you can do something about the circumstances of your life. Should one quarrel with this message? I'm inclined to think not. Is there a theological warrant to propose that God wants us to be poor? Any more than he wants us to be sick? The prosperity gospel contains no sentimentality about the poor. There is no notion here that poverty is somehow ennobling. In that, speaking sociologically, the prosperity gospel is closer to the empirical facts than a romantic idea of the noble poor—a notion reminiscent of another romantic fiction, the noble savage. Such notions, of course, are always held by people who are not poor and who do not consider themselves to be savages. The notions are patronizing. They are implicit in the famous slogan of liberation theology:

"a preferential option for the poor." Mind you, not *of* the poor, but *for* the poor—pronounced, as it were, from on high.[15]

I studied liberation theology at the University of Chicago Divinity School. I was steeped in the thought that the only intellectually sound theology included this *preferential option for the poor*. What this assumes is that those who are wealthy are, by definition, inadequate or suspicious, and that the real problem and trick was to shift wealth from the hands of the rich to the hands of the people—the poor. Without always saying, this was an economic fix. Berger questions the whole understanding of this program, whether it works for those who receive this manna from heaven, or whether this system is helpful for those at the other end, those with wealth and privilege. From Berger's perspective, Rhema Church shifted the whole argument, that the blessings of God are poured out on God's people, some who will go out and create blessings for others, including economic opportunities; others who will educate; others who will care; and others who will teach, all in the name of Jesus Christ, who saves, redeems, and reconciles the whole world unto himself. This is the message of the reconciliation of all things, not just the economy, not just on race, not just between the rich and poor, but of everything; all things are being reconciled. There is no us and them, rich and poor, black and white—no more separation based on tribe or nationhood, but all are one in Jesus Christ. It is a radical message of reconciliation.

Berger is no sap when it comes to how the prosperity gospel can use magical language to create the dream that "if you wish it, you can become rich." The wish for money rarely produces money, but as Berger knew very well, the Protestant ethic, in terms of empirical data, went hand in hand with much of the success of Western nations. Wealth, as a by-product of disciplined desire and hard work, produced and continues to produce some of the great movements toward human progress. Was it purely based on spiritual motivations? By no means, but the ethic and principles internalized a disciplined ethic of innovation and hard work that followed.[16]

Steven Pinker, hated by the left, surely makes empirically clear that the last fifty years of world history have transformed the globe, mostly due to education and neoliberal policies that have freed people to enter the marketplace and work hard (not always, but often, because of the Protestant ethic) to help make their (and their friends' and families') lives better. It is quite

---

[15] Berger, " 'You Can Do It!' "

[16] See Max Weber, *The Protestant Ethic and the Spirit of Capitalism.* Translated by Talcott Parsons; New York: Scribner, 1958. See also Christian Etzrodt, "Weber's Protestant-Ethic Thesis, the Critics, and Adam Smith," *Max Weber Studies* 8, no. 1 (January 2008): 49–78.

clear that wherever we went to look at megachurches, these churches were changing the lives of members, creating a hub of activity that turned churches into small and large epicenters of care and concern for neighborhoods, often in dire circumstances, teaching them not only the gospel, but forms of education and discipline that changed their lives, made them better parents, community members, and human beings who impacted the communities around them. As we've mentioned throughout this study, the service and work of megachurches have rarely been recorded or reported on, so few are aware of how much care, concern for the lonely, food, resources, parenting, and community service these churches have provided. But just because many of us in educated circles tend to dismiss religious organizations as sources of care and opportunity, we should not overlook what is happening on the ground, empirically.

Indeed, Berger is no innocent; he knows that there are many prosperity gospel leaders out there who manipulate their listeners to get themselves rich. But Berger is also willing to give people, including the poor and desperate, the value of their own judgment. They know what's good for them, and what is fool's gold. Berger ends his essay this way:

> People generally know what is good for them, better than the well-meaning outsider. So do buyers in the marketplace, especially if they are poor. Thus the "consumers" of the prosperity gospel generally know what they are "buying." Specifically, they know that the betterment being promised them is not an illusion, and they know and don't care that their preacher has a swimming pool and drives a Mercedes. If they put money in the collection plate, they generally believe that they are getting good value in return. Thus it is not only patronizing to see them as dupes and victims; it is empirically misleading.[17]

Berger doesn't want to speak for the poor or to tell them what they need, or teach them what they "really" need. And in that sense, it seems to us that he is right—people generally know what's good for them. What we saw in the churches in our study were systems that moved folks through very difficult times, helped them to find ways to overcome most of the problems they come across, and created systems of care and redemption, well researched and thought through, that could help individuals and families find jobs, stay together in their homes, and be served food and other necessities, as well as programs that trained them to in turn care for others: for the poor, the displaced, the refugee, the stranger, the lonely one in the neighborhood, the

[17] Berger, " 'You Can Do It!' "

widow, the naked, the last, least, and the lost. This, after all, is the test of discipleship in Matthew 25:44–45 (NIV): "Then they also will answer, 'Lord, when was it that we saw you hungry or thirsty or a stranger or naked or sick or in prison, and did not take care of you?' Then he will answer them, 'Truly I tell you, just as you did not do it to one of the least of these, you did not do it to me.'"

Conclusion

Do megachurches make mistakes? Yes, they have and they will. We do not mean to build them up to be more than they are, nor do we mean to diminish them simply because that is common opinion in certain circles. We wrote this book because we had a question that came from the data: Is all of this too good to be true? We think we answered that question: megachurches *do* create a system that responds to the deepest longings in the human spirit—the desire to find who they are and to do it in a trusted and loving community. Durkheim was deeply skeptical that humans could maintain the balance between individual equanimity and communal satisfaction. We laid out how megachurches achieve this equipoise between persons and the group—through acceptance, a sense of joy, a leader that inspires and offers deliverance, and a community that accepts, equips, and sends people out to serve. To some extent, in hindsight, we can imagine that this all does look too good to be true. The scandals that we examined prove the case that things can go very wrong. But we also made the point that they can also go quite well, and the overwhelming satisfaction of megachurch members shows this to be true. Do megachurches become tied to their pastors? Of course they do. Many become shadows of their former glory following the retirement or the scandal of the founder. But this is not surprising. What is surprising is that for a while something very good percolates in a community of faith, invigorating many to feel welcome, to find release, to be empowered in service and love and reconciliation to others. Too often we look merely into the downside of any movement. We have done both—in fact, we have highlighted the upside of what these megachurches do, and we have explained why and how they work. It is a rare phenomenon but, we think, one that should be examined, both for the good they produce and also how and why they fail. But for now, in the main, we believe megachurches help many people to live lives of integrity, community, and responsibility.

POSTSCRIPT FROM THE PEWS

THE SENIOR AUTHOR has had the fortune of being exposed to any number of megachurches across the world and in the United States. Each has its own genius; that is, its own gifting. The variety is quite remarkable, depending on cultures, country, class, and ethnicity. For several years now, because my family situation changed dramatically, I moved to Seattle, not far from my university. And, without knowing it, my wife and I moved five minutes from a church that I had come to know from research on another book, *Evangelicals vs. Liberals*. I had studied thirty-four active and growing liberal and conservative Protestant congregations. But one stuck out to me throughout my work, a place that I've received permission to use by name, Bethany Community Church. Through some very strange and, as it turns out, wonderful experiences, my new wife, Brooke, attended that church, and so, in time, I have done so as well. Do I agree with everything they say and do? *No*, of course not. But have I grown in respect for this highly unlikely megachurch in the middle of secular Seattle? Yes, I have. They average over 2,000 in attendance, in several sites, and they play a familiar brand of evangelical music, some of which I enjoy. They have ministries and shelters for women, ministries for everything you can possibly imagine—after all, they are one block off Aurora Avenue, one of the toughest areas in Seattle. And most of all they have a teaching pastor, Richard Dahlstrom, who does his biblically devoted sermons every Sunday, always thirty minutes, and I learn more from them than at any church I have ever attended. And it's relevant.

He carefully avoids attacking politicians by name, or anyone else for that matter, but he is guided by scripture to preach good news to the poor, release for the captive, redemption work for sinners, and a strident challenge for those too adjusted to privilege and power. He somehow keeps together a disparate group of middle-class folks, academics, intellectuals, businesspeople, and college students, and he does it with some bravery by upsetting the settled and giving peace to the ones among us who are deeply disturbed. It is an unlikely crew that comes there Sunday after Sunday. Dahlstrom wears jeans and an old wool sweater most Sundays, and it's not to be cool—he's not hip, or a hipster; he's an outdoorsman, someone who lives modestly, and lives to share the good news of Jesus Christ. He doesn't bring much attention to himself; he isn't trying to get famous. But to me, this kind of faithful service is the best of what megachurches do: heal, challenge, and serve justice, peace, and reconciliation. We certainly do need that today more than ever.

APPENDIX A | Data, Methodology, and Descriptive Statistics

S INCE 1992, THUMMA and Bird[1] have tracked the known population of all American megachurches—Protestant[2] congregations with weekly worship attendance of 2,000 adults and children or more—and have compiled them into a Database of Megachurches in the U.S., providing a rough census of American megachurches. In 2007, there were 1,250 such congregations. From this census, Thumma and Bird selected twelve megachurches that closely reflect the national megachurch profile in terms of a wide variety of characteristics, including attendance, region, denomination, dominant race, and church age. While these churches were selected to be representative of the entire population, the sample slightly underrepresents the western region and is slightly larger than the average megachurch.[3] Table A.1 provides descriptive statistics comparing the twelve-megachurch sample to American megachurches in 2008. In 2008, at each church, Thumma and Bird conducted

[1] Scott Thumma and Warren Bird, "Database of Megachurches in the U.S.," Hartford Institute for Religion Research, 2011, accessed February 5, 2011 (http://hirr.hartsem.edu/megachurch/database.html).
[2] Thumma and Travis (2007) note that while "there are many American Catholic and Orthodox churches, and a few synagogues and mosques, that serve over two thousand attendees in an average week," those "churches are organized and led in distinctively different ways that separate them as unique phenomena from Protestant megachurches." See Scott Thumma and Dave Travis, Beyond the Megachurch Myths (San Francisco: Jossey-Bass, 2007), xviii.
[3] Scott Thumma and Warren Bird, "Not Who You Think They Are," Hartford Institute for Religion Research, 2009, accessed February 5, 2011 (http://hirr.hartsem.edu/megachurch/megachurch_attender_report.htm).

TABLE A.I. Descriptive Statistics Comparing US Megachurches to the
12-Megachurch Sample

	% US Megachurches[a]	% in 12-Megachurch Sample (#)
Region		
Northeast	6%	8% (1)
South	48%	42% (5)
North central	21%	33% (4)
West	25%	17% (2)
Average Weekly Service Attendance		
2,000–2,999	43%	33% (4)
3,000–4,999	38%	50% (6)
5,000 or more	19%	17% (2)
Denomination[b]		
Nondenominational	35%	33% (4)
Baptist	26%	25% (3)
Pentecostal/Charismatic	8%	8% (1)
Mainline	10%	99% (4)
Dominant Race[c]		
White	50%	50% (6)
Black	15%	17% (2)
Multiracial	35%	33% (4)
Church Founding		
Before 1946	26%	25% (3)
1946–1980	39%	33% (4)
1981–1990	16%	8% (1)
1991–present	19%	99% (4)

[a] Data comes from the Survey of North America's Largest Churches (see Thumma and Bird 2008).

[b] Percentages do not add up to 100. Data is drawn directly from Scott Thumma and Warren Bird (2009).

[c] 15% or more.

Source: Table adapted from Scott Thumma and Warren Bird (2009). Table is reprinted and adapted with permission from Katie E. Corcoran and James K. Wellman, Jr., "'People Forget He's Human': Charismatic Leadership in Institutionalized Religion," *Sociology of Religion* 77 (2016): 309–333, Copyright [2016], Oxford University Press. Some percentages do not add up to 100 due to rounding error.

focus groups, gave all present church service attendees a survey, and had a key informant, typically the senior pastor, fill out a survey regarding the congregation. The interviews were transcribed and the surveys coded into datasets (one with attendee data and one with congregational data). Leadership Network, a nonprofit consultancy and research group, funded and collected this data, which we use with permission. We also observed at least one worship service for each church and read through various church materials provided on their websites. Further, we incorporate observations of megachurch worship services from other megachurches. While we use the interviews as our primary source of data, we combine these data sources to provide a more comprehensive picture of megachurches.

Qualitative Data and Analysis

Focus groups allow individual participants not only to provide their own responses to questions, but also to prompt the responses of other participants. In doing so, they are particularly useful for identifying group norms.[4] Focus group responses can have a "chain-like" feel to them, where respondents respond, react to, and build off of the responses of other participants. Because interaction rituals, and the collective effervescence they produce, are necessarily group experiences, focus groups are especially useful for capturing emotional group dynamics. Focus groups can include a performative dimension where participants may feel inclined to highlight the power and intensity of their own spiritual experiences. Given that we want participants to fully describe their experiences, this is not a problem, but is in fact a benefit of using this method, as it encourages respondents to reflect and dive deeply into their accounts. The focus groups also allowed a larger array of individuals to be interviewed, which is important given the large size of megachurches. Focus groups, however, also have limitations. Participants may avoid discussing deviant or embarrassing topics or opinions, and shyer individuals may participate less than others. The large-N survey is less susceptible to these limitations as it was anonymous and required written responses. Thus the findings from it complement and further support the focus group results.

During the focus groups, respondents answered questions about how they came to the church, how they became involved in their church, and in what ways they had, or had not, experienced spiritual growth at the church.

---

[4] Jenny Kitzinger, "The Methodology of Focus Groups: The Importance of Interaction between Research Participants," *Sociology of Health & Illness* 16 (1994): 103–121.

Because responses may vary by type of attendee, in each church, three separate focus groups were conducted with newcomers (i.e., have been attending the megachurch for three years or less), longtimers (i.e., have been attending the megachurch for four years or more), and lay leaders (i.e., perform some form of leadership role in the church). The focus group interviews lasted approximately ninety minutes. Our three-person research team read, discussed, and coded transcriptions of the interviews. We coded 282 interviews (150 females, 132 males): 81 newcomers (NCs), 91 longtimers (LTs), and 110 lay leaders (LLs). First, we read through the interviews fully and then each began to create codes separately; we then compared our work and adjusted and consolidated our coding themes. Next, we read through the interviews again, guided by a coding framework emphasizing six major themes: (1) emotional experiences; (2) belonging/solidarity; (3) admiration for and guidance from the leader; (4) feelings of deliverance; (5) feelings of morality and their expression through service; and (6) feelings of spirituality, transcendence, or connection to some form of ultimate.

Expressions relating to sensory or emotional experience were common and cut across all six themes. In addition to extracting illustrative interview quotes, we also conducted word frequencies for the key sensory and affective words used in a context related to the megachurch. This involved identifying every instance in which a word and variations of the word were used (e.g., "love" as well as "loving" and "loves"), then verifying each instance to ensure the context was related to the respondent's megachurch experience.

The theme of leadership was further analyzed based on categories derived from the literature on charismatic leadership as well as our own argument. It is important to note that the respondents were not directly asked questions about their senior pastor, except in rare cases as a follow-up question to a comment already made. This allows us to identify charisma from the ground up rather than labeling a leader as charismatic a priori. In a charismatic community, the group revolves around the leader. The members have a duty to give their "complete personal devotion to the possessor of the quality [charisma]."[5] We also see similar arguments from a micro-sociological perspective in which the charismatic leader becomes the "sacred object" of the group—that is, "the object upon which attention of the group is focused and which becomes a symbolic repository for the group's emotional energies."[6] The leader is the glue that binds a charismatic community together; thus,

[5] Max Weber, *Economy and Society: An Outline of Interpretive Sociology*, edited by G. Roth & C. Wittich (Berkeley: University of California Press, 1978), 242.
[6] Collins, *Interaction Ritual Chains*, 124.

in essence, the leader *is* the group. Based on this, we expected that when asked any question about the group or themselves, the members of charismatic communities would be more likely to respond with a comment about their leader. Although the interview questions did not specifically ask about the senior pastor (who was in all cases male), we identified 270 comments regarding his qualities/characteristics, sermons, and/or how the respondents felt about him or how they perceived he felt about them.

We coded these comments based on three general categories: (1) the senior pastor as having extraordinary abilities, (2) the senior pastor as human, and (3) the emotional or affective relationship between the senior pastor and attendees. We separately read through the interviews with these categories. We then compared our work, discussed themes that emerged from the data, and refined our coding scheme accordingly. Next, we read through the interviews again, guided by the following refined categories. First, the senior pastor as extraordinary: (1a) described as being inspired, led, or called by God, as being a spiritual exemplar, or as being in some way connected to heightened spirituality; (1b) described as being special, unique, or different from other people and/or pastors but without reference to supernatural or spiritual qualities; (1c) his preaching described as being supernaturally inspired. Second, the senior pastor as human: (2a) perceived to have qualities that are human, ordinary, and just like everyone else; (2b) understandable preaching, where the senior pastor is perceived to speak and joke like a normal, average person; (2c) relatable preaching through the incorporation of the ordinary and human experiences of the senior pastor (e.g., discussing his personal life, moral struggles, and everyday human experiences). Third, the emotional or affective relationship between the senior pastor and attendees: (3a) the trustworthiness of the senior pastor; (3b) the emotions the attendees feel from the senior pastor; (3c) the emotions and emotional experiences the senior pastor evokes from attendees. To illustrate the prevalence of these categories and subcategories, we provide the percentage of comments that we coded into each. The categories are not mutually exclusive, and many comments fall under more than one category. To demonstrate the extensiveness of the categories,[7] we provide percentages for their prevalence across focus group participant types (LL, LT, and NC). We present the results in Table A.2. Had the attendees been directly asked about the senior pastor, percentages for the various categories would presumably be higher; however, the fact that participants, without explicit prompting, brought up the same categories

[7] Richard Krueger, *Analyzing and Reporting Focus Group Results* (Thousand Oaks, CA: Sage Publications, 1997).

TABLE A.2. Qualitative Coding of Charismatic Leadership

Coding Categories	Prevalence of Comments, % and (Frequency)		Extensiveness of Comments by Focus Group Type, % and (Frequency)			
	% of total	% within a category	LLs	LTs	NCs	Totals[a]
1. **Senior pastor as extraordinary**	35.19 (95)		44.21 (42)	28.42 (27)	27.37 (26)	100.00 (95)
a. Inspired/led/called by God		53.68 (51)	47.06 (24)	35.29 (18)	17.65 (9)	100.00 (51)
b. Unique without reference to God		43.16 (41)	41.46 (17)	24.39 (10)	34.15 (14)	100.00 (41)
c. Preaching inspired by God		22.11 (21)	47.62 (10)	28.57 (6)	23.81 (5)	100.00 (21)
2. **Senior pastor as human**	35.56 (96)		29.17 (28)	28.13 (27)	42.71 (41)	100.01 (96)
a. Human/ordinary qualities		31.25 (30)	30 (9)	43.33 (13)	26.67 (8)	100.00 (30)
b. Understandable preaching		39.58 (38)	23.68 (9)	18.42 (7)	57.9 (22)	100.00 (38)
c. Relatable preaching (shows human side)		47.92 (46)	28.26 (13)	19.57 (9)	52.17 (24)	100.00 (46)
3. **Emotional bond**	27.41 (74)		35.14 (26)	29.73 (22)	35.14 (26)	100.01 (74)
a. Senior pastor is trustworthy		32.43 (24)	50.00 (12)	20.83 (5)	29.17 (7)	100.00 (24)
b. Emotions felt from senior pastor		29.73 (22)	45.46 (10)	31.82 (7)	22.73 (5)	100.01 (22)
c. Senior pastor evokes emotion		50.00 (37)	27.03 (10)	27.03 (10)	45.95 (17)	100.01 (37)

[a] Row totals for extensiveness of comments only. Percentages over 100 due to rounding error.

Note: N = 270. Categories are not mutually exclusive; some comments are coded as more than one (sub)category. LLs = lay leaders, LTs = longtimers, NCs = newcomers.

Source: Table is reprinted and adapted with permission from Katie E. Corcoran and James K. Wellman, Jr., " 'People Forget He's Human': Charismatic Leadership in Institutionalized Religion," *Sociology of Religion* 77 (2016): 309–333, Copyright [2016], Oxford University Press.

across focus groups and churches is perhaps more indicative of the existence of a charismatic leader, than if the respondents had been directly questioned about their senior pastor, thereby drawing their attention to the topic.

As mentioned, the megachurches were not chosen because they had charismatic leaders, but to be representative. As such, there is variation in the number of senior pastor references in total and within categories across the megachurches, which suggests variation in the degree of charismatic leadership. However, for each category, the majority of churches had at least one comment, usually more, falling under it. The mean number of comments per church is 22.5 with a standard deviation of 15.45, a minimum of 5, and a maximum of 50. In Table A.3, we provide the mean, standard deviation, and minimum and maximum values for the frequency of comments in each coding category across the twelve megachurches as additional evidence for the extensiveness of the categories.

TABLE A.3. Extensiveness of Coding Categories across Megachurches ($N = 12$)

	# of Comments across Megachurches			
	Mean	SD	Min	Max
Overall	22.5	15.45	5	50
Qualitative Coding Categories				
1. Senior pastor as extraordinary	7.92	6.5	0	20
a. Inspired/led/called by God	4.25	3.57	0	11
b. Unique without reference to God	3.42	3.78	0	11
c. Preaching inspired by God	1.75	1.60	0	7
2. Senior pastor as human	8	7.32	1	23
a. Human/ordinary qualities	2.5	2.24	0	7
b. Understandable preaching	3.17	5.39	0	19
c. Relatable preaching (shows human side)	3.83	4.00	0	13
3. Emotional bond	6.17	4.95	0	15
a. Senior pastor is trustworthy	2	2.37	0	7
b. Emotions felt from senior pastor	1.75	2.60	0	7
c. Senior pastor evokes emotion	2.833	2.95	0	7

Source: Table is reprinted and adapted with permission from Katie E. Corcoran and James K. Wellman, Jr., " 'People Forget He's Human': Charismatic Leadership in Institutionalized Religion," *Sociology of Religion* 77 (2016): 309–333, Copyright [2016], Oxford University Press.

Quantitative Data

ATTENDEE SURVEY

At each of the twelve churches, surveys were distributed to everyone age 18 and older at all services during a given weekend. The average response rate was 58% from all twelve megachurches, with a total sample size of 24,900 attendees. Although we use the focus groups as our primary source of data, the large-N survey is useful because it provides sociodemographic data regarding the overall attendee population in these megachurches. It quantifies data about what initially attracted individuals to the megachurch as well as why they continue to attend, and it asks questions about feelings of belonging, morality as expressed through service, and spirituality. The average megachurch attendee is female, white, and has a college education. While females comprise a disproportionate share of our survey respondents (i.e., roughly 60%), this is consistent with the fact that they also comprise a disproportionate share of American Protestant church attenders and American megachurch attenders.[8] We present data for variables using the maximum sample for each measure (i.e., different measures have different sample sizes due to missing data). Table A.4 provides descriptive statistics regarding megachurch-attendee sociodemographic characteristics, their megachurch participation, and their religious participation. The next sections provide a description of the survey question wording and response choices for all nondemographic questions.

Megachurch Participation

The attendee survey asked several questions regarding respondents' megachurch participation. First, it asked how long the respondent has been going to church services/activities at the megachurch (response choices: *less than 1 year, 1–2 years, 3–5 years, 6–10 years, more than 10 years, I am visiting from another church*, and *I am visiting and do not regularly go anywhere*). Second, it asked how often the respondent attends worship services at the megachurch (response choices: *this is my first time, hardly ever or on special occasions, less than once a month, once a month, two or three times a month*, and *usually every week or more*). Third, respondents were asked how their participation in the megachurch's activities has changed in the last two years: whether it has increased, remained the same, or decreased, or whether they haven't attended the megachurch in the last two years. Fourth, it asked what the first step was that moved the respondent from being a spectator

---

[8] Scott Thumma and Warren Bird, "Not Who You Think They Are," Hartford Institute for Religion Research, 2009, accessed February 5, 2011 (http://hirr.hartsem.edu/megachurch/megachurch_attender_report.htm).

TABLE A.4. Megachurch Attendees' Descriptive Statistics

Sex	%	Age	%	Spectator to active participant	%
Male	39.53	18–29	29.69	Doesn't apply	29.71
Female	60.47	30–39	20.58	I can't remember	6.03
		40–49	16.29	General announcement	9.41
Marital status	%	50 and older	27.70	Personal invite	27.65
Not Married	58.78			Inward sense of call	21.37
Married	41.22	*Tenure at megachurch*	%	I took initiative	10.88
		<1 year	19.12		
Race	%	1–2 years	18.7	*Found out about megachurch*	%
Asian/Pacific Islander	3.87	3–5 years	23.05	Friend/family	81.63
Black	21.13	6–10 years	15.86	Media	6.68
Latino	3.45	>10 years	16.57	Saw church facility	11.69
Native American	0.48	Visiting	6.71		
White	69.76			*Mega is home church*	%
Other	1.32	*Attend at megachurch*	%	Yes, only this church	76.18
		First time	4.1	Yes, and other church	12.43
Education	%	Hardly ever	2.29	No	11.38
Less than HS	3.93	Less than once a month	2.18		
HS degree	12.83	Once a month	2.97	*How long Christian*	%
Some college	31.72	2–3 times a month	18.83	< 1 year	4.2
College degree	51.53	Every week	69.62	1–2 years	5.84
				3–6 years	11.0
Income	%	*Participation change in 2 yrs*	%	> 6 years	76.99
<$25,000	16.73	Increased	38.42	Not committed follower	1.96
$25,000–$49,999	21.79	Remained the same	37.19		
$50,000–$74,999	20.20	Decreased	7.31	*Devotions last week*	%
$75,000–$99,999	14.99	Not been here 2 yrs	17.07	Seldom (1 time or less)	30.24
$100,000+	26.29			Often (2–5 times)	39.6
				Nearly Daily (6–7 times)	30.15

to an active participant in the megachurch (response choices: *this question doesn't apply to me, I can't remember, I responded to a general announcement, I responded to a personal invitation from someone, I responded to a personal invitation from someone I did know, I responded to an inward sense of call or spiritual prompting,* and *I took initiative to look for opportunities*). In addition to participation questions, the survey also asked how the respondent first found out about the megachurch (i.e., through a friend/coworker/family member, media, or by seeing the church facility) and whether they consider the megachurch their home church (response choices: *yes this church only, yes but I also attend other churches,* and *no*).

Religious Participation

The attendee survey asked respondents how long they have been a committed follower of Jesus Christ (*less than a year, 1–2 years, 3–6 years, more than 6 years,* and *not a committed follower of Christ*). It also asked how often the respondent practiced personal devotions (times of Bible reading and prayer) in the past week (*seldom: 1 time or less a week, often: 2–5 times a week,* and *nearly daily: 6–7 times a week or more*).

Why They Joined and Stay at the Megachurch

Attendees were asked in separate questions how influential the senior pastor, worship style, the music/arts, "my friends and family are here," reputation of church, adult programs/ministries, children and youth programs/ministries, social or community outreach, self-help or support groups, and denominational ties were for (1) bringing them to the megachurch (1 = *not at all* to 5 = *a lot*) and (2) keeping them at it (1 = *not at all* to 5 = *a lot*). Descriptive statistics for these measures are provided in Table A.5.

Belonging/Solidarity and Small Groups

Respondents were asked if they agreed with the statements (1) "I have a strong sense of belonging to this church"; (2) "I have very few close friends at this church"; and (3) "This church makes a strong effort to help me get involved in the activities and life of the church body" (1 = *strongly disagree* to 5 = *strongly agree*). We coded responses of 4 and 5 as *agree* and all other responses as *disagree/neutral*. Respondents were also asked if they were regularly involved in six different types of small-group activities at their megachurch (i.e., Sunday school/church school, prayer/spiritual discussion/Bible study groups, fellowships/clubs/or other social groups, support/recovery groups, community service/social justice groups, or other small groups). If they marked one or more of these types of small groups, we classify them as participating in small-group activities. Descriptive statistics for these measures are available in Table A.6.

TABLE A.5. Descriptive Statistics: Reasons for Joining and Staying at the Megachurch

Reasons for Joining		Reasons for Staying	
Senior Pastor	%	*Senior Pastor*	%
Not at all (1)	23.26	Not at all (1)	6.12
2	7.01	2	2.57
Some (3)	12.20	Some (3)	8.47
4	13.56	4	17.62
A lot (5)	43.97	A lot (5)	65.21
Worship Style	%	*Worship Style*	%
Not at all (1)	15.79	Not at all (1)	5.10
2	8.12	2	3.83
Some (3)	15.20	Some (3)	11.24
4	19.16	4	22.73
A lot (5)	41.74	A lot (5)	57.10
Music/Arts	%	*Music/Arts*	%
Not at all (1)	28.50	Not at all (1)	14.61
2	9.53	2	6.70
Some (3)	16.98	Some (3)	16.77
4	16.74	4	22.45
A lot (5)	28.24	A lot (5)	39.47
Friends/Family Here	%	*Friends/Family Here*	%
Not at all (1)	37.40	Not at all (1)	26.78
2	9.57	2	10.66
Some (3)	10.09	Some (3)	15.92
4	10.69	4	15.35
A lot (5)	32.24	A lot (5)	31.29
Reputation of Church	%	*Reputation of Church*	%
Not at all (1)	20.21	Not at all (1)	14.20
2	8.03	2	6.01
Some (3)	16.35	Some (3)	13.79
4	19.14	4	18.61
A lot (5)	36.27	A lot (5)	47.39
Adult Programs	%	*Adult Programs*	%
Not at all (1)	41.98	Not at all (1)	23.24
2	11.70	2	9.14
Some (3)	17.02	Some (3)	19.85
4	12.02	4	20.66
A lot (5)	17.28	A lot (5)	27.11

(continued)

Reasons for Joining		Reasons for Staying	
Children's Programs	%	*Children's Programs*	%
Not at all (1)	52.31	Not at all (1)	41.7
2	7.7	2	7.13
Some (3)	11.03	Some (3)	12
4	10.35	4	13.73
A lot (5)	18.62	A lot (5)	25.43
Social Outreach	%	*Social Outreach*	%
Not at all (1)	32.8	Not at all (1)	14.15
2	12.87	2	6.9
Some (3)	19.04	Some (3)	18.44
4	14.61	4	24.76
A lot (5)	20.67	A lot (5)	35.75
Self-Help Groups	%	*Self-Help Groups*	%
Not at all (1)	50.46	Not at all (1)	34.86
2	11.53	2	10.45
Some (3)	14.71	Some (3)	17.79
4	9.1	4	15.22
A lot (5)	14.2	A lot (5)	21.68
Denomination	%	*Denomination*	%
Not at all (1)	45.68	Not at all (1)	38.75
2	9.01	2	8.74
Some (3)	14.36	Some (3)	15.85
4	11.52	4	14.23
A lot (5)	19.43	A lot (5)	22.43

Morality and Service

Respondents were asked whether they agreed that (1) church leaders encourage them to find and use their gifts, (2) the church encourages them to serve in the wider world, and (3) the church doesn't make a strong effort to train me in leadership (1 = *strongly disagree* to 5 = *strongly agree*). They were also asked how frequently they volunteer at the megachurch: never, occasionally (a few times a year), regularly (once or twice a month), or often (three times a month or more. Descriptive statistics for these measures are available in Table A.6.

TABLE A.6. Descriptive Statistics: Belonging, Service, and Spirituality

Belonging		Service (continued)	
Church belonging	%	*Volunteering*	%
Disagree/Neutral	35.14	Never	45.32
Agree	64.86	Occasionally	26.35
		Regularly	12.78
Few friends here	%	Often	15.55
Agree/Neutral	61.37		
Disagree	38.63	**Spirituality**	
		Church size hinders	
Gets me involved	%	*spiritual growth*	%
Disagree/Neutral	31.87	Agree/Neutral	22.80
Agree	68.13	Disagree	77.20
Small group	%	*Spiritual needs met*	%
No	41.37	Disagree/Neutral	24.87
Yes	58.63	Agree	75.13
Small-group types	% Yes	*Felt close to God*	%
Sunday school	25.5	Disagree/Neutral	37.23
Prayer/Bible study	28.12	Agree	62.77
Fellowship/social	12.98		
Support/recovery	6.67	*Growth through mega*	%
Community service	9.54	Other response	57.56
Other	18.9	Agree	42.44
Service		*Spiritual growth*	%
Encourage to use gifts	%	Very satisfied	24.28
Disagree/Neutral	39.62	Somewhat satisfied	43.74
Agree	60.38	Mixed feelings	18.08
		Somewhat dissatisfied	10.42
Serve in wider world	%	Very dissatisfied	3.48
Disagree/Neutral	26.70		
Agree	73.30		
Little effort to train me	%		
Agree/Neutral	31.27		
Disagree	68.73		

Spirituality

Respondents were asked whether they agreed that (1) their spiritual needs are being met by the church, (2) a recent time when they felt closest to God was directly connected to a ministry or activity of this church, and (3) worshipping at a large church hinders their spiritual growth (1 = *strongly disagree* to 4 = *strongly agree*). They were also asked, (4) "How much have you grown spiritually in the past year?" We focused on the response category *much growth, mainly through the ministries of this church*. Respondents were further asked, (5) "How satisfied are you with your own spiritual growth?" with response choices of *very satisfied, somewhat satisfied, mixed feelings/not sure, somewhat dissatisfied,* and *very dissatisfied*. Descriptive statistics for these measures are presented in Table A.6.

CONGREGATIONAL SURVEY

At each of the twelve megachurches, the key informant (typically, and going forward, the senior pastor) was asked questions about the congregation. Senior pastors were asked for their church's denomination, political identity, number of services, number of regular participants, sanctuary capacity, and satellite seating. They were also asked for their congregation's total yearly income, the percent of their income spent on salary, missions, buildings/operations, and programs. This data is presented in Table A.7.

Senior pastors were also asked questions regarding who attends their megachurch: the number of regularly participating adults, youth, and children and the gender, education, age, race, theological identity, and political identity of their attendees. They were also asked whether they agree that the following describes their megachurch: (1) like a close-knit family, (2) spiritually vital and alive, (3) has a clear mission and purpose, (4) is working for social justice, (5) is willing to change to meet new challenges, (6) holds strong values, and (7) welcomes innovation. In terms of worship services, they were asked to what extent the following describes their congregation's largest regular weekend worship service: (1) reverent, (2) contemporary, (3) God's presence, (4) joyful, (5) thought-provoking, (6) welcoming to newcomers, and (7) predictable. Responses of "very well" or "quite well" were grouped together and considered an affirmative response. Key informants were also asked how frequently the following are used or done during worships services: (1) choir, (2) piano, (3) electronic guitar or bass, (4) drums, (5) visual projection, (6) kneeling, (7) communion, and (7) prayers for healing. Responses of "always" or "often" were combined and considered an affirmative response.

TABLE A.7. Congregational Descriptive Statistics

Denomination	%	Number of services/week	
ELCA[a]	8.33	Mean	8.00
Presbyterian USA	8.33	Median	5.00
Southern Baptist	16.67		
National Baptist	8.33	**# Regular Participants**	**%**
Vineyard	8.33	1,500–3,000	18.18
United Methodist	8.33	3,001–5,000	27.27
CCCC[b]	8.33	5,001–7,000	18.18
Nondenominational	33.33	7,000+	36.36
Political Identity	**%**	**Sanctuary Capacity**	**%**
Conservative	25.00	500–1,000	33.33
Somewhat Conservative	50.00	1,001–2,000	25.00
Middle	8.33	2,001–3,000	25.00
Somewhat Liberal	8.33	3,000+	16.67
Liberal	8.33		
		Satellite Seating	**%**
Total Yearly Income (000)		500–2,000	27.27
Mean	$7,772	2,001–4,000	45.45
Median	$5,500	4,001+	27.27
		Annual % Growth Rate	
Spent on Salary	**%**	**(2002–2013)**	
Mean	45.00	Mean	23.13
Median	46.00	Minimum	0.00
		Maximum	73.84
Spent on Missions	**%**		
Mean	15.00	**Media**	**%**
Median	11.00	Website	100.00
		Radio ministry	50.00
Spent on Building	**%**	TV ministry	33.00
Mean	23.75		
Median	21.50		
Spent on Programs	**%**		
Mean	10.75		
Median	8.5		

[a] ELCA = Evangelical Lutheran Church in America.

[b] Conservative Congregational Christian Conference.

Note: N = 12, except where data is missing.

Senior pastors were asked for their age, gender, race/ethnicity, education level, and the activities they engage in (i.e., plans/leads worship, evangelism, visits the sick, counsels people, organizes small groups, represents the church in the community, and recruits and trains lay leaders). This data is presented in Table A.8.

TABLE A.8. Congregational Descriptive Statistics

Church attendees	Mean	Worship Service always/often has	%
# Regularly participating adults	4,034	Choir	41.66
# Regularly participating youth	578	Piano	58.33
# Regularly participating children	1,020	Guitar or bass	91.67
		Drums	91.67
Gender	%	Visual projection	83.33
Attendees 61%–80% female	25	Kneeling	8.33
		Communion	41.67
Education	%	Prayers for healing	33.33
Attendees 61%+ college graduate	42		
		Describes worship service	%
Age	%	Reverent	33.00
61%–80% attendees 35 or younger	42	Contemporary	67.00
1%–10% attendees over 60	58	God's presence	100.00
		Joyful	83.00
Race/ethnicity	%	Thought-provoking	100.00
1%–10% attendees Latino	92	Welcoming to newcomers	83.00
1%–10% attendees black	67	Predicable	67.00
0%–10% attendees Asian	92		
61%–100% white	67	*Senior pastor (SP)*	
		Mean age	48.00
Theological identity of most attendees	%	Male	100.00%
Evangelical	67		
Seeker	17	*SP Race/ethnicity*	%
		White	58.00

Church attendees	Mean	Worship Service always/often has	%
Political identity of most attendees	%	Hispanic	8.00
Somewhat/predominately conservative	75	Black	25.00
		Other	8.00
Agree that megachurch is	%		
Like a close-knit family	42.00	*SP Education*	%
Spiritually vital/alive	83.00	Bachelor's	8.00
Has a clear mission	92.00	MA	58.00
Working for social justice	67.00	Doctoral	33.00
Willing to change	92.00		
Holds strong values	92.00	*SP (quite a bit/great deal)*	%
Welcomes innovation	92.00	Plans/leads worship	58
		Evangelism	42
Visitors	%	Visits the sick	17
Welcome booth	83.00	Counsels people	8
Invited to new member class	83.00	Organizes small groups	8
Invited to small group	83.00	Represents church in community	83
		Recruits and trains lay leaders	17
Programs/activities offered in past 12 months (yes & a lot of emphasis or specialty of mega)	%		
Sunday school	58		
Prayer/spiritual development	75		
Scripture study groups	50		
Fellowships/social	25		
Support groups	75		
Evangelism	75		
Community service	100		
Music program	75		
Parenting/marriage	50		
Young single adult	58		
Sports activities	36		

(continued)

Church attendees	Mean	Worship Service always/often has	%
Political activities	%		
Told in worship of political action opportunities	25		
Groups/meetings to discuss politics	17		
Groups/meetings to get people registered to vote	33		
Groups/meetings to get the vote out for the election	25		
Elected government officials spoke at church	8		
Persons running for office spoke at church	0		
Voter guides distributed at church	8		
Held a big event to attract visitors in last 12 months	%		
Yes	83		
Small groups	%		
Central to member formation	100		
41%–100% of congregation participates in	50		
Mega has a:	%		
Youth minister	100.00		
Youth group	100.00		
Youth choirs or musical groups	75.00		
Youth retreat	100.00		
Youth-led or -planned events	67.00		
Youth counseling	83.00		

Senior pastors were asked about the programs/activities their congregation has offered in the past twelve months: (1) Sunday school, (2) prayer/spiritual development, (3) scripture study groups, (4) fellowships/social groups, (5) support groups, (6) evangelism, (7) community service, (8) music program, (9) parenting or marriage, (10) young single adult, and (11) sports activities. Congregations that said "yes and the congregation places a lot of emphasis on this activity" or "yes and it is a specialty of the congregation" were grouped together and considered an affirmative response. Senior pastors were also asked about the political activities the congregation engaged in: (1) told in worship of political action opportunities, (2) groups/meetings/events to discuss politics, (3) groups/meetings/events to get people registered to vote, (4) groups/meetings/events to get the vote out for the election, (5) elected government officials spoke at church, (6) persons running for office spoke at church, and (7) voter guides distributed at church. Senior pastors were also asked whether their congregation has a (1) youth minister, (2) youth group, (3) youth choirs or musical groups, (4) youth retreat(s), (5) youth-led/planned events, and (6) youth counseling. This data is presented in Table A.8.

APPENDIX B | How Is God "Like a Drug"?
Exploring the Evolution of Social
Affects and Oxytocin
By Kate J. Stockly

W
HAT DOES IT mean to say "God is like a drug"? We chose the
spirit of this phrase—a direct quote from a megachurch member
in our study—as the title of our book for several reasons (not only because
we hoped it might catch your attention). In one sense, it's obviously a hy-
perbolic reference to how *incredible* it feels to perceive yourself as being in
God's presence, feeling God's face shining upon you, and receiving God's
love. The person who said this *meant it.* In fact, he went on to say that
he *can't wait* for his next "hit." And he was not alone—many members
expressed a visceral, physiological yearning for Sunday morning when they
could experience that holy high again, while others emphasized how important it was for them to participate in midweek activities for a mini-dose
to "hold them over" until Sunday.

Readers who aren't familiar with this feeling, or whose memories
of church are a mix of bored sighs, shushing from adults, and shame,
might be wondering: "What?! Why do these churchgoers experience such
pleasure? Where is this joy coming from? What about megachurches
makes attendees feel so good? If *I* went, would *I* feel this alleged high?
How do megachurches evoke such fervor? What is happening in those

big, warehouse-looking buildings?" We sought to address these questions throughout this book by categorizing into six types the felt desires of megachurch attendees (as expressed in our interviews). Then, building on Randall Collins's theory of interaction ritual chains, we proposed the *Megachurch Ritual Cycle* to show how these desires are addressed through social interaction. Leaving aside the question of whether or not the "drug high" feeling really is evidence of God's action or presence, several questions remain. Megachurch participants say they experience their "high" *in the body*; so, what is happening *in their bodies*? Are there any physiological correlates for their feelings? If we assume that all thoughts, feelings, emotions, and sensations, are processed by and manifest in, through, and around the body, then so must megachurch participants' feeling of being high on God. Toward the end of developing such a physiological account, this appendix will do three things: (1) clarify (more explicitly than the main text of the book) what it means to consider the biological body in the study of social and cultural phenomena, (2) explore the evolution of culture and religion, and (3) suggest a testable hypothesis about one possible element of the physiology of the megachurch "high": an evolutionarily ancient neuropeptide called *oxytocin*.

Throughout this book, we've made the argument that the megachurch "high"—which, for now, we'll call *emotional energy*—is a quintessential *social* feeling, emerging within successful interaction rituals.[1] Emotional energy is what animates the ever-present, ever-fluctuating, diffuse affective sense of being pushed, pulled, and compelled, which motivates us to look and think beyond ourselves to engage in social activities and interactions. It's what helps us choose whether to go to a party or watch Netflix alone; and it's what makes megachurch attendees get out of bed on Sunday mornings and drive to church instead of to the ski slopes.

But what *is* emotional energy? In this appendix, I'll explore a bio-social theory of the evolution of human ultra-sociality and hypothesize that a neurohormone called *oxytocin* plays a central role in the physiology of emotional energy: this pivotal, vital, world-changing "energy," the manipulation of which appears to have facilitated not only the massive success of megachurches, but also, more generally, the hyper-sociality of the human species.[2]

---

[1] Randall Collins, *Interaction Ritual Chains* (Princeton, NJ: Princeton University Press, 2004).

[2] As I will explain, I am not suggesting that emotional energy is equal to oxytocin. Just simply that it's a consistent part of the equation.

Embodiment and a Bio-Sociocultural Approach

What do neuroscience and evolutionary biology have to offer a sociological book about megachurches? Potentially a lot. And likewise—this is a two-way street—studying *megachurches* can also offer valuable data for neuroscientists and evolutionary theorists, as they attempt to understand the ways that power structures, social groups, and cultural discourses affect and interact with the human mind, body, and brain. The rise of megachurches, as we've shown in this book, is a fascinating case study of human experience, desire, and social dynamics. We've shown throughout the book that embodiment—the visceral, heart-beating, arms-swaying materiality of the body—is a vital factor for adequately theorizing the complexity of this religious structure, both in its capacity as a social movement and as a site for religious experience.

That being said, studying the body directly has a checkered history within the social sciences and humanities, in some cases causing a "deep-seated distrust of biologically based argument" and even an "axiomatic anti-biologism."[3] So, before we get into how biology applies to a conversation about megachurches, let's explore that complex intellectual history for a moment to see if we can find a productive way forward that refamiliarizes sociological and humanities approaches with the physiological body while keeping intact the wisdom and insight that led them to distrust biology in the first place. If you are most interested in reading about the evolutionary story, feel free to skip to the "Finding Homo Religiosus" section.

AGAINST REDUCTIONISM

With the emergence of postmodernism and poststructuralism, insights about the ways in which language constitutes reality and about the social construction of the categories we embody revolutionized the way we thought about human nature and cultural contingencies. This enriched and enlivened conversations about power, social movements, subjectivity, agency, and culture in vital paradigm-shifting ways. To make their point, these thinkers needed to downplay and challenge the dominance of the role of biology in creating human experience. And given the dominance of biological determinism within modern popular science, this downplaying was a necessary

---

[3] Elizabeth A. Wilson, "Organic Empathy: Feminism, Psychopharmaceuticals, and the Embodiment of Depression," in *Material Feminisms*, edited by Stacy Alaimo and Susan Heckman, 373–399 (Bloomington: Indiana University Press, 2008), 377.

and effective discursive move.[4] After all, unchecked determinism had led (and still leads, when it rears its head) research astray, especially when applied to human bodies. Even though the reductive biological determinism that social constructionists fought so hard to dismantle still remains strong in certain pockets and in popular-science reporting (and given the effectiveness of clickbait headlines, it isn't likely to ever disappear), thanks to these scholars' determination and hard work, it is now losing its grip.

But the problem is, ignoring the role of biology in culture, identity, and agency wreaks its own havoc. Echoing longstanding reservations about evolutionary theories within sociology and anthropology rooted in a legitimate fear of things like the eugenics movement, feminists and social constructionists have generally de-emphasized, dismissed, or even denied the role of the *body* within human experience. Ignoring the materiality of the body reifies the dichotomy between biological nature and social reality. And such a reification does not solve the problem of reductionism; it only swings the pendulum too far in the other direction. Sociologist of religion Manuel Vásquez warns that "remaining ensconced safely in the anthropocentric cocoon of social constructionism and failing to confront the natural sciences in a truly cross-disciplinary dialogue leaves the door open for simplistic and totalizing forms of reductionism."[5] So, for Vásquez, the danger of reductionistic social constructionism looms just as large as the danger of biological reductionism. By excluding the body from their theories, scholars fail to see the material domain in which the exercise of power and social forces is actually felt. In this way, understanding biological factors is just as crucial for doing critical analysis of culture and ideologies as it is for interpreting social movements.

REDISCOVERING THE "NATURAL"

In addition to being potentially socially problematic, the nature/nurture dichotomy is based on a fundamental *misunderstanding* of how human bodies

---

[4] And extra-especially when applied to *female* bodies. For example, the damage done by determinism is especially stark when applied to research about sex and gender; in *Delusions of Gender: How Our Minds, Society, and Neurosexism Create Difference* (2010), Cordelia Fine chronicles the sobering reality that decades of flawed scientific sex-differences research has contributed dramatically to damaging, sexist, exclusionary concepts of "essential" natures of men and women. Cordelia Fine, *Delusions of Gender: How Our Minds, Society, and Neurosexism Create Difference* (New York: W. W. Norton, 2010). See also Rebecca Jordan-Young, *Brainstorm: The Flaws in the Science of Sex Differences* (Cambridge, MA: Harvard University Press, 2010); and Anne Fausto-Sterling, *Sexing the Body: Gender Politics and the Construction of Sexuality* (New York: Basic Books, 2000).

[5] Manuel A. Vásquez, *More Than Belief: A Materialist Theory of Religion* (New York: Oxford University Press, 2011), 13.

work in the first place. As sociologist Vicky Kirby insists, the social *is* natural.[6] Culture is *not* different in kind from "nature." Bringing the biology of bodies into the conversation is not a *return* to reductive scientism or an abandonment of the lessons learned and insights gained from explorations of social constructionism and a focus on symbols, representations, and meanings. Rather, rethinking and refamiliarizing ourselves with nature requires a "deconstruction of the material/discursive dichotomy that retains *both* elements *without privileging either*."[7]

Even sociologists are beginning to see the importance of this reintegration of the body into social theory. For example, feminist sociologist Victoria Pitts-Taylor insists that we need to understand what human embodiment means for our social realities, and when reductionism is kept in check, "the neurobiological body [. . .] can be a rich site of social and biosocial theorizing."[8] The best way to contest reductionist viewpoints, then, is not to *avoid* engaging evolutionary, neurological, or biological theories and research; "it is better," Pitts-Taylor argues, "to insist on the queer potential of nature, and nature/culture, than to deny the imbrication of the biological body in lived experience."[9] By "queer potential," Pitts-Taylor is referring to the diverse ways in which evolution and biology consistently produce forms that appear to resist or challenge the traditional (and now largely outdated) assumptions about natural selection and biology, including things like nonreproductive sexual activity and nongenetic kinship bonds like your "chosen family" and even the "brothers and sisters in Christ" who attend megachurches.

If we are, then, to rethink the roles of nature, bodies, and materiality in social life, what *is* the nature of our material bodies? The material body is far from static, determined, or determining; it is actually dynamic, flexible, plastic, and interactive.[10] The feedback loops between human material bodies and social discourse, action, and structures is one of cocreation, not unilateral determination. This means that just as discourses and cultural values affect embodied experiences, so too does the materiality of our bodies affect social

[6] Vicky Kirby, "Natural Convers(at)ions: Or, What If Culture Was Really Nature All Along?" in *Material Feminisms*, edited by Stacy Alaimo and Susan Hekman, 214–236 (Bloomington: Indiana University Press, 2008).

[7] Stacy Alaimo and Susan Hekman, "Emerging Models of Materiality in Feminist Theory," in *Material Feminisms* (Bloomington: Indiana University Press, 2008), 6 (emphasis mine).

[8] Victoria Pitts-Taylor, *The Brain's Body: Neuroscience and Corporeal Politics* (Durham, NC: Duke University Press, 2016), 11. Acknowledging that such cross-disciplinary work is controversial, Pitts-Taylor continues, "In addition to thinking about representation, we also need to try to say something about ontological realities, about corporeality" (12).

[9] Pitts-Taylor, *The Brain's Body*, 116–117.

[10] Elizabeth A. Wilson, *Gut Feminism* (Durham, NC: Duke University Press, 2015), 5.

action and structures. Our discussion of the embodied experience of megachurch attendance assumes that human bodies are absorbing, responding, negotiating, influencing, and being influenced by the structures, symbols, and social interactions that constitute the megachurch ritual cycle.

A turn toward this socially integrated approach to materially embodied nature is not only the recommendation of feminist theorists; biologists, neuroscientists, and cognitive scientists are jumping on board. Advancements in these fields are making it increasingly clear that researchers *must* understand the formative role that social contexts and structures play if their theories are going to adequately reflect the reality of how human brains and minds develop. Research programs such as neurosociology, the evolutionary cognitive science of religion, and evolutionary sociology are emerging to take on this task.[11] In the introduction to their trailblazing book, *The New Evolutionary Sociology*, Jonathan H. Turner and Richard S. Machalek write, "Evolutionary analysis will not explain everything of interest to sociologists, but it can be surprisingly useful in making sociology a more mature explanatory science."[12]

WHAT'S EVOLUTION GOT TO DO WITH IT?

Feminist social theorist Elizabeth Grosz urges sociologists to reclaim Darwinian evolutionary theory from the grip of modern habits of reductionism and determinacy. The dynamism of Darwin's theory, she says, actually has much to offer in collaboration with humanist and constructivist approaches to human experience.[13] Too often evolution, and therefore also the bodies it produces are understood in reductively deterministic terms. However, renowned geneticist Eva Jablonka and her colleague Marion Lamb

---

[11] For more on evolutionary sociology, see Jonathan Turner and Alexandra Maryanski, "Evolutionary Sociology: A Cross-Species Strategy for Discovering Human Nature," in *Handbook of Evolution and Society: Toward an Evolutionary Social Science*, edited by Jonathan H. Turner, Richard S. Machalek, and Alexandra R. Maryanski, 546–571 (Boulder, CO: Paradigm/New York: Routledge, 2015); and Jonathan H. Turner and Richard S. Machalek, *The New Evolutionary Sociology: Recent and Revitalized Theoretical and Methodological Approaches* (New York: Routledge, 2018); and for more on neurosociology, see David D. Franks, *Neurosociology: The Nexus between Neuroscience and Social Psychology* (New York: Springer, 2010); David D. Franks and Jonathan H. Turner, eds., *Handbook of Neurosociology* (New York: Springer, 2013); and Jonathan H. Turner, *On the Origins of Human Emotions: A Sociological Inquiry into the Evolution of Human Affect* (Stanford, CA: Stanford University Press, 2000).

[12] Turner and Machalek, *The New Evolutionary Sociology*, 12.

[13] "Darwin's work," Grosz says, "offers a subtle and complex critique of both essentialism and teleology." She explains, "It provides a dynamic and open-ended understanding of the intermingling of history and biology . . . and a complex account of the movements of difference, bifurcation, and becoming that characterize all forms of life." Elizabeth Grosz, "Darwin and Feminism: Preliminary Investigations for a Possible Alliance," in *Material Feminisms*, edited by Stacy Alaimo and Susan Hekman, 23–51 (Bloomington: Indiana University Press, 2008), 28.

theorize that there is not one (genetics) but *four* inheritance systems in the evolutionary process: genetic, epigenetic, behavioral, and symbolic (inheritance through symbolic communication like language). They explain that these systems interact and affect one another, culminating in a much more complex and dynamic process than is usually presented by contemporary neo-Darwinian models of evolution.[14] In short, understanding our biological and neurological embodiment *requires* that we pay attention to social forces and our cultural heritage just as much as understanding human sociality and culture requires paying attention to our evolutionary heritage. Wilson explains her use of the word "contingency" to talk about the interwoven factors: "I use 'contingency' here (borrowed from Barbara Hernstein Smith [1988]) to mark that state of *nature-culture entanglement* that is almost impossible to articulate: coimplication, coevolution, mutuality, intra-action, dynamic systems, embeddedness."[15] In other words, a human is not born with a blank slate, waiting for culture to write her story, but neither is she born with a predetermined genetic script. We need to move past "strong adaptationism" or the idea that genetic evolution has instilled in humans a firm, innate set of cognitive "modules" that work the same way regardless of social and cultural influences.[16] This position, which cognitive psychologist Cecilia Heyes calls "High Church evolutionary psychologists," maintains that behind our fancy modern intellect, we continue to operate with Stone Age minds.[17] Without denying the influence of early Pleistocene environments, our evolutionary heritage also tells us a story of the emergence of versatility, adaptability, and resiliency. According to more updated biological and neuroscientific research, our brains and nervous systems appear to be nothing if not *flexible* and *plastic*, which just means open to change.[18] Keeping this in mind should help

---

[14] Eva Jablonka and Marion J. Lamb, *Evolution in Four Dimensions: Genetic, Epigenetic, Behavioral, and Symbolic Variation in the History of Life*, Revised Edition (Cambridge, MA: MIT Press, 2014).

[15] Wilson, *Gut Feminism*, 9, emphasis added.

[16] Agustin Fuentes and Aku Visala, eds., *Verbs, Bones, and Brains: Interdisciplinary Perspectives on Human Nature* (Notre Dame, IN: University of Notre Dame Press, 2017).

[17] Cecilia Heyes, *Cognitive Gadgets: The Cultural Evolution of Thinking* (Cambridge, MA: Belknap Press, 2018). Fuentes and Visala explain that this is, more or less, the position taken by thinkers such as Steven Pinker, David Buss, Leda Cosmides, and John Tooby (7). They also list the four basic assumptions of evolutionary psychology: "(1) computational theory of mind, (2) strong nativism, (3) adaptationism, and (4) massive modularity (23, n. 4). See also Jerome H. Barkow, Leda Cosmides, and John Tooby, *The Adapted Mind: Evolutionary Psychology and the Generation of Culture* (New York: Oxford University Press, 1992).

[18] To summarize contemporary understandings of evolution, which supplant outdated strong-adaptationist accounts, Fuentes lists the following assumptions held by evolutionary theorists: "(a) human evolution is a system *not* best modeled via a focus on individual traits or genic reductionism; (b) feedback, rather than linear, models are central in modeling human dynamics, so niche construction is important; (c) ecological and social inheritance are significant in human systems; and (d) flexibility and plasticity in development, body, and behavior are common." Agustin Fuentes, "Putting Evolutionary Theory to

us fend against the creeping impulse toward "neuroreductionism,"[19] which seems to have become a tantalizing temptation in popular-science reporting and even in some neuroscience research labs.

The influence between culture and the bodies that enact and substantiate culture is always already a two-way street—an eminently complex imbrication of genes, languages, hormones, emotions, beliefs, rituals, ecologies, foods, bones, reproductive strategies, art, etc. The complexity of human life warrants interdisciplinary theorizing. Expediency and accessibility of explanations (it is certainly more efficient to consult only one discipline) sometimes win out over thoroughness, a trade-off that is often necessary and may be appropriate, but there's no reason to deny the reality of the underlying complexity. Our best bet at understanding human phenomena like religion is interdisciplinary efforts that combine the expertise of the social sciences, natural sciences, and humanities.

I can anticipate a similar form of resistance from some of my religious-studies colleagues who might shudder at the idea of studying religious *emotions* outright. Out of respect for the objects and subjects of religious studies research, there is a history of avoiding studying emotions specifically. John Corrigan explains: "Many scholars who studied religion blanched when their investigation of the role of emotion led them to the doorstep of the question 'What is *really* going on here?' They could, after all, be dismissed as *reductionists*, a humanities scare word of the late twentieth century that found particularly good traction within the areas of religious studies and the history of religion."[20] I agree with Corrigan that this hesitancy, while legitimate, keeps us from studying an essential dimension of religion. While sociologists do an excellent job studying religious groups and institutions, they tend to have less to say about *religiosity* as such. Our argument in this book suggests that to adequately explain why some religious institutions succeed and some

Work in Investigating Human Nature(s)," in *Verbs, Bones, and Brains: Interdisciplinary Perspectives on Human Nature*, edited by Agustín Fuentes and Aku Visala, 248–259 (Notre Dame, IN: University of Notre Dame Press, 2017), 252. Fuentes cites Agustín Fuentes, "Re-situating Anthropological Approaches to the Evolution of Human Behavior," *Anthropology Today* 25, no. 3 (2009): 12–17; Susan C. Anton and J. Josh Snodgrass, "Origin and Evolution of Genus *Homo*: New Perspectives," *Current Anthropology* 53, no. 6 (2012): 479–496; Jonathan C. K. Wells and Jay T. Stock, "The Biology of the Colonizing Ape," *Yearbook of Physical Anthropology* 50 (2007): 191–222.

[19] Neuroreductionism is characterized by the idea that human consciousness, thoughts, feelings, behaviors, and personality can be adequately explained by looking at the brain alone—that humans *are* their brains. Even though this approach to brain science was thoroughly deconstructed and replaced with more nuanced and interactionist approaches, people outside the field continue to fear that it will return any second. And not for nothing: it is not unheard of for neuroscientists to lazily make neuroreductionist assumptions in their study designs without taking a moment to reflect on the implications of their hypotheses.

[20] John Corrigan, ed. *Feeling Religion* (Durham, NC: Duke University Press, 2017).

don't, it is necessary to have at least a basic understanding of what human religiosity is and how it arises within bodies, brains, and groups. Based on what our data revealed, we simply could not get at what was driving the growth and stability of megachurches without understanding the central roles played by affect and emotion.

Finding Homo Religiosus

Having set the stage for an interdisciplinary bio-social approach to culture and religion, let's begin the story of how megachurches have come to such prominence. We'll start at the beginning . . . of culture as we know it. In his *New York Times*–best-selling book, *Sapiens: A Brief History of Humankind*, Yuval Noah Harari tells the surprising story of how *Homo sapiens,* who were but one among at least six different human species (genus *Homo*) on earth, survived to see the year 2018, when all other species of *Homo* went extinct.[21] The turning point, about 70,000 to 30,000 years ago, appears to have been the emergence of new and unprecedented ways of thinking and communicating that launched *Homo sapiens* into complete dominance. Harari calls it the "Tree of Knowledge" mutation.[22] However, he explains, it wasn't just language, which allowed the increasingly social *sapiens* to talk about hunting, gathering, reproduction, and protection, that made us dominant; it was the ability to talk about things *unseen*. To share stories and create traditions about legends, myths, and gods. Harari explains, "Many animals and human species could previously say, 'Careful! A lion!' However, thanks to the Cognitive Revolution, *Homo sapiens* acquired the ability to say, 'The lion is the guardian spirit of our tribe.'"[23] *Only Homo sapiens* could do this. Harari is talking about *religion*, or at least proto-religion. Not only are we the only species to have religious beliefs and develop religious structures; these may have been part of the secret to our evolutionary success.

Harari highlights the ability to construct and share stories of things unseen as a defining characteristic of religion. But why, from an evolutionary perspective, would we do such things? In addition to reflecting an insight into and curiosity about the unseen sacred depths of the universe, it turns out that these stories have been incredibly effective tools for connection: they've "enabled us not merely to imagine things, but to do so *collectively*" and *that* is

---

[21] Yuval Noah Harari, *Sapiens: A Brief History of Humankind* (New York: HarperCollins, 2015).
[22] Harari, *Sapiens,* 21.
[23] Harari, *Sapiens,* 24.

the ultimate survival secret.[24] Sociologists Jonathan H. Turner and Richard S. Machalek echo this argument: "The analysis of religion . . . provides a segue into what is sometimes termed 'ultrasociality' more generally because, *without religion, societies on a human scale could not have evolved.*"[25] The massive diversity of religions is one example of the fact that *sapiens* coordinate and cooperate with a flexibility seen in *no* other species, including ants, bees, wolves, and chimpanzees. "That's why *Sapiens* rule the world," Harari says. Humans' *ultra*-sociality, and the intensity of human cognitive, emotional, and behavioral plasticity, was unprecedented and is still unmatched.

However, before we can talk about megachurches as a fascinating contemporary expression of creative ultra-sociality, we need to back up a few million years to discover the roots of our social nature.

HOMO COOPERATIVUS

About eight million years ago, a dramatic climate shift caused the dense, cozy forests that had supported all primate life to thin. The forests full of tall, lush trees that had been our ancestors' home were replaced by large expanses of dry grasslands. As forests and their once-abundant resources became increasingly scarce, our individualistic ape ancestors lost the battle for the trees to monkey species and were pushed into the savanna, in search of food and struggling for protection.[26] In these new and strange environmental conditions, survival strategies that served our ape ancestors well in the forests were suddenly inadequate. The transition from forest to grassland proved devastating for almost all primate species, and most quickly (on evolutionary scales) went extinct. In other words, "the savanna became the graveyard for virtually all apes, except for hominins and humans."[27] So the question is: how are we still here?

The traditional answer to that question is that our unparalleled intelligence enabled us to protect ourselves by outsmarting predators and giving us the wherewithal to invent tools, build shelters, and devise hunting and foraging techniques. And the rest is history. While this is true to a certain

[24] Harari, *Sapiens,* 25.

[25] Turner and Machalek, *The New Evolutionary Sociology*, 3, emphasis added.

[26] Jonathan Turner explains that this is likely at least partly due to the fact that monkeys had "tight-knit social structures revolving around dominance hierarchies among males and matrilines among related females, whereas apes evidence much more loosely structured communities composed mostly of weak ties among adults." Jonathan H. Turner, *Human Emotions: A Sociological Theory* (New York: Routledge, 2007), 17.

[27] Jonathan H. Turner, "Using Neurosociology and Evolutionary Sociology to Explain the Origin and Evolution of Religions," *Journal for the Cognitive Science of Religion* 4, no. 1 (2016): 7–29.

extent, it ignores the actual psychosocial mechanisms at play. "Intelligence" wouldn't have gotten us anywhere if we hadn't been able to cooperate. A better understanding of this whole story can help us understand how our intelligence works, how we build, maintain, and rebuild diverse societies, how social structures and constructs affect the people in them and how people, in turn, affect the social structures and constructs that characterize their world.

One striking difference between humans and the last common ancestor we shared with apes seems clear.[28] In Turner's words, "the conclusion is inescapable: virtually all adult ties among the last common ancestor were probably weak; only the basic mammalian attachment of mothers to offspring was strong in the last common ancestor."[29] This refers to when our forest-dwelling ancestors lived in loose, fluid, temporary groupings, with virtually no strong ties between adults, no permanent hierarchy structures, and very little trust between individuals.[30] This is strikingly different from the ways humans live today—we enjoy incredibly strong, sometimes even life-long bonds with many people who are completely genetically unrelated. We can put millions of humans in a small area like New York City and somehow avoid complete chaos (most of the time).

Our ancestors' individualism was simply not going to cut it on the savanna. Luckily, natural selection stumbled upon a new way to do sociality in the absence of what is called a "bioprogrammer instinct," which is the way that ants, bees, and wolves live in colonies, hives, and packs. The human strategy for sociality built upon, expanded, and emerged from the one strong social tie that *was* evident in our ancestors: the mother–infant bond. This ability to bond tightly to another human (for at least a short amount of time, while the infant is young) was slowly enhanced, generalized, and rendered more flexible. Hominids began bonding not only with their babies, but also with their siblings, other caregivers, and eventually nonrelated adults including sexual partners, friends, and members of their expanding "communities." Humans gradually developed the most intensely diverse, flexible, dynamic, and complex social life ever seen in a mammalian species. Looking at this

[28] To explore the roots of our evolutionary success, which is really the story of our *social* success, Turner and Machalek advocate for the use of cladistic analysis. A clade is a set of species that appear to have evolved from a common ancestor, and cladistic analysis of *Homo sapiens* looks at the particular evolutionary selection pressures faced by *our* ancestors compared to those of the great apes, with whom we share a common primate ancestor—the one ape ancestor who, after climbing down from the trees and trying its luck in the savanna, survived. In this way, we can make inferences about what our last common ancestor looked like and how, since then, humans' brains and social natures have catapulted humans into evolutionary success (for now at least). Turner and Machalek, *The New Evolutionary Sociology*.

[29] Turner, *Human Emotions*, 21.

[30] Turner, *Human Emotions*, 22.

process a little closer will introduce us to the pivotal neurohormone oxytocin I mentioned in my introduction.

HOMO GENEROSUS

In a surprising twist of fate, the mutations that seem to have been the most important for our ancestors happened in the *brain*—instead of our bodies growing faster or stronger, our brains got *bigger*. As our brains got larger and more complex, the size of infant heads grew. Unfortunately, female cervixes did not grow at quite the same rate. Since a baby's survival hinges at least partly on whether they can make it out safely when the time comes, natural selection appears to have gradually shortened humans' gestation period. However, this does not mean that human brains develop faster in utero; rather, it means that human infants are born very neurologically immature and undergo substantial neural growth, pruning, and development *after* they are born.[31] So this means that human babies are less developed and more helpless than any other mammals at birth. This extended period of intensive infant and toddler care massively affected how human childrearing needs to happen.

American anthropologist and primatologist Sarah Blaffer Hrdy argues that this small shift was one of the primary initial impetuses for the evolution of cooperation and hyper-sociality in humans. While other anthropologists and social scientists argue that intergroup conflict and warfare were what made "altruism" and cooperation important, she argues that the initial evolutionary stimulus for cooperation, sharing, trust, and empathy lies in the critical job of rearing children. After all, if the babies don't survive, neither does the species. She notes that aside from intellect, one of the most fundamental differences between humans and nonhuman primates is that human mothers *allow other humans to hold* their newborn babies.[32]

Hrdy emphasizes just how unusual this level of trust among mothers is; for example, an orangutan mother will hold her newborn *100%* of the time, day and night, for about *six* months after it is born.[33] She will not allow anyone to so much as touch her baby. How did human mothers get to be so trusting?

Well, what's a natural process to do? After all, evolution had to find *something* to keep these strangely weak, hairless human creatures alive, and

[31] Turner and Machalek, *The New Evolutionary Sociology*, 317.

[32] Sarah Blaffer Hrdy, *Mothers and Others: The Evolutionary Origins of Mutual Understanding* (Cambridge, MA: Belknap Press, 2009), 73.

[33] Hrdy, *Mothers and Others*, 68. See also Sarah Blaffer Hrdy, *The Origin of Emotionally Modern Humans* [lecture]. October 17, 2011. Published online January 9, 2012. Retrieved from Cornell University YouTube, https://www.youtube.com/watch?v=07YlpVdplqA&list=UUfTfuTTALrsxUWjisrdOWtA.

apparently it did not settle on larger cervixes for larger infant heads; instead it stumbled upon *trust*.[34] Since human infants, compared to other great apes, arrive only half-baked, they are dependent on adults for food, safety, and education long after they are weaned—far longer than any other mammal.[35] This creates an enormous burden for the mother, especially if she has another child before her first has become self-sufficient. In such cases, other members of the community, kin and non-kin alike, would have *had* to step in to help the mother ensure the safety and provisioning of her children. The sheer number of calories needed to rear a child is more than one foraging mother can provide.[36] The future of *Homo sapiens* depended on alloparents: genetically unrelated adults who share parental responsibilities.

Therefore, a mother needed to develop *social networks* ample enough to guarantee the availability, willingness, and trustworthiness of alloparents for her young. Not only that, but the adults who become alloparents must be empathic and generous enough to make them willing to spend resources on someone else's child.[37] For our forest-dwelling ancestors who preferred to wander alone with their (smaller-headed) babies, this type of alloparental arrangement was unthinkable. But without this system of "cooperative breeding," early humans would not have been able to keep their big-brained children alive long enough for them to reach breeding age. In fact, humans (along with marmosets and tamarins, who also exhibit alloparenting) are the *only* primates who, if faced with insufficient alloparental help, will harm their own infants.[38]

ENTER, OXYTOCIN

Alloparental care became a possibility through the expansion and diversification of the oxytocin system through natural selection. During early mammalian evolution, oxytocin appears to have functioned primarily as both a motivator and a reward for maternal care. Oxytocin stimulates muscle contractions during childbirth, promotes milk production in nursing mothers, and helps establish a firm emotional and psychological bond between mother and infant. As the infant grows, oxytocin continues to play an important

[34] Note that, despite my tongue-in-cheek language here personifying evolution, the evolutionary process is not "driven" by any goal or end. The randomness of variation cannot be overstated.

[35] Hrdy, *Mothers and Others*, 31.

[36] Hillard Kaplan, "Evolutionary and Wealth Flows Theories of Fertility: Empirical Tests and New Models," *Proceedings of the National Academy of Sciences USA* 102 (1994): 15294–15298; Hrdy, *Mothers and Others*.

[37] Hrdy, *Mothers and Others*, 31.

[38] Hrdy, *Mothers and Others,* 99.

role: when a mother is separated or hears her infant's cry, oxytocin functions as an incredibly motivating aspect of the stress response, and when she is reunited and able to soothe the infant's distress, she will experience a flood of "feel good" oxytocin, which seems to be a "safety signal" that all is well.[39] Gradually, the oxytocin system seems to have become more and more generalized, facilitating the formation of bonds between infants and fathers, siblings, elders, and friends.[40] This must have been an effective strategy because in modern humans, oxytocin appears to moderate nearly *every* level of social interaction. Neurophilosopher Patricia Churchland theorizes that oxytocin is not only the "hub" of the social hormones, but it also reveals the *root* of human hyper-sociality in the first place.[41] In fact, even though it may function slightly differently in conjunction with varying levels of testosterone and/or estrogen, human men have base levels of oxytocin at least as high as, or even sometimes higher than, women.[42] Oxytocin plays an integral role in the social and mating behavior of many mammalian species, but in combination with humans' cognitive, symbolic, and communicative abilities, our social intelligence and socio-emotional dexterity is unmatched.

Oxytocin is very complicated and difficult to study—for one, because the only way to test it reliably is by drawing blood—but scholars tend to agree that oxytocin helps facilitate the creation of large social groups in which members protect, take care of, and watch out for one another in the absence of genetic relations. In her book *The Brain's Body: Neuroscience and Corporeal Politics,* Victoria Pitts-Taylor analyzes oxytocin as not only being at the core of kinship relations, but also as being one of the core sites of flexibility, creativity, and material agency in human embodiment.[43] In what feels obvious to us now, living in twenty-first-century America, it is the case that affective and

[39] Patricia Churchland, *Braintrust: What Neuroscience Tells Us about Morality* (Princeton, NJ: Princeton University Press, 2011).

[40] Hrdy, *Mothers and Others,* 213. Churchland, *Braintrust.*

[41] Churchland, *Braintrust.*

[42] Omri Weisman, Orna Zagoory-Sharon, Inna Schneiderman, Ilanit Gordon, and Ruth Feldman, "Plasma Oxytocin Distribution in a Large Cohort of Women and Men and Their Gender-Specific Associations with Anxiety," *Psychoneuroendocrinology* 38, no. 5 (2013): 694–701. For example, oxytocin was found to function somewhat differently in men and women in response to stressful social situations and troubled relationships. Laura D. Kubzansky, Wendy Berry Mendes, Allison A. Appleton, Jason Block, and Gail K. Adler, "A Heartfelt Response: Oxytocin Effects on Response to Social Stress in Men and Women," *Biological Psychology* 90, no. 1 (2012): 1–9; Shelley E. Taylor, Shimon Saphire-Bernstein, and Teresa E. Seeman, "Are Plasma Oxytocin in Women and Plasma Vasopressin in Men Biomarkers of Distressed Pair-Bond Relationships?" *Psychological Science* 21, no. 1 (2010): 3–7. See also Shan Gao, Benjamin Becker, Lizho Luo, Yayuan Geng, Weihua Zhao, Yu Yin, Jiehui Hu, Zhao Gao, Qiyong Gong, Rene Hurlemann, Dezhong Yao, and Keith M. Kendrick, "Oxytocin, the Peptide That Bonds the Sexes Also Divides Them," *Proceedings of the National Academy of Sciences USA* 113, no. 27 (2016): 7650–7654.

[43] Pitts-Taylor, *The Brain's Body.*

emotional bonds with your "chosen family" are often significantly stronger than your bonds (if you even have them) with your genetic relations. A social and cultural explanation of this phenomenon can be enhanced by looking at oxytocin and its role in *affective* (vs. genetic) kinship bonds. Pitts-Taylor argues that the oxytocin system demonstrates that it is *not* through genetic relations, but rather interpersonal relationships, that affective kinship bonds are built.

This requires a fundamental reframing of what it means to be "biologically" related; and such a reframing is rigorously supported by research in endocrinology (the study of hormones), biology, and neuroscience. Pitts-Taylor explains, "Being biologically related does not have to mean genetically related; it can mean *having a biological investment in another*, in the form of an inter-corporeal tie to another, that is the product of interaction, intimacy, or companionship."[44] In a bio-social feedback loop, strong social ties produce affective kinship bonds. So this means that Pitts-Taylor is *not* comparing nonbiological to biological relations—but rather showing that affective kinship relations supported by the oxytocin system *are* biological kinship relations even if they are not *genetically* inscribed. Our bodies routinely create strong, enduring, and transformative attachments to people to whom we are not genetically related. So, for example, she explains, quoting Churchland, "the attachment for adoptive mothers 'can be every bit as powerful'—in other words, as biologically supported—'as attachment to a baby carried and delivered.'"[45]

This illuminates a biological dimension for what anthropologists call "fictive kin" networks (though in this case, the word "fictive" is misleading since these bonds are anything but fiction). Think of how frequently religious groups refer to in-group members with familial terms. The Quran says, "The believers are nothing else than brothers" (Surah Hujurat 49:10); the Torah has several references to all people as children of God, and "Israel"—the Jewish people—as God's "firstborn" (Exodus 4:22); Christians are brothers and sisters in Christ, priests are called "Father," nuns are "Sisters" or "Mother," and "pope" comes from the Latin word *papa*; and in Tibetan Buddhism, those who receive tantric initiation together call each other "*vajra* brothers" and "*vajra* sisters" and, according to tradition, *vajra* (which means "unbreakable") relations are carried through death and rebirth to the soul's next lifetime (whereas genetic relations are not).[46] These are explicit indications that

[44] Pitts-Taylor, *The Brain's Body*, 117.

[45] Pitts-Taylor, *The Brain's Body*, 107. Pitts-Taylor quotes Churchland, *Braintrust*, 34.

[46] Martin A. Mills, "*Vajra* Brother, *Vajra* Sister: Renunciation, Individualism and the Household in Tibetan Buddhist Monasticism," *Journal of the Royal Anthropological Institute* 6, no. 1 (2000): 17–34, 24–25.

one of the goals of religious structures is to produce kinship networks in the absence of genetic relations.

Homo Sentimentalis

So where is oxytocin, and what else is in those big brains of ours? Over millions of years, a set of vital shifts and developments took place in our ancestors' brains. It is not only that humans have *substantially* larger brains (proportionally) than any other mammal—the specific *parts* of the brain and the way they expanded constitute evidence for how sociality and emotions work. Turner argues that, from a sociological perspective, we simply "cannot understand the dynamics of emotions and their relationship to social bonds, social structures, and culture without some appreciation for how natural selection worked on specific regions of the brain to produce a *new kind of ape*: one who used emotions to sustain the group, and thereby, survive on the African savanna."[47] Thus it is important to note that *before* we see vital expansions in the brain regions known for managing higher-level cognition such as planning, decision making, and conscious calculations—the prefrontal cortex and the neocortex—we see significant expansion of the *affective* limbic system (including the septum, amygdala, hippocampus, thalamus, and hypothalamus).[48] These subcortical regions, which lie deep inside the brain, facilitate somatic memory, regulate pleasure, and give us our mysterious "spider-sense"—our ability to detect and respond to danger even before we consciously process what is happening. It is also the part of the brain that releases oxytocin. So unsurprisingly, the oxytocin system was involved in the first evolutionary adaptations that began forming the distinctly human brain.

Generally, the limbic system instigates bodily changes that we experience consciously as feelings and interpret as emotions. These affective bodily changes—how we *feel* before, during, and after each interaction—give us vital information about our surroundings and our situations. Affect alerts us, on a deep subconscious level, of the presence of threats both physical and social, and the presence of possible mates; affect motivates and pulls our attention toward enjoyable, exciting, or surprising things; and affect kindles

[47] Turner, *Human Emotions*, 27, emphasis added. He says, "The sociology of emotions must be viewed in this context. What we study represents *an adaptation* to a difficult habitat—at least for an ape . . ." (27).
[48] The neocortex, which is the wrinkled outside layer of the brain, is somewhat differentiated—this is where we get the left brain/right brain discussion—and yet it is also extraordinarily connected via the corpus callosum. All of these size increases are vital for our conversation—limbic, prefrontal cortex, and neocortex. Antonio Damasio, *Descartes' Error: Emotion, Reason, and the Human Brain* (New York: G. P. Putnam, 1994). See discussion in Turner, *Human Emotions*, 45–46.

the "inner torment" of shame in moments of transgression and alienation. As a part of this system, the "feeling" of increases and decreases in oxytocin often manifests on the diffuse level of *affect*.

Lisa Feldman Barrett, who conducts research on the neuroscience of emotion at Northwestern University, describes what affect is and how it works. She explains that each human has what she calls a "body budget."[49] A person's body budget is the status of their body's internal environment, including things like current heart rate, temperature, and blood pressure, as well as *predictions* about what is happening to the conscious person. For example, if the body detects the presence of a danger, the body-budgeting regions predict that you will need to start running, so they will signal the heart to start pumping your blood faster and they may tell the kidneys to release some cortisol for an extra surge of energy.[50] Your body budget works to make sure you have enough energy to make it through the day and stay alive. Barrett continues:

> Your brain must contend with this continuous, ever-changing flow of interoceptive sensations from the predictions that keep you alive. Sometimes you're aware of them, and other times you're not, but they are always part of your brain's model of the world. They are [. . .] the scientific basis for simple feelings of pleasure, displeasure, arousal, and calmness that you experience every day. For some, the flow is like the trickle of a tranquil brook. For others, it's like a raging river. Sometimes the sensations are transformed into emotions, but [. . .] even when they're only in the background, they influence what you do, what you think, and what you perceive.[51]

Oxytocin contributes to the affective milieu of the body in this way. The sensations and feelings that the body-budgeting regions and the interoceptive network produce are close to, but not quite, what we would call "emotions." They are affect. However, emotions and affect are closely related in that emotions are the *social-cultural interpretation* of affective states. Affect helps us navigate the world and social interactions because they summarize so much subtle information and evidence into a physiological cue that is nearly impossible to ignore. Barrett says, "When your budget is unbalanced, your affect doesn't instruct you how to act in any specific way, but it prompts

[49] See Lisa Feldman Barrett, *How Emotions Are Made: The Secret Life of the Brain* (Boston: Houghton Mifflin Harcourt, 2017).
[50] Barrett, *How Emotions Are Made*, 69.
[51] Barrett, *How Emotions Are Made*, 71–72.

your brain to search for explanations."[52] And your brain is quick to respond with all sorts of creative rationalizations. Emotions, then, are *conceptual labels* that we give to the conscious experience of certain culturally common manifestations of affect.[53]

Barrett's concepts of the body budget and the interoceptive network seem to reflect an important insight that has begun flooding into all levels of cognitive science, neuroscience, and endocrinology: that we cannot understand how the brain and body work without also understanding the complex interaction among mind, body, environments, and culture. Cognitive scientists used to study the way humans think with the assumption that the brain is a computer-like processing unit. Now, they realize that you can't study thinking without also looking at affect, emotions, context, and sociality.[54]

Through the complex evolutionary process, humans have developed a revolutionary ability to attach and bond to those around them by capitalizing on an enhanced and expanded oxytocin system. This foundation of oxytocin-supported ultra-sociality played a significant role in facilitating our incredible growth in social intelligence, complex cognition, generosity, mutual care, and cooperation, enabling humans to survive in extremely hostile environments. So, in the story of human evolution, it is not only our brains' wrinkled gray matter (which houses the intellectual capabilities usually considered most impressive), but also changes in our subcortical limbic system, that set us apart. This destabilizes the common misunderstanding that our "higher" brain or the areas of the brain that are "more evolved" function to overcome the "lower" urges of our animal or "reptilian" brain.[55] Even the most ancient

[52] Barrett, *How Emotions Are Made*, 73.

[53] Barrett's theory of "constructed emotion" is an argument against the notion of specific systems for specific biologically inscribed "basic emotions," which has been the dominant viewpoint in the neuroscience of emotion for decades. Joseph LeDoux holds a similar position and explains the emergence of fear and anxiety: "The amygdala, when turned on, activates certain behaviors and releases stress hormones. It activates a lot of body systems. It triggers brain arousal. It focuses attention on the threat. It does a lot of stuff that ultimately contributes to the feeling of fear, but is not the feeling of fear. Fear is not in the amygdala. Fear is a consequence. It's like you've got a lot of ingredients that are non-emotional ingredients that when put together allows the cognitive brain to make the feeling of fear." Charvy Narain, "A Conversation with Joseph LeDoux," *Cold Spring Harbor Symposia on Quantitative Biology* 79 (2014): 279–281, 280.

[54] Damasio, 1994, 87. See also Eric Eich, John F. Kihlstrom, Gordon H. Bower, Joseph P. Forgas, and Paula M. Niedenthal, eds., *Cognition and Emotion* (New York: Oxford University Press, 2000).

[55] For example, in 1992, John Tooby and Leda Cosmides described the "Standard Social Science Model" as one that suggested that since humans' larger brain had enabled culture, culture now essentially replaced the role of biology in directing thoughts and behavior. Although many scholars critiqued this as somewhat of a straw man, it does seem that some sociological theorizing is underwritten with this dismissal of embodied biological functions. John Tooby and Leda Cosmides, "The Psychological Foundations of Culture," in *The Adapted Mind: Evolutionary Psychology and the Generation of Culture*, edited by Jerome H. Barkow, Leda Cosmides, and John Tooby, 19–136 (New York: Oxford University Press, 1992).

features of our brain have undergone dramatic growth, expansion, and development; brain-wide renovations in connectivity have revolutionized the way that areas like the limbic system influence all levels of human functioning.[56] This means that all of our most prized intellectual capabilities were built upon and depended on a highly social brain. So, finally, the idea that the limbic system or the neocortex somehow operate separately, or that some sort of intellectual cognitive reasoning operates independently from the affective emotional systems, is simply inaccurate.

Our evolved cognitive structures that both support and enable religious beliefs and facilitate the sophistication, memory, and representational vibrancy of religious rituals arose out of this social-affective-cognitive adaptive nexus. So hyper-sociality alone did not make religion inevitable in human societies, but hyper-sociality did provide the conditions within which our cognitive scaffolding could flourish and make religion "inevitable." Cognition is inextricably intertwined with emotion; they are never separate.

Our cognitive scaffolding contains innate cognitive biases that enable, encourage, and, indeed, make nearly irresistible the belief in supernatural things. Human cognition also enables the creation of social imaginaries, institutions, and roles that emerge not from some physical cause, but rather via social construction. The cognitive structures that enable the social construction of reality are evolved and universal—even as, of course, their context-dependent constructions are not. In regard to religious cognition specifically, we can, for example, highlight the ability to detect unseen agents and to ascribe thoughts, intentions, and feelings to them through our tendency toward "systematic anthropomorphism."[57] We have the cognitive ability to construct and think in concert with symbolic structures and ritual representations that bring meaning to our social grouping and enhance social bonds. We can also inscribe extremely complex episodic and semantic memories facilitating the creation of what Harvey Whitehouse calls *imagistic* and *doctrinal* ritual experiences, and what Robert McCauley and E. Thomas Lawson call ritual competence, which then help generate

---

[56] This includes renovations in networking throughout the brain and the corpus callosum, which connects the two sides of the brain. This connectivity facilitates a complexity, efficiency, and flexibility in the human brain that outperforms all other mammals. When hominids faced new selection pressures in the savanna, natural selection acted upon the *subcortical* areas first, which set the foundation for sociality, "and then," Turner and his colleagues explain, "only relatively late in hominin evolution, did natural selection begin to grow the size of the *neocortex* of hominins."

[57] Stewart E. Guthrie, *Faces in the Clouds: A New Theory of Religion* (New York: Oxford University Press, 1993); see also Stewart E. Guthrie, "Religion as Anthropomorphism: A Cognitive Theory," in *The Oxford Handbook of Evolutionary Psychology and Religion*, edited by J. Liddle and T. Shackelford (Oxford University Press, 2016), DOI: 10.1093/oxfordhb/9780199397747.013.6. And on agency detection, see Justin L. Barrett, *Why Would Anyone Believe in God?* (Walnut Creek, CA: AltaMira Press, 2004).

the socially constructed meaning systems that we call *religions*.[58] While the primary lens we've used in this book is emotional, the ever-present cognitive phenomena are backing and cocreating social reality and are of utmost importance in understanding the evolution of religion. I will be referring to these cognitive capacities and functions throughout.[59]

Joseph Henrich, a Harvard professor of human evolutionary biology, has written extensively about the evolution of religion, culture, and prosociality, and attends closely to the foundational cognitive mechanisms at play in these processes.[60] His research asks how religion—religious beliefs, practices, and structures—contributes to cultural evolution.[61] Key to this process are effective methods for transmitting ideas throughout cultures. He shows how, based on the evolved cognitive bias toward social learning, religious ritual practices and their associated beliefs can create self-stabilizing systems. These interlocking components together can facilitate commitment to ideas and goals that promote in-group cooperation.[62] For example, Henrich suggests that a person's enthusiastic ritual performance can be a signal of commitment and confident belief, ensuring onlookers that he *actually* believes what he says he does, and therefore enhancing the credibility of the belief itself. Religious ideas, practices, and rituals that are supported by such "credibility enhancing displays" can be contagious—they spread quickly, survive the test of time, and are passed on through generations because they tap into cognitive

---

[58] Harvey Whitehouse, *Modes of Religiosity: A Cognitive Theory of Religious Transmission* (Walnut Creek, CA: AltaMira Press, 2004). Robert N. McCauley and E. Thomas Lawson, *Bringing Ritual to Mind: Psychological Foundations of Cultural Forms* (Cambridge: Cambridge University Press, 2002).

[59] For more on the cognitive science of religion, see, for example, Luther H. Martin and Donald Wiebe, *Religion Explained?: The Cognitive Science of Religion after Twenty-Five Years* (London: Bloomsbury, 2017); and Dimitris Xygalatas and William W. McCorkle, Jr., eds., *Mental Culture: Classical Social Theory and the Cognitive Science of Religion* (London: Acumen, 2013).

[60] See, for example, Joseph Henrich, "The Evolution of Costly Displays, Cooperation and Religion: Credibility Enhancing Displays and Their Implications for Cultural Evolution," *Evolution and Human Behavior* 30, no. 4 (2009): 244–260; Scott Atran and Joseph Henrich, "The Evolution of Religion: How Cognitive By-Products, Adaptive Learning Heuristics, Ritual Displays, and Group Competition Generate Deep Commitments to Prosocial Religions," *Biological Theory* 5, no. 1 (2010): 18–30; Edward Slingerland, Joseph Henrich, and Ara Norenzayan, "The Evolution of Prosocial Religions," in *Cultural Evolution: Society, Technology, Language, and Religion*, edited by Peter J. Richerson and Morten H. Christiansen, 334–348 (Cambridge, MA: MIT Press, 2013).

[61] See for example, Joseph Bulbulia, Armin W. Geertz, Quentin D. Atkinson, Emma Cohen, Nicholas Evans, Pieter Francois, Herbert Gintis, Russell D. Gray, Joseph Henrich, Fiona M. Jordon, Ara Norenzayan, Peter J. Richerson, Edward Slingerland, Peter Turchin, Harvey Whitehouse, Thomas Widlock, and David S. Wilson, "The Cultural Evolution of Religion," in *Cultural Evolution: Society, Technology, Language, and Religion,* edited by Peter J. Richerson and Morten H. Christiansen, 381–404 (Cambridge, MA: MIT Press, 2013).

[62] Henrich, "Evolution of Costly Displays."

mechanisms and are able to evoke such strong affective responses.[63] Henrich insists that in order to understand the emergence of both the cognitive and social elements of religion, we need to frame them in terms of gene–culture *coevolution*—in which there exist complex feedback loops between cultural and genetic evolutionary processes.[64]

Similarly, in their impressively comprehensive analysis of the evolution of religion, Turner and his coauthors of *The Emergence and Evolution of Religion by Means of Natural Selection*, write, "The very forces that pushed hominins to become more social, more group oriented, and eventually more capable of forming enduring ties . . . *are the very same forces* that would make religion *inevitable* in human societies."[65] And, not only that, but they continue, "Without religion, societies on a human scale could not have evolved."[66] These are strong statements—that religion has been both *inevitable* (given the propensities of our brains) and *necessary* for the survival of our species. The reason Turner and his coauthors can make such a claim is because religious structures, since they are centered around and legitimated by *sacred* or *supernatural* forces, often provide significantly stronger potential for community-wide cohesion than other social structures.

Religions deal with matters of life and death, powers unseen, the mysterious and potentially threatening supernatural realm—whatever is deemed to be of *ultimate* importance in a society is what gets called religion. Whether these gods or forces or practices are able to cause rain to fall during a drought, make your sick aunt well again, punish your sins, or liberate you from the bondage of suffering, they are *important*. They have the power to inspire people to make great feats of moral strength, self-sacrifice, generosity, and love; and they also, one must not forget, have the power to inspire acts of hatred, violence, and even genocide.

Homo Duplex

Individuals' survival hinges on their relationality and dependence on others. Thus, compared to our closest evolutionary ancestors, cooperation has

---

[63] For theory on how ritual structures support the transmission of counterintuitive ideas, see: Aiyana K. Willard, Joseph Henrich, and Ara Norenzayan, "Memory and Belief in the Transmission of Counterintuitive Content," *Human Nature* 27, no. 3 (2016): 221–243.

[64] Peter J. Richerson, Robert Boyd, and Joseph Henrich, "Gene-Culture Coevolution in the Age of Genomics," *Proceedings of the National Academy of Sciences USA* 107 (2010): 8985–8992; Peter J. Richerson and Robert Boyd, *Not by Genes Alone: How Culture Transformed Human Evolution* (Chicago: University of Chicago Press, 2005).

[65] Turner et al., *The Emergence and Evolution of Religion*, 2, emphasis added.

[66] Turner et al., *The Emergence and Evolution of Religion*, 3.

become the hallmark of human nature. It's our claim to fame—we are *homo cooperativus*. Sounds great, doesn't it? We have learned to live together in harmony!

Obviously not. While it *is* remarkable that we have built such successful and large societies, no one would claim that we got there through peace and harmony, even if it is a nice thought. After all, one of the most sophisticated manifestations of human cooperation has been large-scale warfare. Nothing about our evolution, our bodies, or our societies is simple. Humans are *also* independent, self-serving, ambitious, and sometimes malicious or even violent. Our sense of *self* matters—we don't only find strength in numbers, but also from within. Essentially, we have constant competing interests and goals. We are *homo duplex*.

We explored this notion of *homo duplex*, first introduced by Émile Durkheim, in Chapter 2. Every single day of our lives is a balancing act between finding ways to meet our individual needs while also meeting our social needs. Our last common ancestor with the great apes was fiercely independent and more than able to fend for herself in the treetops. Our increasingly large brains expanded both our palate for affective and social complexity *and* our penchant for inward thought, self-knowledge, and ambitious ingenuity.[67] In other words, human's natural capacity for and tendency toward creative social living is in constant interaction with individualistic desires and motives.

It is important to note two things that are reflected both in Durkheim's notion of *homo duplex* and in what we know about the brain. First, individualism and sociality are *both* the products of complex bio-cultural processes. This means that it is *not* somehow the case that humans must overcome their "natural" individualistic urges by becoming "cultured" and social. And second, these two sides do not constitute a "'pure' or absolute dichotomy." Jonathan S. Fish explains that Durkheim never intended *duplex* to imply a true dualism. For Durkheim, he says, "The process of becoming human involved much more in the way of moral struggle and effort, as each individual strived to achieve his or her social nature through the forging of attachments with others, as a context for then making important judgements affecting his

---

[67] The shifts, pre-adaptations, and behavioral propensities that eventually enabled the emergence of religion also included things like the capacity for verbal and gestural language, a dramatic increase in the ability to think about the past and future, and an increase in the ability to store and retrieve complex knowledge. Turner, Maryanski, Petersen, and Geertz define a "preadaptation" (also called an "exaptation") as "an earlier trait installed by natural selection or [. . .] a byproduct of selection entailed to an earlier trait." Jonathan H. Turner, Alexandra Maryanski, Anders Klostergaard Petersen, and Armin W. Geertz, *The Emergence and Evolution of Religion by Means of Natural Selection* (New York: Routledge, 2018), 76.

or her own life *as well* as the lives of other people."[68] In fact, as it turns out, satisfaction of our individual needs is almost always dependent upon our social needs getting met also. And so, when Fuentes and Visala rhetorically ask, "Are we naturally inclined toward altruism and selflessness as some classical liberal thinkers such as Rousseau claimed, or is our state of nature war against everybody as Hobbes insisted?"[69] The answer to their question appears to be somewhere between both and neither.

This tension is also reflected in what we know about the way oxytocin influences social behavior. Oxytocin has become somewhat of a popular-science golden child. Journalists and researchers alike have dubbed it the "love hormone," the "cuddle drug," and the "moral molecule."[70] Exciting reports that oxytocin intensifies orgasms and makes men want to interact with their children more have led at least one researcher to make the bold claim that oxytocin might be the elixir we've been looking for to "rebond our troubled world."[71]

However, more recent research shows that while oxytocin may help make humans social, it does not make us *good*. It appears to be active in *all* interactions—both the good and the not-so-good—from protecting marriages against the threat of adultery (according to one study) to encouraging out-group hostility (in defense of the in-group).[72] It is also implicated in vigilance to perceived threats, envy, gloating, and even social

[68] Jonathan S. Fish, "*Homo duplex* Revisited: A Defense of Emile Durkheim's Theory of the Moral Self," *Journal of Classic Sociology* 13, no. 3 (2013): 338–358. See also Mark S. Cladis, "Suffering to Become Human: A Durkheimian Perspective," in *Suffering and Evil: The Durkheimian Legacy*, edited by W. S. F. Pickering and Massimo Rosati, 81–100 (Oxford: Durkheim Press/Berghahn, 2008).

[69] Agustin Fuentes and Aku Visala, "Introduction: The Many Faces of Human Nature," in *Verbs, Bones, and Brains: Interdisciplinary Perspectives on Human Nature*, edited by Agustin Fuentes and Aku Visala (Notre Dame, IN: Notre Dame University Press, 2017), 3.

[70] For example, see: Viola Gad, "Can Oxytocin Get Me a Boyfriend?" *Popular Science*, April 23, 2013, https://www.popsci.com/science/article/2013-04/can-oxytocin-get-me-boyfriend; Lee Dye, "A Love Drug? Oxytocin Hormone Makes Mothers Kinder," *ABCNews*, January 11, 2012, https://abcnews.go.com/Technology/love-drug-oxytocin-cuddle-chemical-scientists-makes-mothers/story?id=15330910; Paul Zak, *The Moral Molecule: The Source of Love and Prosperity* (New York: Dutton/Penguin Group, 2012); see also Paul Zak's TED Talk on oxytocin, "Trust, Morality—and Oxytocin?" TEDGlobal 2011, accessed May 23, 2018, https://www.ted.com/talks/paul_zak_trust_morality_and_oxytocin?language=en.

[71] Mark Honigsbaum, "Oxytocin: Could the 'Trust Hormone' Rebond Our Troubled World?" *The Guardian*, August 20, 2011, https://www.theguardian.com/science/2011/aug/21/oxytocin-zak-neuroscience-trust-hormone?INTCMP=SRCH. On orgasms and men playing with children, see Rachael Rettner, "'Love Hormone' Oxytocin May Intensify Orgasms," *Huffington Post*, April, 4, 2014, https://www.huffingtonpost.com/2014/04/04/oxytocin-love-hormone-orgasm_n_5090992.html; and Maia Szalavitz, "Oxytocin May Forge Bonds between Dads and Children," *Time*, December 14, 2012, http://healthland.time.com/2012/12/14/oxytocin-may-forge-bonds-between-dads-and-children/.

[72] Adultery: Dirk Scheele, Nadine Striepens, Onur Gunturkun, Sandra Deutschlander, Wolfgang Maier, Keith M. Kendrick, and Rene Hurlemann, "Oxytocin Modulates Social Distance between Males and Females," *Journal of Neuroscience* 32, no. 46 (2012): 16074–16079. Out-group hostility: Carsten K. W. De Dreu, Lindred L. Greer, Gerben A. Van Kleef, Shaul Shalvi, and Michel J. J. Handgraaf, "Oxytocin Promotes Human Ethnocentrism," *Proceedings of the National Academy of Sciences USA* 108, no. 4 (2011): 1262–1266.

aggression.[73] Of course, as our book has shown, we should never assume that *religious affects* necessarily make humans good, either. Religious social structures are incredibly diverse living traditions that instill astonishingly strong motivations and social commitments to the in-group's goals and values. Religious affects can be harnessed in a manner that promotes peace and well-being, as easily as they can be exploited for corrupt and violent purposes. And as we saw in Part III, megachurches are clearly no exception.

Humans are a complex mix of cognitive abilities and constraints, physiological drives, desires, needs, and motives. The story of human nature is the story of cultural creativity in the face of biological constraint *and* biological flexibility in the face of cultural constraints. With this in mind, let's now narrow our discussion to explore one way that humans in at least one social structure—the megachurch—rise to this challenge of twenty-first-century America. How do they get the oxytocin and emotional energy flowing? As it turns out, the answer is once again a complex bio-cultural one, and oxytocin remains a main character.

HOMO RELIGIOSUS

What we call *religion*—which has, of course, taken many forms since the emergence of *Homo sapiens*—continues to shape our cultures, groups, and individual minds. On the one hand, religion appears to help humans (*homo duplex*) survive and navigate their complex mix of individual and social needs. But at the same time, it has become a superorganism in and of itself, and it shapes *us* and our minds, just as much as we shape it.

So far, I have discussed the bio-cultural evolutionary changes that happened in the brain and body that enabled ultra-sociality and eventually religion. However, the development of the huge, complex social institutions that we call religions is a much longer and more complicated story. In fact, Turner outlines *five* different types of natural selection, only one of which is a biological mechanism for human organisms. The other four types are sociocultural and have to do with the evolution of group structures, social institutions, and societies. Given the complexity of the issue and to keep this appendix to a manageable length, I can only gesture toward the fact that I have but chipped away at the tip of the iceberg. For a more comprehensive understanding of the evolution of religion, one must also consider levels of selection that emerge with social groups and institutions—for example, Turner suggests

---

[73] Envy, gloating, and aggression: Simone G. Shamay-Tsoory, Meytal Fischer, Jonathan Dvash, Hagai Harari, Nufar Perach-Bloom, and Yechiel Levkovitz, "Intranasal Administration of Oxytocin Increases Envy and Schadenfreude (Gloating)," *Biological Psychiatry* 66, no. 9 (2009): 864–870.

Spencerian Type-1 selection, Durkheimian selection, Spencerian Type-2 selection, and Marxian selection (see brief explanations in footnote 74).[74]

My discussion here focuses on only one sliver of the way that, as each of these levels of selection has done its part to shape and mold all the thousands of religious institutions that we have today, somehow *megachurches* have found success in the sociocultural niche of twenty-first-century America. Especially today when, as Edward Lawler, Shane Thye, and Jeongkoo Yoon explain, "in an individualistic, market-oriented social world, the ties of people to social units—small groups, organizations, communities, nations—tend to be

---

[74] Turner et al., *The Emergence and Evolution of Religion*. See also Turner and Machalek, *The New Evolutionary Sociology;* and Jonathan H. Turner and Seth Abrutyn, "Returning the 'Social' to Evolutionary Sociology: Reconsidering Spencer, Durkheim, and Marx's Models of 'Natural' Selection," *Sociological Perspectives* 60, no. 3 (2016): 529–556; and Jonathan H. Turner, "Using Neurosociology and Evolutionary Sociology to Explain the Origin and Evolution of Religions," *Journal for the Cognitive Science of Religion* 4, no. 1 (2016): 7–29.

The first and primary type of natural selection, which I have looked at here, is Darwinian. This is what most people think of when they think "evolution"—in terms of religion, it refers to the selection of biological traits that enhanced the brain (especially its ability to generate complex affects), the human tendency toward sociality, symbolic communication like language and stories, and the development of need-states and behavioral propensities (which we'll talk about in the last section of this appendix).

Second, when a group faces a new problem that none of their existing coping mechanisms or social structures can help with, Spencerian Type-1 selection kicks in. Very different from Darwinian selection, which involves random gene mutations and biological features, Spencerian Type-1 selection is not random and relies on the creativity and agency of the group. When no existing sociocultural institutions will work, "individuals and [groups] must use their capacities for instrumental thinking and agency to create a new sociocultural formation" (Turner, "Using Neurosociology and Evolutionary Sociology," 19). Spencerian selection tends to kick in when selection pressures arise concerning production, reproduction, regulation/coordination/control of people and groups, and distribution of resources. Turner explains that this is how something we can rightly call "religion" first emerged among very early humans (or late hominins). On the African savanna, humans encountered new pressures concerning production and distribution of resources, reproduction, and regulation and coordination of people. People gradually found ways to address all of these concerns through religion. Constructing stories, rituals, and moral guidelines, and setting expectations that involve the notion of the sacred, *worked*. And the iterations that did not work did not survive. This is a quite different way of conceptualizing selection, but, Turner says, it is "as natural to superorganisms as is Darwinian selection for the evolution of organisms and populations" (Turner, "Using Neurosociology and Evolutionary Sociology," 20).

Third, once humans began developing religious beliefs, rituals, and guidelines, different groups with different religions began competing for resources. Turner calls this process Durkheimian selection. In addition to food and shelter, the "resources" groups are interested in include new members, political influence, and money (provided by loyal members). Religions compete by doing their best to create experiences and attachments that motivate people to not only return, but also to dedicate their own personal resources for the good of the whole.

Fourth, Spencerian Type-2 selection is a conflict model that applies Spencer's infamous phrase "survival of the fittest" to warfare. Turner explains that this type of selection helps us understand the movement from the religions that emerged in small hunter-gatherer bands to huge religious institutions like the Catholic Church, Buddhism, and Protestant Christianity, including, of course, megachurches. For Spencer, religion is closely tied to other geopolitical forces. The power of a society can be dramatically strengthened by a religious system that "legitimate[s] consolidated and centralized power by religion and forces of the supernatural." And so, these religions, with powerful centralized authority, tended to be on the winning side of wars (Turner et al., *The Emergence and Evolution of Religion*, 32).

unsettled and problematic,"[75] how do megachurches maintain their mega-sized crowds?

To address that, let's now take a close look at the megachurch ritual. Part II of the book is an extended discussion of the six steps of our model, the Megachurch Ritual Cycle, so I will invite the reader to refer to that section for more details. Here, I will zoom in even further to look at the Megachurch Ritual Cycle through the lens of oxytocin research. I hypothesize that oxytocin, as one of the most formative biological mechanisms leading to our ultra-sociality, and thus, to religion, may still play a prominent role in religious rituals and megachurch rituals specifically.

Homo Ritualis: Oxytocin and the Megachurch Ritual Cycle

How do we come to be biologically related in the absence of close genetic kinship? We argued in Part I of this book that *religion* appears to have been at least one of the more successful methods of achieving this evolutionary strategy. The scientific study of religion is full of theories explaining the potential role(s) of religious beliefs and practices in human and cultural evolution.[76] In this book, we argued that the *ritual process* is the operative strategy that facilitates affective bonds and large-scale cooperation by creating and spreading what Randall Collins calls emotional energy. However, we also

Lastly, Marxian natural selection refers to the conflicts that arise between major large-scale institutions including political, educational, or scientific institutions. These conflicts often even erupt into violence or warfare. The resources at stake are usually economic, ecological, or demographic, but are very often framed in ideological terms.

[75] Edward J. Lawler, Shane R. Thye, and Jeongkoo Yoon, *Social Commitments in a Depersonalized World* (New York: Russell Sage Foundation, 2009), xi.

[76] Ritual has become a central topic of discussion within the scientific study of religion, which used to be more focused on how and why people *believe* what they do. With the reemergence of the focus on embodiment, and the realization that belief and practice are inextricably intertwined, attention has shifted toward ritual practice. Ritual participation and behaviors may function as signals of loyalty and trustworthiness, signals of fitness, credibility-enhancing displays, and/or cooperative bonding mechanisms. A recent article reviews the psychological function of rituals; Nicholas M. Hobson and his colleagues argue that from the perspective of individual psychology, rituals play a *regulatory* role, helping people regulate three things: emotions, performance goal states, and social connections. For our purposes in this appendix, I'll focus on emotions and social connections. Nicholas M. Hobson, Juliana Schroeder, Jane L. Risen, Dimitris Xygalatas, and Michael Inzlicht, "The Psychology of Rituals: An Integrative Review and Process-Based Framework," *Personality and Social Psychology Review* 22, no. 3 (2017): 260–284. For more on ritual theories in the scientific study of religion, see, for example, Atran and Henrich, "The Evolution of Religion"; Richard Sosis and Candace Alcorta, "Signaling, Solidarity, and the Sacred: The Evolution of Religious Behavior," *Evolutionary Anthropology* 12 (2003): 264–274; Henrich, "The Evolution of Costly Displays."

mentioned that the concept of emotional energy is a bit amorphous. Collins's theory is vibrant and embodied—just reading his book and case studies, the reader gets a visceral and intuitive sense of what emotional energy is. And yet, in terms of how our bodies work, what *is* emotional energy? Collins does not answer this question. However, Collins himself recognizes this gap and invites others to join the conversation. For example, Rossel and Collins admit that the concept of emotional energy is "fuzzy" and needs "further specification."[77] In Chapter 3, we wrote:

> Collins describes EE like a type of capital, similar in some ways to social, cultural, or human capital. These forms of capital (including EE) are all described in the singular but they are made up of a variety of different things (i.e., they are the stock of social, cultural, or human assets and value) and people (or groups) have different levels of them. Collins describes EE as a "feeling of confidence, courage to take action, [and] boldness in taking initiative"[78] and in other places offers other emotional examples of EE, such as joy, awe, or anger. His lack of a clear definition undercuts his ability to measure what it is, how it arrives, and what makes it fluctuate.

Here, I would like to offer a testable hypothesis that emotional energy is mediated, at least in part, by what I call an *oxytocin cocktail.* By this I mean that what Collins calls emotional energy manifests materially in the body as oxytocin mixed with a variable set of other neurochemicals—including things like dopamine, serotonin, testosterone, estrogen, and cortisol—depending on the situation. These other neurochemicals will affect the way that oxytocin influences affect and behavior, even as oxytocin remains the hormonal "hub" of the social interaction.[79]

Empirical research on oxytocin is rapidly expanding, but only a few studies have looked directly at oxytocin's possible role in religion; I think this area is ripe for more research. For example, one study of people who are HIV positive found

[77] Jorg Rossel and Randall Collins, "Conflict Theory and Interaction Rituals: The Microfoundations of Conflict Theory," in *Handbook of Sociological Theory,* edited by Jonathan H. Turner, 509–532 (New York: Springer, 2001), 527.

[78] Collins, *Interaction Ritual Chains,* 39.

[79] See, for example, Sari M. van Anders, Katherine L. Goldey, and Patty X. Kuo, "The Steroid/Peptide Theory of Social Bonds: Integrating Testosterone and Peptide Responses for Classifying Social Behavioral Contexts," *Psychoneuroendocrinology* 36 (2011): 1265–1275. Moana Vercoe and Paul J. Zak theorize that a brain circuit they call HOME (Human Oxytocin Mediated Empathy) is *activated* by oxytocin, but also necessitates the presence of neurotransmitters dopamine and serotonin. Moana Vercoe and Paul J. Zak, "Inductive Modeling Using Causal Studies in Neuroeconomics: Brains on Drugs," *Journal of Economic Methodology* 17, no. 2 (2010): 133–146.

that higher blood-plasma oxytocin levels were significantly correlated with spirituality (but not religiousness) ratings. The same study included interviews coded for evidence of "spiritual transformations." The researchers found that those who had experienced spiritual transformations had *twice* as much endogenous oxytocin than those who had not.[80] Similarly, another study found that endogenous oxytocin was associated with self-reports of spirituality,[81] even while controlling for factors such as church attendance and positive mood.[82] Lastly, a recent study showed that giving oxytocin to males (there were no female participants) increased two self-report measures of spirituality as well as an increase in positive feelings after a twenty-minute guided meditation.[83] None of these studies address ritual practice, so I offer the following hypotheses.

Without repeating our entire theory of the Megachurch Ritual Cycle that we presented in Part II, I will provide a summary interspersed with commentary and hypotheses concerning what role oxytocin cocktails may play in each step of the cycle. As we showed throughout the book, megachurches are *pulsing* with emotional energy; in what follows, I hypothesize that megachurch rituals are also, pulsing with ebbs and flows of oxytocin.

ACCEPTANCE AND BELONGING

As megachurch attendees arrive at the church on Sunday, they are met with hugs and smiles, open arms, and open hearts by a trained "welcome team" with the intention of helping visitors feel that they are being welcomed *home* to their true family (see Chapter 8). In a straightforward manner, assembling for the service accomplishes Collins's first ritual "ingredient": co-presence. In terms of emotional energy and oxytocin, even these first moments are vital for getting the ritual moving and the oxytocin flowing. Starting with hugs, handshakes, and warm touch: in animal models, studies have shown that positive touch alone can trigger the release of oxytocin in the brain.[84] Studies

---

[80] Courtney B. Kelsch, Gail Ironson, Angela Szeto, Heidemarie Kremer, Neil Schneiderman, and Armando J. Mendez, "The Relationship of Spirituality, Benefit Finding, and Other Psychosocial Variables to the Hormone Oxytocin in HIV/AIDS," *Research in the Social Scientific Study of Religion* 24 (2013): 137–162.

[81] The study tested a "homogenous sample of devout Christian" students at Brigham Young University (which is affiliated with The Church of Jesus Christ of Latter-Day Saints). The self-reports consisted of answers to the question "To what extent do you consider yourself a spiritual person?" on a six-point scale.

[82] Colin Holbrook, Jennifer Hahn-Holbrook, and Julianne Holt-Lunstad, "Self-Reported Spirituality Correlates with Endogenous Oxytocin," *Psychology of Religion and Spirituality* 7, no. 1 (2015): 46–50.

[83] Patty Van Cappellen, Baldwin M. Way, Suzannah F. Isgett, and Barbara L. Fredrickson, "Effects of Oxytocin Administration on Spirituality and Emotional Responses to Meditation," *Social Cognitive and Affective Neuroscience* 11, no. 10 (2016): 1579–1587.

[84] Kerstin Uvnäs-Moberg and Maria Petersson, "Oxytocin, a Mediator of Anti-stress, Well-Being, Social Interaction, Growth and Healing," *Zeitschrift für Psychosomatische Medizin und Psychotherapie*,

have also shown that physical touch helps maintain levels of oxytocin for patients in intensive care,[85] and that oxytocin appears to bolster the positive effects of social support.[86] In general, in these situations of positive social touch and interaction characterized by support and acceptance, oxytocin has been found to contribute to a calming effect and can facilitate a feeling of peace and well-being.[87] Of course, it is important to remember here and always that an increase in oxytocin does not solely *cause* these feelings—rather, it is an integral part of a bio-social system that cultivates pleasurable physiological affect and positive emotional experiences.

JOY AND ECSTASY

As the music and worship time begins, attendees are engaged on a psychological level by the words of each song; on a physiological level by standing, singing, and maybe even swaying or raising their arms; and on a social level by being surrounded by people who appear to be feeling and thinking very similar thoughts to their own. A great deal of thought and energy is put into crafting this inspiring moment for attendees—megachurch leaders appear to understand the power of Collins's second ritual ingredient: shared mood. The leaders certainly recognize the affective and emotional power of music, singing, and swaying with a group, which I argue is characterized in part by a surge of oxytocin. One research group looked at the effects of singing on oxytocin levels: after only a thirty-minute singing lesson, participants' oxytocin levels rose significantly, and the amateur singers felt joyful, relaxed, and energized

51, no. 1 (2005): 57–80. Posted online in English at https://pdfs.semanticscholar.org/oac8/c14228b62b9c87636f5b6eb536a434fd04de.pdf, accessed June 29, 2018. See also Mieko Kurosawa, Thomas Lundeberg, Greta Ågren, Irene Lund, and Kerstin Uvnäs-Moberg, "Massage-like Stroking of the Abdomen Lowers Blood Pressure in Anesthetized Rats: Influence of Oxytocin," *Journal of the Autonomic Nervous System* 56, no. 1–2 (1995): 26–30; Kerstin Uvnäs-Moberg, Pawel Alster, Irene Lund, Thomas Lundeberg, Mieko Kurosawa, and Sven Ahlenius, "Stroking of the Abdomen Causes Decreased Locomotor Activity in Conscious Male Rats," *Physiology and Behavior* 60 (1996): 1409–1411.

[85] Maria Henricson, Anna-Lena Berglund, Sylvia Määttä, Rolf Ekman, and Kerstin Segesten, "The Outcome of Tactile Touch on Oxytocin in Intensive Care Patients: A Randomized Controlled Trial," *Journal of Clinical Nursing* 17, no. 19 (2008): 2624–2633.

[86] Markus Heinrichs, Thomas Baumgartner, Clemens Kirschbaum, and Ulrike Ehlert, "Social Support and Oxytocin Interact to Suppress Cortisol and Subjective Responses to Psychosocial Stress," *Biological Psychiatry* 54 (2003): 1389–1398.

[87] Peter Kirsch, Christine Esslinger, Qiang Chen, Daniela Mier, Stephanie Lis, Sarina Siddhanti, Harald Gruppe, Venkata S. Mattay, Bernd Gallhofer, and Andreas Meyer-Lindenberg, "Oxytocin Modulates Neural Circuitry for Social Cognition and Fear in Humans," *Journal of Neuroscience* 25, no. 49 (2005): 11489–11493; Joni Y. Sasaki, Heejung S. Kim, and J. Xu, "Religion and Well-Being: The Moderating Role of Culture and the Oxytocin Receptor (OXTR) Gene," *Journal of Cross-Cultural Psychology* 42 (2011): 1394–1405.

after the session.[88] Another study found that, compared to a group of people who chatted about positive life events, people who engaged in a choral singing rehearsal showed *higher* increases in oxytocin levels and reports of well-being.[89] In our study, congregants reported that the worship music and singing aroused feelings of awe, joy, and amazement. People feel elated and inspired by the presence of God and the Holy Spirit. This is reported as an especially important moment; in fact, many people said that the music and worship was the primary reason they were initially attracted to the church. The multisensory stimulation and embodied participation of each attendee, through singing, standing, and swaying, envelops and demands each person's full attention.

Another potential trigger for oxytocin release is the sense of a shared, contagious, and deeply felt emotion. In many churches, large projector screens display close-up shots of the worship leaders' emotional faces, along with dramatic scans of the worshiping audience, perhaps dwelling on the most emotional faces. Given what we know about mirror neurons and humans' theory of mind, such emotionally evocative images are likely to inspire similar feelings in many onlookers.[90] And indeed, viewing an emotional scene has been found to increase levels of oxytocin in the blood.[91]

[88] Christina Grape, Maria Sandgren, Lars-Olof Hansson, Mats Ericson, and Tores Theorell, "Does Singing Promote Well-Being?: An Empirical Study of Professional and Amateur Singers during a Singing Lesson," *Integrative Physiological & Behavioral Science* 38, no. 1 (2003): 65–74.

[89] Gunter Kreutz, "Does Singing Facilitate Social Bonding?" *Music and Medicine: An Interdisciplinary Journal* 6, no. 2 (2014): 51–60.

[90] Mirror neurons were first discovered in the premotor cortex of monkeys. Researchers found that the neurons discharge *both* when the monkey performs an action *and* when it observe someone else doing the action. It has been suggested that mirror neurons represent the neurological basis for empathy and the theory of mind. If you see another person frown, laugh, dance, or kiss, certain motor neurons fire to simulate the action as if it is *you*. Not only does this help you interpret what the observed person's intentions, thoughts, and feelings are, it also generates, on a neurological level, those thoughts and feelings within you. Oberman and Ramachandran explain:

> Humans have the distinct property of being "like me" in the eyes of the observer. This allows us to use the same systems that process knowledge about self-performed actions, self-conceived thoughts, and self-experienced emotions to understand actions, thoughts, and emotions in others [. . .] internal simulation mechanisms, such as the mirror neuron system, are necessary for normal development of recognition, imitation, theory of mind, empathy, and language. (p. 310)

Giacomo Rizzolatti and Laila Craighero, "The Mirror-Neuron System," *Annual Review of Neuroscience* 24 (2004): 169–192; Giuseppe DiPellegrino, Luciano Fadiga, Leonardo Fogassi, Vittorio Gallese, and Giacomo Rizzolatti, "Understanding Motor Events: A Neurophysiological Study," *Experimental Brain Research* 91 (1992): 176–180; Lindsay M. Oberman and Vilayanur S. Ramachandran, "The Simulating Social Mind: The Role of the Mirror Neuron System and Simulation in the Social and Communicative Deficits of Autism Spectrum Disorders," *Psychological Bulletin* 133 (2007): 310–327.

[91] Jorge A. Barraza and Paul J. Zak, "Empathy toward Strangers Triggers Oxytocin Release and Subsequent Generosity," *Annals of the New York Academy of Sciences* 1167 (2009): 129–189.

That being said, it is not only the presence of other human bodies and emotions that stimulate the mirror neuron system; it also matters *who* those other bodies are, their social relations and representations, and what their symbolic action means to each other. These factors are intimately wrapped up and intertwined with physiological arousal systems, including those that involve oxytocin. For example, in a study examining an important fire-walking ceremony in the small Spanish village of San Pedro Manrique, Dimitris Xygalatas, Ivana Konvalinka, and their colleagues used heart-rate monitors and found dramatic evidence for specific patterns of cognitive states and physiological arousal during the group ritual: the heart-rates of the friends and relatives of the firewalkers displayed "striking qualitative similarities" to the heart-rates of the firewalkers themselves. Heart-raters were synched between loved ones, but there were *no* similarities found in the heart-rates of nonrelated onlookers.[92] This means that those who conceptualized themselves as affiliated with the central ritual participants were not only more physiologically aroused by the ritual than unaffiliated observers, but their bodies displayed stunning qualitative synchronicities with the fire-walkers. So, clearly, such synchronized arousal requires more than simply watching the evocative event: one must feel connected, invested, and implicated in the event. The physiological systems cocreate the conscious experience in concert with psychological and sociological factors. Employing Elizabeth Wilson's framing, quoted in this appendix's "What's Evolution Got to Do with It?" section, this is more than an *interaction* between the biological and the social—it is an entanglement, characterized by "contingencies."[93] We cannot fully understand the phenomenon of physiological arousal without taking the whole entangled network into consideration.

Similarly, in Pitts-Taylor's discussion of how, with the oxytocin system, bodies construct nongenetic, yet still biological, kinship bonds, she adopts neuroscientist Ruth Feldman's term "behavioral synchrony."[94] She explains that these kinship bonds do not simply happen, but bodies *build* them—the oxytocin system becomes entrained to other people through patterned movements and synchronized behavior. In a way that is almost identical to the way Collins describes the mutual entrainment of shared mood and shared

[92] Ivana Konvalinka, Dimitris Xygalatas, Joseph Bulbulia, Uffe Schjødt, Else-Marie Jegindø, Sebastian Wallot, Guy Van Orden, and Andreas Roepstorff, "Synchronized Arousal between Performers and Related Spectators in a Fire-Walking Ritual," *Proceedings of the National Academy of Sciences USA* 108, no. 20 (2011): 8514–8519, 8515. See also Dimitris Xygalatas, Ivana Konvalinka, Andreas Roepstorff, and Joseph Bulbulia, "Quantifying Collective Effervescence: Heart-Rate Dynamics at a Fire Walking Ritual," *Communicative and Integrative Biology* 4, no. 6 (2011): 735–738.

[93] Wilson, *Gut Feminism*, 9.

[94] Pitts-Taylor, *The Brain's Body*, 109.

focus of attention (two steps in his ritual process), Pitts-Taylor describes the affective synchrony that leads to oxytocin-supported kinship bonds: "Here synchrony is an affective, material event in which bodies become mutually attuned and oriented toward each other. It is simultaneously experienced in individual bodies and wholly relational, generated through embodied social interaction with specific others."[95] Not only are megachurch attendees building attachments to each other, they are, perhaps more importantly, building strong foundational attachments to the symbols of the group, the words that are being sung, and the object of those songs, the person of Jesus or God. The "interaction" in this moment with God and/or Jesus can be experienced as not only real, but physical.

TRUSTWORTHY LEADERSHIP

Next, the sermon begins, which channels this vibrant affective glow into ideas and words. Pastors often hold intense amounts of charisma and affective power. By presenting himself as a trustworthy, loving, and faithful guide, the pastor instills confidence in and loyalty to the veracity and righteousness of not only the message, but also the church as a symbol of God's will. His words are laden with affective significance, giving him a great amount of power over the congregants. Political scientists Douglas Madsen and Peter S. Snow explain that the concept of charisma is not only a "skill" of the charismatic person; it also depends on the affects and attitudes of her or his followers. The charismatic bond is "asymmetric, unmediated, and passionate" in both its substance and trajectory.[96] In his own study on megachurches, Kevin McElmurry quotes the lighting director at a large megachurch. She explains the thought that goes into making sure the conditions are ripe for Collins's third ritual ingredient, mutual focus of attention:

> At the very beginning when people are walking into the auditorium we want it to be more brightly lit. We want people to feel OK coming into a bright welcoming space that isn't fluorescent. We try and pick light fixtures that use certain types of light bulbs that cast a softer light. It feels welcoming. But then as the service starts we'll progressively lower the light in the room so you become less and less participatory and more and more engaged within yourself, and pay attention within, and the processes internally. So, by the time we get to Patrick's

[95] Pitts-Taylor, *The Brain's Body*, 110.
[96] Douglas Madsen and Peter G. Snow, *The Charismatic Bond: Political Behavior in Time of Crisis* (Cambridge, MA: Harvard University Press, 1991), 5.

message the room is pretty dim, because we want people focusing on him and focusing on what he's saying.[97]

Presenting the pastor as a loving, parental figure, especially directly following the worship and praise time, during which attendees were pumped with oxytocin, makes him an excellent candidate for a fictive kin relative. As we discussed in Chapter 10, the pastor's rhetoric and presence feed directly into this sense. In addition, not only does the pastor position himself as a reliable leader, as also discussed in Chapter 10, but the theology that he preaches tends to be relatively intuitive (compared to more esoteric religious doctrines) with a few key, attention-catching, "minimally counterintuitive" notions about God and Jesus. For instance, the idea that each person is in desperate and dire need for Jesus's salvific love is experienced as incredibly emotionally evocative.[98]

Pointing to the incredible power that charismatic figures have, scholar of religion Uffe Schjødt and his colleagues used functional magnetic resonance imaging to look at neural activity of Christians listening to prayer. They found that the perceived status of a speaker had a significant effect on listeners' cognitive processes.[99] If the Christians were told that the person they heard praying was a Christian "known for his healing powers," their neural activity differed from if they were told that the person praying (the same prayer) was either a new Christian or a non-Christian. Key brain areas associated with executive and social cognition were *deactivated* when Christian participants listened to someone they were told had healing powers; and the higher the participants rated the speaker's charisma postscan, the more the executive and social cognitive networks were deactivated.[100] Among control subjects (non-Christian participants, who would not have been personally invested in the prayer), *no* deactivation occurred. This study demonstrates the effect that even the *notion* that a person has healing powers, or perhaps is somehow in closer contact with God, has on social cognition. The fact

---

[97] Kevin McElmurry, "Alone/Together: The Production of Religious Culture in a Church for the Unchurched" (Unpublished dissertation, University of Missouri, 2009), 127.

[98] As Michaela Porubanova and John H. Shaver found, whether ideas are intuitive or not, ones that have a somewhat negative emotional valence tend to be remembered more readily than either positive or neutral ideas. Michaela Porubanova and John H. Shaver, "Minimal Counterintuitiveness Revisited, Again: The Role of Emotional Valence in Memory for Conceptual Incongruity," in *Religion Explained?: The Cognitive Science of Religion after Twenty-Five Years*, edited by Luther H. Martin and Donald Wiebe, 123–132 (London: Bloomsbury, 2017).

[99] Uffe Schjødt, Hans Stodkilde-Jorgensen, Armin W. Geertz, Torbin E. Lund, and Andreas Roepstorff, "The Power of Charisma—Perceived Charisma Inhibits the Frontal Executive Network of Believers in Intercessory Prayer," *SCAN* 6 (2011): 119–127.

[100] Schjødt et al., "The Power of Charisma," 125.

that the effect was a *deactivation* perhaps suggests that the Christians were entering a "passive paradigm" in which they "suspend or 'hand over' their critical faculty to the trusted person."[101] This sheds light on the capacity of charismatic authority to lead and influence people. Schjødt and colleagues highlight the central importance of social factors—including the belief in a person's charisma—in these findings: "the effects [. . .] are complex and depend on cultural framing and individual experience."[102]

Also relevant to the role oxytocin may play during the sermon, economic studies have shown that when a person encounters someone who they perceive as trustworthy, their oxytocin levels rise.[103] And not only that, but with those rising oxytocin levels, they are more likely to feel bonded to the trusted person and more likely to take social risks on the trusted person's behalf.[104] In the case of megachurch pastors, the "social risk" at hand may be presented in the very next "step" of the ritual cycle: the altar call.

DELIVERANCE

Ideally, the sermon will have inspired a feeling of conviction and a desire for redemption, liberation, and salvation. The altar call presents an opportunity for just that. As we explain in Chapter 7, for the purposes of megachurches, we recast Collins's fourth ritual ingredient, barriers to outsiders, as an *affective* barrier, rather than a physical barrier. Even though there are physical walls around the church, megachurches do all they can to show that they are open and welcoming to outsiders. Very little special cultural capital is needed beyond what is already shared among contemporary Americans, and megachurch website and branding often assures potential newcomers that you don't even have to like "church" to join the family. However, it seems in practice, there is a clear line drawn between those who have either gone through or who are willing to go through the affective initiation of accepting Jesus into their hearts, and those who haven't or are not interested. The altar call provides the opportunity to experience the strong emotional release that

[101] Schjødt et al., "The Power of Charisma," 125.

[102] Schjødt et al., "The Power of Charisma," 125.

[103] Paul J. Zak and Jacek Kugler, "Neuroeconomics and International Studies: A New Understanding of Trust," *International Studies Perspectives* 12, no. 2 (2011): 136–152; Michael Kosfeld, Markus Heinrichs, Paul J. Zak, Urs Fischbacher, and Ernst Fehr, "Oxytocin Increases Trust in Humans," *Nature* 435, no. 7042 (2005): 673–676; Thomas Baumgartner, Markus Heinrichs, Aline Volanthen, Urs Fishbacher, and Ernst Fehr, "Oxytocin Shapes the Neural Circuitry of Trust and Trust Adaptation in Humans," *Neuron* 58, no. 4 (2008): 639–650.

[104] Kosfeld et al., "Oxytocin Increases Trust in Humans"; Richard A. Depue and Jeannine V. Morrone-Strupinsky, "A Neurobehavioral Model of Affiliative Bonding: Implications for Conceptualizing a Human Trait of Affiliation," *Behavioral and Brain Science* 28 (2005): 313–395.

signals to yourself and to others that you are *in*. By publicly and emotionally accepting Jesus into your life, you become a full member of the family, the body of Christ.

During the altar call, elements of both the previous steps (worship and charisma) will continue to gain strength and energy—the congregation may sing another song or two as the pastor prays with passionate spontaneity, inviting people to the front to receive salvation. According to Collins's theory, emotional energy is at its height here, and so likewise, we might hypothesize that oxytocin levels, too, will have increased significantly by this point. At least two qualities of oxytocin seem pertinent here (in addition to the increased willingness to take social risks): first, Churchland explains that increases in oxytocin help a person feel that what is happening is "right"; and second, oxytocin has been found to encourage both an increased tendency to cooperate and affiliate with members of your own in-group, *and* an increased tendency to *distrust* members of other groups.[105] In this way, it seems that oxytocin may support the construction of *affective boundaries* that determine who is and *who is not* a Christian (or a potential Christian). Those who reject the message of Jesus are construed as *other* and therefore untrustworthy. In fact, oxytocin, it turns out, especially when paired with testosterone, is sometimes linked to increases in *aggressive* behavior against potential threats, to protect in-group members and solidify in-group bonds.[106]

PURPOSE IN SERVICE

The last two "steps" in our model of the Megachurch Ritual Cycle are vital ingredients for megachurches, even though they are not outlined in Collins's theory. However, Collins does refer generally to the idea that emotional energy is temporary and fades with time if not recharged; therefore, we have identified the two general ways that megachurches keep the emotional energy circulating through the congregation during the week. Community service projects and small-group meetings are interaction rituals in and

[105] Churchland, *Braintrust*; Carsten K. W. De Dreu, Lindred L. Greer, Michel J. J. Handgraaf, Shaul Shalvi, Gerben A. Van Kleef, Matthijs Baas, Femke S. Ten Velden, Eric Van Dijk, and Sander W. W. Feith, "The Neuropeptide Oxytocin Regulates Parochial Altruism in Intergroup Conflict among Humans," *Science* 328 (2010): 1408–1411; Carsten K. W. De Dreu, Lindred L. Greer, Gerben A. Van Kleef, Shaul Shalvi, and Michel J. J. Handgraaf, "Oxytocin Promotes Human Ethnocentrism," *Proceedings of the National Academy of Sciences USA* 108, no. 4 (2011): 1262–1266; Carsten K. W De Dreu, "Oxytocin Modulates Cooperation within and Competition between Groups: An Integrative Review and Research Agenda," *Hormones and Behavior* 61, no. 3 (2012): 419–428; Carolyn H. Declerck, Christophe Boone, and Toyo Kiyonari, "Oxytocin and Cooperation under Conditions of Uncertainty: The Modulating Role of Incentives and Social Information," *Hormones and Behavior* 57, no. 3 (2010): 368–374.
[106] van Anders, Goldey, and Kuo, "The Steroid/Peptide Theory of Social Bonds."

of themselves *and* they are links in the larger interaction ritual *chain* (*à la* Collins) that makes up the Megachurch Ritual Cycle. These two steps enact and solidify the strong emotional bonds created during the Sunday worship service. Reinforcing the rhetoric about the Bible, the community, and one's role as a Christian, these steps integrate the church's concepts and emotions into a cohesive personal identity. And when many people do this all at once, it leads to an enthusiastic and cooperative community full of loyal members. Spreading this process throughout the week helps to keep the fire buring between Sundays, and to helps community values and teachings to permeate the rest of each member's life.

The first link, service and outreach projects, gives members an opportunity to, in Collins's terms, practice being an *energy star* for other people and to reinforce the importance of their spiritual gifts. Empowered by the experience of the Sunday worship and equipped with a set of group symbols and ideas that have been infused with personal meaning and salience, members go out into the community to put their new identity "in Christ" into action. As is the case for all the preceding steps, the transformative aspects of establishing a firm identity in a religious group is an extraordinarily complex process, including personal psychological and existential dimensions not covered in this book. Though far from being the whole, megachurch service projects and outreach efforts form an important part of that complex process. It is no secret that the combination of feeling *needed* by others and a high level of self-efficacy is an empowering and confidence-building experience, and this may be reflected physiologically in oxytocin levels too. A famous study by a research team led by Paul Zak found that when people perceive that they are being trusted by others, their oxytocin levels rise. And, in turn, like a self-fulfilling prophecy, higher oxytocin levels are associated with more trustworthy behavior.[107] Very often, these service projects are directed at fellow church members, in which case elevated oxytocin levels may contribute to bonding, attachment, and in-group loyalty.

In the same lab, Jorge Barraza teamed up with Zak to study empathy and generosity. After having participants watch a short video clip of an emotionally distressing scene, which had the effect of raising oxytocin levels 47% (on average) over baseline levels, the researchers found that oxytocin levels were associated with increases in both empathy and financial generosity, especially in women.[108] To study generosity (prosociality), the

[107] Paul J. Zak, Robert Kurzban, and William T. Matzner, "Oxytocin Is Associated with Human Trustworthiness," *Hormones and Behavior* 48 (2005): 522–527.
[108] Jorge A. Barraza and Paul J. Zak, "Empathy Toward Strangers Triggers Oxytocin Release and Subsequent Generosity," *Annals of the New York Academy of Sciences* 1167 (2009): 182–189.

researchers used a popular research tool called the Ultimatum Game. In the Ultimatum Game, the participants are paired up and one person in each pair is given some money (in this case $40). They are then told to offer their partner some of the $40. If the partner accepts, they each go home with their portion of the cash. If the partner rejects the offer, neither participant gets anything. This game was used in another study involving intranasal oxytocin spray (rather than oxytocin that the body had produced endogenously). Researchers had participants play the Ultimatum Game (with $10 this time). When participants were given a sniff of oxytocin, they were more generous with their offers. The researchers report this as an increase in "generosity." However, the same study also had participants play the Dictator Game, in which the second player does *not* have the option to reject the offer; they just get what they get. The oxytocin spray did *not* affect the offers when there was no chance that the offer was going to be rejected. So, was it really "generosity" that was increased, or simply a heightened awareness of social dynamics and *potential social costs?* More research needs to be done on this topic. But for the purposes of our discussion here, both possibilities are interesting and potentially applicable. After all, scholars and the public alike have at times questioned the unconscious motives behind certain forms of outreach and missionizing done by megachurches. Either way, the point is that outreach and service are a vital element of the megachurch model, and I hypothesize that the oxytocin and emotional energy gained throughout the megachurch ritual chain model may help motivate and mediate this action.

Working together on service projects also certainly has a bonding effect in itself. Lawler et al. explain that one of the core principles of their theory of social commitments is that "if a group presents individuals with a joint task and that task generates a sense of *shared responsibility*, people tend to attribute their individual feelings (positive or negative) to the group affiliation and to associate those feelings with the affiliation."[109] Moreover, they say, "Stronger affective commitments lead to more group-oriented behavior, including more effort on behalf of and contributions to the group activities, more willingness to collaborate with others in the group, and more inclination to compromise individual interests when they conflict with group interests."[110] So, if nothing else, it seems clear that service and outreach projects increase levels of solidarity within and commitment to the

[109] Lawler, Thye, and Yoon, *Social Commitments in a Depersonalized World,* xiii, emphasis added.
[110] Edward J. Lawler, Shane R. Thye, and Jeongkoo Yoon, "Emotions and Group Ties in Social Exchange," in *Handbook of the Sociology of Emotions: Volume II*, edited by Jan E. Stets and Jonathan H. Turner, 77–102 (New York: Springer, 2014), 90.

megachurch—thus contributing heartily to the ability to navigate our *homo duplex* nature. In some of the more dubious examples of megachurch social action—certain types of political behavior, perhaps—this observation by Rossner and Meher applies: "Solidarity in a successful interaction ritual is accompanied by momentary bursts of emotional energy or 'charge.' This is a rush of *confidence, invincibility, or power*."[111] In a sense, this may also shed light on the phenomenon of abuse and corruption emanating from the particular brand of "self-sacrificial servant leadership" in soft patriarchalism that we discussed in Chapter 14.

RE-MEMBERING

Last, the sixth and final step, which forms the interaction ritual chain link that cycles back to the Sunday service, is small groups. Small groups are sometimes organized around Bible studies, but often they are simply mixed-generation community fellowship groups. These were highlighted again and again by our interviewees as the aspect of the megachurch model that really strengthened and solidified members' feelings of attachment and kinship with the community. Megachurch leadership emphasizes the vital importance of each member joining and participating in a small group. This is because they understand the power of one of the core human desires: to be known intimately by others—to have a *family*. By creating and supporting a vibrant small-group structure, in which group leaders are empowered to take their group members under their wings, megachurches create a network of intimate spaces that build what they see as the family of God and the body of Christ. As each member is personally enveloped in and cared for by their small group, they feel seen, loved, and needed by others in a way that is difficult to accomplish in the large-scale Sunday rituals. This balances the powerful feeling of riding the wave of the Holy Spirit via the collective effervescence of the Sunday service with a sense of being *chosen*, personally loved, and empowered as an integral part of the megachurch family and a precious child of God.

Here, oxytocin's ability to support nongenetic biological kinship networks, discussed at the beginning of this appendix, is in full force. Citing David Eng's work on kinship, Pitts-Taylor says that affective kinships supported by the oxytocin system are "deeply felt, embodied ties that are experienced

---

[111] Meredith Rossner and Mythily Meher, "Emotions in Ritual Theories," in *Handbook of the Sociology of Emotions: Volume II*, edited by Jan E. Stets and Jonathan H. Turner, 199–220 (New York: Springer, 2014), 208, emphasis added.

in all sorts of kin relations that transcend biogenetic models of family, in-cluding queer and transnational ones."[112] As I already emphasized, the expe-rience of being personally trusted by others is associated with an increase in oxytocin levels, which then in turn stimulates an increased tendency to trust and cooperate with important others. And as Pitts-Taylor explains, oxytocin networks are associated with how we develop motivations for attachment and safety.[113] The social functions of oxytocin—which has expanded *far* be-yond its role as a "maternalizing" hormone—pay no attention to genetic relatedness. Oxytocin-supported biologically evident trusting attachments can form just as strongly between people who are not genetically related as between those who are. Learning to conceptualize symbolically *and* to experi-ence bodily that members of one's small group are their *family* helps solidify the members' loyalty to the megachurch. Understanding the neurohormonal dimensions of affective kinship helps us see how social networks, hierarchies, and desires can be rebuilt and reinscribed.

It is important to note again that oxytocin's effects are not mechanical or global in their range. For example, oxytocin is *not* associated with a *general* increase in trust for *all* people. Indeed, trust is enhanced and solidified only toward those people presented and experienced as worthy of trust. Suspicious outsiders receive the opposite assessment, and oxytocin often increases hos-tility instead of trust. For example, in which participants were given oxy-tocin through a nasal spray, its positive effects "disappear if the potentially trusted other is portrayed as untrustworthy, is unknown, or is a member of a social outgroup."[114] Thus, the most recent research on oxytocin emphasizes its function not as a "moral molecule" or "love drug," but rather as a *socially motivating* factor that heightens social awareness, enhances social cognition, and stimulates social engagement (positive or not). This means that the en-vironmental and situational contexts are vital for understanding the physio-cognitive-emotional effects of oxytocin.

The way that oxytocin influences conscious experience and social behav-ioral patterns depends greatly on moment-to-moment interpersonal contexts. Megachurch small groups are designed and advertised as an explicit effort to

[112] Pitts-Taylor, *The Brain's Body*, 99. See also David Eng, *The Feeling of Kinship: Queer Liberalism and the Racialization of Intimacy* (Durham, NC: Duke University Press, 2010).

[113] Pitts-Taylor, *The Brain's Body*, 101.

[114] Jennifer A. Bartz, Jamil Zaki, Niall Bolger, and Kevin Ochsner, "Social Effects of Oxytocin in Humans: Context and Person Matter," *Trends in Cognitive Sciences* 15 (2011): 301–309, 305; Moïra Mikolajczak, James J. Gross, Anthony Lane, Olivier Corneille, Philippe de Timary, and Olivier Luminet, "Oxytocin Makes People Trusting, Not Gullible," *Psychological Science* 21, no. 8 (2010): 1072–1074; Declerck, Boone, and Kiyonari, "Oxytocin and Cooperation"; De Dreu et al., "The Neuropeptide Oxytocin."

create family, build trust, and foster care for each other. The message, from the person perceived as the most trustworthy of all and supported by the charisma of the pulpit, is that you can and *should* trust the good intentions of your fellow group members. The kinship relationships developed in small groups both enhance the feeling of connectedness and belongingness to the larger megachurch, and are enhanced by the message, symbols, and affective energy of the large worship service. This is a two-way street, a dynamic feedback loop characterized by both "top-down" and "bottom-up" influences. Small groups help fuel members' affective attachment to the megachurch just as much as the energetic residue of the worship service fuels the small groups. By describing, discussing, and connecting over the shared experience of emotional high and release during the worship service, small-group interactions help renew, reify, and give dimension to the somatic markers generated during the Sunday worship service. Kerstin Uvnäs-Moberg, medical doctor and professor of physiology in Sweden, explains that "even thoughts, associations and memories can, most likely, induce a release of oxytocin."[115] Compared to the large-scale interaction ritual during the worship service, small groups are where we see the smaller micro-level interactions that can build oxytocin-supported biological (but not genetic) kinship. As megachurch small groups feed, reenact, and remember the experience of God's presence in their community, it is not difficult to imagine that these might be ideal settings for the socially binding effects of oxytocin—for example, feelings of acceptance, a decrease of stress hormones, an increased likelihood to accept social risks, an enhancement of pair bonds, an increase in compassion, empathy, and generosity, and even potentially a speeding up of physical healing—to influence experience and behavior.[116]

Lawler et al. explain that even though the ties binding a person to a group are "distinct and independent" from person-to-person ties, the latter contribute to the former.[117] In other words, the relationship that a person has to a large group—say, a megachurch congregation— is supported and maintained in large part through the stability of their interpersonal relationships with individuals in the large group. Lawler et al. explain that a vital component of social commitments to large groups like megachurches is the close ties and affective bonds that members build with each other and then *attribute* to the structure of the larger church. It is not only the church's welcoming décor,

[115] Uvnäs-Moberg and Petersson, "Oxytocin, a Mediator of Anti-stress."

[116] In addition to the effects already discussed, on the potential for oxytocin to speed up physical healing, see Jean-Philippe Gouin, C. Sue Carter, Hossein Pournajafi-Nazarloo, Ronald Glaser, William B. Malarky, Timothy J. Loving, Jeffrey Stowell, and Janice K. Kiecolt-Glaser, "Marital Behavior, Oxytocin, Vasopressin, and Wound Healing," *Psychoneuroendocrinology* 35, no. 7 (2010): 1082–1090.

[117] Lawler, Thye, and Yoon, *Social Commitments in a Depersonalized World*, xiii.

inspirational worship, and pastor's charm and moving sermon, or the transformative power of an altar call that get people to keep coming back, but it's also the kinship bonds that hold symbolic value as representative of the larger megachurch family within which they are "nested."[118]

Conclusions and Suggestions for Further Research

In this appendix, I have suggested an approach to conceptualizing and studying the Megachurch Ritual Cycle that takes seriously human biocultural embodiment. In my own thinking, this is only one dimension of a much larger multidimensional approach to religion that includes many other cognitive, psychological, social, neurological, and cultural dimensions. This appendix shines light on one important thread woven through a multidimensional approach. Other important cognitive factors of supernatural beliefs and/or notions of ultimacy, transcendence, and psychological transformation have barely been mentioned.

That being said, in this appendix I tell religion's evolutionary story with a spotlight shined directly on one particularly intriguing neurohormone: oxytocin. There is much more to say and explore about the oxytocin system. Further research, besides testing the hypotheses put forward in this essay, should include attention to the role that genetic factors affecting oxytocin *receptor distribution* may play—as an individual difference among different humans, and as a difference between different species.[119] On a related note, the general limitations of applying animal models to theories about humans (common in oxytocin research) needs further consideration.[120] Similarly, it is worth noting that much research on oxytocin involves using a nasal spray. Studying the effects of oxytocin that is artificially introduced into the body through the nose is not equivalent to studying the effects of endogenous oxytocin that the body produces in response to events, situations, and interactions. Continued attention to the "negative" social influences of oxytocin, especially when paired with certain other neurochemicals, is also vital.

[118] See Lawler's "theory of nested-group commitments," discussed in Lawler, Thye, and Yoon, "Emotions and Group Ties."
[119] On diversity of density and location of receptors, see James L. Goodson, "Deconstructing Sociality, Social Evolution and Relevant Nonapeptide Functions," *Psychoneuroendocrinology* 38 (2013): 465–478.
[120] On animal models, see discussion in Sari van Anders, James L. Goodson, and Marcy A. Kingsbury, "Beyond 'Oxytocin = Good': Neural Complexities and the Flipside of Social Bonds," *Archives of Sexual Behavior* 42, no. 7 (2013): 1115–1118.

And finally, diversity in oxytocin function may potentially shine light on gendered differences in religious behavior and cognition.[121]

GOD IN A BOTTLE (OR A NASAL SPRAY)?

Lastly, unlike what some sensationalized science reporting seems to suggest, I hope it has become clear enough through this appendix that despite the title's suggestion that God is "like a drug," no, you cannot buy oxytocin off the internet and expect it to have the same effect as becoming a member of a religious community. Claims to that effect are examples of the crude reductionism that we want to move *past*, not toward.

In closing, I've used oxytocin as a sort of case study for the potential fruitfulness of bio-cultural theorizing—theories that take seriously human embodiment and our evolutionary heritage, the vibrancy and diversity of our cultural heritage, and the forceful power of socialization. Lest any readers interpret this as a *reduction* of religion to kinship or, even worse, a reduction of God to oxytocin, let me be clear that it is not. Rather, this appendix is intended as a small contribution to an emerging conversation about ritual and embodiment within the context of American megachurches.

[121] James K. Rilling, Ashley C. DeMarco, Patrick D. Hackett, Xu Chen, Pritam Gautam, Sabrina Stair, Ebrahim Haroon, Richmond Thompson, Beate Ditzen, Rajan Patel, and Giuseppe Pagnoni, "Sex Differences in the Neural and Behavioral Response to Intranasal Oxytocin and Vasopressin during Human Social Interaction," *Psychoneuroendocrinology* 39 (2014): 237–248.

| Megachurch Scandals

TABLE C.I PROVIDES information on all the megachurch scandal data we collected from Google News. See Chapter 14 for more information on how we collected the data. The table provides the news source, the date of the article, the person or entity accused, the church related to the person/ entity accused, the position (Pos) of the person or church accused, the type of scandal (Typ), whether the accused admitted to the behavior or was found guilty of it (Ad), and a link to the article.

For position, SP refers to senior pastor, P refers to pastor or pastors, C refers to church, and E refers to elder or elders. For type of scandal, sex refers to sexual scandals, E for economic scandals, V for violence, Alco for alcoholism, and O for other types of scandals or when the behavior was unidentified. For sex scandals, we further coded the data by subtype: (a) affairs or inappropriate sexual relationships; (b) criminal sexual relationship involving minors; (c) not informing the police of sexual abuse, attempting to cover it up, or facilitating it in some way; and (d) homosexuality. We could not subtype one case due to the vagueness of the description "sexual impurity." For "Ad," A refers to admitted, AC for accused, G for Guilty, and NI for no information provided in the article. We only coded information from the articles and we did not code multiple articles on the same story. We did code multiple scandals if they were described in the same news source.

TABLE C.1. Megachurch-Scandal Google News Stories

Source	Article Date	Person	Church	Pos	Typ	Ad	Link
Denver Post	12/10/06	Paul Barnes	Grace Chapel	SP	Sex, D	A	https://www.denverpost.com/2006/12/10/pastor-resigns-over-homosexuality/
New York Times	3/6/07	Ted Haggard	New Life Church	SP	Sex, D	A	http://www.nytimes.com/2007/03/06/us/06church.html
Fox News	11/20/07	Earl Paulk	Cathedral of the Holy Spirit at Chapel Hill Harvester Church	SP	Sex, A	G	http://www.foxnews.com/story/2007/11/20/sex-scandal-rocks-atlanta-area-megachurch.html
Chicago Tribune	2/18/09	Rev. Steve Wu	Willow Creek Chicago	SP	Sex	A	http://articles.chicagotribune.com/2009-02-18/news/0902170688_1_pastor-evangelical-willow-creek-community-church
Newsone	9/18/12	Gaston Smith	Friendship Missionary Baptist Church	SP	E	G	https://newsone.com/2040828/black-pastors-scandal/
Newsone	9/18/12	Creflo Augustus Dollar, Jr.	World Changers Church International	SP	V	AC	https://newsone.com/2040828/black-pastors-scandal/

Newsone	9/18/12	Thomas Wesley Weeks, Jr.	Global Destiny Church	SP	V	G	https://newsone.com/2040828/black-pastors-scandal/
CBS News	9/20/12	Church	Victory Christian Center	C	Sex, C	NI	https://www.cbsnews.com/news/tulsa-megachurch-rattled-by-sex-abuse-claims/
Christian Today	5/16/13	David Loveless	Discovery Church	SP	Sex, A	A	https://www.christianitytoday.com/news/2013/may/three-megachurch-pastors-resign-over-adultery-in-orlando.html
Christian Today	5/16/13	Isaac Hunter	Summit Church	SP	Sex, A	A	https://www.christianitytoday.com/news/2013/may/three-megachurch-pastors-resign-over-adultery-in-orlando.html
Christian Today	5/16/13	Sam Hinn	The Gathering Place Worship Center	SP	Sex, A	A	https://www.christianitytoday.com/news/2013/may/three-megachurch-pastors-resign-over-adultery-in-orlando.html
Atlanta Journal Constitution	6/9/13	Jim Bolin	Trinity Chapel	SP	Sex, A	A	http://www.ajc.com/news/scandal-behind-him-founding-pastor-returns-cobb-trinity-chapel/QSUaJzG3EMLlkAA2HJu6sJ/
Christian Post	6/17/13	Geronimo Aguilar	Richmond Outreach Center	SP	Sex, B	G	https://www.christianpost.com/news/founding-pastor-of-va-megachurch-caught-in-sex-scandal-gets-115k-salary-housing-in-severance-deal-98149/
Birmingham News	8/9/13	Dino Rizzo	Healing Place Church	SP	Sex, A	AC	http://www.al.com/living/index.ssf/2013/08/after_inappropriate_relationsh.html
Phoenix New Times	1/6/14	Mark Connelly	Mission Community Church	SP	Sex, A	A	http://www.phoenixnewtimes.com/news/mark-connelly-phoenix-area-megachurch-pastor-resigns-over-alleged-affairs-6636117

(continued)

TABLE C.1. Continued

Source	Article Date	Person	Church	Pos	Typ	Ad	Link
Christianity Today	2/24/14	David Yonggi Cho	Yoido Full Gospel Church	SP	E	G	http://www.christianitytoday.com/news/2014/february/founder-of-worlds-largest-megachurch-convicted-cho-yoido.html
Huffington Post	2/24/14	Steven Furtick	Elevation Church	SP	O	AC	https://www.huffingtonpost.com/2014/02/24/elevation-church-spontaneous-baptism_n_4849533.html
News OK	5/1/14	Rev. Mark Crow	Victory Church	SP	Sex, A	A	http://newsok.com/article/4745068
Christian Post	5/16/14	Grant Layman	Covenant Life Church	SP	Sex, C	A	https://www.christianpost.com/news/megachurch-pastor-confesses-to-protecting-child-molester-for-years-119877/
Charisma News	5/28/14	Geronimo Aguilar	Richmond Outreach Center	SP	Sex, A & B	G	https://www.charismanews.com/us/44019-scandal-rocked-megachurch-loses-yet-another-pastor
NWI.com	6/3/14	Jack A. Schaap	First Baptist Church of Hammond	SP	Sex, B	G	http://www.nwitimes.com/news/local/lake/ex-megachurch-pastor-blames-underage-victim-wants-out-of-prison/article_2ae9324b-eacf-546e-9f73-c12147f5726f.html
Christian Post	6/5/14	Jerry Sutton	Two Rivers Baptist Church	SP	E	AC	https://www.christianpost.com/news/former-southern-baptist-megachurch-sells-one-of-its-campuses-to-catholic-diocese-121015/
Columbus Dispatch	6/20/14	Church	Vineyard Church	C	Sex, D	AC	http://www.dispatch.com/content/stories/faith_and_values/2014/06/20/church-loses-appeal-on-policy.html
Charisma News	8/27/14	John Munro	Calvary Church	SP	O	NI	https://www.charismanews.com/us/45178-back-to-bible-megachurch-pastor-under-investigation

Culture Map Houston	10/6/14	Church	Second Baptist Church	C	Sex, C	AC	http://houston.culturemap.com/news/city-life/10-06-14-houston-megachurch-slapped-with-sexual-abuse-lawsuit-over-houston-pastors-behavior-asks-for-prayer/
Christian Post	10/23/14	Steve Riggle	Grace Community Church	SP	O	NI	https://www.christianpost.com/news/who-are-the-5-pastors-in-the-houston-sermon-subpoena-scandal-128549/
The Atlantic	11/7/14	Mark Driscoll	Mars Hill Church	SP	O	AC	https://www.theatlantic.com/national/archive/2014/11/houston-mark-driscoll-megachurch-meltdown/382487/
Christian Today	5/22/15	Pastors	Village Church	P	O	AC	https://www.christiantoday.com/article/church-disciplines-wife-for-wanting-to-divorce-husband-who-admitted-paedophile-leanings/54480.htm
The Guardian	11/23/15	Brian Houston	Hillsong	SP	Sex, D	AC	https://www.theguardian.com/australia-news/2015/nov/23/hillsongs-brian-houston-failed-to-report-abuse-and-had-conflict-of-interest-royal-commission
Riverfront Times	2/9/16	Steve Wingfield	First Christian Church of Florissant	SP	Sex, C	AC	https://www.riverfronttimes.com/newsblog/2016/02/09/after-six-months-away-pastor-at-center-of-church-cover-up-scandal-returns
Riverfront Times	2/9/16	Brandon Milburn	First Christian Church of Florissant	SP	Sex, B	G	https://www.riverfronttimes.com/newsblog/2016/02/09/after-six-months-away-pastor-at-center-of-church-cover-up-scandal-returns
Washingtonian	2/14/16	C. J. Mahaney	Sovereign Grace Ministries	SP	Sex, C	NI	https://www.washingtonian.com/2016/02/14/the-sex-abuse-scandal-that-devastated-a-suburban-megachurch-sovereign-grace-ministries/
Christian Today	2/15/16	David Janney	Orlando Baptist	SP	Sex, A	AC	https://www.christiantoday.com/article/woman-sues-florida-megachurch-after-failing-to-get-hush-money-to-keep-affair-with-pastor-a-secret/79598.htm

(continued)

TABLE C.1. Continued

Source	Article Date	Person	Church	Pos	Typ	Ad	Link
Christianity Today	4/13/16	Darrin Patrick	The Journey	SP	O	NI	http://www.christianitytoday.com/news/2016/april/darrin-patrick-removed-acts-29-megachurch-journey.html
The Tennessean	5/5/16	Church	Cornerstone Nashville Church	C	Sex, C	AC	http://www.tennessean.com/story/news/religion/2016/05/05/10-million-suit-against-cornerstone-nashville-church/83943382/
Daily Mail	6/21/16	Church	The Rock Church	C	Sex	AC	http://www.dailymail.co.uk/news/article-2625648/Its-cesspool-sex-Women-sue-director-megachurch-affiliated-rehab-claims-routinely-groped-harassed-laid-slept.html
USA Today	7/11/16	Perry Noble	NewSpring Church	SP	Alco	A	https://www.usatoday.com/story/money/nation-now/2016/07/11/south-carolina-wealthy-megachurch-newspring-fires-founder-perry-noble-alcohol-abuse-strained-marriage/86937078/
Charisma News	7/15/16	Sunday Adelaja	Embassy of the Blessed Kingdom of God for All Nations	SP	Sex, A	A	https://www.charismanews.com/world/58633-nation-s-leaders-punish-megachurch-pastor-sunday-adelaja-after-multiple-affairs
Christian Today	1/11/17	Gu "Joseph" Yuese	Chongyi Church	SP	E	G	https://www.christiantoday.com/article/chinese-megachurch-pastor-arrested-as-crackdown-on-christians-continues/103777.htm

Source	Date	Person	Church/Organization				URL
International Business Times	1/15/17	Bishop Eddie Long	New Birth Missionary Baptist Church	SP	Sex, B	AC	http://www.ibtimes.com/who-bishop-eddie-long-megachurch-minister-embroiled-sex-scandal-dies-cancer-headed-2475759
Christian Post	3/14/17	Johnson Suleman	Omega Fire Ministry Worldwide	SP	Sex, A	AC	https://www.christianpost.com/news/megachurch-pastor-johnson-suleman-accused-of-sex-affairs-bars-church-from-speaking-out-177562/
Courthouse News	4/25/17	Paul Ricky Mata	Water of Life Community Church	E	E	AC	https://www.courthousenews.com/socal-megachurch-sued-investment-fraud/
Christian Post	4/25/17	Chris Hill	Potter's House Church of Denver	SP	Sex, A	AC	https://www.christianpost.com/news/potters-house-denver-pastor-chris-hill-resigns-over-alleged-affair-separates-from-wife-181651/
Korea Exposé	4/28/17	Kim Sam-hwan	Myungsung Presbyterian Church	SP	O	A	https://www.koreaexpose.com/father-son-holy-mess-megachurches/
Christian Today	5/30/17	Kong Hee	City Harvest Church	SP	E	G	https://www.christiantoday.com/article/singapore.megachurch.scandal.pastor.barred.from.running.any.charity.ever/109594.htm
Los Angeles Times	6/6/17	Jan Crouch	Trinity Broadcasting Network	P	Sex, C	AC	http://www.latimes.com/local/lanow/la-me-tcn-history-20170606-story.html
Los Angeles Times	6/6/17	Paul Crouch	Trinity Broadcasting Network	SP	Sex, D	AC	http://www.latimes.com/local/lanow/la-me-tcn-history-20170606-story.html
Los Angeles Times	6/6/17	Trinity Broadcasting Network	Trinity Broadcasting Network	C	O	AC	http://www.latimes.com/local/lanow/la-me-tcn-history-20170606-story.html

(continued)

TABLE C.1. Continued

Source	Person	Article Date	Church	Pos	Typ	Ad	Link
Christian Post	Fred Price, Jr.	6/27/17	Crenshaw Christian Center	SP	O	AC	https://www.christianpost.com/news/crenshaw-christian-center-pastor-fred-price-jr-steps-down-over-personal-misjudgments-189765/
New York Post	Joel Osteen	8/28/17	Lakewood Church	SP	O	NI	https://nypost.com/2017/08/28/pastor-osteen-shuts-church-amid-flooding-crisis/
Christian Post	Michael Hodges	10/9/17	Church of the Highlands, Greystone campus	SP	O	AC	https://www.christianpost.com/news/michael-hodges-son-of-megachurch-founder-removed-as-pastor-due-to-moral-failing-202219/
Miami New Times	Bob Coy	11/14/17	Calvary Chapel Fort Lauderdale	SP	Sex, A, & B	PA	http://www.miaminewtimes.com/news/bob-coy-founder-of-calvary-chapel-fort-lauderdale-accused-of-molesting-child-9827948
Miami New Times	William Graham, Tullian Tchividjian	11/19/17	Coral Ridge Presbyterian	SP	Sex, A	PA	http://www.miaminewtimes.com/news/five-bad-priests-like-florida-megachurch-molester-bob-coy-9839580
KIRO 7	Caleb Treat	11/28/17	Christian Faith Center	P	Sex, A	AC	http://www.kiro7.com/news/local/king-county-megachurch-accused-of-sexual-harassment-in-lawsuit/631178864
Christian Post	Owen and Tammy McManus	3/27/16	City Church of New Orleans	SP	E	AC	https://www.christianpost.com/news/husband-wife-new-orleans-megachurch-preachers-face-arrest-alleged-tax-fraud-164590/

BIBLIOGRAPHY

Alaimo, Stacy, and Susan Hekman. "Introduction: Emerging Models of Materiality in Feminist Theory." In *Material Feminisms*, edited by Stacy Alaimo and Susan Heckman, 1–19. Bloomington: Indiana University Press, 2008.

Almasy, Steve. "Megachurch Pastor Creflo Dollar on His Daughter: 'She Was Not Punched.'" *CNN*, June 10, 2012. http://religion.blogs.cnn.com/2012/06/10/pastor-creflo-dollar-she-was-not-punched/.

American Psychological Association. "Marriage and Divorce." Accessed March 9, 2018. http://www.apa.org/topics/divorce/.

Ammerman, Nancy T. *Congregation and Community*. New Brunswick, NJ: Rutgers University Press, 1997.

Ammerman, Nancy T. "Golden Rule Christianity: Lived Religion in the American Mainstream." In *Lived Religion in America: Toward a History of Practice*, edited by David D. Hall, 196–216. Princeton, NJ: Princeton University Press, 1997.

Anton, Susan C., and J. Josh Snodgrass. "Origin and Evolution of Genus *Homo*: New Perspectives." *Current Anthropology* 53, no. 2 (2012): 479–496.

Aslan, Reza. *God: A Human History*. New York: Penguin Random House, 2017.

Atkinson, Quentin D., and Pierrick Bourrat. "Beliefs about God, the Afterlife and Morality Support the Role of Supernatural Policing in Human Cooperation." *Evolution & Human Behavior* 32, no. 1 (2011): 41–49.

Atran, Scott, and Joseph Henrich. "The Evolution of Religion: How Cognitive By-Products, Adaptive Learning Heuristics, Ritual Displays, and Group Competition Generate Deep Commitments to Prosocial Religions." *Biological Theory* 5, no.1 (2010): 18–30.

Bailey, Sarah Pulliam. "Megachurch Pastor Bill Hybels Resigns from Willow Creek after Women Allege Misconduct," *Washington Post,* April 10, 2018.

https://www.washingtonpost.com/news/acts-of-faith/wp/2018/04/10/bill-hybels-prominent-megachurch-pastor-resigns-from-willow-creek-following-allegations/?utm_term=.d48f5c9c2e99.

Balch, Robert W. "Charisma and Corruption in the Love Family: Toward a Theory of Corruption in Charismatic Cults." In *Sex, Lies, and Sanctity: Religion and Deviance in Contemporary North America*, Vol. 5, edited by M. J. Neitz and M. S. Goldman, 155–179. Greenwich: JAI Press, 1995.

Barad, Karen. *Meeting the Universe Halfway: Quantum Physics and the Entanglement of Matter and Meaning*. Durham, NC: Duke University Press, 2007.

Barkow, Jerome H., Leda Cosmides, and John Tooby. *The Adapted Mind: Evolutionary Psychology and the Generation of Culture*. New York: Oxford University Press, 1992.

Barraza, Jorge A., and Paul J. Zak. "Empathy toward Strangers Triggers Oxytocin Release and Subsequent Generosity." *Annals of the New York Academy of Sciences* 1167 (2009): 129–189.

Barrett, Justin L. *Why Would Anyone Believe in God?* New York: AltaMira, 2004.

Barrett, Lisa Feldman. *How Emotions Are Made: The Secret Life of the Brain*. Boston: Houghton Mifflin Harcourt, 2017.

Bartkowski, John P. "Faithfully Embodied: Religious Identity and the Body." *disClosure: A Journal of Social Theory* 14, no. 4 (2005): 8–37.

Bartkowski, John P. *The Promise Keepers: Servants, Soldiers, and Godly Men*. New Brunswick, NJ: Rutgers University Press, 2004.

Bartz, Jennifer A., Jamil Zaki, Niall Bolger, and Kevin Ochsner. "Social Effects of Oxytocin in Humans: Context and Person Matter." *Trends in Cognitive Sciences* 15 (2011): 301–309.

Bauman, Zygmunt. *Liquid Modernity*. Cambridge: Polity Press, 2000.

Baumgartner, Thomas, Markus Heinrichs, Aline Volanthen, Urs Fishbacher, and Ernst Fehr. "Oxytocin Shapes the Neural Circuitry of Trust and Trust Adaptation in Humans." *Neuron* 58, no. 4 (2008): 639–650.

Becker, Howard S. "Becoming a Marihuana User." *American Journal of Sociology* 59, no. 3 (1953): 235–242.

Bell, Daniel M., Jr. *The Economy of Desire: Christianity and Capitalism in a Postmodern World*. Grand Rapids, MI: Baker Academic, 2012.

Bell, Rob. *What Is the Bible? How an Ancient Library of Poems, Letters, and Stories Can Transform the Way You Think and Feel about Everything*. San Francisco: HarperOne, 2017.

Bellah, Robert. "Civil Religion in America." *Daedalus* 96 (1967): 1–21.

Berger, Peter L. "The Desecularization of the World: A Global Overview." In *The Desecularization of the World: Resurgent Religion and World Politics*, edited by Peter L. Berger, 1–18. Grand Rapids, MI: Ethics and Public Policy Center and Wm. B. Eerdmans Publishing, 1999.

Berger, Peter L. "Further Thoughts on Religion and Modernity." *Society* 49, no. 4 (2012): 313–316.

Berger, Peter L. *Sacred Canopy: Elements of a Sociological Theory of Religion*. Garden City, NY: Doubleday, 1967.

Berger, Peter L. "'You Can Do It!' Two Cheers for the Prosperity Gospel." *Books and Culture*, October 14, 2008. https://www.booksandculture.com/articles/2008/sepoct/10.14.html.

Berman, Eli. "Sect, Subsidy, and Sacrifice: An Economist's View of Ultra-Orthodox Jews." *Quarterly Journal of Economics* 115 (2000): 905–953.

Blair, Gwenda. *The Trumps: Three Generations of Builders and a President*. New York: Simon & Schuster, 2001. https://www.amazon.com/Trumps-Three-Generations-Builders-President/dp/0743210794.

Blair, Gwenda. "How Norman Vincent Peale Taught Donald Trump to Worship Himself." *Politico Magazine,* October 6, 2015. https://www.politico.com/magazine/story/2015/10/donald-trump-2016-norman-vincent-peale-213220.

Blair, Gwenda. *Donald Trump: The Candidate*. New York: Simon & Schuster, 2007.

Blake, John. "How the Ultimate Scandal Saved One Pastor." *CNN,* March 2015. http://www.cnn.com/interactive/2015/03/living/ultimate-scandal-paulk/.

Blau, Peter. *Exchange in Social Life*. New York: Wiley, 1964.

Bourdieu, Pierre. *The Logic of Practice*. Cambridge: Polity Press, 1990.

Bowler, Kate. *Blessed: A History of the American Prosperity Gospel*. Oxford: Oxford University Press, 2013.

Boyer, Pascal, and Charles Ramble. "Cognitive Templates for Religious Concepts: Cross-Cultural Evidence for Recall of Counter-intuitive Representations." *Cognitive Science* 25 (2001): 535–564.

Brasher, Brenda E. *Godly Women: Fundamentalism and Female Power.* New Brunswick, NJ: Rutgers University Press, 1998.

Bruce, Steve. *Choice and Religion: A Critique of Rational Choice Theory*. Oxford: Oxford University Press, 1999.

Bulbulia, Joseph, Armin W. Geertz, Quentin D. Atkinson, Emma Cohen, Nicholas Evans, Pieter Francois, Herbert Gintis, Russell D. Gray, Joseph Henrich, Fiona M. Jordon, Ara Norenzayan, Peter J. Richerson, Edward Slingerland, Peter Turchin, Harvey Whitehouse, Thomas Widlock, and David S. Wilson, "The Cultural Evolution of Religion," in *Cultural Evolution: Society, Technology, Language, and Religion,* edited by Peter J. Richerson and Morten H. Christiansen, 381–404. Cambridge, MA: MIT Press, 2013.

Calulu, Suzanne. "The Delusional Followers of Convicted Felon Jack Schaap." *Patheos Blog,* November 18, 2013. http://www.patheos.com/blogs/nolongerquivering/2013/11/the-delusional-followers-of-convicted-felon-jack-schaap/.

Cavey, Bruce. *The End of Religion: Encountering the Subversive Spirituality of Jesus*. Colorado Springs, CO: NavPress, 2007.

Chaves, Mark. *American Religion: Contemporary Trends,* 2nd edition. Princeton, NJ: Princeton University Press, 2011.

Churchland, Patricia. *Braintrust: What Neuroscience Tells Us about Morality*. Princeton, NJ: Princeton University Press, 2011.

Cladis, Mark S. "Suffering to Become Human: A Durkheimian Perspective." In *Suffering and Evil: The Durkheimian Legacy*, edited by W. S. F. Pickering and Massimo Rosati, 81–100. Oxford: Durkheim Press/Berghahn, 2008.

Coleman, Stephen. "Book Review: The Digital Difference: Media Technology and the Theory of Communication Effects." *Journal of Communication* 67 (2017): E7–E8.

Collins, Randall. *Interaction Ritual Chains*. Princeton, NJ: Princeton University Press, 2004.

Collins, Randall. "The Micro-sociology of Religion: Religious Practices, Collective and Individual." *Association of Religion Data Archives, Guiding Paper,* 2010. http://www.thearda.com/rrh/papers/guidingpapers.asp.

Colson, Charles. *The Body: Being Light in Darkness*. Nashville, TN: W. Pub Group, 1994.

Connell, R. W. *Masculinities,* 2nd edition. Berkeley: University of California Press, 2005 [1995].

Conwell, Russell Herman. *Acres of Diamonds*. New York: Cosimo Classics, 2008 [1890].

Coole, Diana, and Samantha Frost, eds. *New Materialisms: Ontology, Agency, and Politics.* Durham, NC: Duke University Press, 2010.

Corcoran, Katie E. "Thinkers and Feelers: Emotion and Giving." *Social Science Research* 52 (2015): 686–700.

Corcoran, Katie E., and James K. Wellman Jr. "'People Forget He's Human': Charismatic Leadership in Institutionalized Religion." *Sociology of Religion* 77, no. 4 (2016): 309–333.

Corrigan, John, ed. *Feeling Religion*. Durham, NC: Duke University Press, 2017.

Cragun, Ryan, Barry A. Kosmin, Ariela Keysar, Joseph H. Hammer, and Michael Nielsen. "On the Receiving End: Discrimination toward the Non-religious in the United States." *Journal of Contemporary Religion* 27, no. 1 (2012): 105–127.

Damasio, Antonio R. *Descartes' Error: Emotion, Reason, and the Human Brain.* New York: Penguin Books, 1994.

Davidson, Helen. 2015. "Hillsong's Brian Houston Failed to Report Abuse and Had Conflict of Interest—Royal Commission." *The Guardian,* November 23, 2015. https://www.theguardian.com/australia-news/2015/nov/23/hillsongs-brian-houston-failed-to-report-abuse-and-had-conflict-of-interest-royal-commission.

Davis, Kathy, ed. *Embodied Practices: Feminist Perspectives on the Body*. London: SAGE Publications, 1997.

Dawson, Lorne L. *Comprehending Cults: The Sociology of New Religious Movements.* Toronto: Oxford University Press, 1998.

Dawson, Lorne L. "Crises of Charismatic Legitimacy and Violent Behavior in New Religious Movements." In *Cults, Religion & Violence*, edited by D. G. Bromley and J. G. Melton, 80–101. Cambridge: University of Cambridge Press, 2002.

Dawson, Lorne, L. "Psychopathologies and the Attribution of Charisma: A Critical Introduction to the Psychology of Charisma and Explanation of Violence in New Religious Movements." *Nova Religio: The Journal of Alternative and Emergent Religions* 10, no. 2 (2006): 3–28.

De Dreu, Carsten K. W. "Oxytocin Modulates Cooperation within and Competition between Groups: An Integrative Review and Research Agenda." *Hormones and Behavior* 61, no. 3 (2012): 419–428.

De Dreu, Carsten K. W., Lindred L. Greer, Michel J. J. Handgraaf, Shaul Shalvi, Gerben A. Van Kleef, Matthijs Baas, Femke S. Ten Velden, Eric Van Dijk, and Sander W. W. Feith. "The Neuropeptide Oxytocin Regulates Parochial Altruism in Intergroup Conflict among Humans." *Science* 328 (2010): 1408–1411.

De Dreu, Carsten K. W., Lindred L. Greer, Gerben A. Van Kleef, Shaul Shalvi, and Michel J. J. Handgraaf. "Oxytocin Promotes Human Ethnocentrism." *Proceedings of the National Academy of Sciences USA* 108, no. 4 (2011): 1262–1266.

Declerck, Carolyn H., Christophe Boone, and Toko Kiyonari. "Oxytocin and Cooperation under Conditions of Uncertainty: The Modulating role of Incentives and Social Information." *Hormones and Behavior* 57, no. 3 (2010): 368–374.

Depue, Richard A., and Jeannine V. Morrone-Strupinsky. "A Neurobehavioral Model of Affiliative Bonding: Implications for Conceptualizing a Human Trait of Affiliation." *Behavioral and Brain Science* 28 (2005): 313–395.

DiPellegrino, Giuseppe, Luciano Fadiga, Leonardo Fogassi, Vittorio Gallese, and Giacomo Rizzolatti. "Understanding Motor Events: A Neurophysiological Study." *Experimental Brain Research* 91 (1992): 176–180.

Dolan, Bill. "Ex-Megachurch Pastor Blames Underage Victim, Wants Out of Prison." *NWI*, June 3, 2014. https://www.nwitimes.com/news/local/lake/ ex-megachurch-pastor-blames-underage-victim-wants-out-of-prison/article_ 2ae9324b-eacf-546e-9f73-c12147f5726f.html.

Durkheim, Émile. "The Dualism of Human Nature and Its Social Conditions." In *Émile Durkheim, 1858–1917*, edited by Kurt H. Wolff, 325–340. Columbus: Ohio State University Press, 1964 [1914].

Durkheim, Émile. "The Problem of Religion and the Duality of Human Nature." Translated by Robert Alun Jones and W. Paul Vogt. In *Knowledge and Society: Studies in the Sociology of Culture Past and Present* vol. 5, edited by Henrika Kuklick and Elizabeth Long, 1–44. Greenwich, CT: JAI Press, 1984 [1913].

Durkheim, Émile. *The Elementary Forms of Religious Life.* New York: Free Press, 1995 [1912].

Durkheim, Émile. "Individualism, and the Intellectuals." In *Durkheim on Religion: A Selection of Readings with Bibliographies and Introductory Remarks*, edited by William S. F. Pickering. Cambridge: James Clarke & Co., 2011 [1975].

Dye, Lee. "A Love Drug? Oxytocin Hormone Makes Mothers Kinder." *ABC News,* January 11, 2012. https://abcnews.go.com/Technology/

love-drug-oxytocin-cuddle-chemical-scientists-makes-mothers/
story?id=15330910.

Eagle, David E. "Historicizing the Megachurch." *Journal of Social History* 48
(2015): 589–604.

Edwards, Jonathan. *Religious Affections*. Vancouver: Vancouver Eremitical Press,
2009 [1746].

Edwards, Jonathan. *The Works of Jonathan Edwards, Volume 2: Religious Affections*, ed.
John E. Smith. New Haven, CT: Yale University Press, 2009.

Edwards, Jonathan. *A Divine and Supernatural Light Immediately Imparted to the Soul
by the Spirit of God, Shown to Be Scriptural and Rational Doctrine*. Accessed January
9, 2018. https://www.monergism.com/thethreshold/articles/onsite/edwards_
light.html.

Edwards, Kari. "The Interplay of Affect and Cognition in Attitude Formation and
Change." *Journal of Personality and Social Psychology* 59, no. 2 (1990): 202–216.

Eich, Eric, John F. Kihlstrom, Gordon H. Bower, Joseph P. Forgas, and Paula
M. Niedenthal, eds. *Cognition and Emotion*. New York: Oxford University
Press, 2000.

Elder, Lee. "Allegations Continue to Hound Fundamentalist Hyles." *Christianity
Today* 24 (1990): 45–46.

Eliade, Mircea. *The Sacred and the Profane: The Nature of Religion*.
New York: Harcourt, Brace & World, 1959.

Emerson, Richard. "Power Dependence Relations." *American Sociological Review* 27
(1962): 31–41.

Encyclopedia.com. "Thomas Weeks III." Accessed July 8, 2018. https://
www.encyclopedia.com/education/news-wires-white-papers-and-books/
weeks-thomas-iii.

Eng, David. *The Feeling of Kinship: Queer Liberalism and the Racialization of Intimacy*.
Durham, NC: Duke University Press, 2010.

Farley, Harry. "Singapore Megachurch Scandal: Pastor Barred
from Running Any Charity Ever." *Christianity Today*,
May 3, 2017. https://www.christiantoday.com/article/
singapore.megachurch.scandal.pastor.barred.from.running.any.charity.ever/
109594.htm.

Fausto-Sterling, Anne. *Sexing the Body: Gender Politics and the Construction of
Sexuality*. New York: Basic Books, 2000.

Fine, Cordelia. *Delusions of Gender: How Our Minds, Society, and Neurosexism Create
Difference*. New York: W. W. Norton, 2010.

Finney, Charles G. *Lectures on Revivals of Religion*. Createspace, 2015.

Fish, Jonathan S. "*Homo Duplex* Revisited: A Defense of Émile Durkheim's Theory
of the Moral Self." *Journal of Classical Sociology* 13, no. 3 (2013): 338–358.

Frankenberry, Nancy. 1987. *Religion and Radical Empiricism*. Albany: State
University of New York Press.

Franks, David D., and Jonathan H. Turner, eds. *Handbook of Neurosociology.*
New York: Springer, 2013.

Frost, Michael. "Should a Pastor Ever Own a Private Jet or a Luxury Yacht?" April
23, 2018. https://mikefrost.net/should-a-pastor-ever-own-a-private-jet-or-a-
luxury-yacht/.

Fuentes, Agustin. "Re-situating Anthropological Approaches to the Evolution of
Human Behavior." *Anthropology Today* 25, no. 3 (2009): 12–17.

Fuentes, Agustin. "Putting Evolutionary Theory to Work in Investigating Human
Nature(s)." In *Verbs, Bones, and Brains: Interdisciplinary Perspectives on Human
Nature,* edited by Agustin Fuentes and Aku Visala, 248–259. Notre Dame,
IN: University of Notre Dame Press, 2017.

Fuentes, Agustin, and Aku Visala. "Introduction: The Many Faces of Human
Nature." In *Verbs, Bones, and Brains: Interdisciplinary Perspectives on Human Nature*,
edited by Agustin Fuentes and Aku Visala, 1–25. Notre Dame, IN: Notre
Dame University Press, 2017.

Fuentes, Agustin, and Aku Visala, eds. *Verbs, Bones, and Brains: Interdisciplinary
Perspectives on Human Nature.* Notre Dame, IN: University of Notre Dame
Press, 2017.

Gad, Viola. "Can Oxytocin Get Me a Boyfriend?" *Popular Science.*
April 23, 2013. https://www.popsci.com/science/article/2013-04/
can-oxytocin-get-me-boyfriend.

Gao, Shan, Benjamin Becker, Lizho Luo, Yayuan Geng, Weihua Zhao, Yu Yin,
Jiehui Hu, Zhao Gao, Qiyong Gong, Rene Hurlemann, Dezhong Yao, and
Keith M. Kendrick. "Oxytocin, the Peptide That Bonds the Sexes, Also
Divides Them." *Proceedings of the National Academy of Sciences USA* 113, no. 27
(2016): 7650–7654.

Goodson, James L. "Deconstructing Sociality, Social Evolution and Relevant
Nonapeptide Functions." *Psychoneuroendocrinology* 38 (2013): 465–478.

Girard, René. *Deceit, Desire, and the Novel: Self and Other in Literary Structure.*
Translated by Yvonne Freccero. Baltimore: Johns Hopkins Press, 1966
[1961].

Goffman, Erving. *Interaction Ritual: Essays on Face-to-Face Behavior.*
New York: Anchor Books, 1967.

Gorski, Philip. *American Covenant: A History of Civil Religion from the Puritans to the
Present.* Princeton, NJ: Princeton University Press, 2017.

Gottman Institute. Accessed March 9, 2018. https://www.gottman.com/.

Gouin, Jean-Philippe, C. Sue Carter, Hossein Pournajafi-Nazarloo, Ronald Glaser,
William B. Malarky, Timothy J. Loving, Jeffrey Stowell, and Janice K. Kiecolt-
Glaser. "Marital Behavior, Oxytocin, Vasopressin, and Wound Healing."
Psychoneuroendocrinology 35, no. 7 (2010): 1082–1090.

Grape, Christina, Maria Sandgren, Lars-Olof Hansson, Mats Ericson, and
Tores Theorell. "Does Singing Promote Well-Being?: An Empirical Study

of Professional and Amateur Singers during a Singing Lesson." *Integrative Physiological & Behavioral Science* 38, no. 1 (2003): 65–74.

Greenleaf. Accessed July 8, 2018. https://www.greenleaf.org/what-is-servant-leadership/.

Grosz, Elizabeth. "Darwin and Feminism: Preliminary Investigations for a Possible Alliance." *On Material Feminisms*, edited by Stacy Alaimo and Susan Hekman, 23–51. Bloomington: Indiana University Press, 2008.

Gushee, David P. *Changing our Minds: Definitive 3rd Edition of the Landmark Call for Inclusion of LGBTQ Christians with Response to Critics.* Spirit Books, 2017.

Gushee, David. *Following Jesus Out of American Evangelicalism.* Louisville, KY: Westminster/John Knox Press, 2017.

Guthrie, Stewart E. *Faces in the Clouds: A New Theory of Religion.* New York: Oxford University Press, 1993.

Guthrie, Stewart E. "Religion as Anthropomorphism: A Cognitive Theory." In *The Oxford Handbook of Evolutionary Psychology and Religion*, edited by J. Liddle and T. Shackelford. Oxford University Press, 2016. DOI: 10.1093/oxfordhb/9780199397747.013.6.

Haggard, Gayle. *Why I Stayed: The Choices I Made in My Darkest Hour.* Carol Stream, IL: Tyndale House Publishers, 2010.

Haidt, Jonathan. *The Righteous Mind: Why Good People Are Divided by Politics and Religion.* New York: Random House, 2012.

Hamm, Ryan E. C. "Outreach Interview: A New Direction, Stacy Spencer," *Outreach Magazine*, 2012.

Harari, Yuval Noah. *Sapiens: A Brief History of Humankind.* New York: HarperCollins, 2015.

Headspace. 2017. Accessed December 13, 2017. https://www.headspace.com/.

Heinrichs, Markus, Thomas Baumgartner, Clemens Kirschbaum, and Ulrike Ehlert. "Social Support and Oxytocin Interact to Suppress Cortisol and Subjective Responses to Psychosocial Stress." *Biological Psychiatry* 54 (2003): 1389–1398.

Hendley, Matthew. "Mark Connelly, Phoenix-Area Megachurch Pastor, Resigns over Alleged Affairs," *Phoenix New Times*, January 6, 2014. http://www.phoenixnewtimes.com/news/mark-connelly-phoenix-area-megachurch-pastor-resigns-over-alleged-affairs-6636117.

Henrich, Joseph. "The Evolution of Costly Displays, Cooperation and Religion: Credibility Enhancing Displays and Their Implications for Cultural Evolution." *Evolution and Human Behavior* 30, no. 4 (2009): 244–260.

Henricson, Maria, Anna-Lena Berglund, Sylvia Määttä, Rolf Ekman, and Kerstin Segesten. "The Outcome of Tactile Touch on Oxytocin in Intensive Care Patients: A Randomized Controlled Trial." *Journal of Clinical Nursing* 17, no. 19 (2008): 2624–2633.

Heyes, Cecilia. *Cognitive Gadgets: The Cultural Evolution of Thinking.* Cambridge, MA: Belknap Press, 2018.

Hirsch, Arnold R. *Making the Second Ghetto: Race and Housing in Chicago, 1940–1960*. Chicago: University of Chicago Press, 1998.

Hobson, Nicholas M., Juliana Schroeder, Jane L. Risen, Dimitris Xygalatas, and Michael Inzlicht. "The Psychology of Rituals: An Integrative Review and Process-Based Framework." *Personality and Social Psychology Review* 22, no. 3 (2017): 260–284.

Hoge, Dean R., Benton Johnson, and Donald A. Luiden. *Vanishing Boundaries: The Religion of Mainline Protestant Baby Boomers*. Louisville, KY: Westminster/John Knox Press, 1994.

Holbrook, Colin, Jennifer Hahn-Holbrook, and Julianne Holt-Lunstad. "Self-Reported Spirituality Correlates with Endogenous Oxytocin." *Psychology of Religion and Spirituality* 7, no. 1 (2015): 46–50.

Hollinger, David A. *Protestants Abroad: How Missionaries Tried to Change the World but Changed America*. Princeton, NJ: Princeton University Press, 2017.

Honigsbaum, Mark. "Oxytocin: Could the 'Trust Hormone' Rebond Our Troubled World?" *The Guardian*, August 20, 2011. https://www.theguardian.com/science/2011/aug/21/oxytocin-zak-neuroscience-trust-hormone?INTCMP=SRCH.

Hrdy, Sarah Blaffer. *Mothers and Others: The Evolutionary Origins of Mutual Understanding*. Cambridge, MA: Belknap Press, 2009.

Hrdy, Sarah Blaffer. *The Origin of Emotionally Modern Humans* [lecture]. October 17, 2011, published online January 9, 2012. Retrieved from Cornell University YouTube. https://www.youtube.com/watch?v=o7YlpVdplqA&list=UUfTfuTTALrsxUWjisrdOWtA.

Hume, David. *A Treatise of Human Nature*, edited by David Fate Norton and Mary J. Norton. Oxford: Oxford University Press, 2000.

Iannelli, Jerry. "South Florida's Five Worst Religious Leaders, Including Accused Molester Bob Coy." *Miami New Times*, November 19, 2017. http://www.miaminewtimes.com/news/five-bad-priests-like-florida-megachurch-molester-bob-coy-9839580.

Irons, William. "Religion as a Hard-to-Fake Sign of Commitment." In *Evolution and the Capacity for Commitment*, edited by R. Nesse, 292–309. New York: Russell Sage Foundation, 2001.

Jablonka, Eva, and Marion J. Lamb. *Evolution in Four Dimensions: Genetic, Epigenetic, Behavioral, and Symbolic Variation in the History of Life*, Revised Edition. Cambridge, MA: MIT Press, 2014.

Jacobs, Janet. "The Economy of Love in Religious Commitment: The Deconversion of Women from Nontraditional Religious Movements." *Journal for the Scientific Study of Religion* 23, no. 2 (1984): 155–171.

Jacobs, Janet. "Deconversion from Religious Movements: An Analysis of Charismatic Bonding and Spiritual Commitment." *Journal for the Scientific Study of Religion* 26, no. 3 (1987): 294–308.

Jacobs, Janet. *Divine Disenchantment: Deconverting from New Religions*. Bloomington: Indiana University Press, 1989.

Jacobs, Janet. "Abuse in New Religious Movements: Challenges for the Sociology of Religion." In *Teaching New Religious Movements*, edited by David G. Bromley, 231–244. New York: Oxford University Press, 2007.

James, William. *The Will to Believe and Other Essays in Popular Philosophy: Human Immortality*. New York: Dover Publications, 1956.

James, William. *The Varieties of Religious Experience: A Study in Human Nature*. New York: Penguin Books, 1982.

James, William. *Essays in Radical Empiricism*. Lincoln: University of Nebraska Press, 1996.

Jerolmack, Colin, and Douglas Porpora. "Religion, Rationality, and Experience: A Response to the New Rational Choice Theory of Religion." *Sociological Theory* 22, no. 1 (2004): 140–160.

Johnson, Doyle P. "Dilemmas of Charismatic Leadership: The Case of the Peoples Temple." *Sociological Analysis* 40 (1979): 315–323.

Johnson, Jessica. *Biblical Porn: Affect, Labor, and Pastor Mark Driscoll's Evangelical Empire*. Durham, NC: Duke University Press, 2018.

Jones, Terry. *Monty Python's Life of Brian*. London: HandMade Films, 1979.

Joosse, Paul. "The Presentation of the Charismatic Self in Everyday Life: Reflections on a Canadian New Religious Movement." *Sociology of Religion* 73, no. 2 (2012): 174–199.

Jordan-Young, Rebecca. *Brainstorm: The Flaws in the Science of Sex Differences*. Cambridge, MA: Harvard University Press, 2010.

Kant, Immanuel. *Critique of Pure Reason*. Cambridge: Cambridge University Press, 1998 [1781/1787].

Kaplan, Hillard. "Evolutionary and Wealth Flows Theories of Fertility: Empirical Tests and New Models." *Proceedings of the National Academy of Sciences USA* 102 (1994): 15294–15298.

Kelsch, Courtney B., Gail Ironson, Angela Szeto, Heidemarie Kremer, Neil Schneiderman, and Armando J. Mendez. "The Relationship of Spirituality, Benefit Finding, and Other Psychosocial Variables to the Hormone Oxytocin in HIV/AIDS." *Research in the Social Scientific Study of Religion* 24 (2013): 137–162.

Kets de Vries, Manfred F. R. "Ties That Bind the Leader and the Led." In *Charismatic Leadership: The Elusive Factor in Organizational Effectiveness*, edited by Jay A. Conger and Rabindra N. Kanungo, 237–252. San Francisco: Jossey-Bass, 1988.

Kidd, Thomas S. *George Whitefield: America's Spiritual Founding Father*. New Haven, CT: Yale University Press, 2014.

Kirby, Vicky. "Natural Convers(at)ions: Or, What If Culture Was Really Nature All Along?" In *Material Feminisms*, edited by Stacy Alaimo and Susan Hekman, 214–236. Bloomington: Indiana University Press, 2008.

Kirsch, Peter, Christine Esslinger, Qiang Chen, Daniela Mier, Stephanie Lis, Sarina Siddhanti, Harald Gruppe, Venkata S. Mattay, Bernd Gallhofer, and Andreas

Meyer-Lindenberg. "Oxytocin Modulates Neural Circuitry for Social Cognition and Fear in Humans." *Journal of Neuroscience* 25, no. 49 (2005): 11489–11493.

Klett, Leah Marie Ann. "Pastor Kong Hee Sentenced to 8 Years in Prison, Admits He Will Face 'Very Difficult Days Ahead.'" *Gospel Herald*, November 20, 2015. http://www.gospelherald.com/articles/59943/20151120/city-harvest-church-pastor-kong-hee-saddened-by-length-of-sentence-admits-he-will-face-very-difficult-days-ahead.htm?gclid=EAIaIQobChMI3azkj4KL3AIVEttkCh2M-wY_EAAYASAAEgJ_L_D_BwE.

Konvalinka, Ivana, Dimitris Xygalatas, Joseph Bulbulia, Uffe Schjødt, Else-Marie Jegindø, Sebastian Wallot, Guy Van Orden, and Andreas Roepstorff. "Synchronized Arousal between Performers and Related Spectators in a Fire-Walking Ritual." *Proceedings of the National Academy of Sciences USA* 108, no. 20 (2011): 8514–8519.

Kosfeld, Michael, Markus Heinrichs, Paul J. Zak, Urs Fischbacher, and Ernst Fehr. "Oxytocin Increases Trust in Humans." *Nature* 435, no. 7042 (2005): 673–676.

Kosmin, Barry A., Ariela Keysar, Ryan Cragun, and Juhem Navarro-Rivera. "American Nones: The Profile of the No Religion Population, A Report Based on the American Religious Identification Survey 2008." *Trinity College Digital Repository,* 2009. http://commons.trincoll.edu/aris/files/2011/08/NONES_08.pdf.

Kreutz, Gunter. "Does Singing Facilitate Social Bonding?" *Music and Medicine: An Interdisciplinary Journal* 6, no. 2 (2014): 51–60.

Kubzansky, Laura D., Wendy Berry Mendes, Allison A. Appleton, Jason Block, and Gail K. Adler. "A Heartfelt Response: Oxytocin Effects on Response to Social Stress in Men and Women." *Biological Psychology* 90, no. 1 (2012): 1–9.

Kurosawa, Mieko, Thomas Lundeberg, Greta Ågren, Irene Lund, and Kerstin Uvnäs-Moberg. "Massage-like Stroking of the Abdomen Lowers Blood Pressure in Anesthetized Rats: Influence of Oxytocin." *Journal of the Autonomic Nervous System* 56, no. 1–2 (1995): 26–30.

Kuzydym, Stephanie, and Kristine Phillips. "Joel Osteen Calls Claim He Shut Church Doors on Harvey Victims 'A False Narrative.'" *Washington Post,* August 29, 2017. https://www.washingtonpost.com/news/acts-of-faith/wp/2017/08/29/we-were-never-closed-joel-osteens-houston-megachurch-disputes-claims-it-shut-its-doors/?utm_term=.dedab946e0d4.

Lambert, Frank. *"Pedlar in Divinity": George Whitefield and the Transatlantic Revivals 1737–1770.* Princeton, NJ: Princeton University Press, 1994.

Laura, Robert. "Pastor Rick Warren Is Well Prepared for a Purpose Driven Retirement." *Forbes,* March 21, 2013. https://www.forbes.com/sites/robertlaura/2013/03/21/pastor-rick-warren-is-practicing-what-he-preaches-and-getting-ready-for-retirement/#7341c6c44dbf.

Lawler, Edward J., Shane R. Thye, and Jeongkoo Yoon. *Social Commitments in a Depersonalized World*. New York: Russell Sage Foundation, 2009.

Lawler, Edward J., Shane R. Thye, and Jeongkoo Yoon. "Emotions and Group Ties in Social Exchange." In *Handbook of the Sociology of Emotions: Volume II*, edited by Jane E. Stets and Jonathan H. Turner, 77–101. Dordrecht: Springer, 2014.

Lawler, Edward J., and Jeongkoo Yoon. "Commitment in Exchange Relations." *American Sociological Review* 61, no. 1 (1996): 89–108.

Lindholm, Charles. *Charisma*. Cambridge: Basil Blackwell, 1990.

Lipka, Michael. "Many U.S. Congregations Are Still Racially Segregated, but Things Are Changing." Pew Research Center, December 8, 2014. http://www.pewresearch.org/fact-tank/2014/12/08/many-u-s-congregations-are-still-racially-segregated-but-things-are-changing-2/.

Luhrmann, T. M. *When God Talks Back: Understanding the American Evangelical Relationship with God*. New York: Vintage Books, 2012.

Madsen, Douglas, and Peter G. Snow. *The Charismatic Bond: Political Behavior in Time of Crisis*. Cambridge, MA: Harvard University Press, 1991.

Mahaffey, Jerome Dean. *The Accidental Revolutionary: George Whitefield and the Creation of America*. Waco: Baylor University Press, 2011.

Miller, Emily McFarlan. "Former Willow Creek Pastor Steve Carter Breaks His Silence on Hybels Allegations." *Religion News Service*, September 18, 2018. Accessed October 25, 2018. https://religionnews.com/2018/09/18/former-willow-creek-pastor-steve-carter-breaks-silence-on-hybels-allegations/.

Martí, Gerardo. "New Concepts for New Dynamics: Generating Theory for the Study of Religious Innovation and Social Change." *Journal for the Scientific Study of Religion* 56, no. 2 (2017): 157–172.

Martí, Gerardo. "Editor's Note: The Global Phenomenon of Hillsong Church: An Initial Assessment." *Sociology of Religion* 78, no. 4 (2018): 377–386.

Martí, Gerardo, and Gladys Ganiel. *The Deconstructed Church: Understanding Emerging Christianity*. New York: Oxford University Press, 2014.

Martin, David. *On Secularization: Toward a Revised General Theory*. Burlington, VT: Ashgate, 2005.

Martin, Luther H., and Donald Wiebe. *Religion Explained?: The Cognitive Science of Religion After Twenty-Five Years*. London: Bloomsbury, 2017.

Martin, Nancy J. *Small Groups in Big Churches*. Unpublished Ph.D. Dissertation, Department of Sociology, University of Arizona, Tucson, 2007.

McCauley, Robert N. *Why Religion is Natural and Science is Not*. New York: Oxford University Press, 2011.

McElmurry, Kevin L. *Alone/Together: The Production of Religious Culture in a Church for the Unchurched*. Unpublished Ph.D. Dissertation, University of Missouri, Columbia, 2009.

McKnight, Scot. "About Willow Creek: What Do I Think?" *Patheos*, June 27, 2018. http://www.patheos.com/blogs/jesuscreed/2018/06/27/about-willow-creek-what-do-i-think/?platform=hootsuite.

McKnight, Scot. "Willow: Why the Women Went Public?" *Patheos,* July 9, 2018. http://www.patheos.com/blogs/jesuscreed/2018/07/09/willow-why-the-women-went-public/.

Mesterton-Gibbons, Michael, and Lee Alan Dugatkin. "Cooperation among Unrelated Individuals: Evolutionary Factors." *Quarterly Review of Biology* 67, no. 3 (1992): 267–281.

Michael, Larry J. *Spurgeon on Leadership: Key Insights for Christian Leaders from the Prince of Preachers.* Grand Rapids, MI: Kregel Publications, 2010.

Mikolajczak, Moïra, James J. Gross, Anthony Lane, Olivier Corneille, Philippe de Timary, and Olivier Luminet. "Oxytocin Makes People Trusting, Not Gullible." *Psychological Science* 21, no. 8 (2010): 1072–1074.

Miller, Donald, and Tetsunao Yamamori. *Global Pentecostalism: The New Face of Christian Engagement.* Berkeley: University of California Press, 2007.

Miller, Timothy S. *The Birth of the Hospital in the Byzantine Empire.* Baltimore: Johns Hopkins University Press, 1985.

Miller, Timothy S. *The Orphans of Byzantium: Child Welfare in the Christian Empire.* Washington, D.C.: Catholic University of America Press, 2003.

Mills, Martin A. *"Vajra* Brother, *Vajra* Sister: Renunciation, Individualism and the Household in Tibetan Buddhist Monasticism." *Journal of the Royal Anthropological Institute* 6, no. 1 (2000): 17–34.

Moon, Ruth. "Founder of World's Largest Megachurch Convicted of Embezzling $12 Million." *Christianity Today*, February 24, 2014. http://www.christianitytoday.com/news/2014/february/founder-of-worlds-largest-megachurch-convicted-cho-yoido.html.

Moyn, Samuel. 2018. "Hype for the Best: Why Does Steven Pinker Insist that Human Life is on the Up?" *New Republic*, March 19, 2018. https://newrepublic.com/article/147391/hype-best.

Mussumi, Brian. *Politics of Affect.* Cambridge: Polity, 2015.

My Truth Sanctuary. Accessed July 8, 2018. http://www.mytruthsanctuary.com/aboutus_history.html#earlbio.

Narain, Charvy. "A Conversation with Joseph LeDoux." *Cold Spring Harbor Symposia on Quantitative Biology* 79 (2014): 279–281.

Nicholson, Linda. "Interpreting Gender." *Signs* 20, no. 1 (1994): 79–105.

Noah, Timothy. 2016. "Tilting at Windmills: The Futility of Trying to Normalize Trump . . . Dale Carnegie versus Norman Vincent Peale." *Washington Monthly*, September/October 2016. https://washingtonmonthly.com/magazine/septemberoctober-2016/tilting-at-windmills-3.

Novak, Michael. *The Spirit of Democratic Capitalism.* Lanham, MD: Madison Books, 1982.

Oberman, Lindsay M., and Vilayanur S. Ramachandran. "The Simulating Social Mind: The role of the Mirror Neuron System and Simulation in the Social and Communicative Deficits of Autism Spectrum Disorders." *Psychological Bulletin* 133 (2007): 310–327.

Oliver, Robert. *The Psychology of Persuasive Speech*. New York: Longmans, Green and Co., 1942.

Olsen, Ted. "Former TBN Employee Alleges Gay Tryst with Paul Crouch." *Christianity Today,* September 1, 2004. https://www.christianitytoday.com/ct/2004/septemberweb-only/9-13-11.0.html.

Osteen, Joel. *Understanding Your Value*. Accessed January 16, 2018. https://www.joelosteen.com/Pages/Article.aspx?articleid=6465.

Parr, Jessica. *Inventing George Whitefield: Race, Revivalism, and the Making of a Religious Icon*. Jackson: University Press of Mississippi, 2015.

Pew Forum on Religion & Public Life. *"Nones" on the Rise,* 2012. http://www.pewforum.org/Unaffiliated/nones-on-the-rise.aspx.

Pew Research Center: Religion and Public Life. *America's Changing Religious Landscape,* 2015. http://www.pewforum.org/2015/05/12/americas-changing-religious-landscape/.

Pinker, Steven. *Enlightenment Now: The Case for Reason, Science, Humanism, and Progress*. New York: Viking, 2018.

Pitts-Taylor, Victoria. *The Brain's Body: Neuroscience and Corporeal Politics*. Durham, NC: Duke University Press, 2016.

Pitts-Taylor, Victoria. "Mattering: Feminism, Science and Corporeal Politics." In *Mattering: Feminism, Science, and Materialism*, 1–20. New York: New York University Press, 2016.

Pitts-Taylor, Victoria, ed. *Mattering: Feminism, Science, and Materialism*. New York: New York University Press, 2016.

Porubanova, Michaela, and John H. Shaver. "Minimal Counterintuitiveness Revisited, Again: The Role of Emotional Valence in Memory for Conceptual Incongruity." In *Religion Explained?: The Cognitive Science of Religion After Twenty-Five Years*, edited by Luther H. Martin and Donald Wiebe, 123–132. London: Bloomsbury, 2017.

Pritchard, G. A. *Willow Creek Seeker Services: Evaluating a New Way of Doing Church*. Grand Rapids, MI: Baker Books, 1996.

Rappaport, Roy. *Ritual and Religion in the Making of Humanity*. Cambridge: Cambridge University Press, 1999.

Rauschenbusch, Walter. *A Theology for the Social Gospel*. New York: The MacMillan Company, 1917.

Religious Congregations and Membership Study. Accessed January 15, 2012. http://www.rcms2010.org/.

Rettner, Rachael. "'Love Hormone' Oxytocin May Intensify Orgasms." *Huffington Post*. April 4, 2014. https://www.huffingtonpost.com/2014/04/04/oxytocin-love-hormone-orgasm_n_5090992.html.

Richerson, Peter J., and Robert Boyd. *Not by Genes Alone: How Culture Transformed Human Evolution*. Chicago: University of Chicago Press, 2005.

Richerson, Peter J., Robert Boyd, and Joseph Henrich. "Gene-Culture Coevolution in the Age of Genomics." *Proceedings of the National Academy of Sciences USA* 107 (2010): 8985–8992.

Riesebrodt, Martin. *Pious Passion: The Emergence of Modern Fundamentalism in the United States and Iran.* Berkeley: University of California Press, 1993.

Rilling, James K., Ashley C. DeMarco, Patrick D. Hackett, Xu Chen, Pritam Gautam, Sabrina Stair, Ebrahim Haroon, Richmond Thompson, Beate Ditzen, Rajan Patel, and Giuseppe Pagnoni. "Sex Differences in the Neural and Behavioral Response to Intranasal Oxytocin and Vasopressin during Human Social Interaction." *Psychoneuroendocrinology* 39 (2014): 237–248.

Rishmawy, Derek. "Calvin's Multi-Faceted Atonement." *The Gospel Coalition*, 2015. https://www.thegospelcoalition.org/article/calvins-multi-faceted-atonement/.

Rizzolatti, Giacomo, and Laila Craighero. "The Mirror-Neuron System." *Annual Review of Neuroscience* 24 (2004): 169–192.

Rossel, Jorg, and Randall Collins. "Conflict Theory and Interaction Rituals: The Microfoundations of Conflict Theory." In *Handbook of Sociological Theory*, edited by Jonathan H. Turner, 509–532. New York: Springer, 2001.

Rossner, Meredith, and Mythily Meher. "Emotions in Ritual Theories." In *Handbook of the Sociology of Emotions: Volume II*, edited by Jan E. Stets and Jonathan H. Turner, 199–220. Dordrecht: Springer Netherlands, 2014.

Sargeant, Kimon Howland. *Seeker Churches: Promoting Traditional Religion in a Nontraditional Way.* New Brunswick, NJ: Rutgers University Press, 2000.

Sasaki, Joni Y., Heejung S. Kim, and J. Xu. "Religion and Well-being: The Moderating Role of Culture and the Oxytocin Receptor (OXTR) Gene." *Journal of Cross-Cultural Psychology* 42 (2011): 1394–1405.

Schaller, Lyle E. *The Seven-Day-a-Week Church.* Nashville: Abingdon Press, 1992.

Scheele, Dirk, Nadine Striepens, Onur Gunturkun, Sandra Deutschlander, Wolfgang Maier, Keith M. Kendrick, and Rene Hurlemann. "Oxytocin Modulates Social Distance between Males and Females." *Journal of Neuroscience* 32, no. 46 (2012): 16074–16079.

Schjødt, Uffe, Hans Stodkilde-Jorgensen, Armin W. Geertz, Torbin E. Lund, and Andreas Roepstorff. "The Power of Charisma—Perceived Charisma Inhibits the Frontal Executive Network of Believers in Intercessory Prayer." *SCAN* 6 (2011): 119–127.

Schleiermacher, Friedrich. *On Religion: Speeches to Its Cultured Despisers*, translated by John Oman. New York: Harper & Brothers, 1958.

Schmidt, Lee Eric. *Restless Souls: The Making of American Spirituality.* New York: HarperCollins, 2005.

Scofield, Be. "King's God: The Unknown Faith of Dr. Martin Luther King. Jr.," *Medium*, October 13, 2017. https://medium.com/@bescofield/kings-god-the-unknown-faith-of-dr-martin-luther-king-jr-2009-869537387ebb.

Shamay-Tsoory, Simone G, Meytal Fischer, Jonathan Dvash, Hagai Harari, Nufar Perach-Bloom, and Yechiel Levkovitz. "Intranasal Administration of Oxytocin Increases Envy and Schadenfreude (Gloating)." *Biological Psychiatry* 66, no. 9 (2009): 864–870.

Sharot, Stephen. "Beyond Christianity: A Critique of the Rational Choice Theory of Religion from a Weberian and Comparative Religions Perspective." *Sociology of Religion* 63, no. 4 (2002): 427–454.

Slingerland, Edward, Joseph Henrich, and Ara Norenzayan. "The Evolution of Prosocial Religions." In *Cultural Evolution: Society, Technology, Language, and Religion*, edited by Peter J. Richerson and Morten H. Christiansen, 334–348. Cambridge, MA: MIT Press, 2013.

Smith, Mark A. *How Culture Has Trumped Religion in American Politics*. Chicago: University of Chicago Press, 2015.

Solomon, Deborah. "The Whistle-Blower." *New York Times Magazine*, June 3, 2007. https://www.nytimes.com/2007/06/03/magazine/03wwln-Q4-t.html.

Sosis, Richard, and Candace Alcorta. "Signaling, Solidarity, and the Sacred: The Evolution of Religious Behavior." *Evolutionary Anthropology* 12 (2003): 264–274.

Sosis, Richard, and Eric R. Bressler. "Cooperation and Commune Longevity: A Test of the Costly Signaling Theory of Religion." *Cross-Cultural Research* 37, no. 2 (2003): 211–239.

Stace, April. *Secular Music, Sacred Space: Evangelical Worship and Popular Music*. Lanham, MD: Lexington Books, 2017.

Stark, Rodney. *What Americans Really Believe*. Waco, TX: Baylor University Press, 2008.

Sutton, Matthew Avery. *Aimee Semple McPherson and the Resurrection of Christian America*. Cambridge, MA: Harvard University Press, 2009.

Szalavitz, Maia. "Oxytocin May Forge Bonds between Dads and Children." *Time*, December 14, 2012. http://healthland.time.com/2012/12/14/oxytocin-may-forge-bonds-between-dads-and-children/.

Taylor, Shelley E., Shimon Saphire-Bernstein, and Teresa E. Seeman. "Are Plasma Oxytocin in Women and Plasma Vasopressin in Men Biomarkers of Distressed Pair-Bond Relationships?" *Psychological Science* 21, no. 1 (2010): 3–7.

The Liturgists. Accessed December 13, 2017. http://www.theliturgists.com/.

Throckmorton, Warren. "Mark Driscoll Spins the End of Mars Hill Church." *Patheos Blog,* April 9, 2017. http://www.patheos.com/blogs/warrenthrockmorton/2017/04/09/mark-driscoll-spins-the-end-of-mars-hill-church/.

Thumma, Scott. "Megachurches of Atlanta." In *Religions of Atlanta*, edited by Gary Laderman. Atlanta, GA: Scholars Press, 1996.

Thumma, Scott. "Exploring the Megachurch Phenomena: Their Characteristics and Cultural Context." Hartford Institute for Religion Research, 2011. http://hirr.hartsem.edu/bookshelf/thumma_article2.html.

Thumma, Scott, and Warren Bird. "Survey of North America's Largest Churches 2008." Hartford Institute for Religion Research, 2008. http://www.hartfordinstitute.org/megachurch/megastoday2008detaileddata.pdf.

Thumma, Scott, and Warren Bird. "A New Decade of Megachurches: 2011 Profile of Large Attendance Churches in the United States." Hartford Institute for

Religion Research, 2011. http://www.hartfordinstitute.org/megachurch/megachurch-2011-summary-report.htm.

Thumma, Scott, and Warren Bird. "Megafaith for the Megacity: The Global Megachurch Phenomenon." In *The Changing World Map: Sacred Places, Identities, Practices and Politics*, edited by Stanley D. Brunn, 2331–2352. New York: Springer Dordrecht, 2015.

Thumma, Scott, and Warren Bird. "Recent Shifts in America's Largest Protestant Churches: Megachurches 2015 Report." Hartford Institute for Religion Research, 2015. http://hirr.hartsem.edu/megachurch/2015_Megachurches_Report.pdf.

Thumma, Scott, and Dave Travis. *Beyond the Megachurch Myths*. San Francisco: Jossey-Bass, 2007.

Tooby, John, and Leda Cosmides. "The Psychological Foundations of Culture." In *The Adapted Mind: Evolutionary Psychology and the Generation of Culture*, edited by Jerome H. Barkow, Leda Cosmides, and John Tooby, 19–136. New York: Oxford University Press, 1992.

Tremlin, Todd. *Minds and Gods: The Cognitive Foundations of Religion*. Oxford: Oxford University Press, 2006.

Turner, Bryan. *The Body and Society*. Oxford: Blackwell, 1984.

Turner, Jonathan H. *On the Origins of Human Emotions: A Sociological Inquiry into the Evolution of Human Affect*. Stanford, CA: Stanford University Press, 2000.

Turner, Jonathan H. *Human Emotions: A Sociological Theory*. New York: Routledge, 2007.

Turner, Jonathan H. "Using Neurosociology and Evolutionary Sociology to Explain the Origin and Evolution of Religions." *Journal for the Cognitive Science of Religion* 4, no. 1 (2016): 7–29.

Turner, Jonathan H., and Seth Abrutyn. "Returning the 'Social' to Evolutionary Sociology: Reconsidering Spencer, Durkheim, and Marx's Models of 'Natural' Selection." *Sociological Perspectives* 60, no. 3 (2016): 529–556.

Turner, Jonathan H., and Richard S. Machalek. *The New Evolutionary Sociology: Recent and Revitalized Theoretical and Methodological Approaches*. New York: Routledge, 2018.

Turner, Jonathan H., and Alexandra Maryanski. "Evolutionary Sociology: A Cross-Species Strategy for Discovering Human Nature." In *Handbook of Evolution and Society: Toward an Evolutionary Social Science*, edited by Jonathan H. Turner, Richard S. Machalek, and Alexandra R. Maryanski, 546–571. Boulder, CO: Paradigm/New York: Routledge, 2015.

Turner, Jonathan H., Alexandra Maryanski, Anders Klostergaard Petersen, and Armin W. Geertz. *The Emergence and Evolution of Religion by Means of Natural Selection*. New York: Routledge, 2018.

Twitchell, James B. *Branded Nation: The Marking of Megachurch, College Inc., and Museumworld*. New York: Simon & Schuster, 2004.

Uvnäs-Moberg, Kerstin, Pawel Alster, Irene Lund, Thomas Lundeberg, Mieko Kurosawa, and Sven Ahlenius. "Stroking of the Abdomen Causes Decreased

Locomotor Activity in Conscious Male Rats." *Physiology and Behavior* 60 (1996): 1409–1411.

Uvnäs-Moberg, Kerstin, and Maria Petersson. "Oxytocin, a Mediator of Anti-stress, Well-Being, Social Interaction, Growth and Healing." *Zeitschrift für Psychosomatische Medizin und Psychotherapie* 51, no. 1 (2005): 57–80. Posted online in English at https://pdfs.semanticscholar.org/0ac8/c14228b62b9c87636f5b6eb536a434fd04de.pdf. Accessed June 29, 2018.

van Anders, Sari M., Katherine L. Goldey, and Patty X. Kuo. "The Steroid/Peptide Theory of Social Bonds: Integrating Testosterone and Peptide Responses for Classifying Social Behavioral Contexts." *Psychoneuroendocrinology* 36 (2011): 1265–1275.

van Anders, Sari, James L. Goodson, and Marcy A. Kingsbury. "Beyond 'Oxytocin = Good': Neural Complexities and the Flipside of Social Bonds." *Archives of Sexual Behavior* 42, no. 7 (2013): 1115–1118.

Van Cappellen, Patty, Baldwin M. Way, Suzannah F. Isgett, and Barbara L. Fredrickson. "Effects of Oxytocin Administration on Spirituality and Emotional Responses to Meditation." *Social Cognitive and Affective Neuroscience* 11, no. 10 (2016): 1579–1587.

Vandermaas-Peeler, Alex, Daniel Cox, Molly Fisch-Friedman, Rob Griffin, and Robert P. Jones. "Emerging Consensus on LGBT Issues: Findings from the 2017 American Values Atlas." PRRI, 2018. https://www.prri.org/research/emerging-consensus-on-lgbt-issues-findings-from-the-2017-american-values-atlas/.

Vásquez, Manuel A. *More Than Belief: A Materialist Theory of Religion.* New York: Oxford University Press, 2011.

Vercoe, Moana, and Paul J. Zak. "Inductive Modeling Using Causal Studies in Neuroeconomics: Brains on Drugs." *Journal of Economic Methodology* 17, no. 2 (2010): 133–146.

Warren, Rick. *The Purpose Driven Life.* Grand Rapids, MI: Zondervan, 2002.

Warren, Tish Harrison. "It's Not Billy Graham Rule or Bust." *Christianity Today,* April 27, 2018. https://www.christianitytoday.com/ct/2018/april-web-only/its-not-billy-graham-rule-or-bust.html.

Weisman, Omri, Orna Zagoory-Sharon, Inna Schneiderman, Ilanit Gordon, and Ruth Feldman. "Plasma Oxytocin Distribution in a Large Cohort of Women and Men and Their Gender-Specific Associations with Anxiety." *Psychoneuroendocrinology* 38, no. 5 (2013): 694–701.

Wellman, James K., Jr., *The Gold Coast Church and the Ghetto: Christ and Culture in Mainline Protestantism.* Urbana: University of Illinois Press, 1999.

Wellman, James K., Jr., *Evangelicals vs. Liberals: The Clash of Christian Cultures in the Pacific Northwest.* New York: Oxford University Press, 2008.

Wellman, James K., Jr., *Rob Bell and the New American Christianity.* Nashville, TN: Abingdon Press, 2012.

Wellman, James K., Jr., Katie E. Corcoran, and Kate Stockly-Meyerdirk. "'God Is Like a Drug': Explaining Interaction Rituals in American Megachurches." *Sociological Forum* 29, no. 3 (2014): 650–672.

Wellman, James K., Jr., and S. R. Thompson. "From the Social Gospel to Neoconservativism: Religion and U.S. Foreign Policy." *Interdisciplinary Journal of Research on Religion* 7, Article 6 (2001): 1–41. http://www.religjournal.com/articles/2011.php.

Wells, Jonathan C. K., and Jay T. Stock. "The Biology of the Colonizing Ape." *Yearbook of Physical Anthropology* 50 (2007): 191–222.

Whitehouse, Harvey. *Modes of Religiosity: A Cognitive Theory of Religious Transmission.* Walnut Creek, CA: AltaMira Press, 2004.

Wicentowski, Danny. "After Six Months Away, Pastor at Center of Church Cover-Up Scandal Returns." *River Front Times,* February 9, 2016. https://www.riverfronttimes.com/newsblog/2016/02/09/after-six-months-away-pastor-at-center-of-church-cover-up-scandal-returns.

Wilford, Justin. *Purpose Driven Place: Saddleback Church and the Postsuburban Transformation of American Evangelicalism.* Unpublished Dissertation: University of California, Los Angeles.

Wilford, Justin. *Sacred Subdivisions: The Postsuburban Transformation of American Evangelicalism.* New York: New York University Press, 2012.

Willard, Aiyana K., Joseph Henrich, and Ara Norenzayan. "Memory and Belief in the Transmission of Counterintuitive Content." *Human Nature* 27, no. 3 (2016): 221–243.

Wilner, Ann R. *The Spellbinders: Charismatic Political Leadership.* New Haven, CT: Yale University Press, 1984.

Wilson, Jeff. *Mindful America: The Mutual Transformation of Buddhist Meditation and American Culture.* New York: Oxford, 2014.

Wilson, Elizabeth A. "Organic Empathy: Feminism, Psychopharmaceuticals, and the Embodiment of Depression." In *Material Feminisms*, edited by Stacy Alaimo and Susan Heckman, 373–399. Bloomington: Indiana University Press, 2008.

Wilson, Elizabeth A. *Gut Feminism.* Durham, NC: Duke University, 2015.

Witherington, Ben. *Women in the Ministry of Jesus: A Study of Jesus' Attitudes to Women and Their Roles as Reflected in His Earthly Life.* Cambridge: Cambridge University Press, 1987.

Xygalatas, Dimitris, Ivana Konvalinka, Andreas Roepstorff, and Joseph Bulbulia. "Quantifying Collective Effervescence: Heart-Rate Dynamics at a Fire Walking Ritual." *Communicative and Integrative Biology* 4, no. 6 (2011): 735–738.

Xygalatas, Dimitris, and William W. McCorkle, Jr. Eds. *Mental Culture: Classical Social Theory and the Cognitive Science of Religion.* London: Acumen, 2013.

Zak, Paul. "Trust, Morality—and Oxytocin?" *TEDGlobal 2011.* https://www.ted.com/talks/paul_zak_trust_morality_and_oxytocin?language=en.

Zak, Paul. *The Moral Molecule: The Source of Love and Prosperity.* New York: Dutton/ Penguin Group, 2012.

Zak, Paul J., and Jacek Kugler. "Neuroeconomics and International Studies: A New Understanding of Trust." *International Studies Perspectives* 12, no. 2 (2011): 136–152.

INDEX

Note: Tables and figures are indicated by *t* and *f* following the page number

For the benefit of digital users, indexed terms that span two pages (e.g., 52–53) may, on occasion, appear on only one of those pages.

affect, xii–xiii, 1, 8, 10–11, 12–13, 22, 29–30, 31, 80–81, 82, 105, 139, 169, 190, 192, 234, 266–68, 278–79, 282
  vs emotion, 29, 267–68
  like a drug, 252, 258–59
  physiology of, 10–11, 24–25, 266–68
  vs reflective thought, xiii, 10–11, 24–25, 70–71
  religion and, 34, 44, 71, 140, 273–74
affective barriers, 26–27, 284–85
  See also barriers excluding outsiders
affective kinship, *see* kinship, non-genetic
alloparents, 262–64
altar call, xii–xiii, 30, 81, 85, 134, 137–39, 138*f*, 141–42, 149, 284–85

Barrett, Justin L. 11–12
Barrett, Lisa Feldman, 29, 267–68, 267–68n.53
barriers excluding outsiders, 26–27, 30, 81–82, 85, 92, 93–94, 103, 284–85
  See also affective barriers
Bartkowski, John, 75–76
Becker, Howard, 2
behavioral synchrony, 281–82
belief, 6–8, 9–13, 34, 59–60, 63, 164–66, 269–70
Bell, Daniel M., Jr., 217–21
Bell, Rob, 7, 74–75, 116–18, 197–98
  See also Wellman, James K., Jr.
Berger, Peter, 33–34, 97–98, 144–45, 159, 164–65, 222–27
  on the Prosperity Gospel, 222–27
  sacred canopy, 144–45, 164–65

bible passages, 74–75, 96, 97–98,
    112, 117, 119–20, 122–23,
    126–27, 140–41, 150–51, 156,
    159–60, 169, 175–77, 197,
    204–5, 226–27
biology, 15–16, 18–20, 77, 169,
    251–52, 253–58, 255–56n.10,
    256–58n.13, 265–66, 267–
    68n.53, 274–75, 276–77,
    281–82, 288–89
body, xii–xiv, 8, 10–11, 13–14, 24–26,
    75–77, 80–81, 169, 251–52,
    253, 254–56, 267–68, 277
    See also biology; embodiment
body of Christ, 17, 19, 30, 37, 85–86,
    151, 159–60, 165–66, 169,
    174–75, 204–5, 284–85, 288
Bourdieu, Pierre, 79–80
Bowler, Kate, 51, 215n.1

capitalism, 51–52, 217–22
Cavey, Bruxy, 73–75
charismatic leadership, xvi, 27–28,
    30, 40–41, 53–54, 71–72, 81,
    82, 84–85, 115–17, 118–19,
    121, 124–26, 126–27n.14,
    128, 129, 130–35, 141–42,
    192, 195–98, 211–13, 234–37,
    236t, 237t, 282–84
Chaves, Mark, 6–7, 59–60
Churchland, Patricia, 263–65, 285
cognition, 24–25, 29, 71, 105, 137–38,
    143–44, 153–54, 259–60, 266,
    268–71, 283–84, 289
cognitive science of religion, 11–12,
    256–58, 269–71, 283–84
    Boyer, Pascal, 11–12, 143
    costly-signaling, 153–54, 153–54n.2
    McCauley, Robert N. 11–12
    McCauley, Robert, and E. Thomas
        Lawson, 269–70 (see minimally
        counterintuitive beliefs)
    passive paradigm, 283–84

Schjødt, Uffe, 283–84
Whitehouse, Harvey, 269–70
Xygalatas, Dimitris, and Ivana
    Konvalinka, 281
collective effervescence, xvii, 17–18,
    80–82, 94, 103, 142, 288
Collins, Randall, xv–xvii, 2–3, 6–7,
    8–10, 12–13, 20–21, 25–29,
    30–31, 79–80, 81–82, 84–86,
    90, 92, 94, 101–2, 124, 172–
    73, 251–52, 276–77, 278–79,
    281–82, 285–86
Colson, Charles, 5
constructed emotion, theory of, see
    Barrett, Lisa Feldman
cooperation beyond kinship, 2–3,
    16–18, 22, 31, 154–55, 255,
    260, 261, 264–66, 276–77,
    281–82, 286–91
    ultra-sociality, 260,
        261–62, 268–69
Corrigan, John, 258–59
cultural capital, 92–96, 284–85

Damasio, Antonio, 10–11
    See also somatic marker hypothesis
Darwin, 15–16, 64–65, 256–58,
    256–58n.13
    See also evolution
Database of Megachurches in the
    U.S., 231–33
Dawson, Lorne L., 116–17,
    121–22, 124–25
desires, six, xii–xiii, 30–31, 34, 77,
    81, 251–52
    desire for acceptance, 30, 81,
        82–84, 91–92, 95–96, 170,
        174–75, 278–79
    desire for deliverance, 30, 81, 85,
        284–85 (see altar call)
    desire for purpose in service,
        30, 81, 85–86, 156–58,
        170, 285–88

desire for reliable leadership, 30, 81, 84–85, 115–16, 119, 282–84

desire to re-member, 1–2, 30, 81, 86, 288–91 (*see* small groups)

desire for wow/ecstasy, 30, 81, 84, 99, 104, 112, 279–82

Driscoll, Mark, 57–58, 57–58n.34, 119, 190–212, 297

Durkheim, Émile, ix–x, xiv–xv, xvii–xviii, 7–8, 17–20, 18–19n.9, 25–26, 33–35, 37, 39, 44, 58–59, 73, 86–87, 105, 112–13, 137, 153, 158, 171, 227, 272–73
See also *homo duplex*

Eagle, David E., 38–39, 41–42, 48–49

ecstasy, x, 1–2, 99, 109–10, 112, 153–54, 279

Edwards, Jonathan, 2–3, 42–44, 45–46

embodied Choice Theory, 2–3, 24–25, 26, 80–81

defined, 24–25

embodiment, 19–20, 104, 105–6, 169, 181, 198–99, 253–58, 264–65, 276–77n.76, 291

body reflexive practices, 13

study of, 75–77, 254–40

emotional energy, xvi–xvii, 1–3, 6–7, 12–13, 24–25, 28–29, 30–31, 79–81, 82, 104, 115–16, 154–55, 165–66, 169, 171–73, 174–75, 211, 212–13, 252, 252n.2, 276–78, 285–86

critique of construct, 28–29

desire for xvii, 1, 24–25

as a drug 1–3, 104, 251

energy stars, xv–xvi, 27–28, 115–16, 124, 127, 211, 212–13, 286

entrainment, 101–3, 281–82

evolution, 15–17, 22, 64–65, 79–80, 153–54n.2, 252, 253, 255, 256–58, 256–58n.18, 259–60, 261n.28, 262–64, 266, 268–69, 268–69n.56, 270–72, 274–75n.74, 281

gene-culture coevolution, 270–71

Fish, Jonathan S., 18–19n.9, 272–73

focus groups, xvi, 80, 145–46, 233–34

free-riders, 20–22, 20–21n.13, 21–22n.16, 148

free-rider benefit, 20–21

Fuentes, Agustin and Aku Visala, 256–58, 272–73

gender/sex, 106, 180, 184–85, 199–200, 201, 253–54n.4, 263–64
See also patriarchalism

Graham, Billy, 205–6

Great Awakenings, 42–50

Conwell, Russell H., 50–57

Edwards, Jonathan, 42–44

Finney, Charles Grandison, 48–50

McPherson, Aimee Semple, 52–54

Spurgeon, Charles Haddon, 48

Whitefield, George, 45–47

Grosz, Elizabeth, 15–16, 256–58, 256–58n.13

Harari, Yuval Noah, 259–60

healing, 122–24, 134, 137–38, 139, 145–47, 169–70, 244–46, 283–84, 289–90

Henrich, Joseph, 270–71

homo duplex, ix–x, xiv–xv, xvii–, 1, 2–3, 17–19, 22, 25, 31, 35–36, 37, 56–59, 86–87, 137, 151, 187–88, 216, 271–74, 287–88
See also Durkheim, Émile

homo religiosus, x, 259, 274

Hrdy, Sarah Blaffer, 262–64

Hume, David, 23–24

Hybels, Bill, 95–96, 193–96, 201, 211–13
See also scandals

in-group/out-group, 284–85, 289

interaction ritual chains, xvii, 2–10, 25,
28, 30–31, 75, 79–82, 85–86,
90, 154–55, 172
ritual outcomes, 81–82
See also Collins, Randall

international missions, 68–69,
165–67, 216

Jacobs, Janet, 195–96, 197–99, 200–1

James, William, 2–3, 7, 49, 79–80

Johnson, Doyle P., 131–32

Johnson, Jessica, *Biblical Porn: Affect,*
Labor, and Pastor Mark Driscoll's
Evangelical Empire, 190–92, 198

kinship, non-genetic, 154–55,
255, 264–66, 276–77,
281–82, 288–91

Kirby, Vicki, 15–16, 254–55

Lawler, Edward, Shane Thye, and
Jeongkoo Yoon, 86–87, 275–
76, 287–88, 290–91

leadership, 21, 71–72, 84–85, 115–16,
118–19, 123–24, 282–84

LGBTQ, 26–27, 67–68, 69, 180, 183–
85, 199–200, 210–11
homosexuality as a sin, 180,
210–11, 293
same-sex marriage, 26–27, 67–68,
97, 180, 183–84, 210–11
welcome in church, 26–27

liberation theology, 222–25

Madsen, Douglas and Peter Snow,
133–34, 282

marriage, 26–27, 67–68, 158–59, 164,
180, 181–84, 201, 203, 205–6

McElmurry, Kevin, 106–9, 111, 282

megachurch ritual cycle, 30–31,
82, 83*f*, 86, 91*f*, 102*f*, 123*f*,
138*f*, 154–55, 157*f*, 171–72,

173, 174*f*, 251–52, 255–56,
276, 278–91

megachurches, criticisms of, 5, 6–7,
19–20, 23–24, 99, 178–79,
187–88, 215–16

minimally counterintuitive
beliefs, 11–13, 143–44,
270–71n.70, 283–84
See also cognitive science of religion

mirror neurons, 280, 280n.90

missions and missional communities,
63–64, 158–59, 163, 167,
168, 169–70

mother-infant bond, 261–64

music, 10, 81, 84–85, 93–95, 99–104,
106–8, 109–11, 138, 139, 142,
146, 249, 279–80

mutual focus of attention, 27–28,
81–82, 84–85, 102–3,
115–16, 281–82

Novak, Michael, *The Spirit of Democratic*
Capitalism, 220–21

Osteen, Joel, 52, 56, 57–58, 149,
189–90, 300
See also scandals

outreach, 68, 86–87, 109, 156–57,
157*f*, 165–68, 286–88

oxytocin, 251–52, 263–69,
273–74, 276–92
and the Megachurch Ritual
Cycle, 278–92
in popular science, 273
and research on religion, 277–78

oxytocin cocktail, 277–78

patriarchal protest movement,
fundamentalism as a, 199–200

patriarchalism, 187, 194, 198–202,
203–6, 208, 210–11

Peale, Norman Vincent,
49–50, 54–57

Pentecostalism, 40–41, 52–54, 206,
    222–23, 224
Pinker, Steven, 220–21, 225–26
Pitts-Taylor, Victoria, 255, 255n.8,
    264–65, 281–82, 288–89
politics, megachurches engaging with,
    10, 41–42, 70, 97, 180, 184–
    85, 229–30, 249
Prison Fellowship International, 5
prosperity gospel, 41, 49–52, 54–56,
    149, 162, 215–17, 222–27
Protestant ethic, The, 40–41,
    222–23, 225–26

Rappaport, Roy, 9–10
reductionism, 253–55
relational cohesion theory, 86–87
religion, definition of, xvi, 2–3, 33–35

scandals, 21, 187–88, 192–93, 199–
    200, 202, 294*t*
  Cole, Bob, 189
  Driscoll, Mark, 190–92
  Osteen, Joel, 189–90, 300
  finance scandals
    Hee, Kong, 209, 299
    Mata, Paul Ricky, 299
    McManus, 300
    Sam-hwan, Kim, 299
    Smith, Gaston, 294
    Sutton, Jerry, 297
    Yonggi, Cho, David, 209, 297
    Yuese, Gu "Joseph," 299
  drugs or alcohol scandals
    Noble, Perry, 299
  miscellaneous scandals,
    Driscoll, Mark, 297 (*see also*
      Driscoll, Mark)
    Hodges, Michael, 300
    Furtick, Steven, 297
    Munro, John, 297
    Osteen, Joel, 189–90, 300
    Patrick, Darrin, 299

Prince, Fred, Jr., 300
Riggle, Steve, 297
Trinity Broadcasting
    Network, 299
sex scandals, 203, 203n30
  Adelaja, Sunday, 299
  Aguilar, Geronimo, 294, 297
  Barnes, Paul, 294
  Bolin, 294
  Connelly, Mark, 203–4, 294
  Cornerstone Nashville
    Church, 299
  Coy, Bob, 300
  Crouch, Jan and Paul, 299
  Crow, Mark, 297
  Graham, William, and Tullian
    Tchividjian, 300
  Haggard, Ted, 210–11, 294
  Hill, Chris, 299
  Hinn, Sam, 294
  Houston, Brian, 208, 297
  Hunter, Isaac, 294
  Hybels, Bill, 193–96,
    201, 211–13
  Janney, David, 297
  Layman, Grant, 297
  Long, Eddie, 207–8, 299
  Loveless, David, 294
  Mahaney, C.J., 297
  Milburn, Brandon, and Steve
    Wingfield, 208–9, 297
  Paulk, Earl, Jr., 206–7, 294
  Rizzo, Dino, 294
  Rock Church, The, 299
  Schaap, Jack A., 207, 297
  Second Baptist Church, 297
  Smith, Gaston, 294
  Suleman, Johnson, 299
  Treat, Caleb, 300
  Victory Christian Center, 294
  Village Church, 297
  Vineyard Church, 297
  Wu, Steve, 294

sex scandals (*cont.*)
    violence scandals
        Dollar, Creflo Augustus, Jr.,
            209–10, 294
        Weeks, Thomas Wesley, Jr.,
            209–10, 294
secularization, 6–7, 222
seekers, 61, 94–95, 106–7, 148
self-sacrificial, 17, 204
service projects, 85–87, 163, 166–68
    See also desire for purpose in service
sexual abuse, *see* scandals
shared emotional mood, xvii, 27,
        81–82, 84, 94–95, 102–3,
        279–80, 281–82
size of church, 20–21, 68–70, 131–32,
        147–48, 160–61
    downsides of a large church, 161
    See also free-riders
small groups, 30, 69, 81, 86–87,
        167, 171–72, 173–75,
        174*f*, 178–79, 181, 240,
        275–76, 288–91
solidarity, 1–3, 9–10, 27–28, 34, 35,
        54, 81, 82, 154–55, 233–34,
        240, 287–88
somatic marker hypothesis, xii–
        xiii, 10–13, 14, 24–25,
        109, 289–90
spiritual gifts, 19–20, 81, 85–87, 151,
        156–61, 242, 286
Stark, Rodney, 6–7n.5
    and Roger Finke, 21–22n.16
survey of key informant/senior pastor,
        244–49, 246*t*
survey of megachurch attendees, 232*t*,
        236*t*, 237*t*, 238–44, 239*t*, 241*t*,
        243*t*, 245*t*
symbols, 9–13, 28–29, 34–35, 82,
        86, 115–16, 172–73, 211,
        255–56, 286

Thumma, Scott, 193
    and Dave Travis, 5n.2, 20–21n.14,
        231–33n.2
    and Warren Bird, 5nn.3–4, 20–
        21, 21–22n.17, 40–41n.5,
        106n.16, 231–33
Turner, Jonathan H., 15–16n.1,
        256n.11, 259–60, 260n.26,
        261, 266, 274–75
    and Alexandra Maryanski, Anders
        Klostergaard Petersen,
        and Armin W. Geertz, *The*
        Emergence and Evolution of
        Religion by Means of Natural
        Selection, 15–16n.1, 268–
        69n.56, 271, 272, 272n.60,
        274–75, 274–75n.74
    and Richard S. Machalek, *The New*
        Evolutionary Sociology, 256,
        259–60, 261, 261n.28, 274–
        75, 274–75n.74

Ultimatum Game, 286–87
ultra-sociality, 22, 252, 259–60, 268–
    69, 274–75, 276
    See also cooperation across kinship

Vásquez, Manual, 254
volunteering, xv–xvi, 153–54,
    160–61, 166

Warren, Rick, 178–79, 195–96
    and *The Purpose Driven Life*, 178–79
Weber, Max, 222–23
    See also Protestant ethic
WEIRDS, xviii, 3, 6–8, 23–24, 189
Wellman, James K., Jr.,
    Evangelical vs. Liberal: The Clash
        of Christian Cultures in the
        Pacific Northwest, 68–70, 181,
        216, 229–30

Rob Bell and the New American
    Christianity, 7, 74–75,
    116–18, 197–98
The Gold Coast Church and the Ghetto:
    Christ and Culture in Mainline
    Protestantism, 63–68, 70

Wilford, Justin, 96–97
Wilson, Elizabeth A., 253, 255–
    56n.10, 256–58, 281
Wilson, Woodrow, 63–64,
    65, 70
word frequencies, method, 104, 234